ABOUT

# Charles Hughes

Charles Hughes spent four years in the U.S. Navy enlisting in 1948 at the age of seventeen. During the closing weeks of 1950 while the 1st Marine Division was surrounded and fighting their way out of the Chinese Communist trap at the frozen Chosin Reservoir, he and his friend Ollie Langston volunteered for the Fleet Marine Force to serve as hospital corpsmen in a Marine rifle company. He had missed World War II and wanted to find out what combat was like. *Accordion War* is the story of his experience.

Today Hughes is professor emeritus of English at Henderson State University in Arkadelphia, Arkansas. He graduated with a BA in political science from the University of Texas at Austin in 1957 and for the next nine years worked in communication intelligence for the National Security Agency at Ft. Meade, Maryland, and later the Air Force Security Service as a cryptanalyst (Russian), instructor of cryptanalysis, technical writer (cryptanalysis), technical editor, and finally as the Chief of the Editing and Publications Branch of the USAFSS School at Goodfellow AFB, San Angelo, Texas.

He left that position in 1966 to attend graduate school at Texas Tech University at Lubbock where he received an MA (1968) and a PhD (1971) in literature and linguistics after which he was hired by Henderson State where he taught up to and after his retirement in 1996, serving for five of those years as Chairman of the English and Foreign Languages Department.

**www.dochughesbooks.com**

ISBN: 1452827605
ISBN-13: 9781452827605

# From Reviews of and Responses to *Accordion War*

"Hughes, who is professor emeritus of English at Henderson State University in Arkadelphia, Ark., is a gifted writer. . . . This book is hard to put down. The writing is terrific. . . .Well done, Doc."

**GySgt John Boring, USMC (Ret.)**
***Leatherneck Magazine of the Marines, Sept 2007***

"I thoroughly enjoyed reading your book 'Korea 1951.' I always knew that one day an FMF Corpsman would grow up, learn to write and tell their (our) unique story. "Flags of Our Fathers" came close but you nailed it."

**Maxwell Baker, Vietnam/ Korean vet. HMCM USN (Ret)**

"Doc. What can we say? This book is absolutely wonderful—There are so few books written about the Korean War and what our Marines went through. It's a story that needed to be told—and you did it! We are so grateful. We will cherish this book and our 'Doc' that wrote it. Semper Fi "

**Ralph [Marine rifleman, Korean vet.] & Betty Tate**

"Bought the book. Read it. Couldn't put it down. . . .I'm normally a slow reader but I savored this one. Didn't want it to end. It was dejavu all over again. . . Like you I was overwhelmed by the beauty of Korea . Still am. Reminds me of my home state, WV. . . . I have read four books that I consider excellent: *Witness* by Whittiker Chambers; *Falling Water Rising* by Franklin Toker; *Democracy in America* by Alexis De Tocqueville; and *Accordion War: Korea 1951.* You are in good company."

**John Simpson, Marine rifleman, Korean vet.**

"*Accordion War* is a quality read. Your descriptions of that era are like paintings without the sounds, however, your recounting of the artillery barrages was deafening."

**Bob "Doc" Wickman, Korean vet.**

"Your book is great. If you had done it 20 years ago, I believe it would have become one of the key reference genre chronicles of that war and era. I hope it still can. There are actions you tell that I never knew, even though I was usually only a few hundred yards away. Clearly you have done some great research since I first met you. I find especially interesting your musings about the alpha and omega, religion, and our role in the world.  I am trying to spread the word about your fine writing—it makes me wish I had been lucky enough to have been one of your students.  Stay safe.  Semper Fi"

**Nick the BAR-man [Jim Nicholson, MD] Korean vet.**

"This is a gripping work and a must reading. . . .The present day overview/ perspective ties the decades together and makes sense of the cost of war as well as the 'why's' of warfare. . . ."

***Korean War Project Newsletter***

"This is one of the rare books that begs to be read in one reading. . . .the reader can smell both the gunpowder and the kimchi. . . . Well done, Doc."

**Prof. Andrew Lubin, Lead Reviewer,
Military Writers Society of America**

Doc:  I'm deeply honored receiving the book, and also the privilege of serving with you in the 2nd Platoon of How Company. . . .It is certainly accurate from what I remember and beautifully written.  I felt as I was reliving the past.  It also clued me in on where and what the 2nd Platoon was doing prior to my joining How Company.  Great Job.

**Joe Sipolski,
rifleman and Purple Heart veteran of 2nd Platoon, H-3-7**

I have read many books and articles on the Korean War.  This book by Charles "Doc" Hughes is by far the best.  It keeps the interest of the reader while bringing the history of the Korean War to life.  It should be on the shelf of every school library.

**Jean Moore, widow of Wadie Moore,
rifleman and Purple Heart veteran of 2nd Platoon, H-3-7**

"I've now finished both "Fortune Teller's Blessing" and "Accordion War" and have been wowed by both. . . . Thank you for a brace of blazingly beautiful books!'

**Dr. John Wink, Professor of English, Ouachita Baptist University**

www.dochughesbooks.com

*With appreciation to Korean Vet Comrade*

*Charles Anderson*

# Accordion War: Korea 1951

## Life and Death in a Marine Rifle Company

*We Will Never Forget*

*"The Forgotten War"*

*Semper Fi*

*Charles "Doc" Hughes*

# Charles Hughes

HK

*Hell Kreek Book*

www.dochughesbooks.com

*A professional soldier understands that war means killing people, war means maiming people, war means families left without fathers and mothers. All you have to do is hold your first dying soldier in your arms, and have that terribly futile feeling that his life is flowing out and you can't do anything about it. Then you understand the horror of war. Any soldier worth his salt should be antiwar. And still there are things worth fighting for.*

General Norman Schwarzkopf

# Dedication

In memory of Pfc. Alfred J. Smith my foxhole buddy. "Smitty" was a young man caught up in a destructive war, but hurting people was not in his nature. [KIA May 31, 1951]

www.dochughesbooks.com

*Every gun that is made, every warship launched, every rocket fired signifies in the final sense, a theft from those who hunger and are not fed, those who are cold and not clothed. This world in arms is not spending money alone. It is spending the sweat of its laborers, the genius of its scientists, the hopes of its children. This is not a way of life at all in any true sense. Under the clouds of war, it is humanity hanging on a cross of iron.*

Dwight D. Eisenhower   April 16, 1953

*Never think that war, no matter how necessary, nor how justified, is not a crime.*

Ernest Hemingway

# Table of Contents

# Preface

Imagine standing on the back platform of a train watching a town and its landscape fall away into the distance as the train carries you to new destinations. As the town recedes and vanishes from your perception you don't conclude that the town has in fact disappeared; you realize the people in the town are still going about the rounds of their daily lives. The people there have not forfeited their reality by being out of your sight.

Time is closely analogous to space in this respect. Our past, like our view of the town from the rear of the train, is constantly receding from us, growing ever dimmer until it disappears, most of it lost forever. But the past does not forfeit its reality simply because we have forgotten it.

The analogy between space and time, of course, is not perfect. You can at some future time buy a train ticket and return to the town you saw fade into the distance. You can watch the town grow as you approach and when you arrive you can once more walk the streets and talk to the people there. But there is a catch. For the same reason you can never step into the same river twice, you can never visit the same town you left. It's a widely recognized truth that you can't go home again. The fault here lies not with space, but with time.

Time is the problem. We can't buy a ticket to take us back to yesteryear because we live only in the present while time is constantly pushing us into the future. So how can a person in search of lost time reconstruct events that happened a half century ago before they disappear forever over the event horizon? That was the challenge I confronted when I set out to write this book.

Time did provide me one advantage, however. Distance from events provides perspective. The Danish theologian Soren Kierkegaard made that point when he observed that life is lived forward but understood backward. While myriad details of my experiences as hospital corpsman in a Marine rifle company in Korea in 1951 had been irretrievably lost, many memories remained. Time, I found, had performed for me one of the crucial tasks of the writer, and that is the selection of significant detail. Just as the outgoing tide sweeps away detritus and leaves shining and patterned shells resting on pillars of sand, so the passage of time had erased many quotidian details of my experiences in Korea while leaving vivid memories, memories which provided me with my starting point. But I needed much more than those memories to tell the story I wanted to tell.

The task I undertook had something in common with those of archaeologists who reconstruct a past culture or civilization from fallen walls and pottery shards. I was fortunate in that I began my reconstruction with some reliable artifacts. I began by making a long list of specific events, memories that I briefly labeled in phrases and sentences. I was also helped by the fact that I had written some narratives of my Korean experiences while in my twenties, one of which was published as fiction though I had only changed the names. My devoted mother saved all my letters and these were a great help in establishing a time line and clarifying where How Company was and what we were doing at specific times. I relied heavily upon the official four-volume history, *U.S. Marine Operations in Korea* and the official USMC *Battalion Diaries* as well as other helpful sources listed at the end of this book. But the most appreciated contributions came from members of the H-3-7 Brotherhood and their families, from their shared memories, letters and suggestions that helped me to flesh out my narrative.

The payoff for me after two years of work is that I now have a much clearer understanding of what we were doing in the mountains of Korea all those years ago, of what that war was all about. In his excellent and detailed account of the conflict, *The Forgotten War*, Clay Blair explains the place of the Korean War in U.S. history:

> The United States has fought nine major wars, four in the twentieth century. Of these conflicts, the war in Korea, 1950-1953, ranks among the most important, yet it is the least remembered. . . .
>
> The war was a traumatic and momentous chapter in American history. It was a big, long war, during which nearly 6 million men and women served in the armed forces. Americans fought in Korea nearly three times as long as they had fought in World War I and almost as long as they had fought in World War II. The first year of combat was brutal and bloody, often surpassing the toughest battles of any war in American history. Total American casualties in Korea were heavy: 33,629 killed and 103,284 wounded.
>
> The impact of the war on the United States government and society was profound (ix).

Blair goes on to point out that the "blitzkrieg" of the war came in the first year before the two-year positional war set in. That fluid and dynamic phase of the war is the subject of this book, it is what I have termed "the accordion war."

One note of explanation: While we do not experience the manifold buzzing confusion of life as story, we do require the ordering and sequencing of events for understanding; we need narrative to make sense of our experiences. So in this book I have told the story of my experiences in How Company as I remember them. Every personal event I depict derives from the list of memories I first wrote down. I have done my best to establish the proper chronology though it's quite possible I've gotten some things out of sequence. I regret that I can no longer remember the names of some of the men who were my close comrades in Korea. Many I do remember, however, and strange as it may seem, I still remember a number of specific conversations rather clearly, though I might not get every word right or always attribute the words to the right speakers. In this regard I use Marines who were close to me, such as "Hawkshaw," "CP Sam," Smitty, Tardio, Shexnayder, and others as principles in some of those dialogs.

The words spoken on Sunflower How patrol I remember clearly, as well as the words we exchanged sitting in the ditch at the roadblock while covering our freezing legs with straw, and the complaints of the Marine who swore he would do no more walking when he became a civilian, and the words of Tardio after the mortar barrage in the long valley, and Shexnayder's words to me on the Crag as he took potshots at Chinese soldiers scrambling back and forth on an adjacent spur of the mountain—and many more.

Just as with people everywhere many of our exchanges were casual, perfunctory and repetitious since we followed a fairly regular daily routine. Some scenes in the book are conflations of often-repeated activities, such as sick call conducted for villagers, canteen details to find water, and camping in the mountains. Our daily conversations I have reproduced as faithfully as my memory and my ear allowed.

**www.dochughesbooks.com**

# Acknowledgements

A t a memorial ceremony in California in 2003 Charlene Imbrunetti proudly accepted on behalf of her brother his Korean Service Medal. Her son Michael, a Navy veteran who was born twelve years after his uncle was killed in Korea, found his interest in family history stirred by the event. He remembered his grandmother had kept her son's Purple Heart above the headboard of her bed though she rarely spoke of him. The pain from the telegram she had received fifty-two years earlier never left her. Michael's mother, a Registered Nurse, had been a young girl when her brother joined the Marines and was not able to provide her son with many details about his life. So Michael began to search through old family papers and picture albums in an effort to piece the fragments together and gain some understanding of the uncle he had never known. His mother had told him that her brother was in many ways like her father. So Michael now had a good start toward assembling the pieces. His uncle would have been a lot like his Grandpa Harold, the wise and charismatic truck driver, the caring man with many friends who had taught his grandson how to fish.

But Michael wanted to know more. He found the Korean War Project website on the Internet and typed in the name of his uncle. There he found the account I had written about the death of my friend PFC Harold Tardio. We were soon in contact by email. Michael wrote, "It was a sobering moment when I read your entry on the Koreanwar.org remembrance page. So far this is the only information I have found concerning my uncle. Thank you for this." I put Michael in touch with Lt. Col (Ret) George Barnes who had been the leader of our platoon the day Hal was killed and with Dr. Jim Nicholson the BAR man in the fire team from George Company that retrieved Hal's body along with that of Lawrence Hansen from the rocky mountain fortress dubbed "Izabitch."

Our correspondence culminated in a visit Michael and his wife paid to my wife and me here in Arkansas bringing as a gift a beautifully bound book of memories of Harold Tardio. It was from that book that I acquired the letters of condolences to Hal's mother from members of How Company. The pictures of Hal I have included in this book are also from that album which contains other pictures of Hal and his family and friends recording various stages of his short life. Included also are many documents and clippings that Michael assured me were reproductions though they appear to be originals. Among those are the newspaper casualty report with Hal's picture and the telegram to his parents beginning, "DEEPLY REGRET TO INFORM YOU THAT YOUR SON PRIVATE FIRST CLASS HAROLD MICHAEL TARDIO USMCR WAS KILLED IN ACTION IN THE PERFORMANCE OF HIS DUTY AND SERVICE OF HIS COUNTRY."

Michael Imbrunetti's dedication to retrieving something valuable from his family's past served as an example to me in writing this book. To him and all the people named in the chapter "The Brotherhood" and to others I am indebted. I could not have written the book without their help.

To some I must address my gratitude specifically:

For materials, such as photographs and letters I thank Ralph Tate, Joe Sipolski, George Barnes, Bob Nichols, Wadie Moore's widow, Jean, Tom Martin, Hardie Richards, George Brodeur, Jim Nicholson, and my old friend Ollie Langston for the account he provided of How Company's battle for Cloverleaf Hill.

I want to give special thanks to the late Jack Gogan for the inspiration he provided with his first-rate novel, *The Hard Way: The Story of H-3-7, a Marine rifle company. Korea 1951.* Jack, a machine-gunner with our company throughout most of the accordion phase of the war, demonstrates in his novel the point I make in the chapter, "Reserve"—that there was and remains an amazing amount of talent in the men of H-3-7. Anyone interested in a good read might still be able to get hold of a copy by contacting Jack's widow, Joyce Gogan, at 608 Grady St. Scottsboro, AL 35768.

Several people were kind enough to read an early form of my manuscript and offer many helpful suggestions and corrections, specifically Bob Nichols, Joe Sipolski (who pointed out emphatically that his name ends with an "i" not a "y," that his origins are Polish, not Russian), Ralph Tate, Ollie Langston, George Brodeur, Jean Moore, and Jim Nicholson.

While the contributions of all the above were significant and crucial, my greatest debt is to my former platoon leader, Lt. Colonel George Barnes. He was kind enough to go through my manuscript in detail, making copious notes and tactfully pointing out my not infrequent errors and distracting stylistic tics. He gently pointed out to me the redundancy of the statement, "a valley surrounded by hills." (He had a college English teacher who inculcated the elements of style, grammar and usage into his psyche so deeply they remain indelible to this day.) Colonel Barnes' long career in the Marine Corps plus the fact that he is an ardent student of history made his input particularly valuable. He corrected and clarified many of my accounts of the activities of How Company in Korea, and as for any remaining disparities or errors, I am the sole proprietor.

And thanks goes to my family, my son Chuck the talented musician who urged me to write this book, my daughter Cyndi Moorman English teacher extraordinaire who edited and proofread the final draft, and my wife,

Marie, who was the first to read my early efforts and offer helpful suggestions and encouragement and who patiently endured my long periods of distraction and neglect of domestic duties.

Special thanks to Seung A. Lee and Ga Yeong Gim, high-school exchange students in my son-in-law's calculus class, for checking my Korean dialog and providing me with some key words written in Hangul. These young ladies offer reassurance to Korean veterans that the sacrifices our country made in their country years ago have paid dividends.

Finally, while my brothers from How Company have been of great help in my research, they are not responsible for the opinions expressed in this book. They are all my own.

www.dochughesbooks.com

Note: My letters from Korea and the Tardio Book of Memories along with my collection of books on the Korean War including the 4-volume official Marine Corps history of the war have been donated to "Forgotten: the Arkansas Korean War Project" and are available at The Butler Center for Arkansas Studies: The Butler Center, 401 President Clinton Avenue, Little Rock, AR 72201. http://www.butlercenter.org/koreanwarproject/

### Nefarious War

*Last year we fought by the head-stream of the Sang-kan,*
*This year we are fighting on the Tsung-ho road.*
*We have washed our armor in the waves of Chio-chi lake,*
*We have pastured our horses on Tien-shan's snowy slopes.*
*The long, long war goes on ten thousand miles from home,*
*Our three armies are worn and grow old.*
*The barbarian does man-slaughter, not plowing;*
*On this yellow sand-plains nothing has been seen but blanched*
*   skulls and bones.*
*Where the Chin emperor built the walls against the Tartars,*
*There the defenders of Han are burning beacon fires.*
*The beacon fires burn and never go out,*
*There is no end to war!—*
*In the battlefield men grapple each other and die;*
*The horses of the vanquished utter lamentable cries to heaven,*
*While ravens and kites peck at human entrails,*
*Carry them up in their flight, and hang them on branches of*
*   dead trees.*
*So, men are scattered and smeared over the desert grass,*
*And the generals have accomplished nothing.*
*Oh, nefarious war! I see why arms*
*Were so seldom used by the benign sovereigns.*

Li Po (701-762)

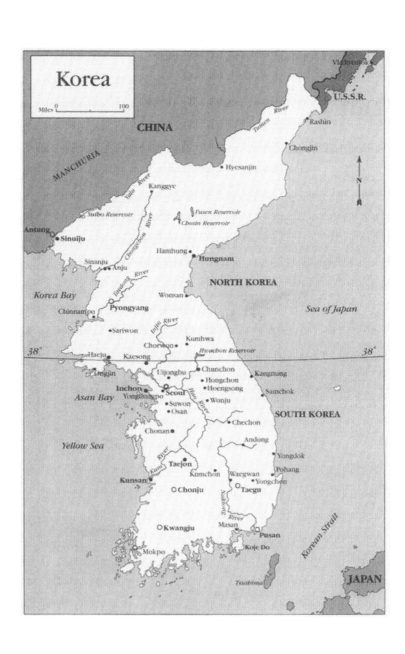

# CHAPTER 1

# Sunflower How

It was bone-breaking cold when we jumped down from the trucks at mid afternoon after a four-hour ride from the east coast port city of Pohang. When I hit the ground I fell to my knees with pain like hot needles shooting through my frozen legs. I managed to struggle to my feet with my heavy pack, rifle, and "Unit One" first aid kit and make my way to the side of the chalk dust road desperate to take a leak. With my left hand I pulled the heavy double mitten from my right and began to unbutton the fly on the outer pair of my three pairs of pants. I managed to get two buttons freed when my hand stopped working. I crammed the hand back into the mitten and beat it against my leg until some of the feeling came back, then I stripped the mitten off once more and began to work on the buttons again. By continuing this process I somehow managed to keep my britches dry, and I learned an important lesson. From then on I never buttoned my fly in Korea in the winter.

We left the truck convoy in the center of a long open valley that stretched ahead of us as it did behind us through the distance we had come from Pohang. Why did the trucks stop here? I couldn't understand the logic of dropping us off in the middle of nowhere, but in a Marine rifle company we weren't required to understand. We followed orders; logic had nothing to do with it.

The empty trucks circled in the dry rice paddies then headed back toward the coast while we formed two columns along either side of the road and continued west into the valley. Our platoon leader Lt. David Lowe passed the word back to "keep the interval," the old infantry practice of keeping enough distance between troops so that a single mortar or artillery shell could not take out so many men. Lowe, who bore some resemblance to Henry Fonda's Tom Joad in *Grapes of Wrath* and stood 6'4," didn't exactly fit his name.

With the walking my blood began to circulate and before long I was reasonably warm in my fleece cap with earflaps, my hooded parka with a helmet on top of the hood, mittens provided with an escape hole for the trigger finger, and shoe pacs (rubberized boots that kept out the snow and water but which, unfortunately, didn't allow our feet to breathe). Of course we had nothing to protect our faces, so throughout that winter of 1950-51 we all tasted the stinging metallic cold on our palates and had a perpetual drop of crystal clear snot dangling from the ends of our red noses.

Ahead of me I could see the two columns of Marines as they moved along the road and from near me and behind me I could hear the shuffle of feet and the clank of M1 Garand rifles and BAR's (Browning Automatic Rifles) against ammo cans and buckles. After we had loosened to the march a considerable amount of kidding and talk started going up and down the lines, but as time wore on the banter trailed off and we all withdrew inward and, as mystics meditate on their mantras, we concentrated on the rhythmic clump of our boots in the dry dust.

Our equipment was new. Our packs were loaded with the standard issue, much of which we would jettison after only a few weeks of climbing the mountains of Korea. We had been given our daily box of C Rations in Pohang that we carried tied to the tops of our packs: three "heavies," (cans of corned beef hash, beans & franks, etc.) and three "lights," (cans of crackers, cookies, and cocoa). Also included in the C Rations was a package containing cigarettes, toilet paper, matches, and a "handy dandy" can opener.

Through the long march across the valley we got periodic orders to "take five" or "take ten" at which times we would fall back on our packs against the far side of the ditch and maybe light up a cigarette while we gathered up energy in preparation for the order to "move out." After two hours of marching we were given a chow break, and then after another hour of trudging down the road I saw the columns ahead begin to move off the road to the left, following the rice paddy levees toward the mountains which lay about a mile to our south.

When we reached the base of the mountains we halted for a while so the platoon leaders could confer with the company commander who had just met with the battalion commander about our orders. Map reading was a particularly crucial skill in the Korean War and the ones our officers used were old Japanese maps made in the 1930's and 40's. The object for the infantry, particularly after General Matthew Ridgway had taken charge of the Eighth Army only weeks earlier, was always to take the high ground, but there was a confounding sameness about the mountainous terrain on the maps. Of course, as the platoon hospital corpsman I was not required or expected to read maps, but I know from several deadly screw-ups that map reading was a problem for infantry officers in Korea.

We really began to feel the weight of our gear once we got into the mountains. Darkness was approaching as we began the climb. A few of the old Chosin Reservoir veterans carried walking sticks cut during their last campaign, sticks which proved their usefulness in the steep ascents. The mountains were not alpine, like the Rockies, but more like the Ozarks, or in some cases the Smokies, wooded all the way to the tops with scrub oaks and pine, but not as tall and dense as those on the American mountains. It was during this the first of my campaigns that I heard the standing joke I would hear again and again throughout my tour in Korea. Sometimes as we would work our way down a steep trail a Marine would slip and fall on his ass, and as soon as he hit the ground some wiseacre would sound off, "Who told you to take five? No one told us to take a break!"

We continued huffing up the rocky trail in the moonlight for some time stopping periodically for the officers to compare their reckonings of where we were and where we were trying to go. We were not yet toughened to the field and were exhausted by the time we were told to scatter on the ridgeline and take up positions for the night. The sky was clear and cold and the moon, almost full, was already high in the eastern sky.

With my entrenching tool I was scraping a place for my sleeping bag on piece of rocky ground when I heard the first burst of gunfire I ever heard in actual combat. It was not directed at us but came from the valley below. I dropped my shovel and moved to a better vantage point. I could see the glowing trajectories of the tracers as they flew through the darkness below us. We watched fascinated, listening to the roar of the gunfire roll up the mountain and reverberate through the canyons flanking us. We speculated on which units were involved but could come to no conclusion since we weren't even sure of our location.

As I watched the tracers streak and ricochet in the velvet blackness of the moon-shadowed valley, I experienced a revelation. Too young for World War II, I had, nevertheless, grown up on John Wayne and William Bendix war movies and had felt cheated that I had missed that war. But now at the age of nineteen I was provided directly an Olympian view of the absurdity of the whole thing. I was not looking at an image on a screen or reading a description of a firefight in a book. Below me there were two groups of men intent on killing one another! It was the sheer reality that awed me now, a reality that can never be captured in pictures or words. I had read about war, I had seen it on the screen, I had spent a good deal of time the past two months imagining what it would be like. They had fired live ammo over our heads at Camp Pendleton while we scrambled on our bellies under barbed wire. But now, watching the bullets fly below me, it all seemed different. My four weeks of combat training had not prepared me for this. I had known, of course, that in combat men try to kill one another, but I had not understood it. As I listened to the gunfire roll up the side of the mountain and watched the golden tracks of the tracers stitching the black night, for the first time I realized the significance of what I had done when I volunteered for duty with the Fleet Marine Force.

It was after midnight before I crawled into the warmth of my goose down sleeping bag and promptly fell asleep.

\* \* \*

We were on the mountain that night as part of an operation that would be unofficially designated the "Gook Chase"—a campaign against guerrillas west of Pohang, the first action the 1st Marine Division had been committed to since the "strategic withdrawal" from the Chosin Reservoir near the Yalu River in the closing months of 1950. My unit, the 1st platoon of How Company, 3rd Battalion, 7th Regiment, like much of the whole division, was made up largely of replacements, since so many Marines had been lost to enemy fire and frostbite in the long retreat from Chosin through Yu Dam-ni and Hagaru-ri to the harbor at Hungnam.

Just days before our entire Division had been loaded on LSTs and brought up the eastern coast of Korea from Pusan to the port of Pohang-Dong where we were unloaded and trucked to a camping area. I wrote home from there on January 22ⁿᵈ:

> We are situated right by an airfield. When we first came up here we were supposed to hold open an avenue of escape for the Army, but now it seems the Army stopped running to catch their breath and looked around and found that the enemy was not within miles of them. So now we are patrolling the parts down here where there are supposed to be enemy troops. We leave tomorrow on a four-day patrol and we're supposed to run into some North Korean troops but it's not certain. I wouldn't be able to tell you about it but we should be back by the time you get this letter....
>
> We are now in a large flat valley. You can see the mountains way off in the distance and boy the wind really comes down off of them & helps make the weather a little more miserable. Night before last the wind was blowing so hard it blew the tin [chimney] cover off of our tent. The only ones that would get up were a sergeant and myself. I climbed up on the tent to put it back on and my fingers and ears like to have frozen. Then we had trouble with our stove. We had to work on it for about an hour...finally when we got the stove cherry red the rest of the guys got up. Our tent has so many holes in it it is pathetic.

I had not enlisted in the Marine Corps. I joined the Regular Navy for three years during peacetime in 1948 and was scheduled to be discharged the following August, 1951, but about that possibility and the war I wrote

> I'm not planning on it [getting discharged in August] because it is very unlikely that I will. A war like this could go on forever,

however I hope we don't withdraw now. We have lost too much already....

Write and give me some local news & let me know what's first on the Hit Parade every Saturday

Write soon. Love Charles

When I wrote that letter I was unaware of how much by the very next day I would be missing that pyramidal tent and oil-burning stove. And the four-day patrol would end up lasting over two weeks.

\* \* \*

Now here on our first night out, weary from the long march and climb up the mountain, I had fallen asleep promptly even though two rocks like spear points were poking me in the back and my head was below the level of my feet because I had tied the strings at the bottom of my sleeping bag to the roots of a tree so I wouldn't roll down the mountain.

I couldn't have been in my goose down sleeping bag much more than an hour, just long enough to get warm in the only place I would ever get warm that winter, when someone kicked my feet and yelled, "Get up! We've got patrol!" I couldn't believe it.

After being jolted out of my deep sleep I crawled reluctantly out of my warm sleeping bag and pulled on my boots and laced them up. I slept in my shirt and pants and socks, so dressing was not that much of a chore. There was no snow on the ground but it was bitter cold. I rolled up my gear, donned my parka and mittens, and picked up my aid kit and my M2 carbine and fell in with the squad members who were gathering around Lt. Lowe. When a squad patrol went out like this often the platoon leader and his runner and the hospital corpsman went along while the other two thirds of the platoon would be exempt. Leaving our gear under the protection of the rest of the platoon, we moved out following a trail down the mountain in the moonlight.

The descent to the valley was not difficult and before long we found ourselves moving along a white dirt road with dry frozen rice paddies on our left and a spur of the mountain we had just descended rising to our right. We moved along the road in two columns keeping our interval in the moonlight. Lt. Lowe told the runner to contact the company CP on the walkie-talkie radio. Once the contact had been made, the lieutenant took the radio and reported on our position and progress. There was considerable static in the communication but I could hear the voice from How Company confirming receipt of Lt. Lowe's report.

We continued down the road as it curved to our right around the mountain spur and then began to angle away from the mountain and leave it behind.

We had now been on the road for thirty or forty minutes. The bright moon was past its zenith, and we could see off to our left across the frozen stubble of the rice paddy a dark line of trees that marked a creek or a dry creek bed perhaps a hundred yards away. We had been making an effort to be quiet; when we spoke we spoke in whispers and were careful to avoid the clanking of arms and gear. We were moving along to the sound only of the shuffle of our boots in the dry dirt when we heard voices. They came from the line of trees to our left, and the words were not English. We all heard them, and as a man, we stopped for perhaps three seconds and looked toward the tree line.

At once a line of fire broke out from all along the creek bed. Just as suddenly fifteen Marines hit the ditch closest to the source of the gunfire and hunkered down to get the maximum benefit of the twelve to sixteen inch embankment the ditch offered. I propped the tip of my carbine over the rim of the ditch and rolled over on my back and turned my face from left to right. I could see the Marines on either side of me, and, inches above our heads, a steady lacing of orange tracer bullets. The deafening explosions of rifle and machine-gun fire engulfed us.

After a minute some Marine several down from me yelled out, "Is anyone hit?"

Word was passed from man to man and I was relieved to hear that miraculously no one had been hit. I was disappointed in myself, however, for as corpsman, I should have been the one to ask that question. But I was relieved that I didn't have to expose myself to that withering fire to get to a wounded Marine.

I could hear Lieutenant Lowe down the line trying to get through on the radio

"Sunflower How this is Sunflower How patrol, over!"

Static

"Sunflower How, this is Sunflower How patrol. How do you read me? Over!"

More static

"This goddamn thing! It's useless. We came around that mountain and this goddamn thing only works line of sight. Piece of shit. Here! Keep trying to make contact!" And he gave the radio back to the runner who frantically kept trying to reach our CP.

Although the gunfire was coming from about a hundred yards distance, it sounded as though our attackers were only a few feet away. And no Marine was contributing to the intensity of the roar of battle because none of us had fired a shot. The fire was so intense and so close that sticking your head above the ditch seemed a certain way to get it blown off.

I had begun to pray the moment I hit the ditch. My prayers weren't imaginative or altruistic or premeditated. They were the basic prayers of a man confronted with momentary extinction, a mindless incantation:

"God, don't let me die! Oh, please God, don't let me die!"

I could see clearly the brief notice that would appear in the *Daily Times Herald* and the *Dallas Morning News*. I could see my family reading the telegram and hear the condolences coming in. I was resentful that I would die in my very first firefight. And there seemed little doubt that we all would die. Here we were exposed on a flat road while our more numerous assailants were firing at us from the cover of the tree-lined creek bed.

After some time Lieutenant Lowe yelled out, "Will someone volunteer to try to make it back to our CP? We can't reach them on this goddamn radio and I don't see any way we can fight our way out of here outnumbered as we are. Will someone try to make a run for it?"

There was no answer. No volunteer.

The lieutenant was new to his command. I was new. Most of the squad were new, being replacements for the heavy losses the Marine Corps suffered after the Chinese entered the war and drove the UN forces back across the 38th parallel to the southern end of the peninsula. There were a few veterans in the squad, however, and one of them, a Chicano, called out to the Lieutenant, "I think they may be friendly forces; they're all using American weapons."

Later we would all learn to recognize the accelerating staccato and rising pitch, the ripping sound of the burp gun and other characteristic sounds of Chinese and North Korean rifles and machine guns, but for now we were all grateful for the perception and presence of mind of this one Marine. And the color of the tracers were further evidence of American firepower. The Chosin vet had provided us our only hope, so we all began to yell out.

"American Marine! No shoot! OK?"

"No Shoot! No Shoot! American Marine! No Shoot, OK?"

We yelled with the energy and enthusiasm of marooned sailors spotting an approaching sail. We yelled up into the tracers that were still flying inches above our heads

"American Marine! No shoot! OK?"

Now the sounds from the road rose and mixed with those from the creek bed as our voices added to the din of the gunfire coming across the rice paddy. The roar from the line of trees continued undiminished.

Then slowly but perceptibly the gunfire began to abate. We yelled even louder with this encouragement and the shooting continued to trail off until it finally stopped. We too fell silent.

"Whatta we do now?"

"Somebody's got to stand up!"

"What if it's a trap?"

"We can't just lay here."

"Who's going to do it?"

Then Lt. Lowe spoke up. His voice cracked as he told us, "I'm going to stand up. If they shoot me you may as well return fire cause there's no way in hell we're going to get out of here."

Then he began to yell across to the darkened line of trees, "I'm going to stand up! No shoot, OK? No Shoot, OK?"

A voice came back from the creek bed, "No shoot."

We watched Lt. Lowe rise slowly to his considerable height with his hands stretched even higher in the air and followed him with our eyes as he crossed the dry rice paddy in the moonlight toward the black streak of trees. We saw him descend into the shadows and we waited as the minutes ticked by.

"What the hell are they doing? He ought to be out of there by now!"

Maybe they did something to him. Maybe they killed him."

"What do we do if he doesn't come out of there?"

At last we saw a tall black shape emerge from the tree shadows and head back to where we were now kneeling in the ditch.

"It's OK! You can get up!"

"Who the hell are those guys?" The squad leader spoke for all of us.

"It's a ROK unit, a road block."

"Those sons a bitches. It's a wonder they hadn't killed us all."

The lieutenant told us the Koreans had asked him if they had hit anyone, and when told they hadn't they began to kid one another for being bad shots. And these, we thought, were "friendly forces." Lt. Lowe had the Chicano Marine go over and stay with the Republic of Korea (ROK) soldiers to make sure they wouldn't fire on us on our return trip down the road.

Lt. Lowe reassembled the squad and got us moving again down the road in the moonlight toward our destination. How he was able to determine where we were supposed to go was a mystery to me and to most of the guys in the squad. Map reading was one of the most crucial skills in this country of mountains where one looked much like another and there were few highways, roads and significant landmarks. And this was a night patrol. The lieutenant did have a flashlight to read his map with, but even though the moon was still bright the terrain was not easy to make out. But we trusted him. We followed orders.

And we followed that road until we came to a mountain spur that descended almost to the road and rose to a dark wood-covered ridgeline to our right. Lt. Lowe had a fire team take the point and we all began the ascent of the ridgeline in single file. The ridgeline took a horseshoe shape and we stumbled along the rocky trail until we reached the highest point and then began to circle back toward the road we had come down. As we were descending we left the ridgeline and were moving down the inner slope toward the road, when at once from the opposing slope small arms fire again exploded aimed at us, but this time we were ready and immediately began yelling, "American Marine, No Shoot!" And this time the shooting stopped promptly and again, amazingly, we were spared any casualties. We had made it through another ROK roadblock.

So we made it back to the company on the mountain and I was able to get back in my sleeping bag for about an hour's sleep before we had to roll out and get ready to move.

*Lt. David Lowe with Chinese skull*

\* \* \*

I had arrived in Korea just four weeks earlier at the port city of Pusan as a member of the 4th Replacement Draft at a time when the future of the UN mission to stem the Communist onslaught seemed in doubt. It was just as well for us replacements that we had no understanding of the big picture at that time; if we had we would not have been in such good spirits when we landed.

We were off loaded from the Japanese ferry *Takuja Maru* and put on trucks for the ride to the city of Masan where the 1ˢᵗ Marine Division was rebuilding after its heroic breakout from the Chinese trap at the Chosin Reservoir. The weather was cold and gray as we made our way through the somber city and on to the unpaved road to Masan passing through outlying settlements where we saw villagers huddled in small groups watching our long line of trucks roll through. Some of them smiled and waved and when we slowed down little children extended their open palms and called out for "chockoleto" or "cigaretto" seeking any item of conceivable worth. Some onlookers waved toy Korean or United States flags. Once through a courtyard and over a wall I saw the bobbing heads of two little girls as they jounced one another on a teeter-totter.

When we got clear of the city we picked up speed. Across from me in the rear of the open truck a row of parka-hooded, brown-helmeted Marines and corpsmen stared out on a patchwork of rice paddies and an occasional cluster of thatched roof mud houses. As our trucks whined along they left in their wake clouds of billowing white dust that sifted and settled on the evenly spaced and flat-cropped trees and the tangle of communication wires stretched along each side of the road.

After some time sitting stiffly in the cold bouncing truck, I saw the dirty puff of a mortar shell burst at the base of a mountain some half a mile in front of us. When the dull report of the explosion reached the truck all the men looked up toward the blast then quizzically toward one another. Several more shell bursts followed in quick succession while our convoy continued to lumber toward the blasts. Was this enemy fire? Were we to be thrown into combat so precipitously? No one told us what to expect. No one told us anything. It was only later that we found out the mortar fire was from our own Marines limbering up their weapons to be ready for the next operation.

We found the Division sprawled out in frozen, rutted bean fields just outside the city of Masan housed primarily in dusty olive-colored pyramidal tents. After we disembarked from the trucks, I and Ollie Langston, the corpsman I had served with over the past year in California at Mare Island Naval Hospital then at Oak Knoll Naval Hospital, and several Marine replacements were directed toward the command post (CP) of How Company, Third Battalion, Seventh Regiment, or H-3-7 for short, a rifle company. We made our way through the tents, stacks of weapons and ammunition, tanks and piles of 90 mm brass shell casings from the tanks to the How Company area where we were met by one of the most colorful characters we would meet in Korea, Gunnery Sergeant Fred Clyde Spell, a World War II veteran who had survived one of the most horrendous battles of that war, Iwo Jima.

I don't offer the following as an objective, photographic description, but as a mental picture I have carried in my head for over half a century. Gunny Spell was of medium height; he had a reddish brown scraggly moustache, a pug nose with a scar on one cheek that looked like a dimple. His arms seemed short for his body and he walked with the right arm held away from his body and bent slightly akimbo like a person whose arm had been broken at one time and not properly set so that the palm of his hand rotated toward the front making him appear to walk with a cocky strut. Often the Gunny's right hand clutched his blackened canteen cup full of coffee. It seemed that steady infusion of caffeine stoked his irascible nature and kept him primed for the ass chewings he dispensed on a regular basis. (I wrote this before I attained the photo below which the reader can check for comparison.)

The Gunny greeted us in a gruff raspy voice, informing each of us which platoon we would be assigned to. I was assigned to the 1st Platoon and Ollie was assigned to the 2nd. Ollie and I were each introduced to the guys in our platoons and taken to one of the pyramidal tents that accommodated about ten Marines, and shown a spot on the ground where we could unroll our sleeping bags and stow our packs and equipment.

*Gunnery Sergeant Fred C. Spell*

During these final days of 1950 the 1st Division was rebuilding after suffering severe losses during its breakout from the trap at the Chosin Reservoir where the Marines had been surrounded and outnumbered by hordes of Chinese Communist troops. Their "strategic withdrawal," fighting their way through the sub-zero snow of the precipitous T'aebaek Mountains, from Yudam-ni through Hagaru-ri, Koto-ri and Hamhung back to the port of Hungnam, added another heroic chapter to the history of the Marine Corps.

We didn't have much in the way of drills and military exercises there in the bean patch, partly I suppose to give those "Chosin Few" who had endured the ordeal of the previous few weeks a well-deserved break, so we spent our days mostly trying to stay warm and scrounge up food. But still we were called out for muster every morning before daylight. Gunny Spell would line us up in the dark and line us out about our daily orders and our deficiencies in conduct and deportment. He kept a "shitlist" of Marines guilty of various minor infractions and seemed to enjoy slapping them with little extra duties and details.

One morning he was particularly wroth about some infraction and was storming up and down in front of the company formation when a voice from the darkness in the back of the ranks said "Fuck you, Gunny!" There was a moment of stunned silence, then a scattered chuckle or two. Gunny Spell charged to the back of the formation in an apoplectic rage demanding to know who the miscreant was who dared such insubordination, but his demands were met with absolute silence. He threatened dire consequences and sputtered about for a while, but when it became clear he was not going to identify the offender he moved on to other topics.

Everyone knows the toughness and the celebrated discipline of the United States Marine Corps, so such a breach of military conduct may seem surprisingly out of character, but over the next nine months I saw more than once defiance from enlisted men as well as officers toward their seniors. The stress of combat can sometimes break down those carefully inculcated reflexes for military discipline and courtesy, and some of those Chosin veterans, after what they had been through over the past few weeks, felt like they didn't need to take crap from anybody. What could happen to them worse than what they had already been through?

That was my introduction to How company.

\* \* \*

But now, just four weeks later, I had survived my first night patrol and had learned in the process what Winston Churchill meant when he said "Nothing in life is so exhilarating as to be shot at without result."

Our company and the whole Division continued its campaign against the guerillas under General Lee Bam Nee of the North Korean Army's 10[th] Division whose object was to interdict the main supply route (MSR) between Pohang and Andong and cut off supplies being sent north to the United Nations forces who were at last making progress against the Chinese Communist Forces and the North Korean People's Army.

Of course we knew none of this then. The top brass felt no obligation to share grand military strategy with rifle companies. All we knew was to follow orders and the orders came on a daily basis.

# CHAPTER 2

# Kitty Dong

We continued to move frequently over the next several days. One night our first platoon was ordered to establish a roadblock. We took up positions in a deep ditch beside a road where intelligence reports indicated guerrilla troops might be moving during the night. The sky was overcast so there was no moon now, and it was bitter cold. We were supposed to keep absolutely still and quiet, though we could not resist the temptation to whisper back and forth. The main topic of our conversation was the cold. There was a pile of straw in the ditch and several of us took some and piled it over our legs for a little extra insulation.

A rifleman spoke up, "You know when we get back to the states we'll all be able to recognize one another."

"How's that?"

"We'll all be arthritic and bent over. We'll look like old men while we're still in our twenties. Walking down the street we'll be able to recognize one another from a block away. 'Hey, there comes another poor fucking Korean veteran, that one there twisted like Quasimodo!' My goddamn knees are killing me."

We all believed him. There would surely be some permanent damage from pain so continuous and intense.

No one came down the road that night. Not even the ROK outfit that gave us such a welcome a few nights before. So the next morning we moved out of the valley and back into the high country.

We took up positions along a ridgeline, heated up some C rations and were sitting around our camp fires watching the light disappear from the sky, drinking coffee and cocoa from our blackened canteen cups, when Lt. Lowe, who had just come from the company CP, told us to turn in because we had a patrol early next morning. The platoon Sergeant arranged the watch for the night and the rest of us crawled in our sleeping bags to warm up and get some sleep.

We were up two hours before daylight. Lt. Lowe assembled the platoon and we were soon joined by a weapons team toting light 30-caliber machineguns and 60 mm mortars and also by Kim the company interpreter. (Every company had its own interpreter and they all were named Kim. All of them had an excellent command of Korean, but as a rule, their English left a lot to be desired.)

A word here about the weapons team: The truth is that most of us in the platoon thought of How Company as a rifle company—three platoons, each with three four-man fire teams. We were not that acquainted with the men in the weapons team who mostly followed along behind us toting light air-cooled 30 caliber machine guns (and light is a misleading term, because those guns weren't light nor were the heavy boxes of ammunition they had to carry). Lugging 60 mm mortars up steep mountain trails along with their required shells was no picnic either.

Machine gunners and mortar men never had to take the point in an assault, so some may have concluded that the weapons guys had a relatively soft job. But one thing I learned in my months in that rifle company was that while machine gunners didn't have to take the brunt in an assault, once the firefight was underway they were called on to set up their guns on high ground to command an effective field of fire, and by doing so they became the magnets which attracted the most ferocious enemy fire. The same was true in defensive operations where the enemy's first objective would be to knock out the machinegun positions. So the weapons team was a vital part of our rifle company and we would find that out on this and many subsequent operations. One of the machine gunners on this operation carrying a light thirty across his shoulder and a can of ammo in his hand was Bob Cameron, a Chosin veteran I would meet again many years later.

We started out down the ridgeline in the dark, but rather than descending to the valley we headed up another mountain steeper and higher than the one we had spent the night on. After struggling up a particularly steep, tree-covered slope, the lieutenant had us take up positions in the trees across and just below the ridgeline. There we waited for daylight.

As the black sky softened to gray and the pale light began to wash down through the trees we found ourselves looking steeply down into a narrow valley. Below us and to our right some 400 to 800 yards away was a village of about seven houses slowly taking shape in the growing light. The trees we were in stopped in a straight line a short distance below us and down below the tree line at the bottom of the precipitous slope a frozen river ran directly toward the village. There was no sign of life anywhere below us. We waited.

Maybe twenty minutes passed after the coming of the first light. Then someone spoke out.

"Hey, there's a guy down there!"

"Where?"

"On the river. Walking down the river. Right there, see him?" He pointed.

We looked, and there was a man all right, walking from our left headed toward our right in the direction of the village. In a few minutes he was directly below us. We could see his clothes were black and that he had a rifle across his back. It wasn't hanging off one shoulder as we carried ours for easy access, but the strap crossed his chest. He walked slowly down the ice, taking care not to slip, totally oblivious that he was the focus of such fascinated attention.

"Kim!" Lt. Lowe spoke up. "Go down to the edge of the trees and call down and tell that guy to put his rifle down and come up here. Tell him we have his ass covered."

Kim worked his way down the steep slope and stopped at one of the last trees and, leaning against its trunk, he cupped his hands around his mouth and yelled something down in Korean. The man on the ice stopped, apparently astonished to hear this voice coming from the mountain. He turned and stared curiously up toward Kim's voice for a moment, then yelled something back that only Kim could understand. He and Kim continued an energetic exchange for perhaps a minute, then, without ever attempting to retrieve his rifle from his back, the man started running down the ice toward the village.

Lt. Lowe yelled out, "Get the son-of-a bitch!"

I had been holding the man in the sights of my carbine that I had steadied against a tree. Although it would fire full automatic, I had it set on semi automatic. As soon as I heard the lieutenant's words I squeezed off three rapid shots and saw three white spots appear on the ice well behind the running man. Then a Marine near me let go with his BAR that was resting on a stump and the black-figured guerrilla hit the ice face down and slid to a stop and did not move.

After the shooting started someone yelled out, "There they go!"

We all looked and saw six or seven guerrillas running away through a ravine behind the village. The light machine-guns, BARs and M1s opened up but the North Koreans had disappeared down the ravine. All the fire was then directed at the houses. Marines were firing the small 60 mm mortars, but the village was so steeply below us that the mortar tubes were pointing almost straight up and the shells seemed to take forever to land; when they did the puffs of WP (white phosphorus, or "Willie Pete") showed they were way off target. But the machine guns and BARs were deadly effective. I could see the tracers crisscrossing and lacing through the mud walls and grass roofs of the houses.

Shortly after we opened fire I saw an old man and a small girl perhaps eight years old emerge from one of the houses. They stood by the door facing us, the old man with his hand on the girl's shoulder, both looking up toward us, toward the trees that were our cover. They stood there for just a few seconds then went back in the house.

By the time the mortars found the target the village was already on fire from the tracers. Smoke was rising from every thatched roof. I had been watching to see if the old man or little girl would appear again but they never did. And the house was burning fiercely now. I don't know how many were in the village, but the only ones we saw escape were the guerrillas who fled down the ravine.

When there seemed no point in trying to inflict further damage, Lt. Lowe gave the order to cease fire. We sat there for a while watching the village burn. The houses blazed and blackened and smoke and embers and whiffs of black straw blew away in the wind down the valley away from us.

Then suddenly there was another burst of gunfire; I looked around to see who was shooting. No one was. The fire was incoming. It was peppering in the trees above our heads. We all immediately scrambled up the hill and took up positions along the reverse slope of the ridgeline and peered back in the direction of the incoming fire, but the trees we were in blocked our view. We had seen earlier another steep mountain across the river facing us; the mountains were close but the distance was far for small arms fire to carry, yet that was the only source for the gunfire we could imagine. We didn't attempt to return the fire because we had nothing to shoot at.

When the gunfire stopped we lay there for a while. Two of the veterans of the Chosin Reservoir were talking, a PFC and a corporal.

"When we had to take a hill just outside U Dam Ni we came up on a ridge line and there was this wounded Chink officer sitting up against a tree in the snow just looking at us. There was something red on his chest like a ribbon or medal, and old Hot Shot there (indicating the corporal) bet me he could hit it with his M1 from where we stood, so I took the bet, a case of beer when we get back stateside."

"Did he hit it?"

"Hell no!" the corporal spoke up. "I missed it by two inches, but I got something out of it. It wasn't a ribbon anyway; it was a goddamn fountain pen. I sold it to one of them rear echelon pogues back there in Masan."

All the way back down the mountain, throughout the rest of the day, and that night in my sleeping bag I kept seeing the figure of the man running along the ice, the white spots exploding behind him and his body sliding face down along the frozen river. And I thought about the old man and the little girl. They must be dead; no one in that village could have escaped. There must have been other civilians in there we never saw.

I surprised myself being the first one to fire at the man on the ice. I wasn't the one who killed him, but that was just a technicality. I had tried. I gave that incident a lot of thought later and decided I wouldn't do that anymore. I was not a pacifist, but I had other responsibilities in the platoon. I did on several occasions later join in giving covering fire, but that was just shooting into a mountainside, into woods and other cover, not shooting at anyone I could see. I suppose I could have killed someone doing that, but I doubt it.

Starting in World War II Navy corpsmen and army medics were issued carbines for their own protection, but they were not required to use them. The old noncombatant approach with red crosses on helmets and sleeves used in World War I had not worked. The red crosses just made good targets. So now the only thing that distinguished corpsmen from other Marines was the first aid bag we carried over our shoulders.

\* \* \*

Every GI in Korea had a story about how he ended up in the war. The hardships we faced, the cold weather, the long marches and mountain climbing, not to mention getting shot at, made us want to find something or someone to blame. Many Marines had signed up in the Reserves before the war broke out never really expecting to be called to active duty. I remember a sergeant who had served in World War II saying he was so happy to be discharged at the end of the war that he signed all the papers they put in front of him, scarcely giving a thought to the fact that he was signing up for the Reserves. What the hell? The war was over! But now, with a wife and kids back home, here he was saddled up again, "snoopin' and poopin'" half way around the world. He had been, as we said in those days, screwed, blued, and tattooed.

Some of the guys in my platoon won some sympathy with their stories. But I could make no such appeals. I had brought this all on myself. Like some other young men of my time I early on acquired an itch for adventure and a strong dislike of school. It wasn't that I didn't like books. I loved to read. The first book that really ignited my thirst for adventure was Twain's *The Adventures of Tom Sawyer*, after that I read *Huck Finn* then everything I could get my hands on by Mark Twain. I read the Penrod books by Tarkington and *Tom Brown's School Days* by Hughes. I read Dana's *Two Years Before the Mast* and Verne's *Twenty Thousand Leagues Under the Sea*. I read John Steinbeck and the Northern wilderness adventures of Jack London and James Oliver Curwood. I was always reading but never the books my teachers wanted me to read. High school to me was a prison and I wanted to escape into that wider world of adventure that I had been reading about in books.

When I was sixteen I rode a Greyhound bus from Dallas to Houston with the idea of signing up with the merchant marines. I had only my bus fare and a few dollars and couldn't afford a hotel so I spent one night sleeping on a piece of plywood in a vacant lot where the mosquitoes feasted on all those parts of me not protected by my jeans and leather jacket. Although my clothes helped me some with the mosquitoes, they did a poor job of protecting me from the cool night air. The next day I went down to the waterfront to inquire about signing up to go to sea. I was asked for documentation of my age and with that request I ran into a brick wall. I hung around the docks a few days with no hope of realizing my dreams of adventure, but I did get to take in those huge rusty freighters from far away places and smell the sea water and diesel oil that for me ever since has become intermingled with the romance of the sea. One night I slept in a chair at the bus station, another in an all night movie. But finally I had to give up. Fortunately I had bought a round trip ticket so I was able to make it back to Dallas.

So I had to go back to school where I was flunking out and wait until I reached the triumphant age of seventeen. As soon as I did, the summer of 1948, I was down at the Coast Guard recruiting office ready to sign up. I had read some of their literature and believed I could find the adventure I was looking for in that organization. I filled out all the applications and took the required tests and was told that I was accepted and would leave for duty within a month. When I told my friend, Robert Pasley, that I was off to join the Coast Guard he said he would like to go with me. We both went back to the recruiting office and told them of our desire to ship out together, but they said unfortunately they could only accept one recruit a month, so Robert and I went to the Navy recruiting office and found we could both be inducted together. We signed up, had our physicals and, along with eight or ten other young men, were ready to be sworn in. But we first had to wait until the Chief Petty Officer and his assistant finished their game of acey deucey.

On the day of our departure we boarded a Pullman train in the grand railroad station at Dallas and began our journey to the Naval Training base at San Diego, California. I was a little taken aback when, as soon as the train pulled out of the station, some of my fellow recruits broke out bottles of whiskey and dice and a deck of cards and began to entertain themselves. I didn't drink or smoke and had never gambled for anything other than matchsticks, but I followed their activities with interest.

The Pullman train offered luxuries that were revelations to me. Porters were on hand to attend to our every need. But since we were teenagers from working class families, we didn't really understand how to make use of such perks. That first night I got a green-curtained upper berth, and found it very restful. It had an air vent that could be turned in any direction to admit the fresh air from outside. So I slept well with the rhythmic clacking of the wheels and the gentle rocking of the car through the night. The next day we passed through the high country of New Mexico where it was raining. After the rain stopped I walked out on the platform between the cars and could see red water falling from a high mesa. I inhaled the fresh ozone and rain smell and knew I was entering a new chapter in my life.

And that chapter was three months of Navy boot camp. The rigors and discipline of boot camp I will not go into here, but I will say that for the unformed youth I was, those experiences were salutary. It was there I got my first experience with Marines. We had to undergo weapons training and the Marines were our instructors. Before our actual target practice we had some preliminaries. We were positioned in a large circle and told to aim at a central point of the circle and pull the triggers of our empty weapons, an exercise called "snapping in." Well, on this particular day I was extremely tired after the exhausting activities of the day before, and while we were lying prone on the ground aiming at that central point, I lay my head over on my rifle and dozed off.

When I awoke a Marine corporal was astraddle my back twisting both of my ears. "How would you like me to send these ears home to your mama, boy? Now get your ass out there and fall into the prone position fifty times. Move it!" So I had to get out in the center of my peers and stand and fall with my rifle fifty times. I never dreamed then I would have much further to do with the Marine Corps.

When I was completing basic training I was called in and asked what specializations I preferred. True to my adventurous spirit I told them I wanted to be a Boatswains Mate or Gunners Mate. The petty officer said those choices sounded great, but they needed a third choice. I had trouble coming up with one so he suggested hospital corpsman. What were the chances, I thought, that I wouldn't get one of my first two choices? So I said, "sure." It was only later that it dawned on me that they were no doubt in need of hospital corpsmen and that I had in effect been set up. But I made the best of the unexpected assignment. I'll never know what would have happened if I'd gone down either of the other two roads not taken, but now with the perspective of years I can say that the road chosen for me did not turn out so badly.

After Hospital Corps School in San Diego I was assigned to Mare Island Naval Hospital in Vallejo, California, and when that facility was closed down Ollie Langston and I and many other hospital personnel were transferred to Oak Knoll Naval Hospital at Oakland. Life at Oak Knoll was pleasant enough. For a while I worked on the proctology ward where I learned about pilonidal cysts, fistulas, hemorrhoids and other afflictions of the human derriere. The high point of that duty was when I got to assist the doctor in a proctoscopic examination of an admiral. During this period Ollie and I put in for sea duty on a fairly regular basis but we had no luck.

Then, shortly after the Korean War broke out in June 1950 we heard they were recommissioning the Hospital Ship *Benevolence*, and Ollie and I hoped we might get duty there, but again we had no luck. Or maybe I should say this time we lucked out. We envied our fellow corpsmen who had been tapped for that duty and wished them well as they set out for the shakedown cruise of this beautiful ship which had gone into service the last year of World War II and then served during the nuclear tests in the Pacific before being retired. With this latest war she had been called back to service and was just limbering up getting ready for her new duties in Korea when on August 20 she collided with the SS *Mary Luckenbach* and sank just off the coast of San Francisco. Oak Knoll Naval Hospital, as well as other medical facilities around the Bay Area, was called on to help in the rescue operation. There were twenty-three fatalities and hundreds of cold, shivering survivors. Soon some of those corpsmen we had envied were back working on the wards with us.

When the news of the war first hit the papers none of us knew where Korea was. We had never heard of it, but we soon learned its location. Not long after the war started some of the first wounded arrived at our hospital and I was transferred to a ward to which a number of them had been admitted. One Marine had been shot in the arm, which was in a cast and threatening to become gangrenous. Another had a hip wound where a bullet had gone through the stock of his rifle and penetrated his leg carrying a lot of splinters with it. And there were other wounded in traction and wheelchairs and in various stages of recovery.

On the wards there in Oakland we were all reading the news about how American and South Korean forces had been pushed to the end of the peninsula to a position called the Pusan Perimeter. Those first wounded we saw were from Lt. Colonel Raymond Murray's 5th Marine Regiment, part of the 1$^{st}$ Provisional Marine Brigade, that had been hastily sent over to aid in that desperate defense. For a while it appeared our forces would have to be pulled out of Korea altogether, but the defending Eighth Army under General Walton Walker and his ROK allies stiffened the defense there and the perimeter held as more reinforcements arrived. At the same time the North Korea People's Army (NKPA) was finding it more difficult to support their forces because their supply lines had become so extended and in addition they were now meeting strong resistance.

The month following the North Korean invasion General MacArthur was appointed Supreme Commander of the United Nations forces in Korea. With the UN forces backed into a corner he believed the time was ripe for a plan he had been contemplating for some time: A Marine amphibious landing at Inchon, the port city near the capital of Seoul. MacArthur had had great success with amphibious operations throughout the Pacific in the last war and he was confident the Marines could do the job now. A successful landing at Inchon would be followed by a rapid advancement by UN forces inland to cut off the NKPA in the south, sever their supply lines, and bring about their defeat. MacArthur was not merely seeking an advantage in the battle; he was seeking victory. General Ridgway in his book *The Korean War* says of MacArthur's plan:

The Inchon Landing, Operation Chromite, the daring 5000-to-1 shot that restored the initiative to our forces in Korea and kept them from being pushed into the sea, was a typical MacArthur operation, from inception to execution. Almost before the rest of us fully comprehended that our nation was at war, MacArthur had begun to plan the amphibious enveloping movement, so characteristic of all his Pacific strategy, that would hit the enemy where he least looked for a blow, would sever his supply lines, and trap him between anvil and hammer. While others thought of a way to withdraw our forces safely, MacArthur planned for victory (33).

But the status of the Marine Corps at the outbreak of the Korean War was somewhat shaky. The Corps had suffered from the post war stand down just as had the other branches of the service. At the end of World War II the Marines numbered over 485,000 strong, but by June of 1950 there were less than 75,000 in uniform and the units everywhere were undermanned and scattered. The Marines were never popular with President Truman who felt the Corps had been too much glorified, and General Omar Bradley had earlier expressed the opinion that the days of amphibious operations were over. Even though the Marines had been told that the famous picture of the flag raising on Mt Suribachi at Iwo Jima assured them of five hundred more years of existence, there were skeptics aplenty, but MacArthur was not one of them.

General MacArthur very much wanted the Marines now and there was a corresponding eagerness on the part of Marine Corps leadership. Immediately after the NKPA invaded South Korea, Marine Commandant General Clifton B. Cates had proposed that Marines be sent to fight in Korea, and on the 15th of July the 1st Brigade consisting of the 5th Regiment and a Marine aircraft group left from Camp Pendleton and arrived at Pusan on the 2nd of August to join in the defense of the Pusan Perimeter. At the end of July "the Organized Marine Corps Reserve was activated; then on 15 August 1950, the Marine Corps Reserve was called up. By September the Marines had activated 33,258 officers and men" (Tucker, 698).

The Inchon landing was a hurried operation for the 1st Marine Division under the command of General Oliver Prince (O.P.) Smith. On September 12 Chesty Puller and his 1st Marine Regiment left Kobe Japan and began their journey around the southern tip of the Korean peninsula and then north in the Yellow Sea. They were joined on the way by the Murray's 5th Regiment which had been fighting with General Walker at the Pusan Perimeter. Those two regiments of the division would soon be followed by the 7th Regiment under the command of Colonel Homer Litzenberg, all headed for their rendezvous near Inchon.

In planning for this operation General MacArthur had taken a questionable step by violating the unity of command and creating X Corps, made up of the Army 7th Division and the Marine Corps 1st Division, and placing them under the command of his Chief of Staff General Edward Almond. The American forces in Korea would have two heads. The X Corps would be independent of General Walker's Eighth Army with Almond operating directly under the command of MacArthur who seemed to believe Walker was not aggressive enough to trust with the Inchon operation. Much friction and conflict was to follow from this decision, for while Almond had the support of the great general and was anxious to carry out his every command, he seemed to rub everybody under him the wrong way, particularly General O.P. Smith and his three regimental commanders.

Many top American military leaders had serious reservations about MacArthur's amphibious operation because the port of Inchon, fifteen miles from the capitol city of Seoul, had some of the most treacherous tides and currents on the planet. The timing of the landing had to be exact or the LST's and other landing craft could be stranded in the mud flats which were the prevailing condition of the port between the brief high tides. Another consideration was that there were no beaches for landing, only high sea walls that would have to be scaled with ladders. Above those walls were hills from which a defending NKPA force with machine-gun and mortar and artillery could rain devastation on the invaders. One of the greatest concerns of all was that the Division had not had a chance to rehearse for the invasion. They were going at it cold, depending on their leadership and the *esprit de corps* of the Leathernecks.

Chesty Puller, the embodiment of that leadership and spirit, was now fifty-two years old with over thirty years in the Corps and he understood this would be his last campaign. Lacking the grandiloquence of a MacArthur, but with brevity and a blunt directness that had more impact on his men, he spoke to a group of his officers just before they went ashore:

> We're the most fortunate of men. Most times professional soldiers have to wait twenty-five years or more for a war, but here we are, with only five years' wait for this one. During that time we sat on our fat duffs, drawing our pay. Now we're getting a chance to earn it, to show the taxpayers we're worth it. We're going to work at our trade for a little while. We live by the sword, and if necessary we'll be ready to die by the sword. Good luck. I'll see you ashore (Davis, 231).

*General Lewis Burwell "Chesty" Puller*

\* \* \*

A battalion of the 5th regiment moved first shortly after dawn on the 15th of September to take Wolmi, a small island in the port of Inchon connected to the port by a causeway, and they succeeded with little opposition. After securing that objective they had to wait until that evening for the next favorable tide when the rest of the 5th Regiment under Murray would take the Red Beach to their north and the 1st Regiment under Puller would land on the Blue Beach to their south. The landing craft came in on schedule and the Marines scaled the seawalls with their ladders. While they met some opposition, it was light and nothing like they had feared. They had only about two hours of daylight to secure the beachhead and the hills just beyond. Both the 5th and 1st Marines quickly secured those objectives and made ready to move toward the capital city the next morning.

And move they did. On the following day as the Marines headed for Seoul, General Walker and the Eighth Army began the breakout from the Pusan Perimeter. The hammer and anvil strategy seemed to work well because the North Korean forces surrounding Pusan, getting word that their long supply lines were in danger of being cut, began to withdraw. And while the NKPA forces at Seoul did attempt to defend against the invasion, their efforts were not that effective, so the Marines were able to continue their methodical advance toward the capital city.

MacArthur and Almond, however, always concerned with public relations, were determined to capture Seoul by the 25th, exactly three months after the NKPA invasion. MacArthur wanted to have a ceremony in that city on that date marking the liberation of South Korea and reinstating Syngman Rhee as President there in the Capitol Building. General O.P. Smith and his regimental commanders, however, were not interested in public relations. They were focused on keeping their units together and protecting their flanks as they advanced, and that's what they did. Murray's 5th Marines raised the American flag above the Capitol Building on the afternoon of the 27th, although Almond, to please his boss, had announced the fall of Seoul just before midnight on the 25th. MacArthur's ceremony took place on the 29th (Tucker, 278).

After their success at Inchon and after securing Seoul and a broad swath of territory east of the city, the 1st Marine Division was relieved by the 7th Army Division and boarded ships to be transported around the southern coast of Korea and north through the Sea of Japan to the eastern port of Wonson, there to go ashore once more and join in the pursuit of the fleeing North Korean Army. What would have been their second amphibious operation at Wonson never took place, however, because by the time they got there the enemy had fled and Bob Hope and his troupe were there to greet them. After that delightful interlude the Marines began their race to the Yalu River.

The Inchon invasion proved to be the most successful American operation of the Korean War. As a result of General MacArthur's daring plan the tide of the war had turned. NKPA forces were now being routed and it seemed the general's forecast of a quick conclusion to the war might well turn out to be accurate. If the great general had not miscalculated the Communist Chinese response to his bold move to take all of North Korea, his prediction that American troops could be home by Christmas might well have been borne out. But while UN forces were moving north China was sending out ominous signals that they would not allow hostile forces to move up to their border. Those warnings were ignored.

Mao Tse Tung was not going to tolerate capitalist forces massing at his borders, so when UN forces approached Manchuria he committed the Chinese Red Army to the battle. Lin Pao's Fourth Field Army, which had begun entering Korea stealthily at night, now began to cross the Yalu in great numbers. Soon the 1st Marine Division, after its stunning success at Inchon, found itself outnumbered and surrounded in the bitter cold snows of the Chosin Reservoir. Now the same Marines who had prevailed at Inchon within the narrow space of two months were about to add another courageous chapter to their history, the "Breakout" from the "Frozen Chosin."

\* \* \*

Back in the USA the nation was completely focused on this first hot conflict of the Cold War. There at Oak Knoll Naval Hospital I was fascinated by the stories of the first wounded veterans of the Korean War. They, in turn, seemed amused by my insistent questions about what combat was like. Because I had been too young in the Big War, I was determined to learn as much about this one as I could. I can't explain to this day what my motives were, but I had a strong desire to go to Korea and see what was happening there.

I went to Ollie again and told him we should volunteer for the FMF (Fleet Marine Force). He was of the same mind, but since we had been volunteering for sea duty so long without any success, we didn't expect results from this latest effort. But were we wrong! Within days after we submitted our request for duty with the FMF we were on a day coach train to the US Marine base, Camp Pendleton, at Oceanside, California.

While we were undergoing our four weeks of combat training at Camp Pendleton the 1st Marine Division was fighting its way back toward the port of Hungnam against hordes of Chinese soldiers while struggling against the bitter cold conditions of a North Korean winter. I don't recall that we had much awareness of this larger picture while we were undergoing our training. The following is an excerpt from a letter I wrote from Camp Pendleton at the time:

> Well, I've been here a little over three weeks now. We were here a week before we started training. When we first started training they issued us all Marine gear. They outfitted us all real nice. I believe I like the Marine uniforms better than the Navy. It's nice to have pockets to put your hands in. They also issued us our combat gear such as packs, rifles, etc. We have real nice little 30 cal carbines. They fire 750 rounds per minute full automatic.

I went on to tell my folks about our "snoopin' and poopin'" exercises where we had to crawl on our bellies. I complained that I was so sore I could hardly walk. But I seemed to be enjoying the experiences. I described a two-day bivouac where it rained on us, and the infiltration course where we lined up in a ditch waiting for TNT charges to go off as our signal to come out of the ditch and start our charge toward our objective. Our progress was complicated by the fact that we had to crawl on our bellies under barbed wire while we tried fruitlessly to avoid the explosive charges all around us. These charges were surrounded by small circles of barbed wire but were so numerous there was no way to escape the blasts. One went off right beside me and set my ears to ringing. We were hardly aware that machine guns were firing live rounds over our heads all this time.

Out of a group of thirty I was the second one to reach the objective. But rather than get a hoped-for word of approval, the sergeant castigated me and the other fellow for getting too far ahead of the group. I'm not sure whether my speed that day was the result of a new Leatherneck gung-ho spirit or whether I was just trying to get away from those TNT blasts.

While undergoing combat training there at Camp Pendleton we corpsmen had a little ditty that we would sometimes sing when marching

> I joined the Navy
> To go to sea
> But look at me now
> I'm in the infantry.

We were only going through exercises, but in Korea the 1st Marine Division was going through the real thing. They succeeded in fighting their way through fierce Chinese opposition and miserable weather to Hungnam harbor. From there they were transported by a flotilla of ships back to the southern tip of the peninsula where they set up camp in the bean fields at Masan. Their goal now was to rebuild their ranks which had been severely depleted by the casualties suffered in the breakout from the Chosin Reservoir.

I don't recall anyone ever telling us why our training was cut a few days short, but no doubt it was to help fill those many vacancies in the Division. So with only two weeks left in 1950, we corpsmen who were part of the 4th Replacement Draft found ourselves aboard a transport plane at Moffat Field seated on canvas benches facing one another, ready for our trip across the Pacific. Once in the air each of us was given a small box of silver tubes with plastic covered needles on one end to add to our first aid kits. These were the morphine syrettes that were, along with an assortment of battle dressings, a crucial part of the corpsman's medical supplies.

But now, six weeks after we had set out to cross the Pacific, on our first operation, the "Gook Chase," the only injured I had ministered to were civilians.

\* \* \*

We who were replacements felt some awe and a little envy when it came to the veterans of the Chosin campaign, but I was troubled by what the corporal and his friend told us up on that mountain while we watched that village burn, how they had used the wounded Chinese officer for target practice. Could it be that what they had endured during that ordeal froze their hearts as well as their bodies? I know How Company was particularly hard hit during that struggle. When the Chinese crossed the Yalu the company was about two hundred strong. By the time they got to Hungnam there were less than twenty remaining.

Martin Russ in his vivid account of the Chosin campaign, *Breakout*, draws upon many personal stories, several from How Company personnel.

And it is clear from his interviews with men like PFC Robert Cameron, one of our machine gunners on this operation, that most survived with their humanity intact. That was true of almost all the "Chosin Few" I knew. But in every war, I suppose, there are closet killers who find in combat the freedom to act on their violent impulses. What do cold-blooded bastards like that do when they go back to civilian life? Do they make good husbands and fathers and friends? Or are they sociopaths who keep their impulses under control until war gives them license?

But with rare exceptions, we weren't sociopaths. We were good young men fighting for what we believed was a worthy cause. I certainly was no killer. But why was I the first to shoot at that guerilla? Why did I even shoot? Once the killing starts, where do you draw the line? I would wonder about these things over the coming days and weeks, and I would continue to see that black shape sliding down the ice.

* * *

I found out while we were on that patrol that there was a name on the lieutenant's map for the village we had destroyed.

It was Kitty Dong.

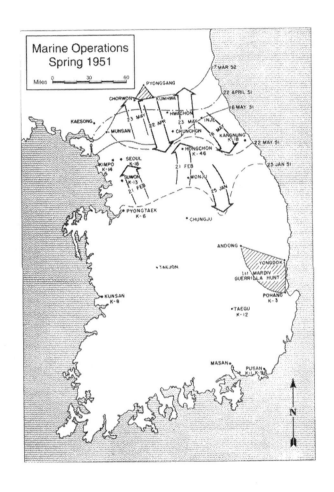

Marine Operations
Spring 1951

Miles  0    30    60

# CHAPTER 3

# Rice Paddy Patrols

Although the weather continued bone-aching cold it snowed little. The most we encountered was a white dusting of the ground. The trees that covered the mountains were not tall or dense, so from the valleys we could see white patches of ground between wooded areas on the rolling mountains and ridgelines. It was on those ridgelines during this guerrilla hunt that I first saw an air strike against the enemy. It was a sight I would see countless times over the next eight months.

We had come down from the high ground and were looking across frozen rice paddies toward the mountains that rose about a half-mile in the distance. Marines from another battalion were engaged with guerrillas there and had called in a close ground support air strike. We watched as four blue, gull-winged F4U Corsairs came in low over the mountains from the south to our right. They passed low over the mountain once to find the bright orange ground panels that marked the Marines' position and then climbed, banking right, where they formed a circle and began to swoop down each in turn on the ridgeline in front of the Marines. First they released the silver, teardrop shaped napalm bombs which tumbled end over end and exploded along the ridgeline sending up curling cauliflowers of black smoke with hearts of flaming red fire. Napalm (jellied gasoline) splatters and sticks to fabric and flesh, sucking oxygen from bunkers and searing the ground and everything touching the ground. After the planes had dropped all their napalm, they began to strafe the enemy positions on the mountain. Arcing up to the right they would gain an altitude of perhaps a thousand feet then circle back to the mountain in power dives; after passing over the Marine position at close to tree-top level they would open up with their wing-mounted 50 caliber machine guns. We could see the discrete puffs of smoke from their guns and seconds later the sounds of the rapid, staccato bursts would reach us as the Corsairs skimmed over the enemy positions. At the end of each run they would pull up sharply, bank right into the circle and continue the process until they were out of ammunition. When they were through, they moved back into formation and disappeared back over the mountains in the direction from which they had come leaving black smoke hanging over the mountain like sooty curtains.

*F4U Corsairs*

We had mixed feelings about those pilots. We appreciated them. We were grateful. They helped us out of many tight spots and undoubtedly saved many infantrymen's lives. And though they were not challenged in the air this far south in Korea, their jobs were not without risks. They would almost always encounter small-arms ground fire, sometimes very heavy. They flew low and their World War II propeller planes were slow and vulnerable.

But we envied them too. They would come in to the combat zone and spend maybe fifteen or twenty minutes over target, and then fly back to their carrier or airbase in Korea or Japan and have a cold beer in the officers' club and sleep between clean sheets at night.

We did notice the different techniques of the pilots. Some would come in low over the treetops and get down in the foxholes with the enemy. Others would strafe from a higher altitude and pull out as quickly as possible. Those flying low we decided were bachelors while the cautious ones must have been married men. We thanked them and we envied them.

*Napalm aftermath*

\* \* \*

We were on constant patrols, now, looking for guerillas. One day we approached a small village and the company commander, Captain Hoey, ordered light 30 caliber machine-guns set up on a rise looking down into the village. Suddenly Marines began firing down toward the three or four thatched-roof houses. Crouching low we approached the machine gunners and joined the men who were firing toward the village. I asked one of them what they were shooting at and he said someone had seen a guerrilla running toward one of the houses, so they had all started firing. The firing continued although I could see no target for anyone to shoot at.

While all this gunfire was ripping into the village a black dog emerged from near one of the houses flying like a greyhound for shelter. Immediately he became the target in a shooting gallery as dirt from the small arms fire sprayed up behind him as he ran. Men who would not normally have even kicked a dog were blasting away in the excitement. Even after the word came to cease-fire the shooting continued for a while before tapering off and

31

ending. The dog managed to disappear behind one of the houses and so far as I could tell escaped with his life, though the experience no doubt left him with some psychological trauma.

Moving along a valley road later that same day we approached another small village that apparently had been abandoned. Lt. Lowe ordered one of the squads to check out the houses, and soon one of the Marines yelled out, "Hey, there's somebody in this one!"

"Who is it?"

"Two old people, a man and a woman. Hey, Doc! The old man's hurt. You want to come take a look?"

I crossed the road and went to the door of the thatched-roof house and peered into the darkness of the room. An old man was lying on a mat; his wife was squatting beside him. There was an ominous stench in the room. I stepped up into the room, went to the old man and kneeled beside him. His wife was speaking rapidly in Korean, which I could not understand, but I could understand the pleading in her voice and the abject fear in her eyes. The old man was trying to speak too, but he was obviously in great pain, and he was weak.

"What is it, Doc?" The Marine with his head poking in the door asked.

"He's been shot in the leg and he has gangrene, clear up to his thigh. That's why he's still here. He couldn't leave when the rest of the village cleared out. And his wife here stayed with him."

"Can you help him, Doc?"

"No, not really. His leg would have to come off."

"Can't you cut his leg off?"

"I don't have the equipment. He would need to be anaesthetized and I don't have a bone saw. And besides, we don't have time."

"What are you going to do?"

"There's nothing I can do. Give him a shot of morphine to ease the pain a while."

I took out a syrette of morphine and showed it to the old man and his wife explaining what I was going to do, knowing they could not understand my words but hoping they would understand my gestures and my tone of voice. They appeared to; the old woman stood and was bowing rapidly and smiling a frightened smile. I emptied the entire syrette in his arm about the time someone from the road yelled, "Come on you guys, we're moving out!"

We had to hurry to catch our platoon which had already moved some distance down the road.

We took up positions that night in the high ground and built small campfires to warm our hands and heat our C rations. We would all swap around to get the cans of "heavies" and the brands of cigarettes we liked.

By this time I had started smoking. It's ironic that over time the cigarettes Uncle Sam gave us would produce more casualties among Korean veterans than the Communist Chinese and North Koreans inflicted during the war. But we were young and strong then and were concerned only with tomorrow, not some vague distant future. Besides, Humphrey Bogart smoked, and the Surgeon General's report on smoking and health was more than a decade in the future.

The C ration cans we opened with "handy dandy" can openers carried on our dog tag chains. We were careful not to go all the way around, leaving enough uncut so we could bend the lid back and fold it down on two sides to make a handle. We would set the can on the edge of the fire and leave it until it started to bubble around the rim, then pull it out, stir it, and place it back to heat some more. The smell of the wood smoke was pleasant and it permeated our equipment, our clothes and our hair. We had been in the mountains now for about two weeks, and we were already much leaner, traveling much lighter, and toughened to the climbing that had become a constant in our lives. But we didn't like it. Sitting around the campfires we talked about it a lot.

"You know, when I get back stateside, I'm not walking anymore!"

"How you going to arrange that?"

"I'm going to get a house with a built on carport where I can step right out of the house into the car. I'll eat in drive-in restaurants and go only to drive-in movies. I tell you I'm tired of this goddamn infantry."

\* \* \*

Most of the medical care I gave during the guerrilla operation was for routine complaints: sore feet, frostbite, headaches, diarrhea, scratches and bruises. Once a Marine, Dick Gilling (we talked about this over fifty years later), brought in a C-ration box full of blood he said he passed from his rectum. I sent him to the battalion aid station assuring him he was OK but fearing he had some serious condition. He was back within two days; it was only hemorrhoids.

If we were in one location for a day or so and I treated a civilian, the word would get out and before long I would have half a village lined up to get what our interpreter told me the people called "magician." It was kind of pathetic, a nineteen year-old Navy corpsman with a medical bag full of battle dressings, morphine syrettes, antiseptics, bandages and APC's, trying to treat everything from pneumonia to intestinal parasites.

To add to the misery of these people who were afflicted with war, poverty and a bitter cold winter, there was a typhus outbreak. The disease contributed some to the defeat of the guerillas who often took refuge in the villages, but it took an even greater toll on the civilians. Once we entered a small village that had been totally abandoned. We had to check out all the houses, and in several of them we found bodies, some of them melting into the floors, all victims of typhus. Korean civilians would usually abandon their homes and villages around the front lines, but in this guerilla operation there were no front lines, so it was not uncommon to find people sometimes in their houses and villages.

Those houses, *hanok*, were built of mud or clay supported by wooden beams on stone foundations and topped with roofs of straw. One ingenious feature of the structure was the heating system built into a stone floor covered with red clay. There would be a kitchen on one side of the house with a fireplace built next to a duct which ran all the way under the house so that when the wood fire was going the heat and smoke would be pulled under the floor and thus heat up the whole house–a low-tech but highly efficient floor furnace. This system, called *ondol*, was an important feature of the traditional Korean house that provided the family with warmth and comfort in the coldest weather.

While it was not uncommon to find people in these villages they were almost always old people and young children. Village elders would be dressed in their traditional *yangban* white cotton "pajamas" with their tiny "top hats" which appeared to be made of black screen wire but were actually woven of horse hair. The elderly, the "Mama-sans" and "Papa-sans," were highly respected in Korean culture, especially the old men.

We would see children at play in all weather. I had seen little girls skillfully launching one another into the air standing on either end of a teeter-totter back in Pusan, and little boys gave me my first demonstration of a hacky sack, though I'm sure they had another name for it. They too exhibited great skill in keeping the tassled projectile hovering in the air from the side of their foot. Could the popularity of that sport later in the United States on college campuses and with the counter culture in places like Woodstock be traced back to these Oriental children? I also remember seeing children chewing on dry squid with the tentacles dangling out of their mouths, a nutritious snack I'm sure. As for infants and toddlers, the clever Koreans solved the problem of the Pamper shortage by simply not putting a bottom in their little suits. All they had to do was squat and go.

\* \* \*

Just a few weeks earlier, back in Masan, on one of those days when Gunny Spell had given us some time to ourselves, I decided to shoulder my M2 Carbine and take to the hills on a "deer hunt." I had never hunted any quarry larger than a rabbit and I have no idea what I could have done with a deer if I'd found one, but since my whole purpose was just to get out and do some rambling none of that mattered.

I started out following a frozen creek that flowed down from the hills outside our camp. After I'd been climbing awhile I heard the laughter of children. As I continued to climb I discovered the source of the voices. I came to a place where the ground leveled off before it rose again to the hills, and there on a frozen pond were eight or ten boys ice skating and riding on small ice sleds. They waved at me and I waved back as I approached them. I stood and watched them for a while then asked them if I could look at their skates. Of course our conversation was carried on in gestures, but we had no problems communicating. Their ice skates were hand made of wood. The blade was a length of thick wire somehow fastened to a wood strip along the bottom, and amazingly with these rustic skates these boys could cut all kinds of didos on that frozen pond.

The sleds were ingenious too. They were small, just large enough to get your bottom and your crossed legs on. They also had wire blades on the runners like the skates. The boys would sit on the sleds, cross their legs and pull their feet up to their butts, then propel themselves with something like ice picks that they held in each hand. After I had watched them awhile, I lay my carbine down and stepped out on the ice and began to push one of the boys on a sled. They thought that was funny and after a while they insisted that I take a ride. I was a little large for the sled, but I finally managed to get on without too much hangover. The boys pushed me around, taking turns, and we all laughed and had a great time.

Music is the universal language, they say. Well it's not the only one; children are too. Those children and I had absolutely no problems communicating. It had not been that long since we eighteen, nineteen, and twenty year old GI's in Korea had been riding our bikes and skates up and down the streets and sidewalks of the USA. All of us GI's would have shared similar childhood experiences being children of the Depression and World War II and sharing in the American culture of the 1930's and 1940's.

The country of these young boys was at war just as ours had been a few years earlier. When I was their age I would have been riding my Western Flyer bicycle around Trinity Heights there in Dallas, selling magazines from door to door, *The Saturday Evening Post, Colliers, Liberty*, and watching little yellow Stearman Kaydet biplanes circling about overhead. Piloting those two-seated open cockpit planes were navy cadets and their instructors from Dallas Naval Air Station at Grand Prairie, young men who had never flown before and who likely had never dreamed they would have the opportunity, but here they were getting to fly and serve their country at the same time. The young men circling above me would get their chance at combat soon. As the war progressed it became commonplace to hear the drone of planes overhead and look up to see huge formations of fighters and bombers flying across the sky on their way to our fighting men. I have not seen such sights since.

But just as this war did not stop Korean children from playing, World War II had not stopped our generation from having fun. In addition to the regular sports of baseball and football, boys of that period had many pastimes to keep them occupied. In early spring we made kites. No one bought kites. We would go to the corner grocer and get an apple box, then slip a butcher knife out of our mother's kitchen and cut our kite sticks from the thin sides of the crate. (I still have a scar on my left index finger from a slip with that butcher knife.) We would mix our own paste from flour and water, tie the sticks together in either the two-stick or three-stick pattern then cover the kite with newspaper and paste it down. When it dried we would attach a tail made from rags torn from an old sheet and head out to the field for a test flight. Maybe they weren't great looking kites, but there was a real sense of accomplishment when we saw them flying knowing we had done the whole thing from scratch.

We found many other things to do in that age before television and computer games. We liked to get old wagon wheels and make soap box cars and take them out to the big hill by Camp's Dairy and go careening down that road risking life and limb.

When I would get a little "jingling money" in my pocket, I liked to go to the Western Auto store and buy reflectors for my bike. (My uncle Howard told me, "A man always needs a little jingling money in his pocket.") I spent many minutes making my selection from all those beautiful reflectors in various shapes and colors; the big round red ones and the red white and blue ones shaped like shields especially appealed to me. I know the Romanovs never got more pleasure from their yearly Faberge Easter eggs than I got from my new shiny bike reflectors—I reveled in the pure joy of my material possessions.

And sometimes we would fasten old playing cards to the front fork of our bicycles with clothespins so the bikes would sound like motorcycles when the cards slapped through the spinning spokes. We made stilts and walked up and down the streets and alleys with them and found many other ways to fill up summer days and afternoons after school.

We were not totally without technology. We had radio and double feature movies on Saturdays. Every GI in Korea in 1951 would have been familiar with radio shows, such as "Jack Armstrong, The All American Boy," "The Green Hornet," "The Shadow," "Gang Busters," "Fibber McGee and Molly," and many other serials and comedies of that period. One I liked that was not so well known was "Jerry of the Circus." The theme song from that show still goes around in my head sometimes.

And the double feature movies on Saturdays were always eagerly antici- pated. Usually they were westerns, with heroes such as Johnny Mac Brown, Hopalong Cassidy, Bob Steele, Tim Holt and Gene Autry. We would emerge from those dark theaters with a swagger, ready to draw on the first hombre that gave us trouble. But we loved the Tarzan movies too, and we all knew then and still know now that the real Tarzan was Johnny Weismuller.

What I'm indulging in here is, I know, nostalgia, and nostalgia is nothing more than selective memory. We all have memories good and bad, and it makes a big difference which ones we choose to hold on to. Our choices will determine to a large extent whether our lives will be happy or sad. Anyway I like the above selections, and all those things were real and they are no more, a fact that evokes the eternal theme expressed so well by Francois Villon and poets through the ages: "Where are the snows of yesteryear?" *Ubi sunt.* Whither flown?

The spirit alive on the frozen pond that day with those kids, the spirit the GI's in Korea had known a decade before, is a spirit that unites humans all over the earth—the magical spirit of childhood. But we all know the problem with children: they grow up to be adults.

Soldiers have always been only a few steps from childhood. I am reminded of a poem from World War II that captures the closeness of soldiers to their childhood, the stark realities of war, and the snow of a particular yesteryear. Pay attention to these words from Richard Wilbur, an infantryman in Europe during that conflict and one of America's finest poets:

First Snow in Alsace

The snow came down last night like moths
Burned on the moon; it fell till dawn,
Covered the town with simple cloths.

Absolute snow lies crumpled on
What shellbursts scattered and deranged,
Entangled railings, crevassed lawn.

As if it did not know they'd changed,
Snow smoothly clasps the roofs of homes
Fear-gutted, trustless and estranged.

The ration stacks are milky domes;
Across the ammunition pile
The snow has climbed in sparkling combs.

You think: beyond the town a mile
Or two, this snowfall fills the eyes
Of soldiers dead a little while.

Persons and persons in disguise,
Walking the new air white and fine,
Trade glances quick with shared surprise.

At children's windows, heaped, benign,
As always winter shines the most,
And frost makes marvelous designs.

The night guard coming from his post,
Ten first-snows back in thought, walks slow
And warms him with a boyish boast:

He was the first to see the snow.

\* \* \*

There were reasons we found only old people and children in the villages. Young men of military age were in the Republic of Korea (ROK) Army or the Korean Marine Corps (KMC). And young women, through some kind of familial legerdemain, were kept away from the armies battling over the land. The reasons are not hard to fathom. Wise parents have always taken care to protect their daughters from transient military suitors. And the Koreans had especial reasons to be cautious. They had only recently gone through a particularly painful thirty-five year period of Japanese colonial rule. During the final World War II years they had 200,000 of their young women taken by that imperial power to serve as "comfort women," that is sex slaves, for the Japanese armed forces. That atrocity, after sixty years, still smolders and disturbs the relationships between the two countries.

Throughout history young women have always been in peril when armies are on the march. The big blowout between Achilles and Agamemnon in the opening scenes of the *Iliad* was over a woman, Achilles' prize of war. Look at what the Romans did to the Sabine women. While both of these stories come from Western mythology there's little doubt they are grounded in common practices. Historical examples of such atrocities are so numerous they seem to be the rule rather than the exception. Chivalry, a romantic ideal, is rarely practiced in reality, especially in war time. Having said this, it is my belief based on what I have observed that no nation has a better record of humane treatment of women in wartime than the United States of America.

For those of us in my rifle platoon young women were no problem anyway since we never saw any. Only once, later in the spring, did I see a young woman. That was when I was called to a house to examine someone who had been injured. It turned out to be a pretty girl about eighteen who seemed to be in a lot of pain. There was another Marine with me, and members of the girl's family were present, but we didn't have an interpreter, so we had to communicate with the few Korean words we knew and with gestures. She was hurting in her back, in the area of her ribcage, and when I asked what happened, an old man gestured with both hands as though he were holding a rifle and hammering something with its butt, and saying "Chun guk, Chun guk!" the Korean word for "Chinese," and since at that time the Chinese were retreating north before our advance we concluded that a Chinese soldier had assaulted her, perhaps raping her. But this was all conjecture because of our difficulty with the language.

Based on that fragmentary information and the fact that breathing for her seemed painful, I concluded that perhaps the problem was fractured ribs. So I had the family raise her little cotton vest so I could tape up the injured area, and as I applied the broad strips of adhesive tape to her back I could see the curvature of the bottom of one of her breasts under her vest. That glimpse of beautiful female flesh disturbed me greatly, but I resolutely kept my focus on the task and, like a hunter trying to keep a bead on his quarry while a fly crawls down his nose, I finished binding up her ribs, and then gave her that magical shot of morphine. I was proud that in my extreme state of deprivation I was able to carry out my responsibilities in such a professional manner.

As the song from that great musical, *South Pacific,* says "there's nothing like a dame!" But as I look back on those months climbing the mountains of Korea I don't recall being preoccupied with thoughts of women, though I did from time to time remember Aiko, a girl I had met in Japan. Maybe I have just forgotten or maybe it was because our energies were depleted climbing mountains and enduring those long marches with our thoughts focused on the hostile forces we faced on almost a daily basis that we were able to concentrate so well on our job.

We know today about urban legends; well there have always been military legends as well. One is the old story that "they put saltpeter in the food." I guess we thought when we heard the phrase that it meant something like "soft peter," some kind of diabolical plan from higher up to keep the military focused on the job at hand rather than being distracted by the siren calls of the fair sex. Whatever the case, the treatment had not been so effective for the American troops when we passed through Japan.

\* \* \*

Back on December 19th, we left Hawaii and continued island hopping across the Pacific headed for Japan. After some time in the air we were told to fasten our seatbelts in preparation for a landing, but when we looked out the windows we could see nothing but ocean. As the plane descended there finally came into view a small dot that grew somewhat larger as we came down until finally we could make out a tiny island with an airstrip that extended virtually from one end to the other. This was Johnston Island, a spot that later would be used as a nuclear waste dumpsite, but which on this day was plump in the middle of the most gorgeous expanse of tropical ocean imaginable. After we debarked from the plane I discovered that just walking through that balmy air with those big white clouds scudding overhead was a sensual experience.

We were there only a few hours while the plane was being refueled. While we waited we walked down to a pier where some sailors were fishing in the perfectly clear green-blue water. Two of them were out on the end of the pier casting out into the water while another behind them in the shallower water was tossing bread crumbs on the surface and slashing at the water with a fishhook on a short pole. When he would snag a small minnow-like fish with the hook he would pass it to one of the anglers who would then bait his line with it and cast out into the surf. I've never known of a place where the fishing was so good. On almost every cast they reeled in a fish, and each one was different. When we asked them what kind of fish a particularly odd-looking specimen was, one of them replied,

"Hell, we don't know. We just catch 'em and name 'em."

We found out the tour of duty there was one year and that the only recreation men on that island had was fishing, reading, and watching movies.

We flew from there to Kwajalein atoll and from there to Guam where we ran into some sailors we had known back stateside. We were there long enough for them to take us on an island tour in a jeep. I recall that there came a rain shower while we were walking somewhere and those of us who were transients dashed for shelter while the old Guam hands just continued their leisurely pace. When we asked why they hadn't run for cover they told us that the rain came so frequently and lasted such a short time and they dried out so quickly it wasn't worth the bother.

I didn't appreciate at the time the fact that recent history was all around us. I was totally unaware that the island we were walking on along with its neighbors Saipan and Tinian was, just six years earlier, the home base for the B29 bombers which had hammered Japan, killing as many as one hundred thousand people in a single night of firebombing during the closing months of World War II. And that was before one of the bombers, the now famous *Enola Gay,* took off from nearby Tinian Island with Paul Tebbets at the controls and dropped the first A-bomb on Hiroshima. The havoc Japan unleashed with their preemptive attack on Pearl Harbor on December 7, 1941, ended up taking a terrible toll on both countries, especially Japan in the final year of the war.

And none of us knew at that time as we toured the island that one of the 22,000 Japanese defenders of Guam, most of whom were killed when

U.S. troops recaptured the island in 1944, was still hiding out on the island. While we were riding around in that jeep Shoichi Yokoi was living in a cave eating nuts, berries, frogs, snails and rats and wearing clothes he had woven from tree bark while waiting for the victorious Japanese army to rescue him. Yokio continued his holdout until 1972 when he was found by a couple of hunters; he was wearing burlap pants and his tree bark shirt. His rifle had long since become rusted and useless. When this 20th century Rip Van Winkle was repatriated after his twenty-six year holdout he was celebrated as a hero in his home country and enjoyed his celebrity until he died at the venerable age of eighty-two.

We took off for the final leg of our flight from Guam. It was dark when we reached Japan and I remember the great expanse of lights below us from the city of Tokyo visible through the windows on both sides of the plane. I knew as we continued our descent that we were about to enter a different world.

\* \* \*

That had been only seven weeks earlier, and now we were winding up my first combat operation, the "Gook Chase."

By early February the guerillas of the North Korea People's Army were pretty much scattered and defeated. They had been star crossed from the start. They lacked some of the key elements necessary for successful guerilla warfare, particularly the support of the local people, many of whom tipped us off to the Communists' whereabouts. And we learned from some of their captured soldiers that General Lee who commanded the guerrillas was despondent and hiding out, no longer leading his men. His mission to disrupt communications and movement of supplies and troops in that eastern area of the peninsula had been a failure. The main supply route from Pohang to Andong had been kept open and now the 1st Marine Division was limbered up for another assignment. And we were ready. The grueling marches, the mountain climbing and the periodic encounters with the North Korean guerilas proved to be excellent training for what we would face in the coming months.

Marine casualties in this operation were 19 KIA; 7 DOW; 10 MIA; 148 WIA; and 1751 non-battle casualties, mostly "frostbite" (USMC Operations in Korea, Vol. IV, 57).

CHAPTER 4

# How The War Began—The Line is Crossed

While we were climbing the mountains and patrolling the rice paddies west of Pohang in the "Gook Chase" the war was continuing in other parts of Korea and it had not been going well for our side. On January 1 the Chinese and North Korean forces had begun a massive offensive. On January 4 they captured Seoul and three days later they captured Wonju. As a general rule men in a rifle company know little of what's going on in the broader war, but as it turned out I had been right when I told my folks about the Army retreating so fast they didn't realize the Chinese weren't pursuing. General Ridgway had given the order to evacuate Seoul but had ordered a systematic withdrawal that would punish the Chinese Communist Forces (CCF) along the way. What actually happened was that the Eighth Army withdrew about sixty air miles in seven days without inflicting any damage on the enemy forces. Instead of withdrawing as a careful rearguard on foot maintaining contact with the enemy, they had evacuated on trucks. Ridgway was furious when he learned what had happened, that his direct orders had been ignored, and wrote to General Joe Collins, the Army Chief of Staff, "The finest of our past infantry leaders must shudder in their graves if their all-seeing gaze now takes in the battlefield performance of some of their descendents" (Blair, 605).

The fallback of UN forces under way in January and February of 1951 was the consequence of China's initial onslaught when they entered the war only weeks earlier. On the 25th of November 1950 the Chinese Army, after infiltrating into Korea in small groups for several weeks, began pouring across the frozen Yalu River in massive numbers in a determined effort to surround the 1st Marine Division and destroy it on their way to vanquishing all UN forces. With this new infusion of Chinese military power, Communist forces were now making a second determined effort to push the defenders of South Korea into the ocean and seize control of the entire peninsula.

\* \* \*

Their first attempt had come seven months earlier when Kim Il Sung gave the orders that launched the Korean War, sending the North Korean People's Army across the 38th Parallel in force and in darkness, catching the South Korean Army and their United States advisors off guard and totally unprepared.

On Saturday evening June 24th 1950, Captain Joe Darrigo, a hard-working American advisor who had gone to bed at Kaesong after his assistant had decided to go to Seoul for supplies and a night on the town, felt a bit lonely being the only American officer at the 38th Parallel. When he was awakened by loud explosions at 0300 hours the next morning he first thought it was his own ROK troops firing their 105 howitzers across the demarcation line in one of the continuing skirmishes and exchanges of fire that had been going on along the Parallel for months, but when he heard small-arms fire and bullets buzzing around him he knew there was something much more serious afoot. He grabbed his shirt and shoes and ran for his jeep followed closely by his houseboy. When he got to the middle of the town he was astounded to see a fifteen-car North Korean train pulling into the station loaded with NKPA soldiers, some of them hanging on to the outside of the cars. The rapid penetration of the enemy troops on that train had completely flanked the 12th Regiment of the ROK 1st Division, the unit he was assigned to advise, so he knew the only course of action was to head south and warn the division commander and the other two ROK regiments positioned there. The NKPA soldiers jumping from the train spotted Darrigo's jeep and opened up with small-arms fire, but he escaped in a hail of bullets and sped south, shirtless and shoeless, to spread the alarm (Blair, 59).

The attack at Kaesong for all its shock and surprise was not the main thrust. The NKPA simultaneously pushed in force down the Uijongbu corridor headed directly for Seoul with infantry led by long columns of Russian T-34 tanks.

The South Koreans in the early hours and days of the war put up a valiant fight, but they could not hold out. The cards were stacked against them. It wasn't long before the outgunned and outmanned ROK forces began to give way under the onslaught and when they did the situation in the south became desperate.

Back in Washington meetings at high levels were hastily called and all kinds of dire recommendations were put forward, from totally withdrawing from the peninsula to using nuclear weapons against the USSR. After urgent conferences with political advisors and consultation with his top military leaders, President Truman decided to draw the line. The United States would stand against this aggression and commit its own troops to the battle. But there was a big problem with this plan. The only troops we had available were the Eighth Army that had been on occupation duty in Japan since the end of World War II and, after working at desk jobs for five years, most of them were soft and totally unprepared and untrained for a combat mission. The United States had made the same mistake it had always made after a big war; it had stood down its armed forces and quickly returned to a peacetime posture naively believing all the trouble was behind it.

The first American troops to land in Korea on July 1, 1950 was a group of about 450 soldiers dubbed "Task Force Smith" after their leader, thirty-four year old Lt. Colonel Charles "Brad" Smith. The task force, from the 1st Battalion of the 21st Regiment of the Army's 24th Division, was flown from Japan to Pusan from which point they moved north for three days until they arrived above the small town of Osan. There Smith had his men set up defensive positions in the hills facing north toward Suwon to await the T-34 tanks that would be coming down the road. In addition to riflemen, his force was armed with a small battery of artillery, two 75mm recoilless rifles and some obsolete 2.36-inch "bazooka" rocket launchers.

After spending a miserable night in the rain, the Americans awoke on the morning of July 5 to see a column of enemy tanks moving steadily toward them. Accompanying the tanks were trucks filled with infantry. When Smith's troops opened up on the convoy, the North Korean soldiers poured out of the trucks and at once began to flank Smith's men there in the hills. The American rockets proved useless against the tanks and the North Koreans quickly knocked out the two recoilless rifles positioned on the front slopes, so Smith ordered his men to withdraw. He was furious when he discovered that his supporting artillery had destroyed their own guns, jumped on the tractors and beat a path to the rear. He was also dismayed when he learned that many of his men's rifles would not fire simply because they had not been properly cleaned and maintained (Hickey, 46).

This was just one of the many debacles repeated again and again as the Communists pushed to the south as the ROK and now American defenders fell before their advance. More American forces were sent piecemeal from Japan until soon the entire 24th Division under the command of Major General William F. Dean had been committed to the conflict. But the same pattern of battle continued: establish a defensive position, get hit, then "bug out." (This was the operation that gave birth to that phrase.)

There was a great deal of panic among both American and South Korean troops. The roads were jammed with civilian refugees fleeing before the Communist invaders, and it was during this frightening time that a tragedy occurred at a railroad bridge near No Gun Ri when American troops fired on civilians attempting to escape the invading North Koreans. This incident has recently generated controversy among Korean War historians, some saying it was a senseless massacre of innocent civilians, and others claiming the Americans had a legitimate concern about North Korean troops disguised as civilians attempting to penetrate allied positions. Also there is some dispute over how many civilians died. One thing seems clear. When you have frightened troops, armed and poorly trained, tragedies are likely to happen. Two informative books have recently been written on the tragedy of No Gun-ri. *

*See "The Bridge at No Gun Ri: A Hidden Nightmare from the Korean War," by Hanley et al; and "No Gun Ri: A Military History of the Korean War Incident," by Bateman.

\* \* \*

There are many gripping stories about this opening phase of the war, but one of the more memorable is the story of General William Dean, commander of the Army's 24[th] Division. He had had a distinguished record as an infantry leader in World War II but he too had recently served as a commander of an occupying army unit in Japan that was predominantly administrative and desk bound, and now he found himself in command of an untrained, understaffed division with few combat veterans armed with obsolete weapons confronting a disciplined and determined well-armed enemy force whose purpose was to drive the American and South Korean forces into the sea. Even though he was handicapped by severe limitations in his forces, General Dean took command of the mission to slow the advance of the NKPA to give General MacArthur and other United States military and political leaders time to move more forces into South Korea to establish a defensive perimeter.

Dean established his divisional CP at Taejon and had his troops set up roadblocks north of the city to intercept the T-34 convoys barreling south down the road. But the pattern established in the first days of the conflict continued. As soon as the American soldiers with their inadequate weapons would fire on the advancing tanks they would receive fierce counter fire from the heavily armed convoy and would then fall back. As panic spread among the defending troops attempts to stop the onslaught were in many cases abandoned and American soldiers were fleeing in disarray.

When General Dean learned that the forces he had sent north had disregarded his orders to hold their ground he was furious. He jumped in his jeep and sped to the crumbling front and confronted his regimental commanders demanding to know who had given the order to withdraw. He summarily dismissed two of those commanders and ordered their replacements to move back into their defensive positions and hold the line. But Dean failed to grasp the magnitude of the disaster going on all around him, and the rout of the 24[th] Division continued until, by the time he finally ordered the withdrawal from Taejon on 20 July, his division was essentially finished as a fighting force.

As he saw his command fall apart around him Dean decided that there was no longer need for generalship, so he organized a small group of soldiers armed with bazookas and set out through the streets of Taejon to destroy some of those T-34 tanks. His first attempt failed when the gunner was unable to hit the tank. It was reported that Dean emptied his 45 at the tank in frustration. Later he joined up with a team with the larger 3.5-inch bazookas; they found a tank and "stalked it through the city streets for several blocks until they found a good firing position from the second floor of a building. Under Dean's directions the team fired three rounds. All hit. As the tank burst into flames, Dean cried exultingly: 'I got me a tank!'" (Blair, 136-137).

By now the NKPA had penetrated far south of Taejon and General Dean, so the remnants of his division that had failed to escape in time were faced with the ordeal of trying to make their way through the enemy forces to safety. By this time the 1st Cavalry Division had landed in Korea and other units were joining in the defensive effort, including some United Nations forces that were now supporting the defense of South Korea.

While these reinforcements were arriving, Dean and a few other stragglers traveled together for days living off handouts from friendly Koreans, hiding out in the hills and cautiously working their way south. Then one night the General, while searching for water, fell off an embankment and was knocked unconscious. When his party couldn't find him they moved on without him. Later, when he came to, he found he had a deep gash on his head, a broken shoulder, and was alone. But he continued to work his way south, and for thirty-six days he continued moving south, living on dried corn, green peaches and other food supplied him by friendly natives. Later he said he even developed a taste for kimchi. Before he made it to safety, however, two Korean men, for a reward of about five dollars, turned him over to the North Koreans. Major General Dean spent almost the next three years in a North Korean POW camp and became the highest-ranking US prisoner of the war.

All this happened while I was working on the wards at Oak Knoll Naval Hospital. We had not yet begun receiving wounded from Korea, but we were reading about the conflict in the papers and speculating about what was going on in that remote and obscure region of the world. By this time we had all expanded our knowledge of geography a bit by learning where Korea was on the map. Reports coming out of there were sketchy and confusing, and now that the United States was involved none of us knew where events might lead. There was always the concern that World War III might be ignited in some part of the globe and we were all hoping Korea would not be that place. We took some comfort in the fact that the Soviet Union's nuclear weapons program was still considerably behind our own, but we all felt uneasy and were worried about what might happen next.

I do remember that one of the big breaking news stories at that time was that General Dean was missing in action. This was a disturbing development that such a high-ranking officer was a casualty so early in the war. No one in this country knew at the time whether Dean was alive, and it was some time before his Communist captors let the world know he was their prisoner. Word did get around about his futile efforts to get his troops to stand and fight and about his final efforts to destroy enemy tanks with his small band of bazooka toting soldiers, and in January 1951 President Truman recommended Dean for the Congressional Medal of Honor, and presented the award to Dean's wife at a White House ceremony.

One of the refreshing traits of General Dean, a man the Japanese called "the walking general" because he preferred going on foot rather than riding, was his self deprecating, down to earth demeanor. He was repatriated September 3, 1953, and when he learned that he had been awarded the Medal of Honor he was dismayed. Of that award and his experiences in Korea he wrote:

> If the story of my Korean experience is worth telling, the value lies in its oddity, not in anything brilliant or heroic.
>
> There were heroes in Korea, but I was not one of them. There were brilliant commanders, but I was a general captured because he took a wrong road. I am an infantry officer and presumably was fitted for my fighting job.
>
> I don't want to alibi that job, but a couple of things about it should be made clear. In the fighting I made some mistakes and I've kicked myself a thousand times for them. I lost ground I should not have lost. I lost trained officers and fine men. I'm not proud of that record, and I'm under no delusion that my weeks of command constituted any masterly campaign.
>
> No man honestly can be ashamed of the Medal of Honor. For it and for the welcome given to me here at home in 1953, I am humbly grateful. But I come close to shame when I think about the men who did better jobs some who died doing them and did not get recognition. I wouldn't have awarded myself a wooden star for what I did as a commander.

He concluded his statement with a characteristic bit of humor. About his time as a POW he says, "I swatted 40,671 flies in three years and counted every carcass. There were periods when I was batting .850 and deserved to make the big leagues"(Blair, 139).

The two men who turned Dean in to the North Koreans were later captured. One of them was sentenced to death and the other to life in prison.

Dean, as those who knew him well would have expected, wrote to the officials in charge and asked that they both be pardoned. There had been enough suffering on all sides during those early days of the war. General Dean's was just one of many stories from the early, frantic, desperate days of the Korean War. These battles had taken place six months before I arrived in Korea and three months before MacArthur's daring Inchon invasion near Seoul in September turned the tide of the conflict. But the general's careful calculations for that landing by the 1st Marine Division were followed by his tragic miscalculations about China's willingness to enter the conflict, as the world learned when UN forces arrived at the Manchurian border. The great general's suggestions that American boys would possibly be home for Christmas proved to be the source of bitter disappointment when hordes of Chinese soldiers poured into Korea in late November.

\* \* \*

While we were chasing guerillas west of Pohang in the opening weeks of 1951, UN forces were pulling back all along the line in the face of the Communist advance. But reinforcements continued to arrive and General Ridgway's leadership was making a difference. The handsome, articulate former paratroop commander of World War II had lifted spirits of the troops by demanding better arms and equipment, warmer clothes, and upgraded medical facilities for treatment of the wounded. He became famous both in Korea and back home for the two hand grenades he wore clipped to the suspenders of his ammunition belt (with their spoons taped down for safety) and for his motivational leadership.

As noted earlier we called this pursuit of guerillas the "Gook Chase." We know today that the word "gook" is not politically correct, and perhaps someone has done some research on the origin and development of this pejorative term, but I have my own theory.

The Korean word for "American" is *Miguk*, for Chinese *Chunguk*, and for Korean, *Hanguk*, so it seems *"guk"* is the term for nationality, thus the term "gook," which was used not only in Korea but also afterwards in Vietnam. This is not to suggest that the term does not have racial connotations; it certainly does. Nations disparage and caricature their enemies, as I remember very well from World War II. Billboards with slant-eyed, buck toothed "Japs" could be seen along US highways, as well as cartoon depictions of Hitler and Mussolini and racist terms were commonly used for Germans and Italians. Most of the United States during the 1940's was still comfortably racist and the war provided an acceptable outlet for those mean sentiments. There was no effective opposition to the rounding up and imprisoning of 120,000 Japanese Americans in 1942, our own citizens, punished for no reason other than their race.

I remember in Dallas a middle aged childless couple with a German name who lived down the block. They were a quiet pair who kept to themselves and didn't sit out on the front porch on those hot, pre-air-conditioned, summer evenings like other folks did when all us children of the neighborhood ran up and down the streets playing hide and seek and red rover. We kids sometimes got in conspiratorial groups and talked about them. Someone said they had a picture of Adolph Hitler on their wall and that when they came in from work they would go up to that picture and give the Nazi salute and say, "Heil Hitler!" We kept a close eye on that couple.

I was ten years old when World War II started and almost fifteen when it ended. I remember poring over silhouettes of German and Japanese aircraft distributed by the government so we citizens would be able to spot enemy planes overhead. We were even provided information to help us identify enemy troops. One curious identifying characteristic of the Japanese soldier that set him apart from our allies the Chinese, I remember, was that the Japanese had a large gap between the great toe and its neighbors while the Chinese didn't. That struck me as strange. Why would two races so historically close have such a physiological distinction? And what were we to do if we encountered a suspicious Oriental? Ask him to take off his shoes? It was only years later that it occurred to me that the explanation for this curiosity most likely lay in the fact that the Japanese wore shoes that separated the great toe from its neighbors. I remember seeing pictures of Japanese sneakers where the big toe was separated like the thumb is separated from the other fingers in mittens. We were told these shoes were a great help in South Pacific islands where Japanese troops used them to shinny up palm trees where they could conceal themselves in thatches of fronds to watch for and snipe at Allied forces. Today how many of us would flunk that toe-gap test because so many of us wear Japanese-inspired thong sandals? And in one of the strange twists of history, in this Korean War the Japanese were now our friends and the Chinese were our enemies.

In war, as in all group conflicts, we call upon those primeval categories, "them" and "us." In the mock wars of athletic competitions we generally keep our perspective and rarely consider "them" as another species. But in real wars we find it necessary to dehumanize our enemies, to make objects of them so the job of killing them won't be so distasteful. Race has always proved to be one convenient marker to separate "them" from "us." World War II was a great struggle against truly evil powers, so maybe that racism toward our enemies is understandable if not excusable. But sadly, in the days of World War II and after, we treated some of our own citizens the same.

It was not until the Korean War that our own armed forces, which had formerly been racially segregated, began the process of integration, thanks to President Truman and other right-minded political leaders. The Korean War was the first conflict in which black and white Marines fought side by side. I saw very few African American Marines in Korea, but one member of our company was a tall sergeant, Melvin "Slim" Sanders. He was the best poker player in the company and once told Lt. Barnes he sent about $1000 home each month, although that sounds a little much.

*Slim Sanders with Chinese burp gun*

We didn't carry much scrip with us there in the mountains, though I did see a lot of money back in Pusan when I was on my way home. Slim was respected and liked by everyone in the company who served with him. How Company, and I believe the Marine Corps in general, was ahead of the curve when it came to integration because there was not a hint of racism in our relationship with Slim or with any of the Hispanics in the company.

It's interesting to note that racial stereotyping and name-calling work in all directions. I remember once in a small village some children who had apparently never seen Americans before were standing in a group watching us and talking excitedly to one another and laughing. When we asked Kim what they were laughing at he told us they were laughing at us. They called us "cow eyes."

\* \* \*

The Chinese offensive that began along the Yalu River November 7, 1950, had not lost its momentum by the beginning of the new year, but by late January of 1951 General Ridgway, who took command after General Walton Walker died on 23 December following a jeep accident, had suc-

51

ceeded in infusing new fighting spirit into the Eighth Army, and as a result the Communist offensive was stopped at the 37[th] Parallel. Soon afterward Ridgway ordered the start of a counter-offensive, the success of which eased fears for the second time that UN forces might be withdrawn in defeat from the Korean peninsula. The pendulum had started to swing once more in our direction.

# CHAPTER 5

# <u>Repose</u>

As the Gook Chase was coming to a close in late February I became a casualty myself but got no medal for my affliction. My wisdom tooth had become impacted and my jaw was swollen. I let it go for two or three days hoping the swelling would go down. When it didn't Lt. Lowe sent me back to the rear to get it fixed.

I was directed to E Medical Company where I found a portable dentist chair had been set up in a pyramidal tent. The dentist, a commander who seemed none too happy to be plying his profession in the desolate winter mountains of Korea, shot my jaw full of Novocain, waited a few minutes, and then started to work.

"Grrgkh!" I groaned as he began to lever the troublesome tooth.

"What's wrong?"

"That hurts, sir. I don't think that anesthetic's had time to take effect."

"It's had time. The goddamn stuff's been frozen and we're having trouble with it. Here, let's try some more."

He shot some more into my jaw, waited another ten minutes then started again.

I broke into a sweat. "It still hurts, sir. It's not working."

"Well, I've already started and we've got to get that tooth out of there, so just hold on and keep quiet."

I somehow managed to keep from yelling out. The tooth broke into several pieces before he got it out while I was sweating and gripping the arms of the chair trying to hold my body still and my mouth open.

That night I got sick and they admitted me to the field hospital. It wasn't much of a hospital, a long tent with folding cots. There were just three or four other patients and we slept in our own sleeping bags on top of the cots. A corpsman came by and took my temperature that night. It was 104 degrees. The doctor came by later and told me they were going to send me back to Pohang.

I had chills that night and diarrhea. The toilet was an open 4-holer some distance from the tent. The wind blew fiercely all night, and it was bitter cold. I tried to control the urges, but it was futile. Lying in my long johns in my sleeping bag, I would prepare for the desperate dash. I would

unbutton the rear flap of my underwear, unzip my sleeping bag, then fly
through the tent door across the frozen ground to the open toilet, do my
business, wipe, and then hobble back stooped over, my arms clenched across
my chest, trying to get back to my sleeping bag before my whole body
stopped functioning. I could not believe how cold it was. Back in my sleeping bag I tried to shiver myself warm and prayed that the urge would not hit
me again. But it did–all through the night.

We were taken back to Pohang in a field ambulance. I remember little
of that trip, but I do remember having my stretcher loaded onto the top of
a motor launch and looking up into a cold gray sky while the launch powered up and headed out to sea. It was a short trip, though, because soon we
pulled up alongside a huge white ship with a giant red cross on the side. It
was the hospital ship, *Repose.* Lines dropped down and were fastened to my
stretcher and before long I was taking a free-swinging elevator ride up the
side of that beautiful ship. I could see sailors and nurses from two deck levels
leaning over the railings watching the operation of the sick and wounded
being taken on board.

As sick as I was, the first thing I insisted on was a hot shower. It was
the first shower I'd had in a month, and, though my teeth were rattling, the
hot soapy deluge was marvelous. Then to put on clean hospital pajamas and
crawl between clean sheets! Streets of gold and pearly gates were, from my
standpoint, a pitifully inadequate description of heaven. It was a luxury
being sick under those conditions.

And I got a lot of attention too, particularly from hospital corpsmen
who wanted to know what it was like in a Marine rifle company. One or
two of them said they would like to trade places with me, and of course I
said that would be fine with me. But we all knew Uncle Sam didn't look
favorably on such informal arrangements.

Within a couple of days I was feeling much better. I had had bron-
chitis and the flu, I suppose. No one ever really told me. Two days after
I came aboard, Lieutenant Lowe showed up suffering from pneumonia.
We got to visit some and talk about our experiences in the "Gook Chase,"
events that happened hardly more than a fortnight ago but which seemed
remote both in time and place from our now comfortable surroundings. I
learned from him that the day after I left, the platoon got into a firefight
and one of our men was killed and another wounded. In my letters home
I referred to these platoon casualties as "my boys." I regretted not being
available when they needed me, but I knew another corpsman was there
for them. We corpsmen took our responsibilities seriously.

After I had been aboard about three days, the *Repose* pulled up anchor
and started south to Pusan. I remember both in Pohang and Pusan hearing
a voice over the intercom call out, "Repose . . .Repose." I asked some crewman why they did that and he told me that it was standard procedure to call

out the name of the ship when the skipper went ashore or returned. If I had been a seagoing sailor I would have known that.

But in spite of all my efforts I never succeeded in becoming a seagoing sailor. Even on my trip across the Pacific I missed that seagoing experience because the 1st Marine Division was so in need of replacements we were flown across the ocean.

\* \* \*

Our first stop was Hawaii. We could see Diamondhead as we approached for our landing. During our short stop there I wrote a postcard to my family back in Dallas mailed on the 19th of December 1950:

> Dear Folks,
> I'm in Honolulu now & it is a beautiful place. We came in by plane and we are just fixing to leave again.
> Been here about 4 hours. No time or space to write much. I hope you are all OK. I am fine. We've flown 2600 miles, one third of the way. I have to close now. Write soon.
> Love Charles

Now, here I was near Pearl Harbor, that place we had to look up in the atlas nine years before when we first got news of the Japanese attack because none of us knew where it was. Soon, however, we were all familiar with the rallying cry, "Remember Pearl Harbor!" But as I write this today there are fewer and fewer of us who were alive at that time, fewer who actually do remember that " date that will live in infamy," Sunday December 7, 1941.

It must have been shortly after noon because we would have gone to church that morning. I was across the street at Ray Tucker's house where he and I were working on a model airplane. We loved to buy Comet model kits for vintage planes, such as Curtis, Grumman, Fokker Wulf,. We'd lay out the paper blueprint on a card table then carefully cut the spaghetti-thin sticks of balsa, pin them to the pattern, then bond them with Comet glue. (It never occurred to us to sniff the stuff; we'd never even heard of such a thing.) One of the last steps was to stretch and glue colored tissue paper over the frame then sprinkle it with water so it would tauten when it dried. When we had it all trimmed and the "rubber motor" and landing gear in place we would be ready for a test flight. Our final product, though generally somewhat lacking in symmetry, would usually bear some resemblance to the picture on the box. We would put the craft through a number of test flights over the next several days until it suffered crippling damage, then we would set it on fire and send it, like the Phoenix, on its last flight, to be reborn only when we built our next model and repeated the process.

Ray also had an old movie projector, but he didn't have much in the way of films. One he had was of a train wreck. We liked to watch the train as it sped toward a stationary boxcar on the tracks, and then see it collide in a silent explosion of steel and wood. But the really fun part was when Ray would reverse the film and we could watch the train miraculously reassemble itself and speed backward in the direction from which it had come. We reran the film often to watch the explosions. But the explosions that occurred on that Sunday could not be undone by reversing a reel, although the years which followed showed that our country was possessed of a phoenix-like strength to rise up from the conflagration of a surprise attack.

We were in Ray's bedroom on that Sunday working on the model plane when we became aware that his parents in the living room were excited about something. We left our project and joined his parents who were standing by the radio transfixed, listening to the voice coming out of the speaker. We could tell they were alarmed. We asked them what had happened and they told us the Japanese had attacked Pearl Harbor. Since children understand the gravity of events primarily through the responses of their parents and elders, Ray and I became frightened. I bolted out of the house and ran across the street where I found my mother and dad and my two older sisters also standing by the radio.

"The Japanese have bombed Pearl Harbor!" they told me.

"Where is Pearl Harbor?" I asked, but no one knew. We had to look it up in the *World Book* atlas. We found it was in Hawaii.

The days and weeks that followed were filled with fear and uncertainty. We were at war and we had no idea what to expect. Would enemy bombers be flying over Dallas? Would the United States be invaded?

Soon we were at war with Germany and Italy as well. My dad was made an air raid warden and was given some pretty basic equipment including a pump-bucket fire extinguisher that would have been useless in anything larger than an ashtray fire. Because of the fear of air raids we had "blackouts," a community drill where no lights were allowed to be seen anywhere in the city. It was my dad's job to go around his several blocks territory during these drills and make sure no lights were showing through the windows of the houses. Some people bought black window shades to make sure the German and Japanese bombers flying overhead could not spot the sprawling city below.

The whole country mobilized. All over the United States young men lined up to join the armed forces. One of them who lived a few houses down from us, Felix Ezell, enlisted in the Marine Corps as soon as he was old enough, and because he had been an outstanding ROTC student in high school we thought that he had been commissioned as a 2$^{nd}$ lieutenant, but actually he was a PFC. I admired this tall young man who seemed to take his responsibilities a little more seriously than most of the youth in that working class neighborhood. I felt honored that he took notice of me some-times, once even inviting me into his room to show me his model planes, which really did look like the pictures on the boxes. What really caught my eye, though, was his desk. It was an ordinary student desk, but on every square inch of it Felix had glued Indian-head pennies. I was impressed. We all took pride in Felix and we all were heart broken when we learned he had been killed on Iwo Jima in February 1945. Sixty years after his death I looked up the names of World War II dead on the Internet, and there he was:

> EZELL,Felix Edwin, PFC., USMCR
> Parents, Mr and Mrs. Willis H.
> Ezell, 3022 Alabama St., Dallas.

We lived at 3050 Alabama.

Many years later I used to run on the football field track at Ouachita Baptist University, here in Arkadelphia, Arkansas, where from time to time I would see a man out getting his exercise walking around the track, shirtless, tapping the inside curb with his stick. This man was Bob Riley, Professor Emeritus at Ouachita University and former Lieutenant Governor of Arkansas. I knew who he was and sometimes I would stop and visit with him while he was toweling off the sweat after his workout. While Felix Ezell and Gunny Spell fought in the battle for Iwo Jima, Bob Riley was wounded on Guam, and though he came away with his life, the battle cost him his eyesight and left scars on his body that he would carry for life. Those wounds, however, had not held him back. He returned to the University of Arkansas and, with a reader provided by the GI Bill, he proceeded to get his doctorate from that institution, an achievement followed by a successful career in academics and politics.

Of course our topic of conversation was often the Marine Corps, and if you talk about the Corps very long the name of Chesty Puller is bound to come up. Puller was the embodiment of the Marine Corps' gung ho spirit. Winner of five Navy Crosses in campaigns going back to Haiti and Nicaragua following WWI and extending to tours of duty in China during those troubling times leading up to World War II and then through that war from Guadalcanal to Peleliu, Puller had fought his last campaign in Korea as commander of the 1st Marine Regiment. Felix Ezell, Bob Riley, Fred Spell and Chesty Puller were just four of the hundreds of thousands of young men who took on the responsi-bility of protecting the world from the evils of the Axis Powers in World War II, and many of them, like Felix, paid the ultimate price.

We on the home front pitched in and did what we could to contribute to the war effort. Certain commodities were rationed, like gasoline and sugar. Families with members in the military, and they were many, proudly placed in their windows small flags with a single star for each service man in the family. We saved newspapers for recycling and grew victory gardens to help in the war effort.

Two years after Pearl Harbor a handsome young sergeant, Johnnie George, from the Army camp at Paris, Texas, came to Dallas and attended church where my family and some of his family were members. There he met my sister, Berle, and they started dating. He was in the Tank Destroyers, and on his shoulder was a round patch with a picture of a panther crushing a tank in its jaws. I was fascinated by that emblem and also by his car, a 1936 Ford sedan. I remember once he had it running out in front of our house and he let me get in it and step on the accelerator. The muffler was not in particularly good shape so when I revved the engine it would roar and belch smoke and the car would rock back and forth indicating that the shock absorbers needed some attention too. But to me that was one cool car.

In 1944 Johnnie learned he was going overseas, so he and my sister decided to get married. He was twenty-one and she was fifteen. Today the idea of a fifteen-year-old getting married gives us pause. But those were exceptional times and with a perspective of sixty years I can attest that theirs was an exceptional union.

Since we had no service-age males in our immediate family, Johnnie became the focus of our family's wartime involvement. He arrived in Europe shortly after D-Day and served under General Patton. We put a map of Europe on our wall and got some colored pins and by listening to newsmen like Gabriel Heatter on the radio and reading the papers we kept up with the movements of the Allied forces, and particularly Johnnie's unit.

Those of us who fought in Korea, with the exception of the senior leadership such as Colonel Chesty Puller and General O.P. Smith and other senior officers and NCOs, were not members of that "greatest generation" of World War II. We were not the sons of that generation either, but more the kid brothers. So my recollections of World War II must have much in common with those of other Korean veterans who were around ten years old when the Japanese attacked Pearl Harbor. Those were grim days and we were all haunted by news of that devastating attack. The rescuers there were horrified to hear for many hours the sounds of desperate banging coming from the sunken battleship *Arizona*.

\* \* \*

On the 23rd of February 1951, I found myself back where I'd been just two months earlier, debarking from a ship in Pusan harbor. But this time, rather than the *Takuja Maru*, it was the hospital ship *Repose*. From there I took that same truck ride down the same dusty road to Masan to be assigned to a casual company while I waited to be reunited with my company. It was still cold but more order had been brought to the campsite in the bean patch. And of course most of the Division was gone from the area having rejoined the Eighth Army in a new operation against the Communist forces near the 37th parallel called the "Killer" offensive. UN forces inspired by the leadership of General Ridgway were beginning to push back.

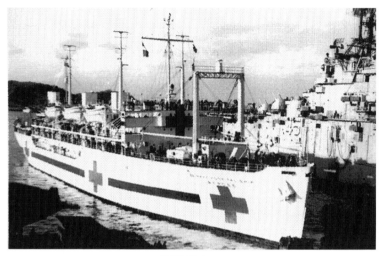

*USS Repose*

The pyramidal tents at Masan now had cots and nice pot bellied stoves. Other amenities that had been added were luxurious four-holer open-air toilets; and we were able to supplement the standard rations with food bought from local civilians who moved fairly freely through the camp. One of the hottest selling items was eggs, which the Koreans called "eggu." We ate lots of eggs there in the casual company. It wasn't unusual for vendors to come up to us and negotiate a deal for their eggs and produce while we were sitting on the toilet. We communicated with them good-naturedly, they using the few English words they knew and we using the few Korean words we knew. Kids would sing to us and we would sing to them the following ditty which someone had arranged to the tune of "My Darling Clementine."

> Cigaretto, Chocoletto
> Sheba Sheba
> Have a no

The words in the first line present no problem. Those in the second referred to that rarest of commodities for infantrymen in Korea, that gift that only women can offer men. I never got a direct translation of "sheba sheba,' but I'm fairly certain today it could be heard only on Korean HBO.

The most popular song in Korea at that time, and I was told by several Koreans that it was always number one on their hit parade, was "China Night." It was a beautiful song sung by a girl with a delicate and beautiful voice. Just about all of us GI's could hum that tune and even butcher some of the words. The title to us sounded like, "She Ain't Got No Yo Yo," but it was actually, "Shina No Yoru." There could hardly be a greater contrast than that between the bleak, cold, war-torn country we found ourselves in and the beautiful, idyllic lyrics of that song whose words evoke images from a minimalist Chinese painting:

> What a night in China
> Harbor lights
> Deep purple night
> Sailing junk
> Ship of dreams
> Ah Ah, I cannot forget
> The sound of the kokyu*
> China Night
> Night of dreams
> China night

> What a night in China
> In the willow window
> A ramp was shaking
> A red bird cage
> A Chinese girl
> Ah sadly
> Singing love songs
> China night
> Night of dreams
> China night

> What a night in China
> Waiting for you
> In the rain at Obashima
> Flowers in bloom
> Like rouge on her cheeks
> Even after parting
> I will never forget
> China night
> Night of dreams

                    * Chinese musical instrument

Repose

This song reflects the historically deeply entwined cultures of three countries, China, Korea, and Japan.

But another popular song was purely native, a Korean folk song, Arirang. But our American ears heard the r's as d's and so for us the song was "Adedong," which we sang as follows:

Adedong Adedong
Ah na de o
Adedong ko ke no
No me ken da

The song describes a trek over the mountain peak at Arirang and laments,

The sorrows in my heart
Are as many as the stars in the sky.

Later, when I went back through Japan, I bought those songs along with a number of other 78rpm records and some cheap, shiny silk-looking jackets with colorful dragons. I thought those jackets looked cool. I bought other souvenirs for my family and a perfect looking "Ronson" cigarette lighter. But to my dismay the lighter quit working on the transport ship on the way home, and when I tried to take it apart to see what was wrong I found on the inside of the metal case some letters from an American beer can.

It was during those years that the words, "made in Japan," warned the buyer of shoddy merchandise. Yet look what they had to work with. Their country had been devastated by the recent war and their economy was in shambles, yet they took account of what the American GI's were looking for and set out to meet those demands using whatever materials they could put their hands on. Pretty ingenious. And it wouldn't be too many years before they gave a completely new meaning to the phrase, "made in Japan," with their automobiles, cameras, and electronic products which set the standards for quality throughout the world.

But of all the souvenirs I purchased, the only ones I have left are the records, and the only way I can play them now is on an antique 1916 Silvertone hand-cranked record player. Every once in a while I'll do just that, and when I do, that same sweet voice on that old scratchy record bridges all the decades and takes me back to that place where I first heard "China Night."

* * *

I don't remember how many days I spent in the casual company, but I found it to be a pleasant interlude. I recall one day we were in our tent fry-

61

ing eggs on our stove when someone came by, poked his head in the tent, and told us the Division commander, General O. P. Smith (celebrated for his leadership in the Inchon invasion, the breakout from the trap at the Chosin Reservoir, and for the phrase, "Retreat Hell!") was in the camp and we should make everything ship-shape. We closed the flap over the door and went back to frying our eggs amused at the thought that General Smith could be interested in a gaggle of Jarheads who were just waiting to rejoin their units.

It wasn't long before someone from outside threw the flap open again, and this time it was a bird colonel who stuck his head in and yelled, "Attention!"

We all jumped to attention, turned to the open flap and saw a helmet with two stars and heard the general's voice,

"How are things going with you men?"

"Fine Sir, just fine!"

"Very good. Carry on."

And he was gone.

\* \* \*

While I was enjoying this respite in Masan the 1st Marine Division had been reassigned to the Eighth Army and the UN forces were continuing to push the Communist forces back north. First there was the "Killer" offensive that had been launched on 18 February followed by the "Ripper" offensive on 7 March. General Ridgway had brought a new aggressiveness and spirit to the campaign. He said our objective should not be to gain and hold territory at any price, but to inflict the maximum damage on enemy personnel and supplies using our superior firepower.

I wrote home at this time that I was going to be flown back to my outfit, but that did not turn out to be the case. What happened was that I and some other members of the casual company were given new equipment and put aboard a train along with the 6th Replacement Draft that had arrived in Korea on 5 March. Among the replacements were Marines like John Tarver, Ralph Tate, Lawrence Hansen and Hal Tardio, men I would be serving with over the coming months in How Company and a tall Texan, Jim Nicholson, who would be assigned to George Company, a man I would meet again decades later.

We were all headed north to find the 1st Marine Division, but the accommodations on this train were nothing like those on the Pullman coach that carried me from Dallas to San Diego. This was a bare-bones Korean train, and rather than being assigned comfortable sleepers, we were unceremoniously loaded into drafty unheated train cars. It was a cold ride but we were able to see some beautiful, bleak winter scenery through the gritty windows as the train rattled its way through the mountains of Korea.

# CHAPTER 6

# <u>Ollie</u>

It was two hundred miles from Masan to Wonju, our destination, and that was as the crow flies, and certainly no sober crow would have taken the route we took. That train ride must have taken twelve hours or more. I don't recall whether we spent a night on the train, but I do remember that it was daylight when we unloaded on the outskirts of Wonju. We were put off behind the Marine front lines in a supply and staging area where pyramidal tents and stacks of ammunition and supplies were scattered about, where trucks, jeeps, tanks and other vehicles were parked or were moving up and down the rocky, rutted roads.

At that point we were all put on trucks and transported to a spot just behind the MLR (main line of resistance), but once there the only instructions we got was that it was up to us to find our outfits, so Hansen, Tate, Tarver, Tardio, I and the other Marines assigned to How Company shouldered our packs and weapons and began to move through the area asking everyone we met if they knew where How Company, 3rd Battalion, 7th Regiment was located. They kept pointing us north and we kept following their instructions until we had left the tents and equipment behind and found ourselves in open mountainous country. Continuing to follow the last directions we received, we finally found How Company positioned along the MLR, otherwise known as the front line, in their accustomed location on the high ground. There we were greeted by Gunny Spell.

The war had not stopped while I was enjoying my respite on the *Repose* and in the casual company at Masan. While we in the 1st Marine Division had been involved in the "Gook Chase," Chinese and North Korean forces continued their offensive, which began on 1 January 1951. Three days into their campaign they recaptured Seoul, and just three days after that they took Wonju. But on the 14th of January UN forces stopped the enemy advance at the 37th Parallel, and then on the 25th began a counter attack, which continued for about two weeks until it was stopped by another Chinese counter offensive. So, for the last two months the war had gone back and forth like an accordion with the outcome of the conflict still much in doubt.

The area where I was now rejoining my company had been bitterly contested during the recent action. The last Chinese counter offensive, which began on 11 February 1951 was halted just four days later at Chipyong-ni, thirty or forty miles west of Wonju, by the 23rd Regiment of the Army's 2nd Infantry Division under Colonel Paul Freeman, along with a French Battalion, the 1st Ranger Company and supporting artillery units. Those UN forces were in fact cut off and isolated, trying to hold on under intense enemy pressure. With the help of airdrops of supplies and ammunition from flying boxcars, however, they were able to use their superior firepower to hold on and repulse the enemy assault.

Up to this point the Chinese had preferred to use smaller units in night attacks, infiltrations, and stealthy probes to encircle or cut off UN forces, but there at Chipyong-ni they began to employ a new tactic—mass assaults in human waves.

One of the greatest challenges facing General Ridgway when he took command in Korea was to raise the morale of his troops and breathe into them the fighting spirit which would be necessary for success. The victory at Chipyong-ni proved to be one of those morale boosters. Bringing the 1st Marine Division back into the line was surely another.

Now I was back with How Company being greeted once again by Gunny Spell. I told him I was ready to rejoin the first platoon, but he told me that wasn't where I was needed now. Another corpsman had been assigned to that platoon, and while I had been gone my old buddy from the states, Ollie Langston, had been wounded so I was to be assigned to replace him in the second platoon. Without knowing it Ollie and I had recently crossed paths, for he was now on the ship I had left only days ago, the *Repose*, and was on his way to Japan where he would undergo treatment for his wound while I was now taking his place in the 2nd Platoon. Tarver and Tardio and several other 6th Replacement Marines were also assigned to the platoon to make up for recent losses.

I discovered I had missed a lot of excitement in the three weeks I had been gone, but thanks to what I learned from Ollie later, I am able to fill in some of the missing history. The following account of the activities of How Company and the 2nd Platoon during this period comes almost entirely from a manuscript supplied to me by Ollie Langston.

\* \* \*

Shortly after I had been evacuated to the *Repose* the "Gook Chase" ended and the Division was back in reserve at Pohang-dong by the sea. Ollie says that after a hot shower and a night's sleep in a heated pyramidal tent, the troops were ready to play. He points out that corpsmen were shown a good deal more deference after this first combat operation. Distinctions between Navy and Marine just evaporated. The Marines valued their corpsmen now and the corpsmen had become integral members of their platoons.

Langston identified some of the platoon members with whom I would now be serving. The platoon leader, 2nd Lt. Walter Kennedy; Sergeant Carl Roach, Platoon Right Guide; a mentally disturbed platoon sergeant he calls "Sergeant Ralph"; the platoon runner, PFC Lou Feinhor; and PFC Joe Rousseau, celebrated for his beautiful singing voice.

Well, it turned out that the Company Commander, Captain James Hoey, who loved and was loved by his men, wanted to show his appreciation for their performance on the Gook Chase by throwing a party for his platoon leaders and other invited guests. (I got to know Captain Hoey fairly well later, and can testify that he would have entertained the entire company if he had had the resources.) Some of those guests included the platoon sergeants from 1st and 3rd platoons, and Joe Rousseau was included for his singing voice, but "Sergeant Ralph" from the 2nd Platoon, perhaps because he had not been a part of the recent operation, was not among those invited.

Somehow the resourceful captain had managed to come up with an open bar. With music supplied by Joe Rousseau accompanied by an equally talented Marine on guitar, all the elements were in place for a great party and the party got underway. As the spirits in the bottles diminished, the spirits of the revelers rose. Joe sang some requests for the partygoers and in between there were animated conversations about the action the company had experienced in the past three weeks. Everything was sailing along nicely when suddenly the merriment was halted by a loud WHOOM! right outside the tent. The explosion could be heard all over the 3rd Battalion bivouac area.

"What in the hell was that?" was the question asked all around the area. Because loud noises had become routine to the troops, however, soon everyone went back to his business. It wasn't until the next day that the mystery of the explosion was solved.

At muster the next morning "Sergeant Ralph" was not present and Lt. Kennedy announced that the 2nd Platoon no longer had a platoon sergeant and that the Right Guide, Sergeant Roach, was temporarily in charge.

Later that day Joe Rousseau explained to some guys in the platoon what had happened. "Sergeant Ralph," one of the "Chosin few," a swaggering combat veteran who carried as his personal weapon a German Luger, had just recently returned from hospitalization in Japan. He had apparently brooded about being omitted from the party's guest list and decided to take revenge. So he pulled the pin on a grenade and tossed it toward the tent that was producing those sounds of merriment. Fortunately for the revelers, the grenade landed outside the captain's tent in a mud hole which smothered and deflected much of the blast. A few shrapnel holes in the top of the tent were the only damage inflicted.

"Sergeant Ralph" may not have been successful in every enterprise he undertook, but he definitely did succeed in putting an end to that party. His second tour in Korea proved to be quite a bit shorter than the first, because now he was on his way back to Japan to see a psychiatrist in Yokosuka.

From what I have read, "fragging," the practice of trying to eliminate hated superiors by tossing fragmentation grenades in their direction, became somewhat common in Vietnam, but this is the only case I know of from the Korean War. It seems clear that "Sergeant Ralph" had preexisting problems and that nothing in the circumstances surrounding this event could adequately account for his violent behavior.

\* \* \*

Just three days after the aborted party at Pohang the word came for the 1st Marine Division to "saddle up" and prepare to board trucks for a move to Wonju in preparation for the UN spring offensive, designated by General Ridgway as operation "Killer." The Commander of the Eighth Army no doubt chose that name to instill a sense of optimism and revive the fighting spirit in those Army forces that had undergone some demoralizing setbacks before their recent success in turning back the Chinese assault on Chipyong-ni. The momentum in this accordion war was shifting again and now the Marines were on the way to lend a hand.

But the weather did not cooperate. It's not easy to generate a fighting spirit bouncing along in trucks through a cold miserable rain with water flowing across the dirt roads, having to get out at every stream and river to build bridges or prepare a ford for crossing. At last, however, in the middle of the night, the trucks stopped in the center of a valley.

After the platoon had climbed down from the trucks, Lt. Kennedy informed them that How Company had perimeter guard for the night. This news made no one happy because it meant they had some climbing to do. With a good deal of grumbling, the platoon saddled up and moved to the higher ground where they set up their shelter halves (pup tents) and settled in for the night.

Ollie and Sergeant Roach fastened their canvas together to make a tent, and then carefully dug a ditch around it to channel the rainwater away. They were not to rest for long, however, because in a couple of hours Lou Feinhor, the platoon runner, gave them a wake up call. It turned out that the Marines they had left down in the valley had been flooded out.

When the 2nd Platoon rejoined their regiment below they discovered that How company was the only dry outfit in the 7th Regiment. Soon the entire regiment was loaded on trucks and moved out of the valley which had now become a shallow lake.

One good thing that came from the flood was that the 7th Regiment was held in reserve to dry out while the 1st and 5th Regiments jumped off from Wonju and pushed the Chinese back twelve miles in two days. But Ollie didn't get to enjoy this rest period because he came down with a bad case of dysentery. For five days he suffered, but on the fourth day something happened to brighten the day. Lt. Kennedy got a package from home with all kinds of "pogey bait:" Baby Ruths, Three Musketeers, Snickers, and best of all, Hershey bars.

It is an ancient tradition for military leaders to share booty with their men, and it was the custom in Korea for anyone getting a package from home to share those goodies with his foxhole buddies. Ollie, Lou Feinhor, and Sergeant Roach waited in anticipation for their rewards. But the lieutenant kept the candy bars stowed carefully in his pack, showing not the least intention of sharing with anybody.

The night before the regiment was to move out Ollie was awakened by a rustling noise in the tent and turned to see Lt. Kennedy rummaging frantically through his pack looking for his candy bars.

"Someone stole my pogey bait!" he howled. "All right! Who did it? I'll court martial 'em!"

A muffled chuckle was heard from somewhere in the darkness followed by more fiery imprecations from the lieutenant as he stormed out of the tent. Sadly, the mystery of the missing pogey bait was never solved. But soon Lt. Kennedy would have more to think about than missing candy bars.

It was now the 27th of February and the regiment was to be moved to the MLR on the following day. That night How Company was assigned perimeter guard. The 2nd Platoon headed up a steep hill to the high ground that overlooked the Battalion bivouac area. From that vantage point they could see across the valley to the MLR and beyond. Around midnight flares were fired into the sky, lighting up the low ground to the front with an eerie flickering light. The Marines of the 2nd Platoon saw red and green tracers piercing the darkness below them, some seeming to come in their direction. This gave them some cause for concern. Could this be a Chinese night attack or were the tracers coming from ROK units that had become a little spooked? As the flares faded from the sky an artillery barrage opened up, the big guns sending devastating high explosive shells all the way across to the MLR to rain destruction on the Chinese forces dug in there.

The next day was the day—the last day of February. The platoon was up at first light for an early start. They saddled up and quickly moved down to the battalion bivouac area where they mustered and drew ammunition and other gear they would need for the coming operation. There they waited until 10AM when a line of six-by Army trucks pulled up to take them north to their jumping off point through the same valley they had looked across just the evening before. Captain Hoey had gone ahead of them with some ROK officers to scout the positions currently held by elements of a ROK regiment which the Marines were relieving, positions the company would occupy later that day.

After they were all aboard, the trucks began to roll north away from Wonju toward the MLR. They had traveled only about half an hour when the trucks turned off the road, forded a swollen river, and stopped on the other side. Word was passed to dismount and the platoon was directed to an area to await the return of Captain Hoey.

Ollie took this opportunity to greet some new replacements and to make sure each Marine had his first aid pack containing a large battle dressing attached to his cartridge belt. He carried battle dressings and medical supplies in his Unit One, the corpsman's first aid kit, but there was not enough room in that kit for bandages for the entire platoon. Besides, corpsmen were mortal too and not always available in a firefight. Marines needed to be able to give first aid to their buddies and to themselves in a pinch.

How Company had about a two-hour wait before Captain Hoey returned around mid-afternoon. The other two companies of the 3$^{rd}$ Battalion, George and Item, had left for their positions long before. The weather continued to be cold and damp, so the troops after the long wait were glad to be moving again, but even though Captain Hoey had previously surveyed the territory, he seemed to be having trouble finding his way.

After they had been trudging along for what seemed like hours they finally stopped for a break. Ollie worked his way down to the company CP and asked the first sergeant how much further they had to go. The first sergeant growled, "If the old man doesn't know where he is, how the hell do you expect me to know?"

After the short break they saddled up again and soon found themselves moving through country that had that blasted look, like it had seen some recent action. There was a dead horse in the ditch alongside the path, and every now and then they would pass unexploded grenades, potato masher types with rag fuses, clearly not GI issue. Finally they started to ascend to higher ground where they stopped on a hillside overlooking a valley of terraced rice paddies filled with winter stubble. Captain Hoey gathered his platoon leaders and they all hunkered down over that most essential and perplexing tool of Korean combat, the map, planning the moves and establishing the objectives for each platoon.

A tremendous artillery barrage accompanied the officers' meeting, the huge shells whistling overhead headed for their targets. Then suddenly the men of the 2nd Platoon were startled to hear a large number of explosions behind them in the area they had just passed through. Those rounds were so powerful some of the Marines said they must be 155 howitzers. Why would their own artillery be landing behind them? About that time another explosion erupted about a half mile in front of them in a rice paddy, then another and another, and still more, and they were coming closer.

George Brodeur, a rifleman, said that these last rounds were from "Chink mortars." With this news the platoon members began to scramble for cover. Then the explosions stopped. Next the word came that the platoon had to get out of that exposed position so they double-timed across a small valley and up the hill on the other side. There they took positions for the night, because it was getting dark. Captain Hoey ordered a fifty percent watch that night; half the company would be on the alert while the other half would try to sleep.

\* \* \*

There were several standard procedures for fighting the war in Korea, in fact for fighting any war in mountainous territory. First, always take the high ground. From that vantage point troops have great visibility and a strong defensive position for directing enfilading fire and mortars. Also gravity lends a hand; it's a lot easier to toss a grenade down a mountain than up a mountain. Second, stay off the skyline. Silhouettes of troops moving across a skyline can be seen from miles away. A third rule is to always build campfires on the reverse slope so the enemy can't spot them.

There was an old saying we had all heard first in boot camp: "There's always that ten percent who don't get the word." One of those new replacements apparently belonged to that ten percent because he proceeded to build himself a fire right on top of the skyline to heat up his C rations. It didn't take long for some of the older hands to douse that fire and bring the new man up to speed on the rules for mountain combat.

Ollie and Carl Roach, who was now platoon sergeant, pitched their tent for the night between a hillside and a grave mound. Those gravesites were common throughout the hills of Korea. Before Buddhism, Confucianism, Taoism, and the infusion of Christian missionaries, the people here practiced an animistic religion that saw spirits in everything in nature, animate and inanimate. One of the most appealing of those spirits was the serene spirit of the mountains, *San-Shin*, so natives found it desirable to be buried on a level spot on the slope of a mountain with a nice view of the valley below. Not a bad idea. The graves, mounds of grass-covered earth about four feet high and ten feet in diameter, were sometimes solitary and sometimes found in clusters.

Although the night passed quietly (except for Ollie who had a return bout of diarrhea), the spirit on the mountain that night was not serene like that of *San-Shin*, but troubled and ominous.

\* \* \*

The next morning, the 1st of March 1951, did bring one pleasant surprise—sunshine, the first the troops had seen in many days. Reveille, however, came in the form of a tremendous artillery barrage, the shells landing in about the same area they had the day before. With a night's rest and better light, the company commander and his platoon leaders were able to focus a little more clearly on their maps, and what they discovered was that on the previous day they had overshot their destination and ended up in "no-man's land." So the company had to saddle up and trudge back over the same ground they had traveled the day before until they arrived at the base of their objective for the day, "Cloverleaf Hill."

The three platoons now spread out to begin the assault. Lt. Kennedy found a trail leading up the mountain to the left and took two of his three squads with him after telling Sergeant Roach to wait five minutes then follow him with the remaining squad. Lt. James Cook took his 1st Platoon to the right and the assault was underway. Ollie remained with Sergeant Roach who kept an eye on his wristwatch until the five minutes passed and then started the remaining squad moving up the trail.

The roar of small arms fire filled the air and it wasn't long before the men began to hear the familiar sound of bullets buzzing by their heads. About that time some of them almost stepped on the first platoon leader and a squad of his men who were hunkered down behind some trees on the slope of the hill. The lieutenant yelled for them to "Get down!" but Ollie told him they had to catch up with their platoon and the squad kept on moving.

Soon Smitty, the new 2nd Platoon runner, emerged from the trees in front of them. Lt. Kennedy had sent him back to find the squad and bring them up to join the rest of the platoon. They found the platoon high on a reverse slope with an enemy machinegun raking the ridgeline with heavy fire. Forward progress had stopped at this point. Every time a Marine would try to take a look over the hill to see what they were up against, a round would fly into the dirt right beside his head.

Lt. Kennedy had a section of two light 30-caliber machineguns with the platoon so he had one of them set up on the crest of the hill in an attempt to fire down the draw from which much of the enemy fire seemed to be coming. But no sooner was that gun in place than the machine gunner was hit in the thigh. He was dragged back down the slope where Ollie examined the leg and, finding no broken bones, bound the wound with a battle dressing.

The next casualty didn't come from the ridgeline. Wayne DeMeuse, the youngest rifleman in the platoon, was hit by what appeared to be a burp gun slug, and he was well down on the reverse slope. It became clear now that there was a sniper or snipers to the rear of the platoon. After Ollie tended to DeMeuse, a BAR man, Gibson, was hit in the side. When Ollie got to him he found a through and through wound. Ollie couldn't tell if the kidney was involved, but there was no hemorrhaging at the wound site. A battle dressing would hold him until he could be evacuated. Now there had been three quick casualties, at least two of them being inflicted from somewhere behind. The apprehension that struck them all at this point was that they were in a spot that exposed them to mysterious incoming enemy fire. They needed to move out of there.

Ollie spoke up, "What are we going to do, Lieutenant, sit here until there is nobody left to fight?"

Lt. Kennedy had come to the same conclusion as the rest of the men, but rather than retreat back down the hill he decided to lead the platoon across the ridgeline into the draw covered by the Chinese machinegun. Like Ollie, he too had been suffering from a bug, although his took the form of laryngitis, but everyone understood his croaked out orders. When he gave the word they all rose and began their dash over the ridgeline and through the draw accompanied by the furious rattle of the enemy gun.

When they reached cover on the other side and looked back they saw what looked like a solid mass of green North Korean tracer bullets. And there, incredibly, was this one Marine, "Arky," still out there in the open, scratching around in the brush looking for something, while bullets were kicking up the ground all around him. The Marines watching this scene were all stunned, and began to yell, "Get out of there, Arky! Get the hell out of there!"

In the mad dash across the draw Arky had dropped his "personal weapon," his pistol, and he wasn't about to go off and leave it. He did find it, though, and came running in to join the rest of the platoon brandishing that pistol above his head like a trophy.

Arky's escape seemed miraculous, but what seemed equally miraculous was the fact that the whole platoon made it across without a single casualty. That was surely a relief for Ollie, because had someone been hit out there he would have been called upon to render aid. There was a saying that went around Marine rifle companies in Korea, "Everybody's pinned down but Doc."

If only the luck the 2nd Platoon had crossing that draw could have continued, but how many miracles can happen in one day? The platoon now found itself in positions behind another low ridge, or berm, in front of which was an open space of a hundred yards or so. The lieutenant gave the word to advance through that area and Sergeant Harold Notsund's squad led the way. They had not got half way across when they came under heavy fire. Sergeant Notsund was hit and, seeking cover from the incoming fire, the squad took refuge behind one of the ubiquitous Korean grave mounds, pulling the wounded sergeant along with them. They immediately began to call for help from the rest of the platoon who had been watching from behind their cover.

Ollie understood the call and rose to a crouch and began sprinting the fifty yards or so to the grave mound, thinking he would bring the wounded sergeant back to the more protected area of the berm. While making the dash he was given covering fire by a redheaded BAR man. As he approached the mound he yelled to his friend, Joe Rousseau, who was closest to the sergeant, to get the wounded man to his feet. When he reached Notsund he grabbed him around the shoulders and at that same moment Rousseau cried out in pain. Joe had been shot through the foot, so that changed Ollie's plans. He had more than one wounded Marine now, so he would have to treat them on the spot. He began to examine Notsund, thinking he probably suffered a chest wound, but as he was searching around for the wound he heard a loud "plop" and something like smoke or dust rose from the sergeant's back. He had been hit again and died while Ollie was looking into his eyes.

But Joe didn't wait behind the mound to be treated. He made a quick crawl back to the platoon's other two squads while the redheaded BAR man who had covered Ollie's sprint across the open area continued to give covering fire from behind the berm. After Notsund took that second hit Ollie sprinted back to find Joe and attend to his foot wound. He learned later that this BAR man who had been so diligent in providing covering fire for them was corporal Reidinger, and that he had himself, unbeknownst to Ollie, been hit in the side while doing so. This had happened while he was protecting his platoon buddies. The bullet hit his cartridge belt and knocked him down. He got up, examined himself, and when he realized he had not been mortally wounded, picked up his BAR and continued to cover his fellow Marines.

Back behind the cover of the berm, Ollie began to be troubled. He had been looking into Notsund's face when he was hit, but everything had happened so fast! How did he know the sergeant was really dead? How could he be sure? He knew he would have to settle the question in his mind, but this time Cpl Reidinger went back across that open space with Ollie to the grave mound where they both confirmed Ollie's first judgment and then ran back to the cover of the berm. There, Ollie gave Reidinger his carbine, because the corporal's BAR had frozen up on him.

By the time Ollie had Joe Rousseau on his way back to safety, the rest of the platoon had made it across that one hundred yard open space and taken the high ground from which Notsund's squad had been fired upon. Since he had given up his carbine, Ollie borrowed a 5-shot revolver from one of the machine gunners positioned behind that low ridgeline. That weapon was good enough for him since he had no plans of being a heavy shooter in this firefight anyway.

Now he had to catch up with his platoon. As he started forward he came across a young PFC lying out in the open with bullets kicking dirt all around him sobbing in fear. Ollie tried to comfort him, telling him everything would be OK and that he would have him evacuated out as soon as things settled down. But that delay in consoling the PFC turned out to be costly for Ollie. When he got going again through that open country to catch up with his platoon and find protection behind the ridgeline ahead he was apparently the only target for the enemy gunners and one of them drilled him through his Unit One, his first aid kit. Ollie said he felt like he had been hit in the hip joint with a baseball bat.

Oddly, one of the first sensations he had was the smell of iodine. Was he hallucinating or did that smell come from his aid kit? He began to hop along on one leg looking for shelter while he felt the blood running down into his boot. His left leg seemed to be just hanging. He became frightened thinking of the possibilities. How bad was he bleeding? Had he been hit in an artery? Was he about to be hit again? He stopped to pull down his three layers of pants trying to find where the wound was, and just at that time two buddies from his platoon, Sergeant Hill and PFC Rinckey saw he was in trouble and pulled him to safety.

When Ollie asked Sergeant Hill how badly he was bleeding, the Sergeant comforted him by saying, "You're bleeding to death, Doc!" When they got his pants down the Sergeant offered further solace by remarking, "I think the bullet came out your asshole." Rather than wearing his dog tags around his neck, Ollie had them in his pocket and the bullet had passed through one of them and exited close to his rectum, fortunately without hitting a bone.

"God help me!" Ollie pleaded. He had visions of a permanent colostomy, an artificial leg, and all sorts of debilitating, chronic afflictions.

At the same time the whole company, in fact the entire battalion, was locked in a difficult battle for Cloverleaf Hill. Captain Hoey had requested that Item Company, which had been held in reserve, be brought up to join in the battle. It turned out that this area they were fighting over was the very spot the Chinese had chosen to make their stand. On the ridgeline above the 2nd Platoon the Chinese had dug trenches and bunkers which crisscrossed the entire area, and they had determined to hold the line right there.

Ollie, in pain from his wound, had given himself a shot of morphine then propped himself up against a tree where he could see the action. He watched the 2nd Platoon Marines in hand-to-hand combat about twenty-five yards above him. At one point the Marines and Chinese were tossing hand grenades back and forth at a distance of about twenty feet. Ollie watched as a Chinese grenade came floating over the ridgeline. He saw a Marine glove it like a pop fly. Then it exploded. The Marine, lost in a cloud of smoke and fire, fell end over end then landed almost at Ollie's feet. Ollie immediately thought that some one should check that guy's dog tags to see who he was, when up rose this apparition, shook itself off, and came up to Ollie, face green-black with powder burns, fingers shredded, and teeth gone, and proclaimed, "It's me Doc! Don't you know me? It's me, Dugger!"

Ollie thought, "Well I'll be damned!" It didn't look like Dugger any more but there was no mistaking that Missouri twang. Those who witnessed this miracle did a little rejoicing that their comrade remained among the living.

A wounded Marine brought news of another KIA, PFC Kayser. Dugger's miracle was not repeated. Kayser died of shrapnel wounds from one of the grenades. The battle above them continued unabated, and the wounded being dragged back down the hill continued to swell the little band of cripples until there were about fifteen. Ollie was finally evacuated by two machine gunners whose gun barrels had melted down from the continued intense fire. One got on each side and helped Ollie down a wide ravine toward safety. They didn't need compass or map to find the direction; they just kept going downhill and away from the sound of battle. On their way down they picked up two more wounded, and at one point they could see in the valley below them a river, later identified by Rousseau as the Han.

When they got to the river's edge they found the 3ʳᵈ Battalion forward aid station manned by a number of hospital corpsmen, none of them happy to see a wounded corpsman. It wasn't just that they hated to see one of their brethren injured, it was the more chilling thought that one of them might have to take his place.

This river, whether it was the Han or not, was the same one they had crossed just the day before in trucks, but now it was at flood stage. It had become a brown roaring torrent. There on its banks Ollie saw the wounded of How company lying in the open on stretchers, being tended to by corpsmen while they awaited evacuation.

The senior corpsman had already established a rough triage. The wounded were to be evacuated to the 1ˢᵗ Regimental Aid Station by small Bell (MASH unit) helicopters. Head wounds were to be evacuated first, then chest and belly, and last wounds of the extremities. That was the plan, but because of the flood conditions, plans had to be modified.

Ollie was evacuated by field ambulance and reunited with his wounded buddies from the 2nd Platoon at an Army Evacuation Hospital below Wonju. Gibson, the BAR man who had been shot in the side, was there. He had only a flesh wound. There was a lieutenant, a Forward Air Observer, who had been shot through the throat and spent much of his time sipping whiskey and suctioning the blood from his throat with an aspirator. Gibson helped the lieutenant with his whiskey sipping. Ollie, after receiving another shot of morphine, drifted off to Opiate dreamland—his peace disturbed only intermittently through the night by the sounds of the lieutenant's suction machine.

From Wonju Ollie was flown to Pusan on a C-47 and soon after found himself on the ship I had recently left, the *Repose*, a name meaning "rest." And healing and rest were what Ollie and the other wounded from How company needed. That is what they would find in the hospitals back in Japan and the United States. Ollie was headed back to Otsu, the town in Japan where we had spent about a week on our way to Korea only two months earlier. And that had been a week to remember.

* * *

I had a strong feeling when our plane was coming in to land in Tokyo that we were entering a different world, and that feeling was borne out in everything I experienced during our passage through that country. In Tokyo we saw buses lined up full of casualties on stretchers from Korea, many of them with blackened feet from frostbite. Most of them were the Marines who had just fought their way out of the encirclement at the Chosin Reservoir.

We spent one night in Tokyo, as I recall, in a dark, gothic looking, drafty building. While some of our group managed to go out for some entertainment, I chose to get some rest. I unrolled my sleeping bag on a flat board bed, or countertop, up against an old battered wooden wall. I had been asleep for a while when I was awakened by a "Thump, Thump, Thump." When I looked to see where the noise was coming from I saw a corpsman leaning over me stabbing his bayonet into the wall above my sleeping bag, grunting menacingly with each stab. I recognized him from our combat training at Camp Pendleton. He had been recognized there for his truculent and aggressive attitude, more the warrior than the caregiver. The alcohol he'd had that night brought out those tendencies even more and he was taking out his aggression on the wall beside me. I said nothing but just lay there until he wandered off to find his own bed. Ollie told me years later that this guy had won the Navy Cross for jumping into a foxhole with several Chinese and killing them with his bayonet, so I suppose he found a good outlet for that aggressive energy.

The next day we were taken about two hundred miles southwest from Tokyo to the city of Otsu, the location of the 7th century Buddhist temple Miidera. The city is also the burial place of the famous 17th century poet, Basho, noted for, among other things, his refinement of the popular Japanese poetry form, Haiku. We were of course totally oblivious of the rich cultural history of the city, having other interests in mind. We were quartered in old Japanese army barracks, and since there was no regimen scheduled for us while we were in transit to Korea we had a chance to go out on the town. We had been provided some of the military money, called "scrip" which the locals were glad to get their hands on, so we were all ready to party.

The weather was cold and gray and the city seemed desolate, but we were young and high-spirited and wanting to have some fun. When we got downtown we hired rickshaws, not the old Chinese kind where the coolie ran along pulling the vehicle between two poles, but the modern tricycle kind where the proprietor rode on his seat up front and pedaled his fares around town.

There weren't a whole lot of sights to see in Otsu, but we did visit some local establishments where delicacies like candied minnows and dried squid were served. One of the lingering sensations of those nights in the little cafes and bars was the sour smell of sake, Japanese rice wine. I tried some of it, but it is obviously a delicacy that takes time to acquire a taste for, and we didn't have much time. There was beer too, and Suntory whiskey, libations more to the liking of American GI's.

The culture we were looking for we found in nightclubs. We saw something remarkable in one of the clubs—a Hank Williams impersonator. There he was in a big white Stetson hat, the star of his country band, singing "Your Cheatin' Heart," and "Move It On Over," in English! All the Hank Williams songs that were big back in the states at that time. What amazing people—and this in a country that had been devastated by the USA in World War II only five years earlier.

But like any group of young men on the town, our interests went beyond the cultural. We had a natural desire for the company of women. And here again the Japanese entrepreneurs in the town were ready to meet those needs. The rickshaw driver, in answer to our request, took us to a house where we were required to take off our shoes and enter through a rice paper sliding door into a room where we were politely invited to sit by a smudge pot, a bowl of glowing coals, and visit with a "Papa-san." As we sat and warmed our hands around the pot, I surveyed a group of young girls sitting behind him. They were all young and pretty, but one of them particularly caught my eye. The Japanese place a great deal of importance on ceremony, so we took some time in getting around to the business of who pairs up with whom and what the price would be. I was, however, successful in getting the girl who caught my eye.

I learned her name was Aiko. I was nineteen on my way to a new war and she was about seventeen and had therefore spent a large portion of her childhood going through the last terrible war. We each had been on different sides in that war, and we spoke different languages, but I felt like we made some kind of real connection. Even though I came from a racist state and even though I had gone through World War II looking at caricatures of slant-eyed, buck-toothed Japanese on billboards and in cartoons, it's amazing how quickly those stereotypes I had been fed vanished when I saw the beauty of Aiko.

We made love on the floor under heavy covers, sharing our body heat in a cold room fragrant of cedar, bamboo and rice paper mingled with charcoal fumes from the smudge pot, talking to each other in different languages but communicating with gestures and laughter and with a sense of freedom I had never known with a girl before. It's true our relationship was commercial. She had no more control over her circumstances than I had over mine, but I wanted to believe that our relationship meant something to her, that it was more than commercial. Perhaps before long Aiko would become a hardened prostitute, but I was convinced at that time she was not. That's what I wanted to believe. Of course I had at best a dim understanding of the different cultural attitudes she brought to our brief relationship.

I did return to Aiko every night I was in Otsu. I told her I only wanted to be with her and she said she felt the same about me. Even seven months later in Korea I was thinking about her. I wrote to my parents in July of 1951 telling them that I was not really serious about marrying a Japanese girl. I had kidded them about that before. I did tell them I met one I really liked, however, and that one was Aiko. I wrote, "They are not like most people think. We used to walk at night and she would sing Japanese songs to me." One of the songs she sang was "China Night."

But one night Papa-san told me Aiko was not available. He said it was that time of month for her. Maybe so, but I was afraid she was with another man.

I knew she had to do whatever Papa-san told her and I brooded about that. I did get to be with her one more time, however, before we left for Sasebo. So Papa-san had lied.

The relationships between transient military men and local women are an old story. I had a number of Catholic buddies and in Japan, Marines and corpsmen, who would go to confession to seek forgiveness for the sin of fornication while we were on our way to join a war where our purpose was to destroy as many of the enemy as possible. I believed then, and I believe now, that the cause we were going to fight for was just, but it does seem strange that we needed God's forgiveness for making love to young women while we asked His blessing in our efforts to kill other human beings.

In the counter culture movement of the 60's and 70's the cry was to make love not war. But here in 1950 the thing we were called on to do was to make war, not love. If we were not restrained by military orders, we had been conditioned by the moral precepts inculcated into us by our churches and families back home. What a paradox! Although I had been raised a fundamentalist Christian, I felt absolutely no guilt about lying naked with Aiko under heavy covers and making love in a cold rice-paper room laced with the fumes from a charcoal smudge pot. It seemed a perfectly natural thing to do. I felt no need to confess my sins. I had been taught to be ashamed of the wrong things.

\* \* \*

I grew up in a Southern fundamentalist church and considered myself lucky that in the wide world of misguided people I was born in a family blessed with "the Truth." It seemed that God would not have put us on earth without some instructions, and the Bible, we all knew, provided those instructions. Our preacher and the elders of the church, we believed, had the one true understanding of the scriptures. We would speak where the Bible speaks and be silent where the Bible is silent. These were good people. They loved one another and helped one another. Once in the depths of the Depression when my Daddy was out of work members of the congregation brought us some groceries. Later my dad became an elder of the church and he worked lovingly with troubled members of the congregation.

There is a great deal to be said for the brotherhood and sense of community that such churches provide. And being raised as I was means the Bible will always be part of me, the great stories—Joseph and his brothers, Naomi and Ruth, the story of Job, Rachel and Jacob, and many others. Then there is the poetry of the Psalms, the Songs of Solomon and Ecclesiastes, the latter which Melville called "the fine hammered steel of woe." The accounts of war, both in the Israelites' victories and slaughter of the Canaanites, and in their defeat and humiliation when taken into captivity in Babylon, tell us a great deal about the horrors of war. They exulted in their victories, but, as Jeremiah tells us, they also grieved for their losses:

> A voice is heard in Ramah,
> Lamentation and bitter weeping.
> Rachel is weeping for her children;
> And she refuses to be comforted for her children,
> Because they are no more.

Where can be found a more eloquent expression of the bitterest cost of war, a mother's inconsolable grief for the loss of her children?

I had a friend, now gone, a philosophy professor, an ordained Methodist minister and a courageous Christian, who said to me about the Bible, "I know they're just stories. But they're *my* stories."

They are my stories too. The Bible has provided most of us who have grown up in America with our spiritual landscape, with many of our cultural stories and symbols. The great gospel songs from my youth still go around in my head. I find myself singing them as I go about my yard work and domestic chores: "We're marching to Zion, beautiful, beautiful Zion, we're marching upward to Zion, the beautiful city of God";"Jesus Hold My Hand"; "Farther Along." We don't know why there is injustice and evil in the world, but "We'll understand it, all by and by." These and scores of other gospel songs are part of me as they are part of America. They symbolically represent deep human aspirations that I think explain their wide appeal. We all want to make it across the River Jordan to that Beulah Land, to meet again in the sweet by and by. There is no purer spiritual expression than that of human voices raising songs of hope, praise and thanksgiving, making a joyful noise unto the Lord.

It's a natural thing to hope that some kind of cosmic attention will be paid to our little lives, just as it seems natural to reach out from our isolation and seek contact with something more enduring than ourselves. Lord knows we all need help as I learned on that Sunflower How patrol and many times since.

Religion can be a great source of comfort, consolation, spiritual and communal meaning and provide what can be called "emotional truth." And while a great deal of good has been done in the name of religion, unfortunately there has also been a great deal of murder and mayhem committed in the same name. Pride was the sin that led to Satan's rebellion against God and pride, it seems to me, is the sin of all those who feel they have such a perfect understanding of any scripture or religious tradition that they can declare with certitude what God wants the rest of us to do. We all need humility in confronting the big questions. Unfortunately many televangelists and preachers make the virtue "Christian humility" seem an oxymoron.

For all the good that came with the religion I was raised in, there was a down side. We weren't much concerned with treating our bodies like the Lord's temple. Brethren would gather on the steps of the church after a good sermon on the evils of demon rum and light up their Camels, Lucky Strikes, and Pall Malls after having had a hearty breakfast of sausage, eggs, and biscuits with plenty of butter. None ever considered that exercise might have a place in the Lord's plan. After all, for people one generation off the farm where families worked from sunup to sundown, who would dream of exercising when he didn't have to? So it was not uncommon for brethren to drop dead of coronary disease in their fifties or even late forties.

Racism was all right in our church as it was with society at large. In the 30's and 40's the congregation would have been mortified if a black person had entered the church door and taken a seat. It was OK to say "nigger" around the dinner table, but you'd better not say "damn." And most people in those days weren't concerned about replenishing the earth. The Dust Bowl, which resulted from our indifference to the land, was recent history. It was common to see folks throwing trash from their cars as they drove down our two lane highways, and see them carrying their junk out to the nearest wooded area and dumping it alongside the way and thinking absolutely nothing about it. This conduct was, I suppose, a holdover from frontier days when there were a lot of wide-open spaces and few people.

Attitudes toward race and the environment in the Dallas, Texas, of the 1930's and 40's can be illustrated by taking a ride on the streetcars of that day. I loved to ride the little trolleys from Oak Cliff into downtown Dallas. I would get aboard and drop my coins or token into a glass box and watch my fare fall to the bottom where the conductor would check it before flipping a lever with his thumb releasing the coins to fall through a trap door to the money box below. I would then walk down the aisle looking for a seat, and when none was available I would grab one of the shiny white loops hanging from the ceiling and hang on as we went rocking down the tracks.

If there were seats available I had to look above the seat on the wall to see whether the little sign said "White" or "Colored." The White sign on the buses had an arrow pointing forward, meaning the seats from that one forward were for whites, and the Colored sign had an arrow pointing to the rear indicating where black passengers must sit. On the streetcars there were no arrows; still the designated seating areas were clear. The clever thing about those little signs was that they were reversible; on one side was written, "White," on the other, "Colored." All passengers had to do was flip them over to adjust the seating to accommodate the ratio of the races on the streetcar. The signs had been ingeniously devised to make sure the races were never mingled and that the black folks always sat at the back of the car.

The reason there were no arrows on the signs in the streetcars was that the streetcars themselves were reversible. When the conductor got to the end of the line there was no round house and no need for one. He simply moved his gear to the other end of the car where there were also controls and started the journey back. As he made his way down the aisle he flipped the varnished hardwood lathe seat backs to the other side and he was soon off in the opposite direction. What had been the rear of the car was now the front, reminding us of that scripture about the first being last and the last being first. But it didn't work out that way for our black citizens; the game was rigged so they would always be last.

The high point of my streetcar ride into downtown Dallas was crossing the Trinity River. The tracks went over a levee then across a wide expanse of river bottom far below, the little streetcar clickety clicking along the trestle, swaying from side to side as passengers looked straight down to the muddy greenery passing below. It was the closest experience I'd ever had to flying, because no matter how hard I tried I could never see anything supporting the car I was on. We were just levitating through space. But there was a price we had to pay for that exhilarating ride—the smell. As we crossed over the river a dank stench rose into the car. It was coming from the Trinity River, nothing more in that day than an open sewer. The city dumped its raw sewage into the river with no more thought than those people throwing trash out the windows of their cars.

It would not be fair to say that our religion was to blame for the way we looked on our black brothers and sisters or that it was responsible for the way we treated the earth, but it is fair to say that those issues were of no concern to our church leadership or to us. Our mission was to save souls, at least white souls. And since we were the unique possessors of the "Truth," we were obligated to spread that gospel to our fellow man. The forces that ultimately elevated our consciousness in regard to civil rights and the environment would have to come from somewhere other than our church.

Science was viewed with some suspicion. The creation myth of the Bible was accepted as literally true and we were all scandalized when rumors spread that they were teaching evolution at SMU. We believed grape juice should be "the fruit of the vine" used for the Lord's Supper, which I suppose meant Jesus changed the water into grape juice at the wedding at Cana. All were expected to accept that a God who is Love had created a burning Hell for those who transgressed His laws, that we whose lives are like grass which flourishes in the morning and is cut down in the evening, or as a Native American sage eloquently put it, "like the buffalo's breath in winter"; that we, who are so tiny and insignificant viewed against the immensities of time and space, are in line for eternal torment for our sins—unless we are among that happy few who make it up the narrow way. But what is the brief span of a human life measured against eternity? Threescore and ten years versus forever? Come on, God! Is that fair? We dared not ask any questions concerning God's sense of proportionality.

We also accepted that a God who was "no respecter of persons" had a "Chosen People," and that the God whose Son said, "Suffer the little children to come unto me," killed all the first born children in Egypt. Reason, which next to love is the greatest gift God has given us, we were not to use. Questions regarding the literal truth of the Bible, whether the earth is really only six thousand years old or how Noah managed to get to Australia and load up two duck-billed platypuses would not have been welcome. For the most part our congregation ignored such issues, but when they came up there were suggestions that those who were teaching evolution were involved in some nefarious plot to undermine God's story of the creation. God, it seemed, had blessed us with the power of reason then told us that if we didn't accept an irrational theology we would burn in hell.

The universe provides enough mystery to inspire deep religious feelings. It's a good thing that God didn't create the cosmos out of tinker toys. If He had we would have figured it out in a very little while and then what would we have done? Just sat around and looked at each other? As it is we have not only Einstein's theory of relativity, but also the big bang, quantum mechanics, string theory, the genetic code, the incomprehensibly vast universe, birth, life and death, and countless other mysteries and avenues of exploration to keep us occupied into the foreseeable future. No matter which way we look, either out far or in deep, the universe appears to be infinitely resolvable.

I think it is likely that we are all genetically disposed to be religious just as we are disposed, under certain circumstances, to go to war. And just as we divide ourselves into clans, tribes, and nations—divisions which create the categories of "them" and "us" and make it easier for us to kill one another in war, in religion we divide ourselves into different faiths and sects, believing we have to label ourselves to win God's approval, each of the labeled groups believing theirs is the label most pleasing to God.

Perhaps the best way to judge religion is, as the American philosopher and psychologist William James said, not by whether it is "true," but by the practical way it influences the behavior of believers. If they are better people for their beliefs—more compassionate, more generous, tolerant and understanding—then that religion is a good thing. By their fruits ye shall know them. Unfortunately there have been too many malignant manifestations of religion throughout the years, from human sacrifices in Meso-America to the Crusades, militant Islam, the Conquistadores, the Jonestown massacre, and today's terrorists and Jihadists. Too many times priests and prophets have served to legitimize war, to place the stamp of God's approval on the slaughter of fellow human beings.

But I am no theologian and in Korea I was a true believer. I accepted the traditional beliefs of my family and community, and other members of our platoon no doubt shared similar beliefs. Some of my friends over there were Catholic, as I have noted. I remember once a Catholic chaplain asked me how come with a good Irish name like Hughes I was not a Catholic. Well, the truth was I didn't even know Hughes is an Irish name.

\* \* \*

There are probably no people anywhere on earth without some form of religion or religious expression. Even in the so-called atheistic Communist states, leaders such as Lenin, Mao Tse Tung, Kim Il-sung, and Kim Jong Il serve in the place of religious icons and receive the adoration and worship of the masses.

The emotional display at the funeral of Kim Il-sung in 1994 equaled in fervor any religious outpouring, with millions of weeping North Koreans lining the streets beating their chests in grief. I recall seeing a film of the funeral on television and hearing the translated words of one of the female mourners watching the procession go by crying out with tears coursing down her face, "Oh dear Leader, why do you leave us? Why can't you take us with you?" Both Kim Il Sung and his son Kim Jong Il skillfully used propaganda to elevate their status to demigods. The followers of Karl Marx who saw religion as the opiate of the people did not abandon that opiate because of his ideology; they only changed the objects of their worship.

There on the mountain ridgelines we would sometimes have gab sessions with our *cargadores*, the Korean laborers who brought our ammunition and supplies up the steep trails. Language was a problem, but we could communicate fairly well with the help of our interpreter, Kim. Once, with Kim's help, I asked one of the men about his religion. He told me that as a child he remembered his parents and other older Koreans going out to pray to a giant tree. That struck me as odd indeed. Of course I was totally ignorant of Korean history, of Buddhism, which entered the country in the 4th century, and of the animism and shamanism, and folk religions that were practiced there from the earliest times. The worker said the old folks sought something larger than themselves, something with an aura of mystery to worship, so in lieu of a St Peters Cathedral, I suppose a giant tree might suffice.

Another thing I learned from the workers was the Korean method of wrestling. We often talked to and kidded around with the *cargadores*. After they had unloaded their A-frames the workers would many times squat on their haunches in circles and talk and laugh, and sometimes they would challenge one another to a wrestling contest. We enjoyed these competitions and sometimes asked if we could join in. They welcomed us into the contests and we gladly accepted. We would strap a belt around our left thighs, then get a good grip on the back of our opponent's waist belt with our left hand and a good grip on his leg belt with our right and try to throw our opponent off balance and to the ground. It was a bit like sumo wrestling. Whatever the outcome there would always be a lot of laughter and good will. What we enjoyed with those Korean workers was fellowship, a crucial ingredient in any religion.

\* \* \*

Those of us in the 4th Replacement Draft had spent the Christmas season a couple of months earlier riding in rickshaws and walking up and down the cold gray streets of Otsu looking at indecipherable storefront signs and visiting sake shops and nightclubs. The Japanese had proved masters at making war. Much of the recent suffering in the world at that time could be attributed to their aggressive militaristic tradition. But there were other sides to their cultural traditions, too; one of them was their literature, which is quite open in accepting physical love between men and women. Basho, Otsu's great contributor to Japanese literature, perfected the seventeen-syllable poem, Haiku. Following is one example of his work:

> The "Inn of the World"
> At this same inn
> Slept pleasure women too.
> Bush-clover and the moon!

Here the poet, on leaving an inn in the morning, has the thought that his experience of the night provided him not only the pleasure of the courtesans, but also the beauty of the shrubbery and the moon. And the title broadens the meaning to the whole world, a world that offers us both the beauty of nature and the pleasures of love.

\* \* \*

It had been only two months since I had left Aiku in Otsu, and now Ollie was on his way back there for treatment of his wound while I was in Wonju ready to rejoin the 1st Marine Division

As it turned out, the apprehension felt by the corpsmen at the forward aid station when they saw Ollie brought in wounded proved to be unwarranted, because now they were safe. I would be the one to take Ollie's place in the 2nd Platoon of How Company.

*Ollie Langston Otsu, Japan 1951*

# CHAPTER 7
# Smitty

The objectives of Operation Killer had been achieved in only sixteen days, and with the Army's success at Chipyong-ni and the Marines' success on Cloverleaf Hill near Wonju the momentum now was clearly with the United Nations forces. Seeking to capitalize on that momentum, General Ridgway sought a new name for his next offensive. "Killer" had worked great, but how do you top that? Well he and his staff came up with a new name they thought would work equally well, or even better: "Operation Ripper." That name would surely inspire the troops to even more victories, they must have thought. The top brass no doubt got excited over the search for macho names for their operations, but I'm not sure those names had much effect down at the bottom of the chain of command. In fact, I doubt if many of the GIs climbing those Korean mountains could tell you what operation they were participating in. But there is no doubt that the advent of General Ridgway into the war did lift morale and turn the tide of the war, and his strategy of using superior firepower to destroy enemy manpower and materiel rather than fight just to hold territory proved highly successful.

On 7 March 1951, How Company along with the rest of the division jumped off in Operation Ripper against Chinese and North Korean forces in the mountains north of Wonju. The enemy had begun to retreat, so we spent much of the time climbing mountains, following ridgelines and sending out probing patrols to smoke them out. After their recent defeats they were in a broad retreat, but some elements remained entrenched in a few strongly fortified positions determined to hold off our advance and give their forces time for an orderly withdrawal. When we encountered one of those entrenched defensive positions a tremendous firefight would ensue.

It was at this time that I met the guy who would be my new foxhole buddy, Pfc. Alfred Smith, or Smitty, as he was known to the platoon. He too was nineteen years old, a native of Pennsylvania, and the new platoon runner having recently replaced Lou Feinhor in that position. What I had heard about him, and I never traced the story down or asked him about it, was that he had told the platoon leader that he would not fire his rifle, that he would not shoot anyone. What do you do with a Marine rifleman who won't fire his weapon? What in the hell was he doing in the Marines, anyway? Some hard-ass officers might have recommended court martial, but in this case a more enlightened approach was taken. Smitty would be the platoon runner.

In the general scheme of things runners were not required to shoot; they were not assigned to a fire team. That didn't mean their jobs were any safer—to the contrary. Runners were required to take the platoon leaders' orders out to the three squads and the company command post (CP). In a firefight it meant they often had to expose themselves to hostile fire to do their job. We saw the risks involved when Smitty was sent to find Sergeant Roach and Ollie and bring that squad up with the rest of the platoon in the battle for Cloverleaf. So Smitty's declaration to the platoon leader was not a ploy to avoid risk to himself; it no doubt came from strong personal conviction.

Smitty was just under six feet tall. He had brown hair and slightly bulging eyes which gave him a sort of excited look; in fact he was often excited in the sense that he showed a lot of enthusiasm. He had a ready smile and moved easily among all the men in the platoon. No one resented the fact that he refused to fire his weapon. He was more or less adopted by everyone and received a lot of good-natured kidding, which he accepted good-naturedly. I don't know what his religious background was but I do know he had some convictions. I would see him from time to time reading the little New Testament he carried in his pack. He was, after all, from the Quaker State, but I don't know what part that played in his conscientious objection to killing anyone. Whatever his beliefs, he didn't try to inflict them on others.

I thought of Smitty as a "natural Christian." Some of us who are not natural Christians try to be "born again," but I don't think that works. It seems to me there's some validity to that old Calvinistic doctrine of the "Elect." Those folks believed that since God is omniscient and omnipotent that He knows the future and the future must unfold as God knows it will, therefore He knows beforehand who will be saved; and since He has all power He in fact must have chosen those in the Elect. The Elect are born good, but most of us are not.

Look at Jesus' Sermon on the Mount. Who can live up to the ethical standards embodied in the Beatitudes and the verses that follow? Turn the other cheek? Are you kidding? If a man sues you for your shirt you're going to give him your coat as well? No way! Many people have pointed out that Jesus' teachings go against human nature. We can flagellate ourselves, fast, wear hair shirts and sackcloth and ashes, but no matter how hard we try, we just can't eradicate those old deadly sins, such as pride, avarice, envy, and wrath, from our hearts.

All of us inherit our virtues and vices in different proportions. The Greeks believed a man's character is his fate and there's little can be done about it. Thoreau came to pretty much the same conclusion. Once while watching a freight train pass pulling flatbed cars stacked with dried ox hides from Mexico he noticed that each of the still attached tails had its own characteristic twist, no two alike. He saw a parallel between those tails and the kinks in human character. You can kill us and skin us but you can't eradicate our inborn character. The modern explanation for the Elect is scientific—genetics. The Chosen are those born with the proper genes. Natural Christians don't even have to be Christians; they can be of any race, culture or religion. (Cultures and religions, however, do affect human behavior, sometimes for the better but too often for the worse.)

I don't offer any of this as a serious attempt to explain Smitty's nature or anyone else's. I am as mystified by the question of human character as anyone. But I do know Smitty was a happy and friendly young man with a big heart, wherever it came from.

When Smitty was made runner he became part of the platoon command post [CP], which sounds a little more elevated than it was. The CP consisted of the platoon leader, a lieutenant, the platoon sergeant, the corpsman, the runner and the platoon right guide. Normally in our movements through the mountains one squad would lead the way followed by the CP and then the other two squads. The leading fire team in the leading squad was called "the point," and since the point was the riskiest position in the formation it was rotated on a regular basis. Squads would take turns taking the point, and fire teams in squads would take turns. Even men in the four-man fire teams would take turns leading the way up those mountain trails. This way every man in the three squads would have an equal chance to get shot first.

\* \* \*

The first day of Operation Ripper went without a hitch. We were moving along the ridgelines meeting no resistance other than the resistance of gravity in our continuous struggle up the steep and rocky trails. The artillery behind us was firing into the mountains to our front, and we could see teams of Corsairs headed north to do their work. We made it through the day without encountering any Chinese and took up positions on a ridgeline with a good view of the valley below.

The place we were in showed signs of recent occupation by the enemy; there were trenches and foxholes and ashes from campfires spotted around. We built our own fires there on the reverse slope, heated our C rations and sat around the fires eating from cans and drinking instant coffee and cocoa from our blackened canteen cups while exchanging banter. In lieu of movies and TV we spent a great deal of time staring into our campfires, into glowing embers and lambent flames, taking comfort from the warmth and the ever-changing kaleidoscope of red and orange, yellow and sometimes blue pulsating light that pushed the darkness back a little. Our attention to fires there in Korea connected us with our enemies who had been there on the mountain before us and with all our human antecedents. We all share a fascination with fire that has changed little since it was first tamed.

It was the ancient Greek Heracleitus who said we can't step into the same river twice, but he went on to say that fire is a better symbol for change than water. In fact he claimed fire is not a symbol at all; it is the ultimate reality. All things are fire he said, ourselves and all the things we perceive around us including the sun and moon and stars. While gazing into the campfires there on the mountain occasionally a pine knot would explode and send tiny embers spiraling up into the sky to mingle briefly with their kindred stars.

Our attention was drawn from the flames when the platoon sergeant came by and set the watch. Those of us not tapped for that duty turned in for the night.

Sometime later I had to take a leak after drinking all that coffee, so I crawled out of my sleeping bag and was walking down the slope in my stocking feet when I stepped on something that felt rubbery and strange. It was too dark to see, so I reached in my pocket and fished out a book of matches. When I struck a match and held it close to the ground I saw a human hand protruding from the dirt, from one of those hastily dug shallow graves the Chinese had used to bury their dead. This soldier had at least been buried. Later the enemy would not always be afforded the opportunity to show such respect for their fallen comrades, being forced to leave their dead by the hundreds lying on the battlefields.

The next morning we moved off the mountain and down into the valley. Captain Hoey had learned from 3$^{rd}$ Battalion HQ that Able Company of the 1$^{st}$ Battalion had encountered one of the mountain fortresses the CCF were using to slow down the UN advance, and we were called on to come to their assistance.

We had proceeded down a road through the valley for some time when the company column turned off to the west and began to move toward a mountain ahead. Soon we could hear the firefight underway and the sounds grew louder as we neared the mountain. Our artillery rounds were exploding all along the crest and now we could hear the furious exchange of small arms fire. As we continued moving along rice paddy dikes toward the battle another sound was added to the din—the slap, slap, slap of helicopter rotors.

When we looked down the valley to the south we saw a little Bell 47 chopper, the pilot encased in his Plexiglas bubble, approaching low to the ground. He continued toward us until he reached a spot abreast of the mountain where he suddenly began to climb almost straight up. He hovered just below the skyline for a few moments, then rose quickly, sidled up to the mountain, and dropped down. The few seconds he was exposed above the skyline brought a hail of gunfire from the Chinese troops who could no doubt hear the chopper and were just waiting to get a shot. We could see tree limbs flying around the little craft and we marveled at the pilot's daring and skill.

What we learned later was that Able and Baker companies had found a flat area just below the ridgeline where they laid out their colored air panels to guide the choppers and were bringing their seriously wounded there for evacuation. We also discovered that there was more than one skillful and courageous chopper pilot, because after the first one took off in a hail of bullets, another one arrived to repeat the procedure. Each chopper could carry only two wounded, one on each side in a wire stretcher basket. We continued to watch their daring maneuvers until we entered the wooded area at the base of the mountain and began our ascent.

Some of the wounded had been brought down the slope there and several corpsmen from the 3$^{rd}$ Battalion Forward Aid Station were working over them. The corpsmen and Marines up on the mountain had apparently worked out some kind of triage and were evacuating the critically wounded with a good chance of survival by helicopter, while bringing the less seriously wounded and those with no hope down the trail where we were. Three Marines lying on stretchers had not made it. Their faces and bodies were covered with ponchos. The feet of one of the dead Marines were sticking out from under the poncho and I thought as I walked by, "those are the socks he pulled on this morning, the shoes he tied."

Before long we were meeting walking wounded and other Able and Baker people on the trail. They told us they had encountered a heavily defended position and had suffered many casualties. After climbing for some time we began to see signs of those fortifications and signs of the battle. Trees were splintered and broken and the ground was blasted and pock marked. From time to time we would see dead enemy soldiers in their tan, quilted, pajama-looking uniforms wearing thin canvas shoes that could have offered little protection against rain, snow and ice.

When the trail began to level to horizontal we stooped to a crouch because now the battle was right in front of us. We came up on Able Company Marines in defensive positions in holes and behind trees so we spread out and took up positions with them. They told us the worst of it was over but that there were some holdouts on the ridgeline in front of us.

There was a forward air controller (FAC) near us with a radio someone later told me was an ANGRC-9, or as they called it, "Anger-9." Another Marine was cranking a generator with both hands, like pedaling a bicycle, thereby enabling the FAC to communicate with the pilots. That was what he was doing as we watched, calling in an air strike to hit the holdouts in front of us.

A big limb crashing to the ground in front of us announced the arrival of the air strike. I turned and looked up through the trees behind us and saw a blue gull-winged Corsair with guns blazing coming directly at us. I could clearly see the determined expression on the pilot's face behind his canopy as he swooped down on us, right above the treetops. We all hit the dirt immediately and as we did so we could hear that FAC on the radio:

"Pull up! Pull up! You're too low! You're hitting us! Pull up!"

The crewman was cranking that Anger-9 like mad and his efforts must have paid off because the next pass of the Corsairs was farther on down the ridgeline where the holdouts had taken their stand.

The air strike had the desired effect, I suppose, because after the planes left, there remained only some mopping up to do on the mountain. How company accomplished that with little trouble, relieving Able and Baker companies so they could pull back, regroup, tend their wounded and replenish their forces.

(An account of Able Company's battle on this day by Major Allan C. Bevilacqua appears in *Leatherneck,* and can be found at http://www.mca-marines.org/Leatherneck/OpRipperArch.htm).

\* \* \*

Now in the aftermath of the battle, How company was taking up positions in this former stronghold of the Chinese. The 2nd Platoon was positioned where we commanded the approaches to our area, and after some consultation between Captain Hoey and the platoon leaders we all settled into our routine of building fires, heating up our C Rations, and setting up our shelter halves.

The weather largely determined whether we would go to the trouble of setting up our pup tents, and the consideration of how long we would be in one location also was a factor. But that afternoon the weather became overcast and threatened rain, so Smitty and I decided to button our shelter-halves together and have some protection for the night. Some of the guys would just wrap up in them to keep the water away.

It was at this time that I was getting to know the men in the 2nd Platoon. Some of them were new like I was and had ridden to Wonju with me in that old Korean train. There was Hal Tardio from Stockton, California, and John Tarver who I believe was from Oklahoma. I met Marcel Shexnayder from New Orleans, a party guy from a party city. There were a number of the older hands, like George Brodeur, Joe Rousseau, and Lou Feinhor. One colorful guy we called "Hawkshaw Hawkins" after his favorite country singer by that name from West Virginia, though this Marine's real name was Bill Hannah. And then there was "CP Sam."

I learned later that Sam got that moniker because he was always hanging around the platoon and company CPs, soaking up and distributing whatever scuttlebutt he could latch on to, stories he would embellish for dramatic effect.

He could spin some real yarns of derring-do, often with himself at the center of the action. His stories were generally met with laughter or scorn from those who knew him. He fell somewhat into that literary stereotype, "the braggart soldier," like Shakespeare's Falstaff. But Sam was more scrawny than portly, physically more an Ichabod Crane than a Falstaff. And he was not nearly as articulate as Prince Hal's sidekick. Sam's favorite expression was, "Ratshit!"

After we finished our C Rations some of the guys started exploring the holes and bunkers around the mountaintop to see what they could find. There were a number of dead Chinese soldiers strewn about the recent battle site. When they could the Chinese took the weapons from their dead as they retreated, but sometimes one of our guys would find something like a rifle or burp gun. As a general rule, though, it is not infantrymen who come home with war trophies. They come upon them first, but there is a practical reason they seldom get home with them. An infantryman would have to add the weight of his trophies to his already heavy gear and almost no one was willing to do that. I do know, however, that for a while John Tarver did carry a burp gun. But war souvenirs generally ended up in the hands of what we called, "rear echelon pogues," those people who came in behind us to survey the battlefields and collect the spoils.

Smitty and I and some others who had not joined the scavenger hunt were sitting around a fire talking when Hawkshaw came running back up the slope, excited.

"Hey, one of them down there is alive! He's alive! He was lying back up in a bunker and I saw something sticking out of his coat pocket! I thought he was dead and when I started to crawl in and find out what was in his pocket he raised up and looked at me!"

"Let's go see," someone said, and we all got up and followed Hawkshaw down the slope.

CP Sam grabbed his M1 saying, "If he's alive we can take care of that."

When we got to the spot, Hawkshaw stooped and pointed into the darkness of the bunker where we could see the soldier staring sullenly out at us.

"There's no need taking chances," CP said as he brought his rifle to his shoulder.

"Put that down," Smitty ordered. "He's not armed; they took his weapon. Besides he's hurt pretty bad. He's not going to do anything."

"Let's get him out of there," I said, and Smitty and I went into the hole and grabbed the man by the shoulders and worked him out onto the open ground. I could see his leg had been shattered, so I went back up the slope to get my aid kit and asked the platoon sergeant if he could have someone bring a stretcher up from down the ridgeline.

It had started to rain by the time I got back to the prisoner. I cut away his uniform to expose the wound and could see fragments of bone protruding from the hole in his leg. I bound the wound tightly with a battle dressing and gave him a shot of morphine. Before long the stretcher arrived and we managed to get the man up on the stretcher and cover him with a poncho to protect him from the rain. All we had to do now was wait for the Korean workers to come up and take the injured man back down for treatment and interrogation. We carried him back up the slope to a spot near our pup tent; by this time it was starting to get dark.

I was about ready to turn in, but Smitty went to his pack and retrieved a can of beef stew and took it to the fire which had been almost extinguished by the rain and began to work to rekindle the flames and heat up the can. I crawled into the tent and looked out through the flap where I saw Smitty stirring the can of stew, and then I saw him go over to the prisoner and squat down and start to feed him with a plastic spoon. The prisoner accepted the food slowly, but glared at Smitty all the while, sullen and inscrutable. Now the rain was coming down harder.

\* \* \*

Early next morning the rain had slacked off and Korean workers of the Civilian Transport Corps, CTC, the *cargadores*, arrived bringing ammunition and supplies on *ji-gae,* their sturdy A-frame packs. Normally we exchanged pleasantries with these men, joking back and forth with the few words in their language we knew, and even at times entering those wrestling contests with them. I once or twice took part in the wrestling matches and did pretty well, I thought. The contests were a lot of fun and offered no danger to the combatants except to our pride.

But while there was good will between American GI's and South Korean workers, the same was not true between those workers and North Korean and Chinese prisoners. When we told them they would have to take the prisoner back down the mountain, one of the *cargadores* walked over to the man lying on the stretcher and kicked him in the face. Smitty ran to the worker and grabbed him around the shoulders and yelled, "No, no! No kick! No hurt!"

We tried to impress on them that they were not to harm the man and they clearly understood us. When they left two of them picked up the litter and we watched them disappear into the trees down the ridgeline.

The rain started again the next day, sometimes mixed with sleet falling from slate-gray skies. It was still cold even though it was the beginning of the spring thaw, and the weather was miserable; there was mud everywhere.

The roads, which were barely passable in good weather, were quagmires now so it became necessary to supply the 1st Marine Division by air. C 119 "Flying Boxcars" were called into service, planes with twin tail assemblies astraddle a fat cargo fuselage, a design similar to World War II P 38's.

When they dropped their parachutes into the valleys behind us we liked to watch from the ridgelines. The planes came over with the rear door of the big central cargo compartments open to make it possible to shove out the supplies. It was on this particular drop that the 2$^{nd}$ Platoon witnessed something perhaps no one had ever witnessed before. We were sitting on the reverse slope watching the orange, yellow and red parachutes float down to the valley below us when someone shouted out, "Hey, look! Look there," pointing. "That's a guy! Isn't that a guy falling?"

We looked where he pointed and were all amazed to see a man falling to earth, wheeling slowly head over feet in a long dive, passing the parachutes and gaining speed as he plunged to the valley below.

We sat there for some time in stunned disbelief. Had we really seen what we thought we saw? I know there have been times when a parachute has not opened and people on the ground have witnessed the tragedy. And there have been a very few times when someone has fallen from a plane without a parachute, but I doubt there were ever any witnesses on the ground. But here the entire 2$^{nd}$ Platoon, and no doubt many other Marines in the mountains surrounding that valley, saw the man fall to his death.

How could that have happened, we wondered? We knew nothing about the way crews on those flying boxcars worked, but we speculated that they had the supplies set on skids and crewmembers there to push them out. (I later learned they are called "kickers.") But surely those men would wear safety harnesses! Maybe this guy was just overconfident; or maybe he was forgetful that day. Did his foot get caught in the rigging? Did the plane hit an air pocket, or did the suction at the open door pull him out? We never found out.

We did learn, however, that we had not been hallucinating. A few days later one of our men who had been to the Battalion HQ for some reason came back with a harmonica. He told us he had gone to Graves Registration and was told by a friend there that a young man had indeed fallen to his death from that Flying Boxcar, and that one of the things they found on his body was this very harmonica.

\* \* \*

Earlier, when describing the Chinese prisoner Smitty was feeding, without even thinking, I used the word—"inscrutable," an adjective we in the West have used for years to paper over our ignorance of the Far East. Who were these people we were fighting? The truth is we didn't really know.

What we did know was that they were fierce and determined fighters. That they could travel for days through the mountains on meager diets, often only a bowl of rice a day and maybe some beans and soy flour, carrying heavy equipment and supplies, was amazing enough. But when you consider the overwhelming firepower they confronted every day, the tremendous price they paid in hundreds of thousands of casualties, their courage and tenacity were remarkable. I'm not sure how much their Communist ideology influenced their determination to fight against such great odds. No doubt the militant spirit that carried them through the long struggle with the Japanese imperialists and later with the Chinese Nationalists was still strong in these fighters.

The Korean War was the first hot conflict in the Cold War. Western powers saw North Korea's invasion of South Korea as further evidence that Communism was an aggressive, monolithic menace which threatened free countries everywhere. It took decades for the world to understand what a colossal failure Communism was. Behind that militant, threatening façade and all the slogans hailing workers and the brotherhood of man was a failed, rotten totalitarian system that if not transformed would ultimately collapse from within. But this peasant Chinese army we faced was still very much under the control of Chairman Mao and that early Communist zealotry and had no doubt been convinced they were fighting to protect their homeland against capitalistic imperialists.

One of the greatest advantages the UN forces had was the control of the air. We had just had a taste of what the enemy forces experienced every day when we looked up and saw that Corsair blazing away at our position. We were able to call them off in that case, but the Chinese and North Korean troops could never do that. And they were frequent victims of that most fearsome weapon—napalm. There are many more high tech weapons than wing tanks filled with jellied gasoline, a weapon that was developed just at the end of World War II, but few more nightmarish. Watching the sorties come in and bomb and strafe and smear napalm across those ridgelines was a daily thing for us. The air attacks were usually at a distance where we could not see the enemy troops or the destruction inflicted on them, but one time we were close enough. I saw a Chinese soldier jump from a flaming bunker, dash headlong down the slope burning fiercely and then collapse. Even though we rarely witnessed such scenes close up, they were surely repeated over and over.

Another problem for the enemy was supplies. We had truck convoys and C 119's. We could move our supplies day or night. They had a few trucks, Mongolian horses, and human bearers, but they could move only at night. We controlled the air north and south, and with their forces now below the 38th Parallel their supply lines were very long.

I wrote a letter home at this time telling my family,

> We are now sitting on a hill overlooking a small valley and
> then more mountains. Everything is pretty quiet now, except
> for mortars and artillery. We are giving the Chinks a beating.

I see the planes circling to my right preparing for an air strike. They sure make it miserable for the Chinese.

From the reports we've gotten from prisoners they say their morale is mighty low. They have to go on long marches at night with heavy equipment then they are kept awake all day by air strikes.

My company is now the farthest most point of any UN troops so I guess you can find where I am on the map. That's what we're waiting for now, is the rest of the troops to catch up . . . .

The sun has come out and it is very warm. We are all running around in shirtsleeves. It is pretty muddy with all the snow melting but if this sun keeps up it might dry up some.

There is a machinegun chattering away below us. I don't know what they're shooting at but there are a lot of civilians standing around watching. He must be firing right over their heads. These people are crazy. When the shooting starts they just stand around and watch. I fixed up a little boy's hand this morning where he had been shot. He was bringing up water to us.

It's good that we had a sunny warm day because there weren't many of them that March.

I tell more in this letter than I usually did. I didn't want to worry my mother so I usually censored my letters home. Mother was a strong good woman with unshakable religious faith, but she was also straightforward and blunt. She worried about me a great deal, and after I sent home a letter in which I described some of the action we had been through she wrote and told me that if we didn't meet again in this world, we'd meet in the next. Well, that was just exactly the kind of mail I didn't need to be getting from home, so from that time on I gave her few specific details about military operations. For the most part I would assure her that everything was fine and sometimes I would even go so far as to tell her that I wouldn't want to be anywhere else. But at times my weariness and frustrations would show.

I doubt that those Chinese soldiers got regular letters from home. They were lucky to get supplies. It was not only our control of the air that hurt them, but the fact that we had heavy artillery, 105mm and 155mm Howitzers, tanks and numerous other weapon systems to inflict grievous destruction. In spite of our superiority in weapons, however, the Chinese and North Koreans were formidable adversaries. What they lacked in weaponry, they made up in numbers and determination.

They had recently thrown those numbers at UN forces at Hoengsong, Chipyong-ni and Cloverleaf Mountain in a struggle that J.D. Coleman, a retired Lt. Colonel who fought at Chipyong-ni, called the "Korean Gettysburg" in his book of the same title. During the closing days of April 1951 and early March the two sides committed their main forces against one another in a crucial and decisive battle. And like that great watershed battle in 1863 where the North finally gained ascendancy over the South, these battles coming at the turning of the seasons in Korea in 1951would prove to be the tipping point of this war. Since the Chinese entry into the war all the victories had gone to the Communist forces, but from this point on things would change. UN forces were now seasoned and strong with control of the air and possessed of tremendous firepower, so for the Communists, numbers would no longer be enough.

Just as the United States Marines played a key role in the previous war by stopping the Japanese expansion in the Pacific in the crucial battle for Guadalcanal, they were again playing a major part in Korea as they had done in stopping the Communists here at Wonju. That victory along with the Army's brave stand at Chipyong-ni cheered General Ridgway and the leadership of the Eighth Army, but nothing could compensate for the terrible losses we had suffered only four weeks earlier at the battle of Hoengsong.

It was our 7[th] Marine Regiment that gave that tragic battle its name.

CHAPTER 8

# Massacre Valley

The next day we moved down from the mountain where the 1st Battalion had taken so many casualties and began to move once more in pursuit of the enemy. The delay the Chinese holdouts had provided with that battle gave their comrades time to clear out of the area. Now it was our objective to move quickly and reestablish contact again and keep them off balance.

When How Company made it to the valley and got back on the road we had come up the day before, we turned north. A cold rain was falling as we formed our two columns, one on each side of the road, and settled into that old hypnotic rhythm of the march. The other companies of the 3rd Battalion soon joined us and before the day was done the entire 7th Regiment was moving north.

The UN's victories at Chipyong-ni and Cloverleaf Hill at Wonju, had stopped the Chinese, but the offensive the Communist forces had launched on February 11th leading up to those battles caught our forces by surprise and exacted a heavy toll. As we began moving through the narrow valley north of Hoengsong our regiment was the first to see how costly that Chinese offensive had been and to witness directly the aftermath of a horrible military miscalculation.

A regiment is a large body of men, somewhere between three and four thousand, and on this day a number of Marine units had preceded the 2nd Platoon down the road where engineers had plowed and pushed the slush and debris to the side. We were used to seeing dead Chinese and North Koreans, but we were not prepared for what we saw as we followed the curving road around a steep bluff. What came in view were American vehicles headed south, but they weren't moving. They were in the ditch. There were jeeps, trucks, and M-16 half-tracks, most of them riddled with bullet holes. There were tanks as well, some with their tracks blown off.

The 7th Regiment Marines ahead of us had discovered hundreds of dead GI's in this narrow Hoengsong valley, some of them still in their riddled vehicles, others lying in the ditches alongside the road. Many of them had been stripped of their clothes and boots. A few had been executed with their hands tied behind their backs. Tanks were found with the whole crews dead inside and others tanks and vehicles had simply been abandoned. The stark and grisly convoy we discovered had been frozen in time since that awful night four weeks earlier, its members no longer aware of the cold rain and sleet that had since continued, sporadically, to fall on their rigid bodies.

The first Marines going through had to drag dead soldiers off the road so they wouldn't be run over by our vehicles. They were assisted by an Army recovery team from the 2nd Infantry Division, which had been sent to retrieve the bodies of Support Force 21 and the equipment that had been lost when that unit was overwhelmed by the Chinese offensive.

By the time the 2nd Platoon passed through the area the bodies had been pretty much collected, but whiffs of decaying flesh were in the air. For a few weeks now we had noticed that the bodies that had been frozen in the winter were beginning to thaw. We humans like to set ourselves off from other creatures as being different, maybe with some justification, but in death there is no distinction. All decomposing mammalian flesh smells the same. We had to this point been exposed mainly to enemy dead, bodies left unattended or hastily buried. Sometimes there was the smell with no bodies—only flesh and fragments of bone and teeth and tatters of brown uniforms mixed in with dirt and gravel that graders had pushed to the ditches as they cleared the road.

What we saw and smelled on this day drove home the realization that it is much easier to look upon the dead "them" than the dead "us." These were Americans who had died here. This realization fell on us like a pall. All banter stopped as we marched through the valley. We looked quietly to the left and right as we passed through the scenes of destruction, each man deep in his own thoughts.

There was only one happy note in this grisly discovery. A number of survivors were found hiding under some houses. They had held out there for over four weeks with almost no food or water and came out of hiding only after hearing the Marines speaking English moving through the area.

The name we gave to this area was "Massacre Valley." It was obvious that an army convoy had been ambushed, but we didn't know how it came about and we had no time to inquire. We were moving north.

Infantrymen never get the big picture, or even a very large snapshot, and the picture here was not one many would want to look at. The American and UN commanders were certainly not anxious to publicize this debacle either. It was not until much later that the story came out. What had happened was this:

\* \* \*

In late January and early February General Almond, the unpopular Commander of the Army's X Corps who had commanded the 1st Marine Division at Inchon and later during the advance from Hungnam to the

Chosin Reservoir, had developed a plan to put ROK forces on the line and have them supported by US Army artillery units. This had not been done before. Perhaps he wanted to give encouragement to our South Korean allies and prove the two armies could work together. Whatever his reasoning, he placed the ROK 8[th] Division in the mountains in the area of Changbong-ni north of Hoengsong with the US Army's 21[st] SF (Support Force) in the valley behind to back them up with 105 and 155 Howitzers, M-16 AAA half-tracks, and other heavy weapons. A detachment of US infantry accompanied the heavy weapons force to guard their perimeter. Almond planned for the ROK 8[th] division to launch an attack from that point and push the Chinese back, but this proved to be a grave miscalculation and a major failure of intelligence. It turned out the Chinese had recently moved several divisions into the area in preparation for a major offensive of their own. And on the night of February 11 they launched a fierce assault on a broad front north of Hoengsong.

When they hit the ROK 8[th] Division and quickly flanked them, the South Koreans fled in disarray. SF 21, with its big guns ready to offer their support, lost all radio contact with the Korean division in front of them. They learned of the Chinese attack shortly before midnight. It wasn't long before ROK soldiers were fleeing south past the artillery pieces out in the field. These were the very troops the artillery was supporting, the troops that were supposed to hold the front line, the only buffer between the American artillerymen and the Chinese. The commander of SF 21, Lt. Col John Keith Jr., realizing the desperate situation his unit was in, called his division commander and requested permission to withdraw about three miles to an earlier position. In the meantime Lt. Col William Keleher's infantry detachment was trying unsuccessfully to halt some of the fleeing ROK soldiers and get them to join in a perimeter defense. And there were command and control problems. Since the 8[th] ROK Division had disintegrated it was not clear who could give Col Keith permission to withdraw.

There followed scenes of frantic confusion as Col Keith continued to try to get permission to withdraw and to get the big guns lined up on the road behind their tractors with all the troops and vehicles ready to move. One member of SF 21, Lt. Paul G. McCoy, 82AAA, D Battery, remembers that night:

> On 11 February, prior to midnight, we received word that the 8[th] ROK Division was under severe attack by Chinese forces. This soon turned into a collapse of the ROK units, and SF 21 started a delayed effort to load vehicles and attempt our own withdrawal. . . . Our withdrawal did not start until 0200 hours, 12 February. By this time the Changbong-ni area was inundated with fleeing ROK forces being closely followed by elements of several Chinese divisions.

Lt. McCoy says that no sooner did the convoy get moving than they came under machinegun and rifle fire from the hills along the road and the progress stopped. He says he was "ranked out" of the front seat of his jeep by a captain, and that rather than sit there in the back seat of a jeep that wasn't moving he decided to jump out and move forward and see if he could find out what was holding up the convoy. That decision, he realized later, was what saved his life.

As he moved forward he found that many of the vehicles were missing their drivers. It wasn't that they had been killed, but they had apparently left the drivers seats when they came under fire. He estimated that one in ten of the vehicles were without drivers, so he set out to find volunteers. One man said he could drive but that he didn't have a driver's license. Lt. McCoy decided he would risk breaking the rules and have the man get in a vehicle and get it going. He got some of the vehicles on the move but the tie-ups continued, so the lieutenant continued his progress toward the front of the column and toward the town of Hoengsong.

The Chinese forces, employing time honored military tactics, had followed up their initial success in routing the ROK division with rapid pursuit of the fleeing enemy. The Chinese had taken positions commanding the road to Hoengsong and established roadblocks at key points along the way. Not only was the column being attacked from the flanks, it was now being attacked from the front and rear as well.

At one point Lt. McCoy felt he had outpaced the Chinese because fire from the flanking ridgelines had ended. He came upon a couple of tanks, one of which had been abandoned by its commander, and took charge of them. He appointed a sergeant the new tank commander and got the two tanks moving down the road. Expecting to soon meet US forces Lt. McCoy rode on the back of the second tank so he could explain to friendly forces when he met them what was going on. But as they approached a bridge north of Haktam-ni, the lead tank was hit by a burst of machine gun fire from a Chinese roadblock at the bridge. That first tank veered into a ditch with all guns firing while the tank the lieutenant was on tried to pull around it. Just as they got abreast of the first tank they were hit with a rocket launched missile and the lieutenant was blown off. The entire crew inside the tank was killed.

The lieutenant and two survivors from the first tank joined forces in the ditch beside the road and continued to work their way south. They eventually did get around the bridge and cross over the river. They experienced a great feeling of relief when at last they made contact with US forces, the 3rd Battalion of the 38th Infantry.

At first Lt. McCoy could not understand why this US battalion had not come to the rescue of his comrades who were being attacked back up the road. He had not understood the magnitude of the Chinese offensive until he was told that now the road between where they were, Saemal, and Hoengsong had been cut off. The Chinese had the entire battalion surrounded! The ordeal was not over for the lieutenant.

By sunrise on 12 February a few other stragglers from SF 21 had made their way into the battalion perimeter. Of the entire unit there were only about twenty-five men and four or five M 16 half-tracks left.

Now the 3rd Battalion was coming under heavy attack so the order was issued to move south toward Hoengsong. Lt. McCoy writes, "About noon we started a breakout with an infantry company on each side of the road with the remaining M-16's providing support for the infantry." [M-16 half-tracks, which had quad 50 caliber machine guns mounted on the rear, were designed for antiaircraft defense, but they could also be deadly effective when used against ground forces.] The lieutenant commanded one of the M-16s as the new convoy started on its way toward Hoengsong.

He goes on with his account:

> On one point on the road, a Chinese mortar had zeroed in on a bottleneck, which could not be avoided. My M-16 went through the impact area, but the vehicle behind me appeared reluctant to follow. So, I left my vehicle; counted the pop from the mortar and attempted to encourage the commander to follow. However I missed a pop, and a mortar round hit my left foot. My momentum was sufficient to propel me out of the impact area, and a bit of crawling into a ditch provided some protection, at least until the Chinese put a machine gun into position so as to be able to rake the ditch.

But the lieutenant did manage to escape from the ditch after he got his wound treated and a shot of morphine from a medic. He climbed into a jeep, was tossed an M1 rifle and a bandoleer of ammo, and he and his comrades began their desperate dash through the Chinese gauntlet to the town of Hoengsong.

As they sped on their way a concussion grenade bounced off the canvas top of the jeep and exploded near one of the wheels. Then the lieutenant took a shot through the thigh, then another through the calf of his leg. And as if this weren't enough, as they were passing an M-16 while they were still under fire, thanks to the effects of the morphine, he failed to draw his right leg in fast enough and his foot struck the half track. The impact broke his right ankle. (www.patriotfiles.com/article/php?sid =345). But he escaped from Massacre Valley

So many didn't. Lt. McCoy's was one story. But there were many others, most of which will never be told—dramatic stories of chaos, panic, confusion, and courage.* We know of famous lost battles—Thermopylae,

The Alamo, The Little Bighorn—but who knows the story of the Battle for Hoengsong?

*[One of Lt. McCoy's fellow officers, however, did relate his harrowing experiences during the battle of Hoengsong forty years later in The Graybeards March-April 2005, a publication of the Korean War Veterans Association. Lt. William R. Webster was not as fortunate as Lt. McCoy. He tells the story of how he was shot in the knee and taken prisoner and sent back north with other walking wounded, many of them Chinese soldiers. His harrowing story of captivity and escape is noteworthy for a number of reasons, but one point of interest is the kindness shown him by his wounded Chinese captors. In this war, as in all wars, there were atrocities on both sides, but there were also many occasions when the combatants recognized their opponents as brothers in arms.]

All of us who walk the earth walk through history every day without knowing it. I had not long ago done that on Guam, and in Tokyo and Otsu, and that's what we did in the 2nd Platoon when we marched through Massacre Valley. Of course we saw clear evidence that something terrible had happened there. A large armored Army convoy had been ambushed with tragic consequences, but we had no idea how it happened or why. The sounds of battle, the desperate voices were silent now.

And this tragedy had happened only four weeks earlier. The Chinese army that had wreaked this destruction was the same one that had been repelled by the US Army at Chipyong-ni and by the Marines on Cloverleaf Hill, the same one that the 2nd Platoon was battling when Ollie was wounded.

The Army lists the casualties from this attack for the period from nightfall on 11 February until daylight on 13 February at around 11,800—9,800 South Koreans, 1,900 Americans, and 100 Dutch. The exact number will never be known. The army recovery team that accompanied us into the valley recovered over 250 American bodies in a few days. Many others members of SF 21 were taken prisoner and many died in captivity. The equipment toll was also heavy: twenty-eight 105 mm howitzers, six 155mm howitzers, six tanks, and hundreds of crew-served weapons, and hundreds of vehicles were lost (www.army.mil/cmh-pg/books/korea/ebb/ch17.html).

But now the Chinese army had been stopped and was on the run, and we were in rapid pursuit.

\* \* \*

The closeness of troops in war is peculiar. Dissention was almost nonexistent in the 2nd Platoon. And we weren't men who had known each other for a while, like the Civil War units made up of men from a single town or area who had known one another before the war and stayed with one another for the duration. We met our platoon members when we were rotated in, and left them—the great majority of them forever—when we were rotated out.

The turnover of personnel was not rapid but continuous. Most of us knew each other for only a few months. Yet the bonds between us were strong and unlike any others we would likely ever make again in our life-times. Though we never spoke of it, we all understood that we had only one another to rely on. Human organizations in other circumstances are fraught with conflicting personalities, ambitions, and motives, but every one of us in that rifle platoon had the same motive. We wanted to get out of Korea alive and we could only do that by working together. Often grand ideals are invoked to explain why men are willing to face death in battle—freedom, democracy, the fatherland—but the primary reason men risk their lives in combat is for their comrades, for one another. Egotism and selfishness had no place in the 2nd Platoon.

Accounts of war inevitably focus on battles. But any foot soldier can tell you that the overwhelming portion of his time is spent in marching and climbing, slogging through snow and rain and mud, up mountains and down mountains, following roads and trails or just striking out through brush and trees but always following one another and the directions of the officers with the maps. Who was it that said that combat is ninety-eight percent boredom punctuated by two percent pure terror? The only thing we had to dampen the terror a bit was the knowledge that we could depend on our buddies, and all we had to protect ourselves from boredom was one another. Here also the 2nd Platoon was particularly fortunate because we had a number of entertaining members.

We knew each other primarily by only one name, sometimes the first, but more often the last. A few were known by nicknames, such as "Hawkshaw" and "CP." I was "Doc." Few if any men in that group knew I had another name. (The same was true for all corpsmen in Korea.) Of course NCOs like platoon sergeant Roach and the squad leaders Nolan, Noreiga and Putnam we could just call "Sarge." Most of the platoon, however, was made up of PFCs any one of whom would tell you that he wished those initials stood for "poor fucking civilian." One of the replacements who rode up with me on the train from Masan, Tardio, proved to be a real morale booster. He kept the platoon laughing with his good nature and wisecracks. He and Hawkshaw made a good comedy team.

We saw enough of the How Company CP for them to seem like part of our 2nd Platoon group as well. Captain Hoey, our company commander, was a fairly large-boned man who gave the impression that he might be friendly with the bottle when he got the chance. He was older than the rest of us, and in those mountains a few years could make a big difference. (I remember one rifleman, thirty-five years old, who could not keep up with the march.) But Captain Hoey was always right there with us. He was one of those officers who cared more for the men under him than the brass above him. The company not only respected him but had genuine affection for him.

Another member of the company CP was Gunny Spell. He was always coming into our area with that canteen cup of coffee in his fist, growling out the orders of the day, gruff and comical, much as he had been down in the bean fields of Masan. Our old buddy, Kim, the interpreter was still with us, and the tall Lt. Lowe had rejoined the company, but now he was executive officer, assistant to Captain Hoey. He and I visited some and talked about our experiences on the "Gook Chase" patrols. I noticed that he now wore two canteens on his belt rather than one. Men got thirsty climbing mountains.

\* \* \*

It wasn't long before we left the road through Massacre Valley and moved back to our familiar territory, the high ground. The somber mood that had fallen upon the platoon as we passed through that valley of death very slowly dissipated as we climbed the jagged ridgelines.

For several days we continued our advance through the mountains without any contact with the enemy. Often we would hear gunfire from neighboring ridgelines, but generally we couldn't tell whether a firefight was underway or whether someone had just become overly excited. Each evening we would take up defensive positions for the night and go through our normal routines of preparing a place to sleep, setting the watch, and building fires to heat our C Rations.

Our movement along the ridgelines during the day was generally accompanied by the sounds of artillery echoing through the mountains. The skies were often overcast and sometimes the booms from our artillery were reinforced with rumbles of thunder. The two sounds intermingled in my mind and remained associated for years. Many times after I got back home when skies grew dark and thunder rolled a mood would come on me, and I would find myself back in the mountains of Korea listening to artillery reverberating through the valleys.

\* \* \*

We were now approaching the town of Hongchon and our mission was to keep moving north until we reestablished contact with the enemy. We were still carrying out operation Ripper, and our first objective had been attained. We had reached phase line Albany, just south of the city. It was at this time, the 14th of March, when Seoul to our west was retaken by UN forces without a struggle. It had now changed hands four times in nine months. This time would be the last.

After continuing to follow the ridgelines north we finally came in sight of Hongchon spread out in the valley ahead. The city was still some distance away but there were a few thatched-roofed houses at the base of the mountain below us, and where there were houses there was always a water supply. It was customary for us to take turns going for water. Those on the water patrol would go around gathering canteens from their buddies and bind them together like bunches of coconuts, then head down the hill. On this day Smitty and I agreed to make the journey so we set about gathering canteens. Lt. Lowe happened to be passing through the 2nd Platoon area, so we offered to bring him some water too. He was the only man in the company I knew of who carried two canteens during this cool weather, but still he said yeah, he could use some water, so he gave us the one from the right side of his belt, keeping the full one on the left as his reserve.

As runner Smitty still carried his M1, but that was for form rather than function. He grabbed his rifle and I picked up my carbine and aid kit. Together we shouldered the canteens we had strung together on belts and began our descent into the valley.

About thirty minutes later we found ourselves approaching the yard of one of the houses we had seen from the mountain. The area surrounding the house appeared to be a garden, which was fallow now since it was not yet the growing season. As we neared the house we called out, "Hello! Hello! ...Yoboseo?"

We saw no one and no one answered so we went to the door and looked in. We got a bracing whiff of *kimchi*, that potent Korean dish of fermented cabbage seasoned with garlic and other powerful condiments, but again we saw no one.

We knew most of the houses built up against the mountains were there because of a water source, usually a spring, so we began to search around the house until we found a path leading back toward a ravine at the base of the mountain. Sure enough, we discovered a stream coming out of the rocks falling into a basin about the size of a pup tent, so we immediately set to work filling the canteens with ice-cold water.

While we were thus employed we heard a sound behind us and turned to see an old man in the traditional homespun white *hanbok* outfit, bowing and smiling apprehensively.

"Anyung haseo." He said, continuing to bow.

"Hello," we replied. Then holding up our canteens we said, "Mul, mul. We've come to get water, mul."

"Ah," he smiled, "mul."

He had apparently come from one of the houses close by that we had seen from the ridgeline above. And it wasn't long before we noticed other villagers approaching cautiously behind him. He turned and said something in Korean that apparently reassured them, so they moved up a little more quickly to join him. They all stood looking curiously at us as we threaded the full canteens back on the belts.

"We are Americans, Miguk, Miguk!" Smitty told the small group standing there watching us who obviously already knew who we were.

There was a thin, stooped, wizened old woman that we took to be the old man's wife, with several children standing behind her. None of them spoke.

"Miguk!" Smitty said again and pointed up to the mountain where we had come from. The children, who had apparently been reassured by our talk and gestures, began to move in closer to examine us and our equipment. We were used to dealing with children, so we kidded around with them a bit while we shouldered our canteen belts.

I looked at the old man and asked, "Papa san, have you seen Chinese? Chunguk? Chunguk?"

"Ah, Chunguk! Chunguk! Ne, ne!" And he turned and pointed north. Then he spoke more in Korean that we couldn't understand and held up three fingers. We knew that more than three Chinese had been through here so we thought maybe he was telling us that they had passed through three days ago.

As we started back toward the trail up the mountain Smitty said, "Hey Doc, see that boy over there, the one leaning on that stick? Look at his leg. Something's wrong with his leg."

When I looked I could see there was something definitely wrong with his leg. I set the canteens down on the ground, approached the boy, then squatted down and said, "eeteewa, eeteewa cipsio" and motioned for him to come to me. He looked to be about ten or eleven years old. He limped toward me leaning on his stick and when he got near I motioned for him to sit on the ground, then had him extend the injured leg toward me and pointed to the injury, indicating that I wanted to look at it. The wound was between the calf and the ankle and had been wrapped in some coarse, home-spun material. But I could tell from the redness that extended beyond the bandage that there was infection and inflammation there. I got my surgical scissors out of my aid bag and cut away the bandage and found some kind of brown smelly goo had been applied to the injury, no doubt some Korean home remedy, so I took some gauze from my kit and began to wipe that substance away to get a better look.

The boy grimaced as I worked, but he was very good at holding his leg still. I expected to find a bullet wound, but the three-inch gash I found looked more like shrapnel. Or it could have been one of those injuries active boys often suffer. Some stitches would have helped earlier on, but now with the infection the only thing to do was clean the wound, apply some antiseptic ointment and dress the leg with clean bandages. That's what I did using water from one of the canteens to wash the leg. Some penicillin would have been helpful, but front-line corpsmen were not equipped to give long-term care. The Battalion Aid Station would be setting up here in Hongchon in a few days and the boy would be able to get some follow-up treatment there.

Before we could shoulder our canteens again the old Papa-san came up to me and pointed to the old woman and spoke rapidly pointing to his neck and shoulders and then pointing to the same places on her. I gathered from all this that the woman was in some pain from arthritis or osteoporosis. What could I do? I shook him out about eight or ten APC tablets and tried to make him understand that she was to take only two at a time and wait at least four hours between doses.

"Komapsumnida!" He said. "Komapsumnida!"

"Komapsumnida! Thank you!" We responded. "Komapsumnida!" Finally we were on our way back up the mountain with our canteens.

\* \* \*

When we rejoined the platoon the campfires were going and everyone seemed in fairly good spirits considering the pall that had fallen over all of us as we had passed through Massacre Valley. Tardio was going from fire team to fire team trying to make a C Ration swap. "Who would like to have a delicious can of corned beef hash? I'll take any of those undesirables, like ham and lima beans, franks and beans, even chicken and noodles! Better hurry, this offer can't last long! Step right up!" He was having no luck making the trade. Someone else called out, "Who likes Chesterfields? I'll trade for some Lucky Strikes!"

We got a box of C Rations daily and, since we had so little to look forward to, we made the most of the contents of that box: three heavies and three lights. There were about a dozen different selections on the heavy's menu—meat and beans, pork and rice, meat and spaghetti, and so on. The lights were always the same—coffee, cocoa, cookies, jellies, jams and crackers. Also in the box were cigarettes, matches, toilet paper and other useful items.

As noted earlier the box also contained one of the greatest inventions in the Western world—the handy dandy can opener, also known as the P-38. I understand that the invention got that name, not from the World War II fighter plane, but from the fact that it took exactly thirty-eight punctures to open a can of C Rations. I never counted them but I always made sure I didn't go all the way around so I could bend the lid back and make a handle so I could warm the can on the fire. With that box of C Rations we had Christmas every day.

Smitty and I joined Tardio, Hansen, Tarver, and Shexnayder around a fire and had our evening meal. We were still talking about our morning march through the valley of death. We couldn't understand how such a thing could happen. Marines always set themselves apart from the army believing they are superior warriors. I heard Marines taunt army guys in Korea saying, "I'd rather have a sister in a whorehouse than a brother in the army!" But that was just talk, friendly rivalry, though there were some real questions about the relative performances of the two organizations. But there was little that army group SF 21 could have done to avert the disaster that fell upon them. Fighting men are often victims of the mistakes made by their commanders, and Massacre Valley was clearly an example of that.

The conversation shifted to the cold ride some of us had shared on the train from Masan to Wonju. It was hard to believe that it had only been a couple of weeks since Tardio, Tarver, several others and I had been aboard that train. I mentioned before how that ride contrasted with the luxurious ride I'd had in the Pullman train from Dallas to San Diego after I joined the navy. Later Ollie and I had ridden a day coach from Oakland to Oceanside after we had signed up for the FMF. But there was one more memorable train ride in my recent past, and that was the ride we took in Japan from Otsu to Sasebo on our way to Korea.

\* \* \*

When we left Otsu I had to say *sayonara* to Aiko. She assured me that she wouldn't be a butterfly, but what were the chances of that? We both knew it was a lie. She was no more a free agent than I was.

We passed through some striking landscapes on that train ride through Japan. The sky was overcast, the weather bleak and cold, and large patches of earth were covered with snow, but the rolling wooded hills were beautiful and I got that feeling again of being in a strange, alien place, almost like being on another planet. The woods sometimes gave way to terraced rice paddies, a few times we crossed trestles over rivers, and frequently we would pass farmhouses, villages, and towns, and there were times when the train slowed down as we passed through cities.

If outside the train the weather was cold, inside it was warm and, as always with a group of GIs on an outing, there was a lot of kidding and horseplay going on. If any of us were concerned about the fact that we were headed for a war it didn't show. Although this wasn't a Pullman train like the one I rode to San Diego, it did have amenities. We had a Japanese porter, a young man probably in his late twenties, who was anxious to attend to our every need. He could speak a little English so we kidded around with him and peppered him with all kinds of questions.

One question I asked, because the issue had puzzled me for some time, was how the Japanese military had recruited kamikaze pilots in the recent war. He told us that the military leaders would hold rallies for these young men and whip up their patriotic fervor with passionate speeches, regale them with plenty of sake, and when emotions were at a high pitch, align them in formation and ask for volunteers to raise their hands. If no hands went into the air, the porter said, the leaders on the stand in front of them would say, "Oh, there are some brave men at the back, raising their hands!" This trick would start the bandwagon going and before long hands would be shooting up all over the place.

That's what the porter told us. I suspect now that he was mostly telling us what he thought we wanted to hear. The story of the Kamikaze was much more complex and deeply rooted in Japanese history and culture. The name itself means "divine wind" and it goes back to the 13th century when a massive invasion force of the Kubla Khan was destroyed by a typhoon off the coast of Japan. The Japanese believe their salvation resulted from the prayers of their emperor and other holy men and that the storm was a "divine wind." Ritual suicide was also an honored tradition, so when Japan was clearly losing the war in 1944 they called upon that ancient power, the human "divine wind," or Kamikaze, to protect them from the coming Allied invasion as that typhoon had protected them in 1281.

Such massive suicide attacks carried out by the Japanese were new in the history of warfare and were totally alien to our traditions and ways of thinking. We had brave men who would undertake missions with a slim chance for survival, such as Lt. Col. James "Jimmy" Dolittle and his men who staged the daring B 25 raid on Tokyo not long after Pearl Harbor. They flew sixteen bombers off two aircraft carriers with little chance of finding landing places and with great chances of being killed, or captured and tortured. But it was not literally a suicide mission. That idea is alien to the American mind. And it was certainly alien to those of us in the 2nd Platoon sitting up on that mountain overlooking Hongchon.

\* \* \*

It turned out we had some drama in our own ranks that evening. Just as in Greek tragedies where the mayhem takes place off stage, we in the 2nd Platoon learned of this latest catastrophe second hand from CP Sam. Sam had just returned from the company CP (yes, he liked to hang out there too) with a tale to shiver one's spine.

What had happened was that Gunny Spell a day or so ago had been looking for some water to make a cup of coffee. He had emptied his canteen and was looking around when he spotted a canteen belt lying on the ground with two canteens, more water than a man actually needed. So he tore open a package of instant coffee, dumped it in his canteen cup, then poured the liquid from the purloined canteen into the cup, stirred it a bit, and walked over and placed the cup on the fire to heat up. But wait a minute! What was that smell? He raised the cup to his nose for a moment and then his expression began to change; something like panic started to spread on the face of this crusty old Leatherneck.

The Gunny who was always cool under fire was now shrinking in fear as the painful realization dawned on him that he had attempted to make his coffee with Lt. Lowe's whiskey! That was why the lieutenant had been carrying those two canteens. Gunny pondered his predicament for a few minutes. A canteen cup holds a lot of liquid so surely the lieutenant would miss what he had taken. What could he do now? Unfortunately the sergeant made another bad choice. He went back, unscrewed the lid and poured the contents of the cup back into the canteen. From that point on the Gunny had more to worry about than the Chinese. It didn't take him long to realize that pouring the coffee back into the canteen was not such a good idea. For the next day and a half he was filled with foreboding as he waited for Lt. Lowe to make the fateful discovery. And that was what had happened while CP Sam was visiting the How Company CP.

CP told us in gory detail how Lt. Lowe let out a roar when he made that discovery. He had been carrying that whiskey for weeks, ever since he had left the *Repose*, and it wasn't that Japanese whiskey, Suntory, but good old American straight bourbon whiskey. He had wanted to save it for a celebration once we got to go in reserve, but now some dimwit had poured coffee in his canteen and had blasted those plans. There would surely be dire consequences for the miscreant who had defiled the lieutenant's ceremonial libations.

Gunny kept a shitlist of Marines in the company who were guilty of minor infractions and indiscretions and was always coming up with little extra duties and details for those unlucky ones to perform. Often these extra assignments were administered with a good butt reaming. So of course the best part of CP's story was when Gunny Spell had to step forward and acknowledge that he was the culprit. We all liked the Gunny but at the same time we took some pleasure in seeing him for once on the other end of an ass chewing.

Those of us listening to CP kept pushing him for more details, which he gladly provided with more and more elaborations. But when even his fertile mind grew weary of the questions and needling from some of his audience, he cut off the conversation with, "Ratshit!" and walked off.

# CHAPTER 9

# The Long Valley

The old Papa-san had told Smitty and me that the Chinese had left Hongchon and the following day the 1st battalion of the 7th Marines confirmed that intelligence when they sent a motor patrol through the battle ravaged city without encountering any opposition. One vehicle did blow out a tire when it struck a butterfly bomb that had been dropped by our own aircraft. Crews were sent to clean up the little 4-pound bombs with spinning fins that had been dropped to hamper the retreat of the CCF army. The 7th Regiment then began to move toward the town and the high ground surrounding the town.

How Company left the mountain on the same trail Smitty and I had followed the day before in our quest for water. We passed by the houses where we had talked to the villagers and moved on until we came to a larger group of houses a couple of miles on the outskirts of the city. We stopped there while Captain Hoey met with the battalion commander to receive the latest intelligence and the company orders for the next phase of Operation Ripper.

While we were sitting around waiting for the captain, Gunny Spell was going from platoon to platoon checking to make sure all weapons were in good working order and that ammo supplies were adequate. He seemed to have regained his accustomed grit and gruffness, so apparently his atonement for the great coffee fiasco was going well. Perhaps Lt. Lowe had discovered the pleasures of Irish coffee.

I didn't get to sit very long because Kim came up and asked me to follow him. He took me around a couple of houses to where a large group of villagers were standing. Kim told me they wanted me to help them like I had helped the boy and old woman the day before. He told me they believed I could do magic things to make them well. If in the valley of the blind the one-eyed man is king, I suppose in a town with absolutely no medical facilities, a nineteen year-old corpsman with a first aid bag is the Mayo Clinic.

Needless to say I felt totally overwhelmed by the variety of ailments and injuries standing there before me. There was everything from gunshot wounds to intestinal parasites. And Kim's English was not good enough to make the symptoms very clear. But I did learn one thing–the power of faith. Those people believed I could help them, and just that belief seemed to lift them up. Through the ages shamans and medicine men with less knowledge and technology than I had must have witnessed the same effects in their patients. Having such power is a sobering responsibility.

So I dressed some wounds, dispensed some APC's. But most of I all looked at them, touched them, and listened to them with the help of Kim. In this age of high tech medicine there is still something to be said for the laying on of hands.

Word came for us to move out before I could attend to all those who had lined up, but I told Kim to tell them the battalion aid station, or "hospital," would soon be set up in the area and that they would be able to get help there.

We didn't get to enter Hongchon after all because Captain Hoey had come back from his meeting with the word that we were headed back to the high country, so we took a road east toward the mountains and before long we were back climbing ridgelines.

If anyone had thought the Chinese had completely cleared from the area, we discovered to our dismay that wasn't the case when after an hour or more of climbing a mortar shell splintered a tree about fifty yards to our right. When another burst followed the first one we spread out and took cover, and soon Captain Hoey called for our 81mm mortars to come forward and take up positions to return fire. George and Item companies were moving up adjacent ridgelines and they too had come under fire, so a bombardment exchange was quickly underway. The Chinese had artillery zeroed in on our positions, so we in turn called upon our artillery.

Forward observers often accompanied rifle companies in order to direct fire against enemy positions. There were FO's for artillery, FO's for heavy mortars, and there were forward air controllers like the one I had witnessed calling in the air strike for Able Company when that Corsair almost got us. Also, the lieutenant who was shot through the throat and hospitalized with Ollie, the one who spent the night suctioning the blood out of his throat and sipping whiskey with the BAR man, Gibson, was a forward air observer.

This small cadre of FO's in Korea used some sophisticated tools and techniques to triangulate and zero in on enemy mortars and artillery. These guys were unobtrusive and we seldom even noticed their presence, but I do remember talking to a couple of them one time. They explained one technique they used, a technique called "flash bang," which worked best late evenings or at night. What they would do was watch for the flash of the enemy artillery muzzle then time how long it took for the bang to arrive. They would then use that information to pinpoint the location of the artillery.

When they believed they had located the source of the enemy mortars or artillery the FO's would call for WP (white phosphorus, or "Willie Pete") rounds. These shells could burn victims severely, but they mainly served as visual markers for the FO's to help them get the fire on to the target. Once they got the WP on target they would call for so many rounds of HE (high explosive) and that target was in big trouble. Enemy gun crews must have started to shake when a WP shell went off close by.

Another great tool we had for silencing enemy artillery were the little two-man observation OY planes called "Mosquitoes." All they had to do was fly over enemy territory where artillery was located and their guns would fall silent. The Chinese had learned from hard experience that if they fired their artillery while the OY planes were in the air, destruction would soon fall upon their heads. The crews of those planes carried maps with them and could notify our troops of the exact locations of enemy artillery. That was of course in the daytime. Later it was discovered that the Mosquitoes could even silence enemy artillery at night. The pilots couldn't read their maps in the dark but the Chinese didn't know that, so when they heard the little planes flying over even at night their guns fell silent.

The Chinese put up stiff resistance on this hill which was marked on our maps, 356, and kept us pinned down the rest of that day, but ultimately the 105 and 155 howitzers, under the direction of their forward observers, made the difference. They did a good job of pinpointing the target and for hours our artillery fluttered close over our heads and exploded on the ridgelines ahead of us, shaking the ground. We did lose three of our six 81mm mortars, but by the next morning we were able to move forward through a soft rain and take our objective.

The scene on top of the mountain was a familiar one. Trees were splintered and blasted, and powder-burned craters and broken rocks were everywhere. The Chinese did have dug-in fortifications—trenches crisscrossing the ridgeline and several reinforced bunkers, so they had determined to defend the position. But the extended bombardment of the previous day had been too much to withstand.

They had not been able to remove all their dead. Two were still in a collapsed bunker, one was lying in a trench, and one was sitting against a tree with his eyes open, looking as if he had just sat down for a rest. But a closer look at the soldier revealed he was not resting, that those were not tears from his eyes—the top of his head had been sheared cleanly off. The brain was gone and the rain that had fallen through the night had filled the empty brainpan and was now spilling over and running down his face.

We had prevailed in this battle largely with the help of our mortars and artillery, but on the following day the 1st Battalion met strong resistance on Hill 399 and had to resort to grenade attacks going from bunker to bunker.

The next day, March 17, while the 1st Battalion was still mopping up on Hill 399, the commander of that battalion, Major Sawyer, received some surprising guests. The 71-year-old General Douglas MacArthur, along with General Ridgway and Marine General O.P. Smith, had ridden all the way from Wonju in jeeps because MacArthur wanted to visit Marine troops in the field. The visit had not been announced in advance, nevertheless there were a number of cameras on hand as the celebrated general shook hands with the officers of the 1st Battalion. MacArthur, the legendary military leader, was also a master of PR.

So far as I can remember we in the 3rd Battalion knew nothing about this visit from the big brass. We were still occupied with the Chinese in the mountains east of Hongchon; although after their defensive struggles to hold hills 356 and 399, the enemy took to their heels again and for the next few days our biggest problem was the rainy weather and muddy conditions as we continued in pursuit.

As noted earlier, the US Marine Corps is organized by threes: three regiments to a division, three battalions to a regiment, three companies to a battalion, three platoons to a company, three squads to a platoon, and three fire teams to a squad. Down to the company level it is standard practice to always have two units up front while keeping one in reserve. This arrangement provides each unit with periodic relief and ensures that there will always be some backup in cases of extreme need. The 7th Regiment had been on the line for some time and was due some relief, so the 5th Regiment moved into our positions and relieved us and we were able to return to the valley for a few days rest and re-supply.

\* \* \*

When we had a little time like this we would set up our pup tents in rows with walks, or "streets" separating the rows. Since we were forced to lead such an unrooted nomadic life, we would often use the luxury of being in one place for a few days to do a little homesteading. We would outline our walks with rocks, and some guys would even find little bushes or trees to poke in the ground to satisfy their landscaping instincts. Smitty was especially artistic when it came to landscaping, so he and I often had the best looking pup tent on the block.

Sometimes we would go scrounging for anything novel or that could be of use. Mostly, though, we scrounged for food, anything to supplement that steady diet of C Rations. I remember once one of the guys managed somehow to appropriate a large can of peanut butter and a big metal spoon. He opened it with his little handy dandy and went around for a couple of days with the can tucked under his left arm while he wielded that big spoon in his right, just daring anyone to challenge him for it. It was one of those primate things. On about the third day, though, his enthusiasm began to wane (too much of a good thing), and finally he relented and let some of the other guys swoop in with their little plastic spoons.

But the Marine Corps, not wanting us to become too comfortable, always managed to throw in a little training while we were in reserve. Once

I wrote home complaining that we spent a month on the line fighting the Chinese then, when we finally got to go into reserve they had us in training, learning how to fight the Chinese.

During this particular break I took the opportunity to write a couple of letters home. In the first one, dated March 20, I said,

> The 7th Marines are now in reserve and we're not doing anything but training. We were relieved several days after we crossed the Hongchon-gang River, and we are now set up in the valley of that river. I don't know where we will go from here but we will probably relieve the 1st Marine Regiment.

I also added that there was scuttlebutt saying the 1st Marine Division was going to be relieved to go back to the states. We got a steady diet of scuttlebutt. We chased after it like a will-o-the-wisp. I often wrote home that my replacement was on the way, that I would soon be relieved to go "back to the rear with the gear." But like a mirage that always recedes with your advance, that replacement continued tantalizingly there in front of me for months. Hope springs eternal in the foot soldier's breast.

A few days later I wrote again,

> We are now up on an outpost on a mountain overlooking our tent area. We have to come up here once every six days and stay for a day and a night. Smitty, the platoon runner, and I have us a pretty nice little place fixed up here. It's made of four poles with a poncho over the top and some tin we picked up around the sides. It keeps the cold wind off.

Employing our ingenuity, Smitty and I had arranged these fine accommodations even for our second home. But all we were doing really was following that great Leatherneck credo, "if you don't have the equipment you need for the job, improvise!"

I went on to tell my folks that we had had a regimental inspection that morning and had stood in the same spot for three and a half hours. I also broke the bad news that we were going back to the front the next morning. I added, "We are all hoping and praying that we don't have to cross the thirty eighth" [Parallel]. I also expressed some negative views about President Truman, views that I, with the perspective of years, no longer hold and which I now attribute to the callowness of youth and the pressures I was feeling at the time.

It turned out that there actually had been some plans to relieve the 1st Marine Division, but those plans had been changed. The 7th Marines were to be moved up from our reserve location near Hongchon to be attached to the Army's 1st Calvary Division for the attack above Chunchon. And so we saddled up once more and started north.

We now had a new platoon leader, Lt. George Barnes, from Massachusetts. We learned that he was a stickler for personal safety. Many of us had discarded our helmets, or at least we carried them on our packs rather than wearing them on our heads, but the new lieutenant stressed at every opportunity the importance of wearing those helmets. We had also become lackadaisical about digging foxholes. Unless the incoming mail was pretty steady, we wouldn't bother. What was the point in going to all that trouble and effort if we were never in one spot very long? But Lt. Barnes drove home to us the importance of digging good deep foxholes and his advice could possibly have been responsible for saving lives in the 2nd Platoon.

My hope that we would not re-cross the 38th Parallel was of course, vain. On 4 April the 7th Regiment was among the first UN troops to cross that crucial line of demarcation. Then on 8 April General Ridgway ordered the rest of the 1st Marine Division to join the 7th Regiment on the Kansas Line replacing the 1st Calvary Division in preparation for another move north.

*Lt. George Barnes 2nd Platoon*

The general was concerned about a Chinese buildup in an area known as the Iron Triangle, one of the few relatively flat places in this mountainous country. It was pretty much an equilateral triangle, each side about fifteen miles in length, with the bottom or southern side running between the towns of Chorwon and Kumhwa, and the northern point at the larger town of Pyonggang (not to be confused with the capital of North Korea, Pyongyang, some distance northwest of Pyonggang). The Iron Triangle was an ideal staging area for the CCF and they were now busy there in an apparent buildup for another offensive. While we had absolute command of the air, the Chinese and North Koreans had adapted to that disadvantage by moving their forces and supplies only at night. They had motorized vehicles, of course, but they supplemented those with human carriers and with pack animals, some of which were little shaggy Mongol horses that could follow trails no vehicle could navigate.

I had hoped we could remain on the Kansas Line until some kind of peace arrangement could be worked out, but now, much to my disappointment, we were on the move again. The rain had stopped as we came down from the mountains north of Chunchon and moved northeast on the road toward the town of Hwachon located just west of a reservoir of the same name. We had a long hike that day in our regular formation, a column on each side of the road, as always taking care to maintain our interval. We started out on fairly level ground but after we had been marching an hour or more the road began to climb over a mountain pass. It wasn't a high mountain and when we reached the top the road switched back to the left to ease the angle of descent. After a while it turned back to the right and we found ourselves looking into a long valley that stretched out before us.

The land here looked different. There were very few trees on this slope of the mountain, and the road was white and rocky. I could see the two columns of Marines far ahead of me and when I looked behind I could see both columns all the way back to the skyline following us down the road. It was all infantry, perhaps the whole 3rd Battalion, but I do remember a radio jeep passed through us, the long antennas bent forward forming an arch over the little vehicle.

As we came down off the mountain we had a clear view of the long valley ahead of us. On the left of the road was a low range of hills, the main ridgeline of which ran parallel to the road. On the right was a wide stretch of fallow rice paddies with some mountains farther off in the distance. As we continued our descent we could see ahead of us where the road leveled off into the valley a dry, stony creek bed with a few houses, or, actually, ruins of houses, scattered about. The head of the two columns had just passed through this area when a series of explosions hit the creek bed and the nearby houses. At that moment we saw the Marines below us scatter to each side of the road seeking cover.

When I saw the mortar rounds go off I dropped my pack and ran down the hill toward the creek bed. By the time I got there the barrage had let up so I moved around among the men there looking for wounded but amazingly found no one had been hit. I started to go back to retrieve my pack when another round of mortars began to go off all around us. The big white boulders in the creek and the walls of the ruined houses offered us protection as we hunkered down against this latest barrage. After a few minutes it stopped so I started back up the road to get my pack.

As I was going back to look for it some Marines told me that someone had picked it up and carried it down to where I had been. When I got back to the creek bed, there was my pack where some thoughtful Marine had left it. I shouldered it and began to double-time it to catch up with my platoon.

We continued to move through the valley and the mortars continued to fall. Apparently the enemy was at a point in the high ground where they commanded the area of the road around the creek bed through which all our troops had to pass, and that was where most of the enemy fire was directed. Some of it continued to come in our direction and now and then we would have to take cover until the incoming let up.

But we kept moving up the long valley. Lt. Barnes had the map that showed our destination to be at the far end of the valley on the western slope of the hills. When we finally got there we didn't go to the high ground, as was the usual practice, but took up positions low on the slope. For some reason Smitty and I moved ahead of the rest of the platoon and began to scratch our way up the side of a hill thinking to dig us some kind of protection from the mortars which were still raining in on the valley behind us. We sat there on that hill for a few minutes, and then we heard this sound, "thunk, thunk, thunk," and looked at each other. What we were hearing were Chinese mortar rounds being dropped into the tubes and they sounded like they were right above us. We had unknowingly come right upon the position of the Chinese who had been lobbing mortar rounds at us as we had come through the valley. I believe I could have thrown a rock and hit that mortar crew.

Well Smitty and I were not the two to go charging up that hill to take out those mortars, so we went back to Lt. Barnes and the rest of the platoon and found that we had overshot our mark and needed to pull back to find our correct position. We did that and again took up a spot low on the slope and began to dig foxholes for protection against the continuing mortar barrages. The fire at this time was mostly directed at the Marines still coming into the valley behind us, so we were able to make a lot of headway with our entrenching tools and even find time to have a break for our afternoon C Rations.

After our meal several of us were standing around talking, Smitty, Tardio, Shexnayder, Hawkshaw, and I with my hand braced against a small tree. Suddenly a mortar round exploded right below us. Fortunately we had dug our foxholes as Lt. Barnes had encouraged us to do, so we scattered out and jumped into whatever hole was most convenient. I ended up on top of Tardio and we all lay there until the barrage let up.

When we finally felt safe enough to climb out, Tardio said, "Hey, Doc, you're bleeding. You bled on my shirt."

I immediately examined myself and found that the index finger on my left hand was split on the end. It was bleeding pretty good so I had to go to my aid kit and get some gauze and tape to staunch the bleeding.

You got a purple heart there, Doc. Write it up," Hawkshaw said.

Purple Hearts were given based on the battle tags corpsmen tied to the wounded. And I suppose I could have made out a tag for myself on this occasion, but I wasn't going to do that. I didn't know how my finger got that wound. I did have my hand against the tree when the mortar shell exploded, but at the same time I had quickly jumped into the foxhole and could have cut it then. I didn't believe my injury was deserving of such a commendation and felt I would likely have other opportunities for that award in the future.

Tardio spoke up and said, hey Doc, you know how you can tell when I've been wounded?

"How's that, Tardio?"

"My blood will be red white and blue, with little stars!"

"Yeah, I'll remember that."

**PFC Harold Tardio**

\* \* \*

The next day Captain Hoey tapped the 2nd Platoon to make a move against the enemy. Four heavy Pershing tanks had been brought up to give us support and when they began to grind north up the road we moved with them.

Tanks in Korea were often a big help for the infantry. They provided a good shield when put between us and incoming fire. From time to time we were permitted to hitch a ride on tanks, and anytime an infantryman can hitch a ride he'll jump at the chance. (I remember warming my hands over exhaust vent grills of their engines as we rode along.) And of course tanks are able to provide great covering fire. Their 50 caliber machine guns could tear up a hillside. The flat-trajectory 90mm rifled cannons were effective even at long ranges with their high muzzle velocity and optical sights, and when fired at close range they were devastating.

But tanks had a downside for infantrymen—they attracted enemy fire. No doubt the enemy became fearful and edgy when they saw tanks approaching their positions and called on every weapon in their arsenal to fire away at the tanks. The tanks were armored to give the crews some protection, but the soldiers around them had no such protection, so often the wise thing for the infantryman to do was to put some distance between himself and the tanks when going into action.

We stayed with the tanks on the road for a while, and then turned east, away from the hill where Smitty and I had heard the Chinese mortars dropping into the tubes, crossed a creek and moved out onto open rice paddies. To our right was a group of houses and ahead of us, across the rice paddies on the east of the valley was a high range of wooded hills or low mountains that formed the other boundary of the valley we were in. As we moved across the rice paddies toward those hills we came under heavy mortar and machinegun fire. The tanks had moved out into the fields on either side of us and were now firing into the mountain ahead of us. The muzzle blasts from their cannons shook the ground and bounced blankets of dirt from the dry paddies each time they fired. All of us in the 2nd Platoon did what we always did in such circumstances—we looked for cover.

I jumped in a wide, shallow ditch with a number of other Marines and we continued moving up the ditch in a crouch toward the mountain. Mortars were whistling in and exploding all around and the sounds of small arms and machinegun fire from the mountain mixed with the returned fire from our tanks engulfed us all. We had progressed some way down the ditch when I got that dreaded call.

"Hey, Doc, they need you!"

"Where?"

And then the Marine, raising his hand up above the rim of the ditch and pointing, yelled,

"Out there!"

"Oh God!"

I climbed out of the ditch and began to sprint in the direction he had pointed. I ran by a tank out in the rice paddy firing its 50 caliber machine guns into the mountain and passed some Marines hunkered down behind hummocks and berms. One of them seeing me coming pointed toward a rice paddy dike. As I ran in that direction I saw a Marine lying face down. I ran up to him, bent down beside him and grabbed his shoulder and pulled him over. When I did his intestines slid out on the ground and lay there beside him. He had taken cover behind the low dike but it had not protected him from the mortar shell that landed right beside him.

I double-timed it back to the ditch, jumped in and rejoined the column of Marines moving toward the mountain. After a short while our progress stopped.

Someone behind yelled, "What's the holdup up there? Get it moving!"

Then a Marine up ahead said, "This guy won't move! We can't get by him!"

I could see about three guys ahead of me a man down on the ground curled up in a fetal position apparently sobbing.

"Kick him in the ass!" the voice behind me yelled.

And then the Marine behind the sobbing man kicked him in the ass.

"He still won't move!"

"Then climb over him!"

That's what we did. We all climbed over him and continued to move toward the mountain.

In Korea we learned some things about assaulting mountains. The times you are most vulnerable are when you are approaching the mountain and when you get near the top. As you are approaching the mountain, as we were crossing the open rice paddies, the enemy in the high ground can see you coming and will throw everything they have at you. Once you reach the base of the mountain you are in the cover of the trees and out of their line of fire and vision. Then you can begin to move up to seek them out and they can't see you coming. But when you arrive they will see you again, and all hell will break lose.

The mortars hitting us were coming from high on the ridgeline ahead of us. About this time an FO in an OY plane spotted the Chinese mortar crews and called in artillery and quickly knocked them out. When Captain Hoey got the word the mortars had been hit, he radioed Lt. Barnes to move out. As we moved forward and passed by the deserted houses we could see our objective ahead.

We were approaching the base of the mountain now and could see two Marines of our platoon leading the way. Somehow they had gotten far ahead of us and were determined to take out the Chinese on top of that hill. Our 3rd Squad leader, Corporal Lawrence Nolan and a BAR man were scratching their way up the slope. But just at this time Lt. Barnes got another radio message from Captain Hoey who had been observing the action from a hillock behind us. The Skipper told Barnes to abort the attack and return to our former positions. We began to yell at our two gung-ho Marines to stop and come back to us, but they seemed reluctant. After repeated calls we finally got them to come down off the mountain and rejoin us. I don't know how the others felt, but I certainly was not disappointed to have the attack called off.

I learned later that the tanks picked up the Marine who had broken down in the ditch and the one who had been killed by the mortar round. I didn't recognize the dead Marine at the time and only learned many years later that he was Corporal Donald Robert Gross, twenty-one years old.

\* \* \*

Later we assembled back at our position at the base of the western slope and had our evening C Ration meal. Even though we had pulled back from our assault, I believe the Chinese had felt the pressure and had withdrawn from the area since the incoming mortar fire we had been receiving the past several days had stopped. While we were sitting around the fires the lieutenant said, "We saw what you did out there today, Doc."

Unfortunately there had been nothing I could do for Gross. But I have to admit I was glad I didn't have to stay there in that rice paddy long, glad that I was able to get quickly back to the ditch and to cover. As I ran through that din of machinegun fire and incoming mortars, I uttered that same old selfish prayer I had uttered the night of the Sunflower How patrol and all our firefights thereafter, "Oh God, please don't let me die!" I never came up with a significant variation of that incantation during my entire tour of duty in Korea–purely selfish–nothing heroic in that. I was terrified.

I didn't want to die. I had thought about it a lot. Some people said if death came they wanted it to be sudden, but I didn't. Most of all I feared being hit in the head, being snatched from life in an instant. I even tried to imagine what it would be like–a sudden starburst in the head and then...?

It's sad to say, but most of us find it much easier to contemplate someone else's death rather than our own. I guess that's because, even though we can imagine the beginning of the universe and speculate on its demise, even though we can study the history of life and man on earth and imagine what things were like before we came and what things might be like after we're gone, we all know, really, that the only world we'll ever know didn't exist until we were born and that it will perish when we die. And that will be it. It's an amazing thing. The potential to be us that had existed since the big bang will be gone. It's the same for everybody. Every time somebody dies they take a world with them. That's why killing people is such serious business.

It's hard to come to terms with mortality. Our lives are so short, the universe is so vast, and we are so small—no wonder man is religious. That Native American sage captured our predicament poetically when he said, "mans life is like the buffalo's breath in winter." Animals like the buffalo instinctively fear danger but they don't know death. Our knowledge of death is the price we pay for consciousness, for Adam and Eve biting into that apple. That act turned the light on in our heads and separated us forever from the rest of nature; and since knowledge and guilt are a package deal, mankind was from that moment forever fallen from grace. That was a tough bargain.

By this time I had seen enough of death to understand that, while the living may be filled with fear of it, the dead don't care. Being dead doesn't bother them a bit. It's the living who suffer. Walt Whitman made that point in his beautiful elegy for Abraham Lincoln, "When Lilacs Last in the Dooryard Bloom'd":

> I saw the battle corpses, myriads of them,
> And the white skeletons of young men, I saw them,
> I saw the debris and debris of all the slain soldiers of the
>     war,
> But I saw they were not as we thought,
> They themselves were fully at rest, they suffered not,
> The living remain'd and suffer'd, the mother suffer'd,
> And the wife and the child and the musing comrade
>     suffer'd,
> And the armies that remain'd suffer'd.

Of course it's one thing to say that the dead are fully at rest, but that's little comfort. We all know that as long as we're alive we don't want to be dead. Like the song says, "everybody wants to go to heaven but nobody wants to die." Still many people take comfort in the thought of an after-life, although somebody said that the only thought worse than death is the thought of living forever. If, as Ecclesiastes says, there's nothing new under the sun, it might get a little tiresome seeing the same old events eternally cycling by.

Mark Twain could always put things in perspective. About the hereafter he said, you want to go to heaven for the climate but you want to go to hell for the society.

I don't recall ever trying to make a deal with God like some guys did. You know how the deal goes: "God if You'll get me out of this I'll be good and go to church and quit cussing, drinking, gambling and chasing after women!" I wasn't above making such a bargain; I just figured God was too smart to fall for it.

But one of the good things about being young was that the fear came only during the action. Afterwards we were pretty much kidding and care-free, and for the most part we gave little thought to the morrow, unless we had intelligence of some impending conflict. As my mother used to say, "sufficient to the day is the evil thereof." We were resilient and overall our morale remained high.

\* \* \*

The following day we moved to positions on the high ground and it became clear that the Chinese had moved out of the immediate area and given up the positions from which they had lobbed mortars on us for the previous several days. We were still in the vicinity of the Kansas Line at the west end of the Hwachon Reservoir and expecting a CCF offensive to be launched at any time. They did hit our left flank the night of 11 April, but the attack had been easily repulsed and we all knew that the big one was yet to come.

The weather at this time was very changeable. I wrote home on the 13<sup>th</sup>,

> The sun is shining now and it's pretty warm, but day before yesterday it rained, sleeted, snowed, and the sun shone all inside of an hour. The weather over here is hard to describe, also the mountains. I don't know if they're really high or not, but every time you think you've reached the top you look up and there's a higher peak above you, and when you're sure you've reached the top all you can see is still a higher one.

That day of the changeable weather and that Chinese attack on our left flank, 11 April, was also a date of change for UN forces in Korea. That was the day President Truman relieved General MacArthur of the command of all UN forces and replaced him with General Matthew Ridgway. Then on 14 April General Van Fleet was appointed to the former position of General Ridgway as head of the Eighth Army.

MacArthur had for some time been issuing foreign policy statements at variance with official US policies and had been openly critical of those policies. When the Chinese entered the war he spoke in favor of an all out war even to the extent of using nuclear weapons. He never acknowledged his own errors of judgment in saying the Chinese would not enter the war and that our troops would be home by Christmas of 1950.

Fortunately President Truman saw the danger of a nuclear war with China and the Soviet Union. With the support of General George Marshall, Secretary of Defense, and the Joint Chiefs of Staff, he issued the order to recall MacArthur. So an unpopular Commander in Chief recalled a very popular field commander and then faced the public outcry that followed. But Harry Truman was not a man to shrink from tough decisions. This former haberdasher and artillery captain understood the chain of command and the unacceptability of insubordination, even if the legendary general did not. That momentous decision to fire General MacArthur, however, had virtually no effect on the 2nd Platoon. We had more practical concerns.

In the letter quoted above I also announced the good news that we had been issued inflatable mattresses. No more rocks poking us in the back at night. I didn't know then how short-lived that luxury would be though, because after all the huffing and puffing to blow them up we discovered the rocks that had been poking us in the back easily poked holes in the mattresses. So we all discarded the mattresses within a few days, except for Tardio. Ever resourceful, PFC Tardio fashioned himself a raincoat out of his, cutting the bottom out of one end and armholes and a head hole in the other, then slipping his torso into the affair. Voila! He cut quite a figure in that improvised raincoat and gave us all a lot of laughs as he paraded around for our amusement.

I had written home for my folks to check the newspapers for photos, because from time to time we would pass by news photographers who would snap our pictures. So far as I know none that I was ever in made a publication, but Tardio made it, and it may have been because of that raincoat. The photograph, which I believe appeared in the *New York Times* and other publications, was taken about two weeks later as we were headed south once more. Joe Sipolski tells me that the guy behind Tardio is George Nightwine of the 3rd Squad and he recognizes the fellow two places behind him as another member of that squad which was headed by Corporal Nolan, the Marine who had to be called back from his assault on the mountain in the long valley. It shows Tardio in front with his BAR balanced on his pack wearing, not a helmet, but a stylish flat-brimmed hat, both hands resting on his ammo belt, and that mattress raincoat extending to his knees.

To get a sense of the effect Tardio had on our platoon all one needs to do is look at the expressions on the faces of the Marines following him to see the good humor he brought to our group. He had no doubt made some comical remark as we passed the photographer that had the men behind him laughing.

*Hal Tardio leading George Nightwine and members of 3rd Squad 2nd Platoon H-3-7  April 1951*

\* \* \*

We left the long valley and it looked like our assault on the mountain there may have had some effect because the Chinese forces were now nowhere to be seen. We continued to move north toward a phase line designated Quantico. The rain had stopped and now we were confronted with smoke—brush fires, grass fires and sometimes tree fires. My mother cut a picture out of the local paper showing Marines running through the smoke; those Marines could well have been us.

At the time I thought WP shells or napalm had started the fires. Only later did I learn that the Chinese, who were trying to prevent our OY planes from observing their buildup in the Iron Triangle, had lighted them. They had even sent infiltrators behind our lines to set fires. And the enemy had become very aggressive in firing at the little Mosquito observation planes. It was clear to our intelligence people that a major CCF offensive was in the works, but they didn't bother to share that information with those of us in the 2nd Platoon, so we went on about our business setting up positions in the high ground west of the Hwachon Reservoir and conducting regular patrols.

# CHAPTER 10

# The CCF Spring Offensive

In the war that North Korea launched on June 25, 1950, South Korea reacted much like a recoiling spring. When the blow fell its army gave way rather quickly, but as the Communist forces pushed farther to the south, rather than collapse, thanks to the infusion of American forces, the tension in the spring grew. By the end of July, with the help of the US and now with the support of the UN, the defenders of South Korea were maintaining a toehold on a small piece of real estate on the southeast tip of the peninsula dubbed the Pusan Perimeter. With increasing US and UN forces coming in and with US dominance on the sea and in the air, the fear that allied forces would be pushed into the sea diminished and a new resolve infused the defenders of South Korea. The situation, however, was still precarious. Up to this point the North Koreans had won virtually every battle; but that changed in August 1950 when, after a bitter struggle and heavy losses, the 1st Marine Brigade drove the NKPA from their heavily defended positions on Obong-ni Ridge (a.k.a. "No Name Ridge") in the "Battle of the Naktong" (US Marine Operations in Korea, vol I, 189-206). Thanks to the U.S. Marines the UN forces now had their first victory.

Undeterred by that one setback, however, at the beginning of September the North Koreans renewed their determined efforts to push the defenders of South Korea into the sea and unify the country under the rule of Kim Il-sung. But their offensive was halted two weeks later when again the Marines carried the day with the successful landing of the entire 1st Division at Inchon. General MacArthur, who had had great success with amphibious assaults in the Pacific in World War II, had called upon that proven tactic one more time. When the North Korean forces besieging Pusan discovered the Marines were moving in behind them threatening to cut off their supply lines and their avenues of retreat, they began to pull back. At that moment the UN forces defending the Pusan Perimeter went on the offensive. Now with the Communist forces in danger of being caught in a pincher movement, the coiled spring of UN forces defending the Pusan Perimeter began to rebound.

For the next two months UN forces under General MacArthur made steady progress. On the 7th of October US forces crossed the 38th parallel. Then, ominously, the next day Mao Tse Tung ordered Chinese "volunteers" to cross the border into Korea. On the 19th of October the UN captured Pyongyang, the capital of North Korea. But a week later the Chinese went on the offensive, and a week after that, on November 1, they intensified that operation. Now MacArthur notified the UN that the Chinese had soldiers fighting in Korea, but he was undeterred in his "Win the War" campaign and had even suggested that our troops would be home by Christmas. President Truman had assured the world that the United States had no intention of invading China. But the Chinese clearly had no intention of permitting US forces to mass along their border.

As they had been warning all along, the Communist Chinese unleashed an all-out offensive on November 26 (the day Bob Cameron, a machine gunner who would be with us at Kitty Dong a couple of months later, joined How Company). The Eighth Army was the first to be hit by the onslaught, and by the next day the Chinese hit the Marines at Yu Dam-ni. Soon the enemy had the Division surrounded at the Chosin Reservoir. The dynamic spring of that struggle began once more to recoil as the UN forces again headed south.

The heroic battle, the breakout from the Chosin Reservoir, we touched on before. It was General O. P. Smith who was given credit by a reporter for answering a question about the retreat of the 1st Marine Division with, "Retreat, Hell! We're just attacking in a new direction!" When asked later about that quote, he didn't say he said it but he did say that comment exactly reflected his attitude and the attitude of his staff.

Moving in opposite directions was a pattern established early in the war, beginning with the NKPA's rapid push to the Pusan Perimeter followed by the Eighth Army's equally rapid advance to the Yalu River. This pattern of advance and retreat marked the first fifteen months of the three-year Korean War. I can think of no other war where two armies made such dramatic advances and retreats and covered so many miles in such a space of time. It was because of the fluid nature of the early months of the conflict that the struggle was sometimes called the "yo-yo war" or the "accordion war."

The entry of the Chinese into the conflict dramatically changed the dynamics of the struggle and led to the second broad pullback of the defenders of South Korea. By December of 1950 UN forces had been pushed back to another defensive line near the 37th parallel in the southern half of the peninsula. That was when I arrived with the 4th Replacement Draft.

After the 1st Marine Division's campaign against the guerillas in the "Gook Chase" in January and February east of Pohang, the recoil/rebound pattern continued. The UN push north was halted by the CCF offensive of February 11th that led to Massacre Valley. After that enemy offensive the

1st Marine Division rejoined the Eighth Army and the tide was turned once more with the Army victory at the battle of Chipyong-ni and the Marine victory at Wonju. Our victories at those two locations had brought a halt to the Communist offensive. The United Nations forces then followed up those successes with Operations Killer and Ripper. H-3-7 had done its part in this effort at the battles of Wonju at Cloverleaf Mountain and in the hills around Hongchon, and most recently by routing the mortar firing Chinese from the long valley we had just left.

Now we were in the high country near the Kansas Line on the western bank of the Hwachon Reservoir after succeeding in pushing the enemy back across the 38th Parallel. But something was brewing in the Iron Triangle.

\* \* \*

It was mid April now. How Company was kept busy going out on daily patrols trying to make contact with the enemy, and we continued to struggle through smoke that swept across the land, smoke that was part of the enemy's attempt to conceal the buildup for their spring offensive. The Chinese took other steps as well to prevent our getting a look at or interfering with their preparations. The little OY planes came under unusually heavy fire when they ventured into the area of the Iron Triangle. The Chinese brought heavy anti aircraft guns into that area and used them against any of our planes venturing near. They even set out decoy trucks, tanks, and other vehicles to lure our fighter-bombers overhead so they could shoot them down. They posted lookouts on top of the mountains around the buildup area and when they saw our planes approaching they would signal from mountaintop to mountaintop by firing their rifles.

The valley of the Iron Triangle, about 40 square miles, was an ideal staging area for the Communists. In addition to providing cover and concealment for gathering troops and supplies, a railhead there linked them to their supply sources in Manchuria. The Iron Triangle also served as a bastion to defend their capital of Pyongyang to the northeast. So they had many powerful motives for protecting that area from our aircraft, and they had some success with their defensive tactics, shooting down sixteen Marine planes during the period from 1 April to 21 April.

But now the 1st Marine Division was advancing toward that fortress. On the 19th of April I found time to write home:

> We are still on the Kansas Line but we go north again tomorrow. I sure hate to go but we have no choice. The news around here sure was getting good for a while. I was about convinced the war was over . . . The next line we go to is Quantico which is a few miles farther north and I hope and pray we will stop there. The

good news is that I made another rate, I am now HM3 or third class petty officer which is equivalent to a buck sergeant.

Near the end of the letter I said, "I would be the happiest man in the world if this war would end and I could come home again. It's been a long long time." There may have been enthusiasm for this campaign among the high brass, but there was little among the ranks, and I certainly reflected none in this letter. But in another letter I gave my folks the good news that I was now making $115.00 a month.

The Chinese were trying desperately to keep their activities secret, but all their efforts at concealment availed little for a number of reasons. Foremost among those reasons was their failure to provide their soldiers with any training or code of conduct to guide them in the event that they were captured. And the prisoners we captured on a fairly regular basis had been freely telling us for the past several weeks that the next CCF Fifth Phase Offensive would begin on 22 April.

This news, however, did not cause us to stop and take up defensive positions. We continued our northward advance. On the 18th KMC units moved almost completely unopposed into the town of Hwachon while the 1st Marine Division continued its progress toward phase line Quantico. As we moved forward we knew we were getting close when some Marines encountered crude signs on a road saying, "Your Folks Like See You Home," and "Forward Means Death."

Undeterred by these warnings the 1st Marine division moved out at 0700 hours on 21 April continuing its push toward Line Quantico. Our 7th Regiment was on the left, the 5th Regiment was in the center, and a KMC regiment was on the right with the 1st Marine Regiment in reserve. Although green wood smoke limited our visibility to a few hundred yards, we were able to make good progress against negligible opposition advancing 5000 to 9000 yards that day. We did have one problem, though. We lost contact with the 6th ROK division on our left flank. That division was ordered to reestablish lateral contact with us, but as we continued to move forward the next day and into the following night they still had been unable to link up with us.

Throughout the afternoon of April 22, the 3rd Battalion passed through a valley, crossed a stream, then continued on to the right of a curved ridgeline later identified as "Horseshoe Ridge." The name of the mountain described its shape: The open side of the horseshoe pointed south, the curved front faced east, north and west.

How Company moved up into the ridgeline about 1000 yards east of Horseshoe Ridge, and when we got to our positions we used what daylight we had left to dig foxholes and make other defensive preparations. George and Item companies took up positions along the ridgelines on our right flank. As far as we knew the plan was for us to continue our advance north on the following day.

But at 9:20 that night word came that the 6th ROK Division on our left flank was under heavy attack. A short time later platoon leaders and platoon sergeants were called to the company CP for a conference, and when they returned, the word was not good. Our platoon sergeant told us that the Chinese had broken through on our left flank and were moving rapidly to the south in an effort to encircle us and cut off our route of withdrawal. The 6th ROK Division on our flank had disintegrated and visions of Chosin and Hoengsong came readily to mind. We in the 7th Regiment now had a particularly acute problem with that exposed flank and with the Chinese pouring into the gap.

Lt. Barnes set a fifty percent watch for the night and we continued very much on the alert, establishing forward outposts to warn of any attacks. We worked on our defensive positions, sent up flares, and watched the ridgelines to our front for any signs of advancing Chinese. All through the night our artillery pounded the mountains in front of us.

The skies were overcast and, to illuminate the ground to our north, the Marines had brought in mercury arc searchlights and set them up in the valley behind us. These were the same kind of lights used to search for enemy aircraft in World War II and later to attract crowds for grand openings at shopping malls. Here they were aimed up at the clouds so the light would bounce back down in front of our positions and give us some visibility. These lights contributed to an ominous atmosphere that was only intensified when flares were fired into the sky where they popped and floated slowly down on parachutes, squealing eerily as they spewed their flickering phosphorescent ghostly glow on the wooded ridgeline to our front.

We took advantage of this extra light to continue work on our defensive positions. The fifty percent watch for the night meant at any time half of us could be asleep, but there wasn't going to be much sleeping in the 2nd Platoon. The squad leaders, Sergeants Putnam, Noriega and Nolan, had their men busy working on their defensive positions while Smitty and I were digging us a good deep foxhole. While we were busily employed in these activities gunfire and a series of explosions erupted on the hillside to our right. We moved in that direction to see if we could figure out what was happening, and after a few more minutes of the gunfire one of the searchlights dimmed and then went out. What had happened? Had the Chinese infiltrated our lines and shot out one of those lights? We had no way of knowing.

We continued our preparations for the expected attack, and while at that work we were interrupted by a sound we had not heard before, the roar of big bombers overhead. We all stopped to listen, and before long we were shaken by the loudest noise we had ever heard in Korea. The bombers we heard flying over dropped their payloads on the ridgelines to our front and the explosions literally shook the ground we were standing on. Anyone who has never been on the ground near one of those bombardments cannot begin to understand the power of such demolition. That was the only time I knew of when such big bombs were dropped on enemy troops.

I heard later from Lt. Barnes that the bombers were US Air Force B 26's that had been headed north to attack military and industrial targets. Because of the CCF offensive, they had been rerouted to give us some help there near Horseshoe Ridge. OY spotter planes had sighted thousands of Chinese in the valley in front of us and the bombers were called in to take advantage of this target of opportunity. Those bombs jarred us in How Company, but they must have been a devastating hell to the Chinese troops they fell on.

When the word spread of the rout of the ROK 6th Division, the 1st Marine Regiment, which had been held in reserve near Chunchon, was called forward with the 1st Battalion of that regiment to take up positions on Horseshoe Ridge to defend our exposed southwest flank. As these 1st Marines were moving north in trucks they met many ROK soldiers heading south, but, like the SF 21 infantry detachment at the battle of Hoengsong, they had no luck in getting the frightened soldiers to turn around.

The 1st Battalion of the 1st Marines (1/1) did succeed in taking up positions on Horseshoe Ridge to our rear in time to meet the assault from determined CCF units that came that night in an effort to turn our flank. There was a 1000-yard gap between our positions and Horseshoe Ridge. On the left of the 1st Marines there was no one. So our positions were particularly vulnerable. But the shape of the ridgeline worked in our favor as 1/1 was able to fire in three directions, north east and west, and with the deadly effective artillery support from the 11th Marine Regiment they were able to hold their ground.

The Communists attacked Horseshoe Ridge at 10:00 that night to the sound of trumpets and cymbals. They came en masse illuminated by the light of their eerie green flares. For four hours the Chinese tried to push 1/1 off the ridge with machineguns, burp guns, mortars, and hand grenades, but after four hours of furious battle the Marines succeeded in beating them off.

Lt. Reisler, a platoon leader who was positioned on an outpost in front of Charlie Company on Horseshoe Ridge, said of that attack,

> They came in wave after wave, hundreds of them. They were singing, humming, chanting, 'Awake Marine. . .' In the first rush they knocked out both our machineguns and wounded about 10 men, putting a big hole in our lines. We held on for about 15 minutes, under mortar fire, machinegun fire, and those grenades—hundreds of grenades. There was nothing to do but withdraw to a better position, which I did. We pulled back about 50 yds and set

up a new line. All this was in the pitch black night with Chinese cymbals crashing, horns blowing, and their god-awful yells (US Marine Operations in Korea, Vol. IV, 113).

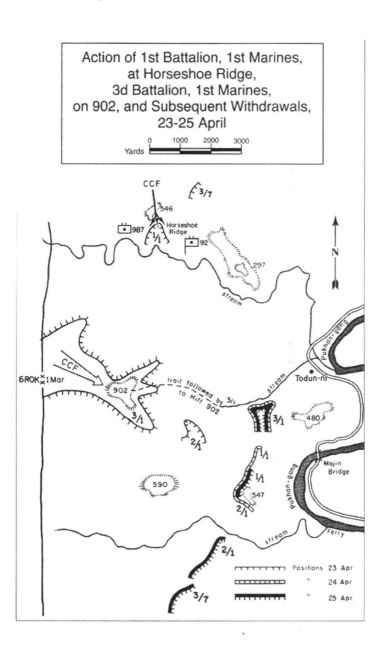

Action of 1st Battalion, 1st Marines,
at Horseshoe Ridge,
3d Battalion, 1st Marines,
on 902, and Subsequent Withdrawals,
23-25 April

The 1st Marine Division's greatest problem was that with the collapse of the 6th ROK Division, our entire left flank was exposed to the Chinese army that had already penetrated far to our south. We were now faced with the task of defending ourselves not only from the north but from the west as well.

The Division could not ignore the ominous possibility that, as in the battle of Chosin, it might have to fight its way south once more.

To help protect the Division's western flank, the 3rd Battalion of the 1st Marines was dispatched to hill 902, south and slightly west of Horseshoe Ridge. This hill, 3000 feet high, commanded much of the valley and the Marines had to race the Chinese to the top, but they won. So now the Division had some protection on the left. The line had been bent to defend the Division from two directions.

We listened that night to the battle going on behind us on Horseshoe Ridge and wondered if we would have a way out in the morning; we wondered if 1/1 could hold and prevent the enemy from encircling us. How Company had been told that the Chinese were massed to our front and that we would be pulling out at daylight to head south. The most disturbing news was that How Company would be the rear guard.

We made it through the second night receiving only harassing and probing fire from the Chinese. The next morning we held our positions serving as rear guard while the other companies of the 3rd Battalion passed through us and descended to the valley below. We had anticipated there would be a real battle as we held off the Chinese while the other companies passed through us, and were relieved when the attack didn't come. After the other companies had all cleared through we then followed, platoon by platoon, until we all had left the mountaintop and were descending back into the valley.

The Chinese had hit Horseshoe Ridge behind us during the night but the Marines there had held. As we came down off the mountain we saw a phalanx of tanks positioned nose up on the slopes facing the ridgeline we were coming down with their 90mm cannon and 50 caliber machineguns aimed at the ridgelines to hit any CCF forces that might be pursuing.

I suppose the Chinese had decided the cost would be too high to sustain their attacks against the 1st Marine Division, that it would be much easier to move south through the gap left by the collapse of the ROK division on our western flank. It was clear the enemy knew what units they were facing and that when they went on the offensive they always struck what they believed was the weakest link. So while How Company escaped the brunt of the attack that night, there is no doubt that the resistance the enemy met from 1/1 on Horseshoe Ridge and the attack from the B 26 bombers with their devastating 500 lb air-bursting bombs also played a role in discouraging the Chinese from continuing their assault on the Marine positions.

Retreat, as everyone knows, is not a word in the Leatherneck vocabulary. It is also a tactic absent from Marine history in cases of a toe-to-toe battle between reasonably equal forces, or in many cases unequal forces with the Marines on the short end of the stick. But in cases like Chosin or here at Horseshoe Ridge where the force has been surrounded or is in the process of being cut off, the only tactical choice is to move in the opposite direction. But the word "retreat" in these instances is neither acceptable nor accurate, so, in the case of the battle at the Chosin Reservoir, the appropriate term was "strategic withdrawal," and for the battle at Horseshoe Ridge the term was "April Retrograde." This first year of the Korean conflict truly proved to be an accordion war.

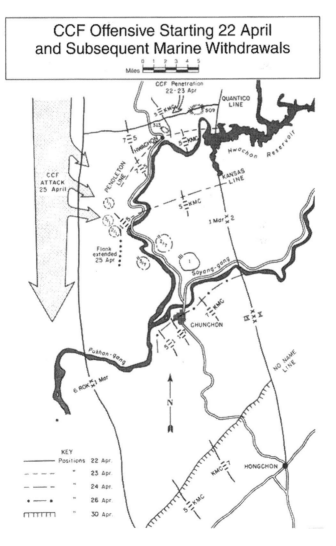

135

As we moved past Horseshoe Ridge into a much broader valley a remarkable scene unfolded. Coming down from the mountains from every direction were columns of Marines. Never before and never again would I see so many Marines, thousands of Marines, all in one panorama. The entire 1st Marine Division was filing onto the road that day to begin a long arduous journey south in a race to frustrate the CCF effort to cut us off and surround us.

Overhead our aircraft continued on sortie after sortie to pound the enemy north and west of us. Our artillery continued to thunder, the shells exploding along the mountaintop we had just vacated sending up great puffs of dirt, jagged shrapnel and shards of rock. Looking back over our shoulders we could see curling flames of napalm smearing across the ridgelines leaving clouds of black smoke to drift away in the wind.

Just as we reached the valley floor two jeeps each pulling trailers carrying 36, 4.5 rocket launcher tubes, turned off on a side road, whipped around so the tubes faced over the ridgeline we had just come down, and prepared to fire. Once the rocket men had their weapons properly aimed, they let them rip. One by one in rapid sequence the rockets blasted out of their tubes in balls of fire, kicking up huge clouds of dust behind the trailers. When the last one had fired the men bounded back in the jeeps and made it quick time out of there. They weren't going to stick around and give the enemy a chance to answer their volley.

As we converged with other troops coming down from the mountains we saw that the Division consisted of much more than rifle companies. We considered ourselves the premier component of the Corps, but the scene on this day made it clear that rifle companies require a great deal of backup. There were vehicles in every direction—trucks, tanks, artillery, weapons transports, jeeps, trailers of all kinds—all queuing up to get on the road to begin the journey south. Rifle companies may be the vital element in the Marine Corps, but they depend on many supporting units and here, for once, we could see them all in one place.

The Pukhan-gang River meanders through the valley we were moving through. Running parallel to the river was the road that went to Chunchon—the road we would all have to take south. The little town of Todun-ni was on that road about four miles southwest of Horseshoe Ridge and about six miles south of that town on the curving Chunchon road was the Mojin Bridge that crossed the Pukhan-gang River at just about the 38th Parallel. Now the 1st Marine Division's western flank was exposed and the Chinese had penetrated many miles south of us, so this bridge was a critical point in our withdrawal and had to be guarded to protect the troops and vehicles moving out of the valley.

Four battalions were tapped for the job—the 1st Regiment's 1st and 2nd Battalions, the 5th Regiment's 3rd Battalion, and us, the 7th Regiment's 3rd

Battalion. So, for the second time in two days we were going to serve as the rear guard, this time for the entire division as it made its exit from the valley. We in the 3rd Battalion had already crossed the Mojin Bridge on our way south but were called back and had to re-cross the bridge to find our assigned positions west and south of the bridge and the road.

To get to our defensive location we had to move through rice paddies and take up positions that provided good fields of fire to defend the bridge. We found those positions, dug in and waited. We were now south of the bridge while the other three battalions were north of us; the river lay between our positions and the road. We remained there through the day and much of the night while the long procession of vehicles and troops moved south down the road. Then in the early morning darkness we got the word to saddle up and move out.

The other three battalions had already moved on to the road, some of them having been able to cross the bridge over the river and stay on the road. In our position that was not an option. We had to wade the Pukhan-gang with our packs, weapons, and all our gear. Fortunately the engineers had strung cables across the river to facilitate our crossing, but the going was still difficult. Even though it was now late April the water was ice cold, and as we stepped out into the river we gasped a bit from the cold and took great pains not to slip. The water grew deeper as we got to the middle rising up to our chests. I held my carbine and aid kit above my head with one hand and held the cable with the other. In spite of our best efforts a few Marines lost their grip on the cable and slipped and had to be grabbed by buddies and helped to the other bank, soaked through to the skin.

But we made it to the road and joined the caravan moving south. Everyone was wet and cold. But once into the rhythm of the march we began to loosen up. After an hour or so we had warmed up pretty well and our clothes had started to dry. When the column stopped to "take ten" the men fortunate enough to have dry socks in their packs put them on. We had to take care of our feet.

At first How Company was near the end of the column, but as different infantry units held back to take their turn as rear guard we passed through them, and when the convoy of vehicles on the road halted from time to time we would pass some of them as well. So slowly we made our way forward in the column.

After a while there in the morning darkness our spirits lifted a little. We felt relieved that we had escaped that valley that had seemed to threaten some kind of impending Armageddon. Even though we had had little sleep in the last several days, the men of the 2nd Platoon now seemed spirited. Tardio, who would have a news photographer take his picture later that morning wearing his mattress raincoat, and Hawkshaw were exchanging quips. There was a lot of talk going on up and down the line about where we had come from and where we might be going.

But as the march wore on the talking stopped except for an occasional comical remark from Tardio, who could always lighten the burden a little. Then, as mile stretched on to mile, we did as we had always done in these circumstances; we turned inward and picked up that unconscious rhythm of the march, our old hypnotic plod. We didn't have the term "cruise control" then; maybe we knew "automatic pilot." Whatever the term, we had developed the ability to remove ourselves to some tiny remote spot leaving only our bodies to the grueling job of placing one foot in front of the other and slogging on down the road.

The sun came up and we kept moving. We did stop occasionally to "take five" or "take ten," often not even removing our packs, just flopping back against the ditch wall on the side of the road. Mostly we kept moving. We were also given chow breaks at the appropriate times. A few lucky guys carried "canned heat"; the rest of us had to eat our C Rations cold.

The morning hours passed into afternoon. Weary and sore, we continued moving down the road accompanied only by the sounds of shuffling feet, clanking equipment and the smell of exhaust fumes from the trucks and other vehicles passing between us.

Those trucks bothered us! All the drivers had to do was step on the gas pedal and move on down the road. And they could do that while they were *sitting*! Where was the justice?

The grind was starting to tell on all of us. The weapons guys, the machine gunners and mortar men toting their heavy loads, along with older members of the company were slowly falling behind. All of us were exhausted and footsore, but we kept getting the word, "Don't get on the trucks!" I had had several members of the platoon come to me with physical complaints, telling me they couldn't keep up because of sore feet, sore backs, or because they were sick. Each time I presented their cases to Gunny Spell I got the same response, "Nobody gets on the trucks!"

Many of the trucks passing through had room; some of them were empty, but still the word was, "Don't get on the trucks!" What kind of crazy crap was that? You've got weary, sick Marines and empty trucks and the word is "Nobody gets on the trucks"?

Even though we couldn't see it, there was a reason for this order. The whole Division was moving down this road to take up new defensive positions. It was vital that units not become separated so that when we arrived each unit would be intact. General Ridgway's replacement, General Van Fleet, had issued the orders to keep all units together. If infantrymen from different units were permitted to hitch rides on the trucks no telling where they would end up or what kind of confusion would result.

But I did succeed in one case. Smitty brought a man to me who was in real distress. He couldn't breathe without severe pain. After I talked to him I concluded that he was suffering from pleurisy and that he could not possibly continue the march, so I went to the Gunny and then to Captain Hoey and got permission to put him on a truck.

But the rest of us continued all through the day trudging down the road to Chunchon. It's easy to dramatize the conflict of a firefight, but for me the most agonizing memory of the CCF Offensive was that grueling slog from Horseshoe Ridge to Chunchon.

\* \* \*

The Eighth Army commanded all UN forces in Korea. The 1st Marine division during the period of the CCF Spring Offensive was attached to the IX Corps of the Eighth Army, and in spite of the breakthrough on our left flank, we had been able to hurt the enemy by employing General Ridgway's policy of not fighting to hold real estate, but inflicting maximum damage on personnel and materiel, by using our superior firepower, and remaining flexible and mobile.

There was one piece of real estate however that we did want to hold on to, and that was the capital city of Seoul west of Chunchon. And the Chinese wanted badly to retake that city, some reports said, as a May Day gift for Mao Tse Tung. They made a determined effort to do that the same night they had attacked in our area, on 22 April, and were met at the Imjin River about 40 miles north of Seoul by the British 29th Brigade.

Elements of the Brigade had defensive positions south of the river on a rise dubbed Castle Hill. During that first night the Chinese were successful in infiltrating around that position and inflicted heavy casualties on the British. By mid morning the next day only one officer of Company A was left. The Chinese succeeded in taking Castle Hill, but the next day the British made another valiant effort to retake the hill; still the Chinese kept coming in great numbers. By the evening of that first full day of battle the British Brigade faced a full division of Chinese forces.

The Gloucester Battalion of the 29th Brigade, from this day forward known as the "Glorious Glosters," was surrounded by the swarming Chinese and was in effect destroyed with 20 KIA, 35 WIA and 575 missing, presumably captured. But the massed enemy forces arrayed against the British made excellent targets for our fighter-bombers, which proceeded to inflict heavy destruction on that army, and the efforts of the British 29th Brigade, costly though it was, contributed to the frustration of the Chinese plan to recapture Seoul (Forty, 76).

Although the British suffered heavy losses, they held back the CCF Offensive in their area for three days and frustrated Communist efforts to retake the capital city. For their heroic stand they were awarded the United States' Presidential Unit Citation. The Communists had occupied Seoul twice but, thanks to the Glorious Glosters, they would never do so again.

Orders from the Eighth Army were for its forces to withdraw to the Kansas Line so I Corps north of Seoul drew back to an area six miles north of the capital city. Later the decision was made to pull back farther in several phases in the central area of the peninsula. Our "retrograde" maneuver finally stopped on what General Van Fleet designated "No Name Line" between Hongchon and Chunchon.

Around this time there were changes in the top brass of the 1$^{st}$ Marine Division. On 24 April General Gerald C. Thomas replaced General O.P. Smith as Division Commander. General Smith, the "Retreat Hell!" general, the same one who had poked his head in our Casual Company tent at Masan, had provided great leadership of the Division from the Inchon landing through the breakout from the Chosin Reservoir up to the current battles of the CCF Spring Offensive. The highly respected General was an oddity in the Marine Corps since, as a Christian Scientist, he didn't smoke, drink or swear. These changes in the high ranks, however, were little noted by us gravel crunchers, even though decisions at the high levels always had profound effects on troops at the front lines.

**General O.P. Smith**

We had lost quite a bit of ground to the Communist forces during their April offensive. The Chinese had begun that effort with the boast that this time they would succeed in pushing the UN forces into the sea, but they had fallen quite short of that ambitious goal. Our lines had been breeched and we had been forced to pull back many miles to close the gap, but now we had restored the integrity of our front line, and after a week the vaunted CCF Spring Offensive had run its course. The Chinese army had failed in their attempt to present Mao Tse Tung with Seoul as a May Day gift.

The CCF Spring Offensive had petered out, and that's the way we felt by the time we took up our positions on No Name Line. For a solid week we had been moving—marching, wading rivers, climbing mountains and, sadly, re-crossing the 38th Parallel. Now we were back in our accustomed locale, camped out in the high ground.

\* \* \*

We were tired all right, but considering what we had been through, we were in pretty good shape—in two ways. We were lucky that most of the company had made it through the ordeal, and we were "lean and mean" from months of climbing mountains and enduring marathon hikes. Like wealth, good fortune is relative. We now felt fortunate that we were once more able to build fires and heat our C Rations. And being lean and mean and young meant that we were resilient, so it wasn't long until good nature returned to the campsite.

CP Sam had gone over to the Company CP to see what scuttlebutt he could pick up and no doubt to entertain folks there with the details of his exploits on this last operation. Tardio, Shexnayder and Nightwine were cleaning their weapons and shooting the breeze. Tardio was a BAR man and those weapons required particular care. They are basically a one-man machinegun with tremendous firepower, but they are easily jammed when dirt or dust gets into the breech, so special care was required to keep them clean and in working order. The BAR is heavy too, twenty pounds plus twenty more pounds of ammunition carried around the waist in a pocketed belt, so toting them and their ammunition was a burden. The assistant BAR man helped by carrying another twenty pounds of BAR ammo, and he had the additional responsibility to drop his M1 and take up the BAR when the BAR man was disabled so as not to lose that extra firepower.

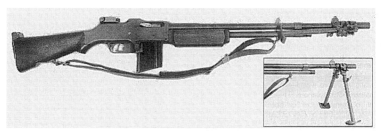

*Browning Automatic Rifle (BAR)*

Smitty and I had set up our pup tent and had a nice fire going, and he and I and Hawkshaw and his foxhole buddy, Brodeur, were heating some meat and beans, meat and noodles, and corned beef hash. Tarver was sitting up against a tree writing a letter home when the sound of laughter rose from somewhere below us where some of the guys were congratulating

Sgt. Putnam on the news he'd just got from his wife that he was a new daddy. Strange to say the atmosphere on that mountain around the tents and campfires was pleasant and comforting.

* * *

Why do we find the smell of wood smoke pleasant? Why does it seem to stir deep atavistic feelings in people? Just as we walk through history every day without knowing it, as we did back on Guam and at Otsu, I suspect we do things all the time we feel are unique and novel to us, which are really reenactments of ancient patterns.

For hundreds of thousands of years humans followed wild herds through Africa and Europe and Asia, and finally to the Americas. The smell of camp or home was always the smell of wood smoke, the smell that signaled food and warmth and comfort, and came to symbolize the center of family life— the hearth. Ancient hunters and warriors traveled in bands and gathered around campfires where they prepared their food and readied their weapons for the hunt and for battle. And no doubt they socialized around their campfires, just as we in the 2nd Platoon were doing in Korea in 1951.

Today, while transplanting a burning bush in my backyard, I dug up a perfect flint arrowhead which I added to the collection my son and I gathered some years ago from Caddo Indian campsites along the Ouachita River that runs through our town here in southwest Arkansas. History, which is always right beneath our feet, we seldom take notice of. We drive over the past in our SUV's talking on cell phones on the way to Wal-Mart.

But sometimes the past intrudes upon the present and captures our attention as it did with the story of Otzi the Ice Man. The discovery of a frozen body by a couple of hikers in the Alps in 1991 was first thought to be just another Alpine fatality. As the rescuers pried the body from the ice they weren't particularly careful and did some damage to the remains, and then someone discovered the man was carrying a copper axe. Experts were called in and after months and years of careful scientific analysis it was learned that Otzi (rhymes with "tootsie") had died some 5,300 years ago. He was a Neolithic European hunter/warrior dressed in animal skins wearing leather shoes stuffed with grass for insulation, and he was carrying a pack, a quiver of arrows, a stone knife, and a bow that he was working on that was not finished. He had apparently lost his bow and was in the process of replacing it.

How he had died was the question that challenged the scientists. Many theories were put forward, but after several years of study a remarkable discovery was made. A dark spot on one of his ribs in an X ray, thought to have been a fracture, was in fact an arrowhead. Otzi had been shot in the back. He also had a cut on one hand that had the characteristics of a wound received while fending off an attack. So one of the leading theories now is that he was in some kind of battle. He had lost his bow and retreated to the high country (his body was found at 10,000 feet) and was being pursued. The angle of the wound showed that his assailant shot the arrow from somewhere below. So Otzi, our Neolithic European ancestor, was caught up in the ancient practice of warfare, doing what we were doing here in the mountains of Korea.

The scene of the 2nd Platoon on that mountain would not have been unlike one of a Neolithic hunting party or an early Native American war party, and apart from the different dress and weapons, it would have been a scene familiar to Otzi and our ancient forebears.

But we can never hear from them, except in a few cryptic ancient cave paintings, because they had no alphabet, they couldn't write down their thoughts and stories. They were clearly intelligent, like us they had names and families and plenty of adventures to tell about, but when they died they took all with them. Just in recent times, since the invention of writing, have human voices been able to span generations. And the voices we are most curious about are the earliest, both because they are remote in time and because their voices are few. The alphabet was like a seed crystal in human affairs. Before it appeared past generations were silent to history. Writing took hold slowly, but soon it exploded in a geometric progression. Today literacy is virtually universal and it seems everybody has a story. But the abundance of the supply diminishes the value of the tale. The first stories, by virtue of being the first, provide us with our archetypes; the greatest warriors were those early men who sat around their campfires entertaining one another with tales of their exploits. Where are the heroes to rival Achilles and Odysseus?

\* \* \*

Words, words, words. All of this speculation would have meant nothing to us there. We were on a real mountain, around real fires cleaning real guns, eating real C Rations and involved in a very real war.

Tarver's family would be happy to get that letter from him. His writing might not span generations, but it would span the ocean and bring comfort to his family back home. Plus he was enjoying one of the great benefits of the military in Korea—free postage. Every three cents counted.

I took advantage of that free postage privilege about this time and wrote home,

> Don't get the impression that we all go around with long faces or are bitter at the world. We still gather around the fires in the evenings and sing and joke and have good times.

And that we did, and that's what we were doing this evening.

But soon CP Sam returned with his scuttlebutt from the Company CP. It seemed, according to him, that we were not going to enjoy this respite on the mountain for very long; that there were plans afoot to start moving north again, to go out on probing patrols to find where the Chinese had settled in after their breakthrough to the south. None of us was happy to hear this, and as always there was a lot of skepticism about any news CP brought to us. After all, this was the kind of information we would be getting from our platoon leader and platoon sergeant, not from CP. But he insisted this was the straight scoop.

He also told us Lt. Lowe still carried those two canteens, so we determined that the lieutenant believed his whiskey was salvageable and that he could still hold that celebration once we got to go into a long reserve.

But as always, CP got more and more carried away with his stories, and when he began to recount some of his exploits in the mountains near Horseshoe Ridge, several members of the platoon who knew better challenged him. CP responded by making even more extravagant claims, and then the skeptical listeners broke out in laughter.

CP's reaction was predictable. "Ratshit!" he exclaimed, and walked off in a huff.

# CHAPTER 11

# Izabitch

It was now the 1ˢᵗ of May, but Mao Tse Tung had not been able to celebrate that great Communist holiday with the recapture of Seoul, for the city was still firmly in UN hands. The Communists didn't come up with that holiday anyway. It is one of the oldest in human history, going back over the horizon of the past to dim antiquity.

Ancient man was never sure that life would return to the earth after the death that comes with winter, so he developed religious rituals to appease the gods, to win their favor so crops would grow once more and animals and humans would give birth. For our ancestors those rituals always worked. Spring always returned. May Day has from earliest times been a celebration of the rebirth of life, of fertility, of the coming of spring. In the West we celebrate the return of fertility to the earth with the fecund Easter Bunny and all those eggs, and Christians celebrate the coming of spring at Easter with their belief that Jesus was buried and rose from the dead as the seed is buried and then brings forth new life.

We didn't erect a maypole there on the mountain, but we could look out on the valley and the slopes of the mountains and see for ourselves that spring had come to Korea. Seeing the countryside while climbing mountains in the infantry might not be the most congenial way to experience the landscape, but it's the most intimate. Even through the bitter cold and hardships of the past winter–the Gook Chase west of Pohang, the steep mountains overlooking the frozen river and the little town of Kitty Dong, the train ride from Masan to Wonju, the campaign that took us all the way to Horseshoe Ridge–we couldn't help but notice the bleak beauty of this country. Now that spring had come, the bones of winter had fleshed out into a beautiful misty green.

On our way to this position we had passed some of the solitary grass-covered domed graves positioned on the mountainsides to overlook the valleys below. No urban crowding here, no jumbled crowd of markers and headstones—only *San-Shin*, the spirit of the mountains. It was easy to see here on this May Day morning why the Koreans called their country, "The Land of the Morning Calm."

But we weren't carried away in transports of ecstasy over the view; we had much more immediate concerns. I did note the season change in a letter home, but I also commented on the travails of the infantryman in Korea:

> Spring is here now and the mountains are green and I guess if we were not here for the reason we are it would be beautiful. It's getting pretty warm here too. Climbing these mountains with heavy packs can really get a man down. We will be marching along sometimes and I will start thinking about those biscuits & butter and peach preserves, sweet milk & etc. I can certainly understand now why people give thanks before they eat.

I don't recall what kind of grace we said when we got our daily C Rations.

Along with those daily C Rations we got our daily orders, and that was about as far into the future as we could see. As noted before, the foot soldier is not privy to the grand plan, the big picture. But there were changes taking place in this war even if we were unaware of them. The time when one side could push deeply into the territory of the other was coming to an end because the forces on either side were too strong, too evenly balanced. We had the technology, the firepower; the Chinese had the manpower. The accordion phase of the war was coming to an end.

MacArthur had wanted a different conclusion to this war. He had wanted to cross the Yalu, to attack Communist China. He was a great general who could accept no outcome but total victory. But even as a teenage noncom fighting this war in the mountains of Korea I could see the misguided nature of his ambition. What could have been the end of such an adventure? Even at that time China had close to a billion people, and the war MacArthur sought would have been on their territory. Of course the General had that big saber to rattle, the nuclear bomb; but the Soviets had the bomb now too, and what would have been the consequence of using it? Would the Soviet Union have stood by and watched us invade China and attack with nuclear weapons, then permitted us to march up to their border as we had marched to the Yalu? Had MacArthur been allowed to follow his "victory at any cost" proposal the result would very likely have been World War III and the human toll would have been incalculable.

Fortunately we had as our President that unpretentious former WWI artillery captain with a level head and a strong backbone who saw the folly of MacArthur's grandiose ambition and relieved him of his command. While Truman was vilified for his decision, MacArthur returned home to a ticker-tape parade and a hero's welcome. He was given the honor of addressing a joint session of congress where he gave his thirty-four minute "Old Soldiers Never Die" speech in slow, measured organ tones that had many congressmen in tears. One congressman overpowered by MacArthur's lugubrious eloquence exclaimed, "We heard God speak here today, God in the flesh, the voice of God!" In such emotional responses to champions of war lie one of the greatest dangers to world peace and our country's principles.

President Truman's reaction to the speech was, "a bunch of damn bull shit!" (Quoted in Whelan, p305).

As has often been noted, old men make wars and young men fight and die in them. Here in Korea we were proud to be Americans and proud to be Marines, and we believed in the cause we were fighting for, though at times we may have become discouraged and questioned the wisdom of our leaders. Freedom, democracy, equality, these are values worth fighting for and these were the values our country represented. But when you think about it, we in the 2nd Platoon could not take credit for choosing the right side; it just so happened that we were born in the USA. If we had been switched in the cradle with Chinese, Soviet, or just a few years earlier with German or Japanese babies, we would have been fighting on the other side. Some of us might have been flying those Kamikaze planes in World War II.

The point is that old men, the leaders of nations, are the ones who choose to go to war, but young men, and today young women as well, of whatever nation, never have the choice of which war to go to. They fight the war *du jour*. The United States has as good a record in fighting for worthy causes as any nation in human history, but we have made mistakes, and as citizens of a democratic society we need to think carefully before we let ourselves get caught up in emotions and the drumbeat and call to war.

Two months earlier MacArthur himself had foreseen how this war would end. He had said,

> Assuming no diminution of the enemy's flow of ground forces and materiel to the Korean battle area, a continuation of the existing limitations upon our freedom of counter-offensive action, and no major additions to our organizational strength, the battle lines cannot fail in time to reach a point of theoretical military stalemate (Whelan, 307).

Here on the first day of May 1951 we were getting close to that point, although few if any of us thought about such things. We were merely concerned with the day to day.

After our pullback from Horseshoe Ridge to No Name Line, the Eighth Army had reestablished a front line extending all the way across the peninsula; all units now had secure flanks and were backed with highly efficient heavy weapons and effective air power. In all our battles the Chinese suffered disproportionately large casualties because of our superior firepower and dominance in the air. The enemy had developed tactics to try to minimize those disadvantages, such as operating primarily at night in order to avoid our artillery bombardments and air strikes. With the UN lines solid again they had backed off out of range of our artillery, which had been exacting heavy tolls from both Chinese and North Korean armies throughout the war. The strategy in the 1ˢᵗ Marine Division now was to send out patrols and establish forward outposts to locate the enemy in order to bring that firepower to bear on their positions. And even though the CCF offensive of 22 April had failed, word was that there would be another one in May, so our objective was to probe the enemy's lines, feel them out, and keep them off balance.

\* \* \*

As it turned out CP's scuttlebutt was accurate for once. Lt. Barnes and the platoon sergeant had been called for a conference with Captain Hoey, and when they returned we got the word that we would be moving out the next morning on a company combat patrol. Some of us had made ourselves pretty comfortable accommodations on this mountain and weren't happy to get this word, but that was the way it always went.

We started north early the next morning following the ridgelines, staying in the high country, keenly aware that we were in no man's land and on the alert for any sign of the enemy. We ranged the area in front of our own front lines that day, but the only other person we met was a Dutch officer scouting the area in front of his lines. I had noticed before that the British and Australians would also sometimes send out one, two or three man scouting parties. No doubt that was an effective tactic, although it must have been a lonely assignment.

We took up positions in the high ground that evening and got word that an OY plane had spotted enemy troops on a hill some distance from us, but one we could see from our position. They called on the 11ᵗʰ Regiment artillery to strike the target, but this time rather than fire in sequence, the guns fired their rounds simultaneously so they all struck the target at once. It was quite a show. It demonstrated clearly why the Chinese were so anxious to keep out of range of our artillery, but it also showed us there on that mountain that if we needed that kind of help it was available.

Being in no man's land we remained on high alert, but the night passed without event. The next morning we learned that the 2ⁿᵈ Platoon would have the point as we continued to follow the ridgeline to the west. On patrols in the mountains we normally moved in single file along the ridgelines until we encountered resistance. When we encountered the enemy we would scatter to either side of the trail, take cover, and form skirmish lines.

So How Company started out this day with our 2ⁿᵈ Platoon leading the way. The objective was a hill some distance to the west. We continued moving along the ridgeline for some time until the hill finally came into view. As we were studying our objective off in the distance, someone in our group said he could see one or two people on top of the hill. Lt. Barnes reported that intelligence to Captain Hoey who told us to just keep moving. There was some word now that the whole 7$^{th}$ Regiment might be moving forward to form a regimental outpost just south of Chunchon, and Captain Hoey was of the opinion that anyone on that hill would likely be "friendlies."

As we neared our objective it became clear that this was no ordinary hill. In months of climbing mountains in Korea I had never seen such a monolithic obstacle. Where the surrounding mountains were wooded and green and for the most part gently sloped, this citadel of stone rose up from the ground like a monstrous Gothic fortress.

We had not seen any other movement on top of the hill since that first report, but as we approached our objective Lt. Barnes positioned one squad of our platoon on a rise which commanded the crest of the hill and left our attached machinegun section of two light 30 caliber guns with them. He told the squad leader, Sergeant Noriega, that if there was any trouble to rake the top of the hill with all the firepower they had.

Smitty and I and the lieutenant, along with the other two squads, continued to move down the trail toward that dark looming promontory. We could see that the top of the hill was a natural fortress with stony and jagged walls steep and sheer. We followed the trail down from the ridgeline to the base of the rocky crest and found it took us to a wide crevice in the stone face of the hill, a crevice that natives apparently used when they wanted to scale this precipice. We explored the base of the hill to the left and right trying to find an easier access, but there was none. The only way up was this narrow steep rocky passageway. Our mission was to gain the top, so we started up in single file. During all my months in Korea, that was the only time I remember when we had literally to crawl using our fingers and toes to reach an objective.

We tried not to make noise as we climbed but that was impossible. Our weapons and gear banged on the rocks as we struggled to maintain our holds and keep our footing, and now and then a rock would be dislodged and go bouncing back down the mountain. Our weapons were slung on our shoulders, since there was no way to hold them at ready and at the same time use our hands to scale this steep crevice. I could see the squad of Marines ahead of me working their way toward a spot of sky above us that marked the top of the hill. If anyone was up there we could only hope Captain Hoey's speculation was right, that they were friendlies.

We continued up the crevice for a few minutes more until the point of the column seemed to penetrate the spot of sky, and at that moment a tremendous burst of machinegun fire exploded right above us. Other small arms fire joined the machinegun, and the concussive reports of enemy hand grenades added to the roar.

When I looked up I saw a squad of Marines cascading toward me, so I turned and joined the avalanche of men to the bottom of the hill. We took shelter up against the base of the steep precipice while Chinese hand grenades continued to be lofted from up high to explode harmlessly below us. We gathered around the platoon leader and squad leaders to take a count and assess what had happened. Was anybody missing? The fire team leader who had been the point man looked around and said, "Where's Tardio?"

We began asking one another who had seen Tardio. Some yelled out, "Hey, Tardio!" But we got no answer.

Then the point man told us what had happened. He had led his four-man fire team up the crevice, his rifleman behind him, next the BAR man, Tardio, followed by the assistant BAR man. Feeling some relief at finally reaching the end of this tough climb, he poked his head up to take a look at the top of that stony fortress and found himself looking down the barrel of a machinegun with Chinese soldiers all around. He immediately pitched backwards as did his rifleman, and they began that avalanche back down the crevice as the Chinese cut loose with their fusillade. But now Tardio was missing, and maybe others.

When the shooting started squad leader Noriega had the light 30 machineguns open up and rake the top of the hill. The covering fire we were getting from that squad put an end to the rain of hand grenades and provided us an opportunity to move back to Sergeant Noriega's squad and get the platoon all together again. Now also was the time to call in the artillery, so we needed to get away from the mountain so as not to be caught in our own artillery barrage. We called again for Tardio but got no response.

Attempting to climb back up that crevice to find him was not an option because of the difficulty of the climb and the fact that the Chinese would be looking down our throats; for them it would have been like shooting fish in a barrel. So reluctantly we crouched and withdrew under the covering fire of our two machineguns and the riflemen in Sergeant Noriega's squad.

When we reassembled Lt. Barnes had the squad leaders count noses, and when they did another Marine was missing, PFC Lawrence Hansen.

"Hansen! Hansen! Anybody see Hansen?"

We all talked among ourselves trying to find out who saw him last, where he might have been, but no one could come up with an answer. So now we had two Marines up on that mountain.

Lt. Barnes reported this news to Captain Hoey in his position to our rear. The Skipper told us to pull on back because he was about to call an artillery strike on the target. As we were moving back to rejoin the company the artillery started to fall on that rocky fortress.

It occurred to me later that the Chinese soldiers must have seen us coming from the time a member of our platoon spotted someone on top of that hill. They must have watched us move down the trail toward their position and withheld their fire as we moved along the ridgeline toward them. Just as in our assault on the hill in the long valley, and as is the case in any assault on a fortified mountaintop, the most vulnerable times for the attackers are when they're crossing the open area in the approach to the objective and again when they come up on the defenders on top. When they reach the base of the hill they are out of the line of fire of the defenders.

Why then had those Chinese not fired on us when we were in the open? Why had they permitted us to reach the base of the hill unopposed? I can think of two possible reasons: First, they knew we had only one way up and since they commanded that crevice they calculated that they could wreak the maximum damage on us there rather than at the much greater distance while we were out in the open. They knew we couldn't come storming out of that crack in the ground in sufficient numbers to be a threat to them, so they felt secure to play their waiting game.

Another possible motive was their fear of our artillery. That hill was a tough climb, so they may have thought we would not attempt it, that we would just bypass it and move to another area and leave them undisturbed. If that had been their hope they had been sorely disappointed because now our artillery was splintering the rocks there in their citadel.

Some Korean civilians we met a few days later told us the Chinese had removed 75 casualties from the hill. If that was true they paid a heavy price for their strategy. And we had succeeded in our objective, which was to ferret out enemy forces so we could bring our firepower to bear. Our purpose was not to occupy ground, but to destroy enemy personnel and materiel and that's what we did on this day.

But we too had paid a dear price. Hansen and Tardio were still up there somewhere in that crevice. Marines don't leave their dead on the battlefields, so their bodies were marked for recovery. But we would not be the ones to get that assignment because How Company had been ordered to disengage and move into a new position.

I was unaware then that Marine units kept daily diaries but they did, and the official record of How Company's activities on those two days in 1951 reads in part as follows:

> 2 May: . . ."H" Company was assigned the mission of moving to said patrol base to conduct further patrolling to vicinity TA9786: to establish observation post for purposes of detecting enemy activity and intentions. No enemy contact throughout this period.

3 May: "H" Company reinforced in moving to establish observation post vicinityTA9786: received heavy smallarms and automatic fire. After a heavy engagement of six hours "H" Company was ordered to disengage and establish night defensive positions vicinity TA9683. While in contact with estimated enemy battalion, "H" Company employed smallarms, automatic weapons, 60mm and 81mm mortars, artillery and air support resulting in an estimated 125 enemy casualties while suffering two (2) Marines killed in action and no wounded.

In any firefight each man will have a different perspective and a different story, and every story may well be true even though there may be apparent conflicts. My memories, though very vivid, do not coincide exactly with the official diary, but they're close enough.

Bill Wills gives another first hand account of that day in a letter to Hal's mother from Camp Otsu Japan dated 28 January 1952:

> Dear Mrs. Tardio,
> I was just reading the January issue of "Leatherneck" magazine and noticed your ad in the "mail call" column. I knew and also served with your son Harold in "H" Co. He was in the 3rd Squad of the second Platoon and I was in the 1st Squad so was in fairly close contact with him most of the time....
> I only knew your son for a couple months before his death, but I can say he was a great moral[e] builder in the whole company. We especially remember his humor when we were retreating from North Korea the last part of April. You probably received the picture of him dressed in an old rubber mattress and rain hat walking down the road in the rain. He always had us forgetting our trouble by his antics even when the going was tough....
> I'll try and explain what happened the day he was killed. We had finally stopped retreating from the Chinese and had set up a defense line north of Hongchon, South Korea. "H" Co. was sent out on a 2-day patrol about 2000 yards in front of the lines to try and locate the enemy since we had had no contact with them for a few days. We set up the first night on a hill just south of the Chunchon valley. The second day we patrolled on to this second hill which was our main objective. We didn't receive any enemy fire as we went up the hill, but as we neared the top we had to go single file because of the rocky terrain. The 3rd Squad had the point and Harold was the 3rd man in line from the front.... I was about five men behind him when

I heard this heavy machine-gun start firing and the guys came running back for cover. The Chinese had waited till we got in a narrow draw and then opened up on us with their machine-gun and grenades.

The first two men in front escaped with only shrapnel wounds, but Harold and the Marine behind him were killed instantly by machine-gun bullets....

The loss of your son was a heart-breaking blow to the whole platoon and we missed him very much. Hope this letter helps a little in answering any questions you may have had.

Yours respectfully

Bill Wills

John Tarver also wrote to Mrs. Tardio from a hospital in Japan where he was recuperating from wounds suffered on 12/1/51:

You know there is always one guy who is the life of the party. Harold was that guy. He always kept the group laughing when we felt like crying, and when you felt low, after talking to him for a few minutes you felt like you were sitting on top of the world.

When he was killed it was quite a shock to all of us. I know the platoon will never be the same, and there will never be another guy like Harold Tardio.

On May 4 George Company came out of reserve and occupied our position while we backtracked and took up their old positions in reserve. The following day George Company had the assignment to go back up on that hill and retrieve the bodies of our two Marines and, knowing what had been on top of that hill two days earlier, those who got that assignment approached it with some trepidation.

It so happened that one of the men chosen for the job was the BAR man, Jim Nicholson, the same one who had ridden the train from Masan with Tardio, Hansen, me and other Casual Company and 6th draft replacement troops to join the Division at Wonju in early March. It also happened that he knew both of the men who had been killed.

Nicholson later wrote:

IZABITCH: Hal Tardio and Lawrence Hansen were killed on this precipice by the Mongol cavalry. I had been in advanced combat training with both of these Marines. They were with How Company, 7th Marines caught on patrol, partially up IZABITCH. The Mongols dropped grenades down on top of them and their bodies lay in crevices for two days.

IZABITCH was named by some Marine within my hearing who when looking at this formation from a distance said "Jesus Christ, that is a bitch!" The idea of climbing this structure knowing there were already two dead Marines up there was a rather intimidating idea.

Our policy, of course, was that no Marine, dead or alive, is left to the enemy. It fell to George Company, and specifically to my fire team, to retrieve their bodies. . .

Menehune, Nick's fire team leader, also had some memories of that day when they climbed Izabitch. They had drawn cards to see who would get the privilege and it was not Menehune's lucky day:

I drew the 3 of spades. To this day when I see a 3 of spades it gives me the shivers. . .

As we moved along the base of the mountain a shower of rocks came tumbling down—my adrenaline was so high my heart could have been heard ten feet away. The climb was very difficult. We felt the Chinese were on top of the hill when we began climbing because of the falling rocks. By the time we got to the top however, they were gone. A small hut was at the top of the cliff and a fire was still burning in it. No Chinese were found in the area. We did find our KIAs from How Company. KIAs were Nick's buddies who had been in Tent Camp 2 with him.

*Izabitch 1.5 miles distant*

After reaching the top and seeing how far the Chinese could overlook, I don't know if I would have had the courage to do this again (George-3-7th Marines—a brief glimpse through time of a group of young Marines. "Izabitch." Unpublished manuscript by Jim Nicholson, MD).

This last comment of the George Company fire team leader confirms my speculation that the Chinese saw us coming that day and that their decision not to fire on us while we were in the open was a tactical calculation on their part.

*Here it is up close. . .*

Here it is up close. A sight I haven't seen in over half a century, but one that has remained vivid in my memory all those years. This photograph from Jim Nicholson presents Izabitch just as I have remembered it. The vertical crevice on the right is the one we scratched our way up. Unfortunately the four men in the point fire team were the only ones to reach the top and two of them did not make it back down.

*James Kee Tom and Jim Nicholson*

Thanks to these men and their comrades in George Company, 3rd Battalion, 7th Marines the bodies of Hansen and Tardio were recovered.

*Lawrence Hansen*

*Hal Tardio KIA three weeks after the picture was
taken of him in his mattress raincoat*

\* \* \*

Hal Tardio's father was a truck driver as was mine. Probably many of us in H-3-7 were from similar backgrounds. We were born at the beginning of the Depression and many of our parents were the first generation off the farm. Where I grew up in Dallas, in Trinity Heights on the then outer fringe of the city, many of that transitional generation brought their country ways with them. It was common for people to raise chickens in their backyards, to have vegetable gardens, and even as we did for a while keep a milk cow, a pretty little jersey. So even though Daddy's depression level income may have been lacking, we were able to supplement it with our own milk, eggs, vegetables, and chicken. Mother would take a straightened coat hanger with a hook on the end and go out and catch a hen by the leg then wring its neck and we would watch it flop until it stopped, then she would pluck it, singe any remaining pinfeathers off, clean it, cut it up and we would have a great Sunday fried chicken dinner. We could make do.

And for us kids there was no lack of entertainment. Just two doors down from my house was a large open field, often planted in oats. Beyond that were woods and a creek which were always inviting. Five Mile Creek I suppose would never compare romantically with Wordsworth's "sylvan Wye," but it gave me many hours of pleasure exploring its natural mysteries. I early on developed a passion for reading and adventure and those woods and fields provided me with a great imaginary realm. I would take my dog, Buster, a wonderfully good-natured part chow with a blotchy blue tongue and a half bobbed tail, and we would go off to our wilderness to hunt field mice and anything else that we could scare up. I can't speak for Tardio's experiences as a child, but I expect many in that generation shared experiences similar to mine.

Hansen and Tardio were just two of the 34,000 young men killed during the three years of the Korean War. Just as in the story of Izabitch, there was a story behind each one of those deaths; in each case a life was cut short before it was fairly started. But few of their stories will ever be told.

I wish we had been able to go back that day and retrieve Hansen and Tardio. I was closer to Tardio than I was to Hansen because Tardio kidded around with me and we talked a lot. It hurt that we could not save them, that we could not go back up that rocky crevice and bring them down.

\* \* \*

I have wondered since, if we had been able to recover their bodies that day, would Hal Tardio's blood really have been red white and blue with little stars?

# CHAPTER 12

# The CCF Offensive— Phase Two: Morae Kogae Pass

By early May of 1951 General Ridgway was Supreme Commander of United Nations forces in Korea and General Van Fleet was in command of the Eighth Army. After the Chosin campaign General Ridgway kept his word and never again had O.P. Smith serve under Almond and X Corps. But after General Smith had returned to the United States to a well-deserved hero's welcome the 1st Marine Division, now under the command of Major General Gerald Thomas, was once more returned to X Corps. These changes in the high brass had little effect on How Company. We were much more focused on our own leadership, and we too had some changes at this time.

A day or two after we lost Tardio and Hansen on Izabitch, Lt. Barnes was transferred to the 3rd Platoon and we got a new platoon leader in the 2nd Platoon. He was 2nd Lt. Thomas L. McVeigh, twenty-two years old, a graduate of Colombia University who hailed from Stewart Manor, NY, where his father was a high police official, as I recall, in one of the large boroughs of New York City. McVeigh, who had been leader of the 2nd Platoon during the Gook Chase while I was in the 1st Platoon with Lt. Lowe, had been wounded in February and was just returning to duty and wanted his old platoon back.

Lt. McVeigh was called to active duty in the Marines shortly after he had entered law school at St. John's University. Not your typical spit and polish Marine line officer, McVeigh was personable and informal and moved easily among all the guys. He insisted that we not call him "Lieutenant" or "Sir," but that we just call him "Lefty." A star athlete in high school, he had natural political skills that seemed to bode well for his future. I wrote home that the word was he had been wounded in the Gook Chase and cited for the Silver Star. He never mentioned it so I don't know if the story was true, but I do know he fit the mold of the daring young platoon leader.

The first two weeks in May the 7th Regiment continued to patrol the mountains north from our position above Hongchon toward the city of Chunchon, probing to find the Chinese who had recently suffered heavy losses during their disastrous April 22nd offensive. Now they were trying very hard to keep out of range of our artillery and hide from our aircraft while they prepared for the second phase of their Spring Offensive. On their first attempt they had failed to push us into the sea as they had boasted they would, but they were determined to make another effort. It was our job to stay in contact with them, keep them off balance, and inflict as much damage as possible in order to cripple their efforts to launch another effective attack. In order to maintain contact with the enemy the 1st Marine Division sent out units in front of the MLR, which was still at No Name Line, to set up outposts and use those outposts as bases from which to send out patrols to probe deeper into no man's land and ferret out the locations of the now elusive CCF units.

How Company was very much a part of these operations, going out on daily patrols, climbing the ridgelines, always on the lookout for the enemy. The OY spotter planes were also busy searching out targets for our artillery, and in good weather there was always the steady over flight of Corsair quartets from the Marine Air Wing (MAW) headed north to unload their cargos of destruction on enemy positions. During the April 22nd CCF Offensive the 11th Regiment had run short of ammunition and had to ration its support to front line troops. Now the ammo was in plentiful supply and the big guns were primed to respond.

But enemy targets were not easy to find now, for the enemy had pulled back and were hiding from our aircraft and artillery. Still, intelligence reports at this time indicated that the second phase of their spring offensive was in the offing, that the quiet spell we were experiencing was merely the lull before the next storm.

The intelligence reports again proved accurate when on the evening of the 16th of May the Chinese launched their assault. The intelligence got the timing right, but it missed the location. General Van Fleet had expected the attack to be directed at Seoul so he had been strengthening defenses above that city, but when the blow fell it hit the ROK divisions of our X Corps which were positioned between the U.S. 2nd Infantry Division on the 1st Marine Division's right flank and the east coast. Almost no one had expected the attack to come in this area of rugged and forbidding terrain with terrible roads where the attackers would be vulnerable to the big guns of U.S. Navy warships sitting offshore in the Sea of Japan.

By seizing the element of surprise and once more striking the ROK divisions, which continued to be the weak link in the UN lines, the Chinese were able to succeed in the initial stages of their offensive. As the official USMC history reports, "Six CCF divisions spearheaded an advance on a 20-mile front that broke through the lines of the 5th and 7th ROK Divisions. Pouring into this gap the Communists made a maximum penetration of 30 miles that endangered the right flank of the U.S. 2nd Infantry Division." (US Marine Operations in Korea Vol. IV, 123) Clay Blair puts the number of enemy higher in his description of the attack: "The Communist offensive burst upon Almond's X Corps and the ROKs to the east early in the evening of May 16. About fifteen CCF and five NKPA divisions—some 175,000 men—swarmed at the UN lines, blowing the familiar bugles and horns and firing flares. The weather was poor, overcast and rainy" (Blair, 874).

General Van Fleet, after assessing the situation and consulting with General Almond, agreed to send the Army 3rd Division, his reserves which were backing up the line for the expected attack on Seoul, for a 70-mile all night truck ride to the east to staunch the rapid penetration of CCF forces there. He continued to worry about a possible attack on Seoul but understood that he had to respond to this clear threat in the eastern sector. The generals concluded that the objective of the Chinese appeared to be either to move south along the coast toward Pusan to threaten UN supply lines or to move south and swing west in an attempt to encircle the 2nd Army and 1st Marine Divisions.

* * *

Things started off routinely that day for the 3rd Battalion. Early that morning George Company was sent on a patrol north toward Chunchon while Captain Hoey sent Lt. Barnes with his new 3rd Platoon back toward Hongchon to sit on Morae Kogae Pass with instructions to return to the company area at 1600. But after the day's quiet beginning the situation changed drastically when word of the Chinese attack reached the other front line units of X Corps that evening.

When the 7th Regiment learned of the breech in the UN lines to the east, Colonel Herman Nickerson contacted his battalion commanders and conferred with them regarding necessary preparations and precautions, and one thing they all agreed on was the critical need to protect the regimental supply line, the Chunchon-Hongchon highway. They all knew the most vulnerable spot on that road was Morae Kogae Pass.

The 3rd Battalion was tapped for the job of defending the pass and Lt. Colonel Kelly was happy to report to Colonel Nickerson that Captain Hoey already had Lt. Barnes' 3rd Platoon sitting on the pass and that they would hold it until the rest of the battalion arrived. But there was a problem. Retired Lt. Colonel George Barnes shares his memory of his experience at Morae Kogae Pass that day:

> During the day I reported a patrol 3-4000 yards away believed to be enemy because their march discipline was excellent. It was off my map but I gave an azimuth from my position and an estimate of distance. After lunch my radio stopped transmitting but I could receive and about 2:30 or so heard the radio operators chatting and one stated that "Nucleus" (the 3/7 call sign) was moving. I tried repeatedly to call battalion but got no answer.

My orders from Capt. Hoey were to be back by 1600 to the company area. So about 1500 I saddled up the platoon and we marched back. My arrival at the battalion CP was a very unwelcome surprise as Col. Kelly had just told the Regt. (or Division) that one of his platoons was occupying the pass.

Captain Hoey was livid—probably having forgotten his orders to be back at 1600. So I turned around and *ran* the platoon back to the pass (Barnes, notes).

The rest of the battalion except for George Company, which had not returned from its patrol, soon followed and took up positions in roughly a rectangular formation to guard the pass. How Company was assigned to the ridgeline on the west side of the road and Item Company defended the pass from the west to the east rims while facing north. George Company returned from their patrol around midnight and took up defensive positions in the hills facing east. After we had dug in and set the watch we waited.

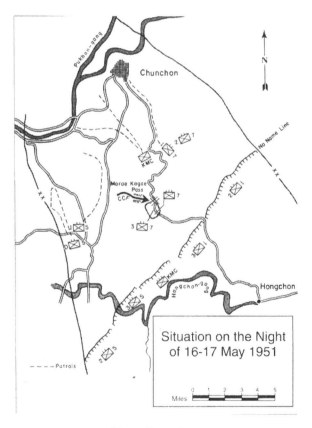

*Morae Kogae Pass*

As was usually the case I had little understanding of what we were doing, why we had been sent in such haste to occupy these positions above this stretch of the Chunchon-Hongchon road, but the Chinese well understood the strategic importance of that real estate and had sent a large well-armed regiment to occupy it. They were unaware that we had beaten them to the spot, but they were about to make that discovery.

We learned of their arrival during the early morning at 0245 hours. Those of us not on watch were in our sleeping bags when a volley of gunfire followed by several loud explosions erupted from the ridgelines to northwest of us, from the area of Captain Stoyanow's Item Company. The first eruption was followed by a short pause and then the firefight began in earnest. All of us in How Company were now up and on the alert. Lt. McVeigh set three fire teams forward as outposts and the rest of the platoon took up defensive positions, searched the dark ground to our north and west for any sign of movement, and waited.

The Chinese Regiment that attacked that night had not come down the Chunchon-Hongchon road but had followed a trail through a dry creek bed from the northwest, and that trail led them right into the position of Item Company and the five tanks. The Chinese were obviously surprised to be met there because some of their forward troops were carrying heavy weapons, mortars and machineguns. But they quickly adjusted to the unexpected situation and proceeded to put up a determined fight to take the pass away from the Marines.

Some of the Marines were surprised too. A couple of tank men were lying outside on their tank when the shooting started, and before they could both get back inside, a Chinese soldier was up on the tank and engaged in a tug of war with the last Marine in who was trying desperately to close the hatch while the Chinese soldier was determined to pull it open and toss in a grenade. Fortunately the Marine won the contest and got the hatch shut.

Other Chinese swarmed over the tanks, which had to turn their guns on each other to sweep them off. Some attackers carried satchel charges and one of them succeeded in blowing a track off one of the tanks. But of course the 50 caliber machineguns on the tanks exacted a high price from the daring attackers.

The fight continued on through the night, sometimes slacking off and then intensifying again. Some of the gunners in How company joined in the fight, firing down onto the slope north and west of our position, but it was Item Company ahead of us on the ridgeline that was getting the brunt of the attack. Our artillery had the coordinates and proved to be a decisive force in the battle. George Barnes shares more of his memories of the battle for Morae Kogae Pass and the effects of our artillery:

> I did not hear much artillery fire that day until Item Co. FO fired in his concentrations for night protective fires somewhat before dusk. [When the attack came in the early morning darkness] he adjusted fires from those concentrations to envelop the Chinese regiment in a wall of fire so intense some 80 of them laid down under the machine gun fire to await the opportunity to surrender after dawn (Barnes, notes).

By the time daylight approached it had become clear to the Chinese that they were not going to succeed in taking Morae Kogae Pass, so they began a withdrawal. Unfortunately for them by this time our artillery had precisely zeroed in on their escape route, so as they began to pull back the artillery opened up with deadly results. Many Chinese were slaughtered in their attempt to flee from this battle. And by mid-morning the fighter-bombers from the MAW were on the scene and proceeded to assail those who had escaped the artillery barrages. For those Chinese it was a terrible ending to the second phase of the CCF Spring Offensive.

How terrible it had been became evident with the morning light. The Marines who walked out in the area northwest of Item Company's position the next morning were stunned to see the number of Chinese bodies strewn out before them. The attackers had come in close ranks and provided rich targets for our mortars and artillery. The official count was 112 dead and 82 prisoners, but that was in the immediate vicinity and did not include the wounded and the mortally wounded who were dragged away and those that were caught by our aircraft some distance from the battlefield. Our losses were 7 KIA and 19 WIA (USMC Op. in Korea, Vol. IV, 125). This was not an unusual ratio in a war that pitted people against firepower. Our artillery units were now at full strength with plentiful ammunition and orders to expend it freely, and the Chinese with their close order attacks were providing a new dimension to the term, "cannon fodder."

George Barnes' memory of the aftermath of that battle differs somewhat from the official USMC history. He says Lt. Ed Powers, a good friend of his in D Engineers, buried the Chinese with his bulldozers. Barnes says Ed told him "that he counted 450 Chinese dead and did not count all of them before the bulldozers hid them under dirt" (Barnes, notes).

*Morae Kogae Pass:  The Price Paid*

*Morae Kogae Pass.  More of the same (Barnes)*

\* \* \*

Because of the breech in our lines to the east, the 1st Marine Division and other elements of X Corps were pulled back to No Name Line while the 3rd Army Division was plugging the gap on the right flank of the 2nd Division. Within less than a week, however, the Communist offensive had ground to a halt and General Almond, always eager for the dramatic tactic, believed it was time for the counterpunch. He got the approval of Generals Van Fleet and Ridgway to launch a strike northeast up the Chunchon-Inje highway in an effort to beat the enemy at their own game, to encircle them before they could make their getaway back north. The force that would carry out this daring plan was the 187th Airborne Combat Team designated Task Force Baker. Since time was the crucial element in the plan, the 187th would have to speed to their objective up the road in vehicles—trucks and tanks and jeeps. There was one problem, however. Their objective was miles away and the country between No Name Line and that objective was still enemy territory. But Almond was resolved. Clay Blair explains the predicament of the 187th:

> Almond stood the 187th staff on its ear. Owing to the enemy withdrawal, he said, it was imperative that the 187th get moving at utmost speed for Inje. The staff was first to form a battalion combat team (an infantry battalion, plus no fewer than two tank companies and support units), dash to the Soyang River, and grab a bridgehead. The team was to leave by noon. The staff was to send the rest of the 187th to the bridgehead as fast as possible by truck.
>
> The staff properly regarded this assignment as suicidal. The Soyang River was fifteen miles north of the 187th CP and the X Corps front line. The staff had heard nothing of an enemy withdrawal. All intelligence indicated the territory was still held by three or four—or more—CCF divisions. One battalion of infantry—even paratroopers!—plus two tank companies (twenty-four tanks) attempting to make that dash was certain to be annihilated before the rest of the 187th could get more tanks and follow. Probably the full 187th with a whole battalion of tanks would be annihilated (894).

There were problems getting the convoy underway and Almond dropped in by helicopter from time to time, raging at the 187th staff to get moving up the road. The pressure from the general for speed was so insistent that by the time the first group moved out the force had been reduced to twelve tanks, a recon squad, and the engineer platoon under the command of Charles Newman. Following Almond's orders they proceeded up the Chunchon-Inje road at twenty miles an hour, blasting away at groups of Chinese forces with 76-mm guns and 30 and 50 caliber machine guns. Somehow they were able to get through and establish a tenuous bridgehead near the Soyang and, ironically, gather some Chinese prisoners who came forward to surrender.

But bad news reached them after they arrived at their destination. Intelligence reports told them that there was a force of 4000 Chinese just north of them and when the tank commander, Douglas Gardiner, handed the message to Newman he asked, "What are we going to do now?"

"Newman replied without hesitation: 'We're going to attack the Chinks. If we turn back we'll run into General Almond'" (Blair, 896).

And attack they did. After calling in a devastating air strike on the enemy in front of them they formed a skirmish line and moved forward with the tanks until they reached the Soyang-gang where they established a small perimeter along the riverbank and waited for reinforcements. Almond had the rest of the 187th Airborne on the Chunchon-Inje road and through the day, unit by unit, the remainder of the task force joined the perimeter.

Still, an armored regiment with several enemy divisions around it is in a precarious spot, so to back them up Almond tapped the 1st Marine Division. The truth was he was not fond of so-called "elite" forces, such as paratroopers and Marines, and his recent conflicts with General O.P. Smith and his regimental commanders was likely still a sore spot. But the Marines were back under his command now, so when he told General Thomas he needed a regiment to follow the 187th up the Chunchon-Inje road, the 7th Regiment drew the short straw.

After the Chinese offensive on May 16th and our defense of Morae Kogae Pass that night, the 7th Regiment had been ordered back to No Name Line above Hongchon along with the rest of the 1st Division. We had been there about a week conducting our regular patrols when we learned of our new mission as part of General Almond's daring plan. But of course, as was always the case, no one in How Company was in on the big picture, the grand plan. We just shouldered our gear and went where we were told.

We did hear, however, that there was an Army paratroop unit surrounded somewhere north of Chunchon and that our mission was to move up the Chunchon-Inje road to reinforce them. The unusual thing about this operation was that we were to proceed up the road through enemy territory in trucks with a tank escort. From the scant information we got, I assumed the paratroopers had dropped into the spot they were in. I didn't know they had motored to the spot just ahead of us.

We waited in the rice paddies alongside the road while the trucks were brought up from Hongchon to transport the regiment, and we were told the 3rd Battalion was to lead the way in the convoy. When the trucks arrived the 2nd Platoon of How Company was assigned the point, so I climbed in the fourth truck with other members of my platoon. Three tanks had moved out ahead of us on the road, and when everyone was aboard the convoy started to move north toward the city of Chunchon.

We continued down the road until we came to the last outpost of UN forces, a 2ⁿᵈ Army Division unit occupying the high ground east of the road. The convoy stopped there while the Battalion CO, Lt. Col. Bernard Kelly, and company commanders, Captain Hoey of How Company, Captain Airheart of George Company, and Captain Stoyanow of Item Company, climbed up the hill to confer with the officers there.

When they returned the word we got was that the Army officers had told them there was no way we could continue down that road because after the 187ᵗʰ had passed through the Chinese had moved back and occupied the high ground to the north and had for some time been exchanging fire with the Army positions there. Our leaders conferred with one another for a while about this latest intelligence and consulted with the Regimental Commander by phone. With pressure no doubt still coming from General Almond, our leaders, like those of the 187ᵗʰ Airborne, concluded that orders were orders, so they got back on the trucks and our convoy resumed its progress north.

The tanks moved out ahead into the valley and we followed in the trucks. On our left to the west was a fairly wide expanse of rice paddies backed by a ridgeline of mountains running north and south. The mountains were closer to the road on the east in front of the Army position. The light colored stony road rose straight ahead of us toward Chunchon and we were on our way to link up with the paratroopers. If the enemy were on the ridgelines ahead of us the tanks would certainly grab their attention, just as they had in the rice paddies of the Long Valley.

The Chinese were there, all right, because we had gotten no more than a thousand yards into the valley when a barrage of mortar shells erupted all around the head of our convoy. One hit the first truck and a geyser of steam shot up from its radiator. At that same moment Marines up and down the road cleared out of the trucks and took to a ditch that ran along the right side of the road. Fortunately it was a deep ditch that provided good protection from the mortars and from the small arms and machinegun fire that had now joined in the attack.

I had just hunkered down in the ditch with other members of my platoon when the word was passed back, "Hey Doc, up there! Somebody's been hit up there!"

At first I thought I might be able to work my way up the ditch and get to the wounded man that way. I tried crawling over several Marines but I soon saw that going that way was much too slow, so I jumped out of the ditch and began to run in a crouch toward the head of the column. Now the tanks were firing into the hills north and east of the road and the Army had apparently called in an artillery strike on those targets, so as I ran, chanting under my breath that old self-preservation mantra I had first used on that Sunflower How patrol, I was surrounded by a tremendous din of small arms, mortar and artillery fire.

Since I was the only one up on the road and running I felt all that fire was directed at me, but I had no way of knowing. I just knew I wanted to find the wounded Marine and get back in the ditch. As I ran the world seemed to close in around me and everything became a frantic blur. The trucks had some distance between them, so I had a way to go down the road, but I kept looking to the ditch for some signal that I had found the place. Finally I saw a hand stick up and immediately ran to that spot and dived in with a gasp of relief to find that the hand was only pointing forward down the road.

Once more I thought I might work my way ahead through the ditch over the Marines crouching there. I assumed the enemy had seen where I jumped in the ditch and I didn't want to jump out in that same spot. I did manage to move a little way forward before I had to leap back out on the road and continue my sprint to find the wounded Marine. I got encouragement from the guys in the ditch this time. As I ran I heard their voices,

"GO, DOC! GO!"

The next signal I got was from the ditch right beside the first truck, and this time when I dived in I found him. He was a tall Marine from the 2$^{nd}$ Platoon that I knew well, although today I can't remember his name. He had been hit in the subclavian artery and every time his heart beat blood would spurt out. He had already lost a fair amount of blood and told me he was afraid he was bleeding to death.

I took a battle dressing from my aid kit and reassured him as I worked that we could take care of the situation and that he was not going to bleed to death. The thing this wound required was pressure, so simply tying the dressing around his shoulder would not be sufficient. To stop the hemorrhaging I placed the thick dressing up against the wound and pushed hard. While I was doing this I looked him over for other wounds and found none, and inquired of the other Marines in the ditch if anyone else had been hit. Fortunately none had. He had apparently been hit by shrapnel from that first mortar round that blasted the radiator of the truck he was riding in.

All the time I was busy with this wounded Marine the battle was raging in the rice paddies and ridgelines around us. This was our first contact with the enemy since Morae Kogae Pass, and just as in that battle our forces once more had a chance to apply superior firepower, to use the now plentiful artillery shells to exact a toll on the enemy. When our tanks nearby added to the fusillade with their 90mm cannons they shook dirt from the walls of the ditch we were hunkered down in.

Meanwhile my arms had grown tired pressing the battle dressing against the wound, so I finally leaned my head on my hands to help maintain the pressure. Blood from the wound covered my hands and soaked my shirt, but at last the flow was stopped, and the Marine, though pale, was still conscious and seemed to be doing OK. I replaced the soaked dressing with a new one and this time tied it tightly around his shoulder, but I kept the pressure on the wound to continue to staunch the bleeding.

After a while the sounds of battle changed. Our forces continued to pummel the ridgelines, but the incoming fire had diminished and possibly stopped—it was hard to say. Some of us started to peep out of the ditch and we could see the trucks behind us toward the Army position backing down the road, one by one. The tanks were still on the road in front of our position there in the ditch beside the crippled truck, and they were continuing to fire sporadically at the ridgelines to the east.

When I looked behind us I saw that Lt. McVeigh had hopped back out on the road and he and Smitty were moving in our direction. As he walked by his platoon there in the ditch he brandished his carbine and encouraged his men to join him on the road. After filling out a wound tag and tying it to the wounded man's shirt, I left him in the care of one of his fire team members and told that man to try to get his buddy on the truck behind us when the driver came to back it out.

The rest of us began to climb out of the ditch to follow Lt. McVeigh up the road toward the high ground on our right where the fire had been coming from. We took the precaution of bunching up on the left sides of the tanks that were now continuing north on the road, putting them between us and any possible enemy fire from the eastern slopes. We stayed with the tanks as the road rose steadily on an upward grade toward a mountain pass ahead.

After some time we arrived at a position adjacent to the ridgeline on our right without being fired on. At that point the tanks stopped and the lieutenant, after conferring with Captain Hoey on the radio, led us off the road to our left and through some fallow rice paddies toward a mountain spur that pointed toward us like the foot of a staircase. When we reached its base we began a slow ascent which soon brought us into some scattered tree cover. We moved up slowly, fully expecting to meet some resistance after what we had encountered on the road, but we were able to move into defensive positions on the high ground without any problems.

Since our convoy up the Chunchon-Hongchon road had been halted, the 7th Regiment was now fanning out into the surrounding hills and into the valley behind us. As we climbed we could see from time to time elements of our own 3rd Battalion setting up in the valley below. Our artillery continued to whistle overhead, and once there was a terrific explosion in the valley behind us. We thought it must have been one of our artillery's short rounds. Only later did we learn that a round from one of our large 4.2 mortars had hit an overhead phone wire and exploded, with devastating results for the mortar crew.

How Company continued to move north on the ridgelines west of the road for much of the day until we were told to halt and dig in. After setting up our watches for the night we settled in and let the artillery continue to punish the enemy positions. We gathered dead wood from around the area, built our fires on the reverse slope and proceeded to heat up our C Rations and water for cocoa and coffee, our daily routine.

Smitty, Lt. McVeigh, Sergeant Putnam and I, and several others were gathered around a fire talking when Hawkshaw came by and said "Hey, we're going to have to call you 'Bloody Doc' now!" I was bloody for a fact. I had washed the blood off my hands with water from my canteen but there was no way to get it off my shirt, so that name would fit until I could wash my clothes or get me a change, and there were no streams in this high country.

Sitting around the campfire that evening we smoked cigarettes, drank coffee and reviewed the events of the day, and after we had hashed it all over those of us not on watch crawled into our sleeping bags.

\* \* \*

By the next morning, the 26th, General Almond had gotten word that his bold and daring tactic had failed, that the Chinese had fled north so rapidly they had escaped the trap before any X Corps forces could cut them off. He was furious. He blamed the 7th Marine Regiment for the failure. But even if we had been able to get around the crippled truck it would have been impossible for us to make it to the 187th in time to cut off the fleeing enemy. We in How Company knew nothing of the general's displeasure, and even if we had we wouldn't have cared. Our self-esteem came from another place; it didn't depend on the general's approval.

Now rather than going in search of the 187th Airborne, we would continue putting pressure on the defeated and demoralized CCF forces. The second phase of their spring offensive had failed much more dramatically than did the first, and it was becoming apparent that a new and perhaps final chapter of the war was at hand. UN forces seemed powerful enough to drive the Chinese from North Korea but General Ridgway, sensitive to the political ramifications of the war, saw UN strength as a means to get North Korea to the bargaining table. So the object now was to keep pressure on the enemy.

We learned that same day we had a new assignment. We would be going on an extended combat patrol north into no man's land, and the word was that while on this mission we were to take no prisoners. To this day I don't know if such orders are official or legal or where that word came from, but that was what we were told. The rationale was clear enough. Since we would be out of contact with our front lines and with any other units, we would have no way to guard or care for prisoners. It certainly would be inconvenient to say the least to carry out our mission dragging along a troop of Chinese prisoners. The hope was we wouldn't be faced with that problem.

We set out on our patrol and soon found ourselves in a scattering of low trees that grew thicker as we climbed. We followed wooded mountain ridgelines all morning then stopped in a good defensive position and took a lunch break. Lt. McVeigh went to exchange information with Captain Hoey while Smitty, Hawkshaw, CP Sam and I sat around our fire heating C Rations and talking about our experience in the convoy and in our earlier battle for Morae Kogae Pass. After seeing all those bodies we agreed that being a Chinese soldier was a tough proposition. CP thought they didn't mind dying, that their lives weren't worth much anyway. What did they have to live for? Why else would they charge by the hundreds into such meat grinding, withering fire?

Hawkshaw said we had to give them credit. They were damn brave soldiers and tough fighters. "How would any of us stand up under the hardships and destructive firepower they faced?" He asked.

CP said they were just crazy damn Chinks, and he wasn't going to waste time analyzing them. It was easier to just kill them. That's what we were there for anyway.

But there sure were a lot of them.

The lieutenant came back and sat down with us around the fire and heated a can of C Rations. The rest of us heated up water in our canteen cups and made instant coffee, and while we were enjoying it someone brought up Gunny Spell's misadventure with his coffee and Lt. Lowe's whiskey. We all got a good chuckle out of remembering that episode, which continued to provide How Company with moments of levity even during our down times.

Lt. McVeigh enjoyed the story too, although he had not been with us when that dramatic episode occurred. As I noted before, this Ivy League educated platoon leader blended in easily with his predominantly working class charges, some high school graduates, and some, like me, high school dropouts. He had those qualities that quickly won the respect of the platoon, and what is amazing to me after all these years is that he was only twenty-two years old. Lt. McVeigh was a natural leader.

The lieutenant told us we had a way to go that day before we reached our objective, so after our lunch we all saddled up and resumed our journey along the rugged mountain ridgelines.

About two hours into our hike we were startled when out of the woods to our right came three unarmed Chinese soldiers. They walked right into our column and joined our procession up the ridgeline. One of the soldiers appeared injured or wounded and the other two, one on each side, were helping him along. We all stopped at this point and sent the word up the line to hold up while we examined the soldiers and decided what to do. Lt. McVeigh called me to examine the injured man, so I approached him and had his two helpers sit him down so I could take a look at him.

I examined him from head to toe looking at his uniform for any sign of gunshot or shrapnel wound, but there was none, no blood anywhere. He had some kind of marking or insignia on his collar which the other two did not have, so I concluded he was probably an officer and the other two were his men who were trying to get him some help. They could have been survivors of the battle for Morae Kogae Pass or a later firefight who either could not keep up with their fleeing brothers or had simply had enough and wanted to surrender. While I was checking the officer he rolled his head around and seemed to babble incoherently, but since it was Chinese I couldn't say for sure. But I did wonder if he might have been on some kind of drug from the way he was acting.

I told Lt. McVeigh I could find no wounds on the prisoner. Now we were faced with the problem of what to do with them. We had gotten the order, "take no prisoners."

That order might be all right in a firefight where you kept shooting until the last enemy was dead. But what do you do when they walk unarmed right into your midst? Do you line them up and execute unarmed men? That would have been no problem for almost any army throughout the history of warfare, but that approach went against all the values we had been taught. Who could shoot in cold blood unarmed men? If we did such things then how could we claim to be the good guys?

Of course even in America, unfortunately, there are a few who would have no qualms about such brutal measures. And we had one there in the 2nd Platoon. CP Sam, who was never the bravest man in a firefight but always the most bellicose in a bull session, approached us there with those prisoners with his M1 at the ready and said,

"The orders are to take no prisoners, so by God we need to follow those orders!"

"What are you going to do, Sam, shoot 'em? Smitty asked.

"You're Goddamn right I'll shoot 'em. Those are our orders!"

"Hold up there, Sam." Lt. McVeigh said. We're not going to shoot them. I'll go talk to Captain Hoey and we'll decide what to do with them."

When the lieutenant returned he said we would keep the prisoners with us until we got a chance to send them back to the battalion area.

CP was disappointed by this order, and as he walked off he was muttering to himself; one of the words sounded like, "Ratchet!"

We kept a guard on the prisoners that night although it was pretty clear they were no threat to anyone. Before we turned in we sat around our campfires and listened to the artillery rumbling through the mountains and occasionally glanced at the three prisoners whose enigmatic faces were illuminated in the flickering firelight.

Thunder and smoke were our constant companions in Korea. If not thunder from the clouds, then thunder from the artillery, or often both blending together in somber harmony—and smoke—if not from enemy grassfires then from our own campfires.

For many years afterward the sound of thunder and the smell of wood smoke would take me back to the war, to the days of living on the rocky ridgelines with the 2$^{nd}$ Platoon in the mountains of Korea... thunder and smoke.

The following day a group of Korean *cargadores* was able to find our position and bring us C Rations, water and other supplies. We took that opportunity to turn our captives over to them for safe delivery to the rear. Those amazingly strong and courageous Korean workers with their A-frame back packs were crucial to our war effort; they were the ones who kept us supplied with food, ammunition and water day after day while we were moving through the high ground.

Over the next few days we continued to move north with no opposition. The three prisoners were the only enemy we saw. After their initial penetrations of UN lines on the eastern front the Communist forces were first contained and then pushed back, and within just a few days the second phase of their spring offensive turned into a retreat and in some places a rout. The UN lines were now moving north at full strength and intact all across the peninsula, backed by unprecedented firepower, both on the ground and in the air.

\* \* \*

Eleven months after the NKPA had awakened Captain Joe Darrigo when they came shooting their way into Kaesong at three o'clock in the morning, and six months after the Chinese crossed the Yalu and surrounded the Marines at Chosin, the answer to the question of who would prevail in the struggle was becoming clear. UN forces were unmistakably in the ascendancy. During the month of May the Communists suffered 200,000 casualties, 17,000 dead and thousands taken prisoner (Whelan, 313). Earlier in the war Chinese soldiers would often choose to die rather than surrender, but now they were surrendering much more readily, sometimes as units.

But the struggle was by no means over. The enemy had not abandoned the field. They had pulled back to establish strong defensive positions below the Iron Triangle, the Hwachon Reservoir, and the town of Yanggu where they were determined to stop us.

It was clear now we were headed back across the 38$^{th}$ Parallel. This would be the third time I had crossed it and the fifth time UN forces had crossed it. But this would be the last time.

# CHAPTER 13

# The Crag

The enemy offensive of May 16th had run its course and now the Chinese were pulling back in the face of our advance, leaving NKPA units to slow us down while they made their getaway. The accordion phase of the war was in its last stages and the positional war that would last another two years was about to begin. By late spring of 1951 the United Nations forces were probably strong enough to make another big push into North Korea, but the United States and its allies could see no possible end to the war by following that path. It seemed that MacArthur's prophecy that the war would end in a stalemate would be borne out, that it was in fact inevitable. The objectives for both sides now would be to secure as advantageous positions along the 38th Parallel as possible in order to hold a strong hand if and when negotiations began. This did not mean, however, that the fighting was about over. There would still be some very bitter battles to take and hold those advantageous positions.

I had made it from the brutally cold days of winter to the beautiful warm days of the Korean spring, and over those months my mood and outlook naturally changed with the weather and with my circumstances. Unlike many of the guys I served with, I really had no right to complain since I had volunteered to go to Korea. I had literally asked for it. But of course I did complain at times, though at other times I expressed no regrets. Following are some comments from my letters home reflecting my changing attitudes toward the war:

Jan 22: Pohang-dong. [I had just told my folks because of the war I probably wouldn't be able to get out when my enlistment was up in August.]

> A war like this could go on forever, however I hope we won't withdraw. We have lost too much already. I hope ya'll don't worry about me too much, because I'm not the same boy that used to step out of his pants and leave them on the floor & leave the bathroom all messed up.

Feb 22:

> Most of the guys here are tired of traveling and want to go home to stay. I may be crazy but there are a lot of places in this

world yet where I want to go.... I just feel sorry for boys that are born in a town, are raised, married and work all their lives and die in the same town, never seeing anything but the surrounding country....

America is the best and greatest country in the world and if there's even a chance this war is doing any good it's worth taking. I think the greatest trouble with people back home is that they take everything for granted.

I never changed my attitude about my country, but after weeks and months of climbing mountains and battling the Chinese and North Koreans my views of the war fluctuated.

Apr 1:

Well, we got the bad news today. We are going back up to the front tomorrow morning. We are all hoping & praying that we don't have to cross the thirty eighth. All I have to say is I am a Republican, and I hope ya'll never vote for Truman.

In those days I knew absolutely nothing about politics, but like people generally, I needed someone to blame for my misfortunes and President Truman was the obvious target. A week later we had crossed the 38th Parallel and my spirits had lifted a bit. There was now talk about the possibility of some kind of settlement between the two sides.

Apr 7:

I'm hoping we can make some kind of agreement with the Chinese. Our original plan was to set up along this Kansas Line and just send out probing patrols until we could make an agreement with China.

We hit it a little rough now and then, but don't think we have lost our spirit.

Apr 19:

I would be the happiest man in the world if this war would end and I could come home.

And then, after the Chinese Offensive of April 22nd, after that battle and the grueling "retrograde" march to close the gap on our left flank when the

10<sup>th</sup> ROK division disintegrated on our flank I was weary and discouraged. I wrote home:

> I'm beginning to get pretty disgusted about this whole deal though. I read Mac[Arthur]'s speech you sent me. I guess I've had the old boy wrong.... I do know whoever's responsible for this war is one of the worst kind of criminals there is.... It's a privilege to fight for your country, but it would take a fast talker to convince me I'm fighting for the US.

But I didn't lose my sense of humor, sardonic though it was. In that same letter I said:

> It's a funny thing that over here you can live like a dog and never get sick or injured, but probably when I get home I'll trip over a curb & break my leg and come down with the double pneumonia.

I tried not to say things in my letters that would cause my mother to worry because she worried so much anyway. But sometimes the discouraging remarks would escape from my pen or pencil. Then mother would write expressing even more concern. To one of those letters I responded:

> I want to talk to you about the way you have been worrying about me. I don't know how you have it pictured over here, but the way you talk you must think it's like the Bataan death march. Believe me, it's not near as bad as you think.... The reason I volunteered to come over here was because I figured that if I stayed in California much longer one of those California drivers was sure to get me.

I'm glad my mother never knew what happened to How Company on that last day of May 1951. She didn't know then and she never found out because when I got back home I never told her.

\* \* \*

This is what happened. After the battle at Morae Kogae Pass and our aborted attempt to reach the 187<sup>th</sup> Airborne by truck convoy and cut off the fleeing CCF forces, we continued our advance north until we once more crossed the 38<sup>th</sup> Parallel. Our objective now was to take the town of Yanggu, an important road center on the eastern edge of the Hwachon Reservoir.

While the Communist forces had been withdrawing ahead of our advance, they were by no means giving up the battle. They were pulling back to protect the town of Yanggu and to establish strong defensive positions to hold in the likelihood that there would be truce talks. And the terrain there was ideal for fighting defensive battles—high mountains and rugged and rocky ridgelines and peaks. Our leaders too understood by now that the war was likely to end somewhere in the middle of the peninsula, so they were determined to grab the most favorable real estate before the line was frozen. The accordion phase of the war—lightning penetrations by one side and then the other, long advances and long retreats covering many miles—was coming to an end. The last two years of the war would be fought from trenches and bunkers and see pitched battles to gain only a few hundred yards or the next ridgeline.

Before going into many of our earlier battles the 2$^{nd}$ Platoon had not had a great deal of time to reflect on what was about to happen. We had often come up on conflicts suddenly; they had been pretty much unpremeditated engagements, like the battle in the rice paddy at the end of the Long Valley where Corporal Gross was killed, and Izabitch where we lost Tardio and Hansen. The same was true for the battle at Morae Kogae Pass and the attack on our convoy that came on us suddenly, giving us time to think about events only after the fact. Before most of those battles we had derived some comfort from the hope that the enemy would not show up, not materialize, that they would flee before our advance. So many of our firefights were precipitous; we found ourselves in the thick of it before we had time to think about it. We did have some time to worry about the CCF Spring Offensive, but except for the losses in Item Company and the long grueling march south, the 3$^{rd}$ Battalion came out all right. Now How Company was about to be confronted with something different—a looming battle with plenty of concern aforethought.

For several days after we had sent the prisoners back with the *cargadores* we continued to move north with only light opposition, generally along the high ground but occasionally moving down the roads when our flanks were secure. Then on Memorial Day, Wednesday afternoon the 30$^{th}$ of May, (twenty years later Congress would convert that solemn memorial to a three day holiday weekend) we took up positions in rolling hills overlooking a road down below, a stream beyond that, and rice fields stretching off to the base of a very large mountain in the distance. The sky was overcast and our artillery was thundering, and its target was that mountain.

Lt. McVeigh had the platoon dig in and set up defensive positions and after that we built small campfires and heated our C Rations for the evening meal. Smitty, Hawkshaw, CP and some of the other guys and I squatted around the fire carrying on the usual conversations, but on this day talk was unusually quiet and subdued. All the while we were sitting around our campfires and milling around the platoon area we kept looking at the mountain. I had bad feelings about that mountain; I think we all did. Then when the lieutenant came back from a meeting with Captain Hoey, our worst fears were confirmed. The enemy, either CCF or NKPA or both, were dug in on the mountain in force and were determined to hold it and keep UN forces from taking the town of Yanggu which lay behind it. How Company had been given the assignment to take the central peak of the mountain on the following day. We would be jumping off at daylight.

While Lt. McVeigh called the squad leaders together–Sergeants Nolan, Putnam, and Noreiga–to look over the map and the plans for the following morning, the rest of us looked across the valley to the mountain. Later someone in the company called that mountain "the Crag" and the name stuck. That name had a kind of psychological validity since what we saw standing out there in the distance seemed so daunting, so foreboding. But to me it looked more like a monstrous starfish high at its radial center, or perhaps an octopus with ridgelines like tentacles reaching out towards us. Or perhaps it more closely resembled a monstrous tree stump with three gnarled roots clawing the ground in our direction like the talons of a Tyrannosaurus Rex. The mountain was not alpine but it was huge, and while there were mountains behind us and to our east and west, the Crag stood out in the panorama across the flat rice fields—solitary, massive and menacing, with no visible connections to the other mountains around it. It seemed reaching out for us, waiting for us.

Compared to the surrounding terrain the Crag was a grand mountain, and under any other circumstances it might have stirred feelings of awe and appreciation for the beauty and grandeur of nature. But knowing what we knew about what awaited us up there in that high ground we could feel no sense of appreciation at all. To add to the somber mood the sky was still overcast, meaning there likely would be no air support to aid in our assault.

Because the clouds were threatening rain Smitty and I put our shelter halves together and made a pup tent for the night. We crawled into our sleeping bags shortly after dark, knowing we would be rousted out early the next morning. We were not looking forward to it.

\* \* \*

The call came shortly before daylight and it didn't take much to wake us up, those of us who had managed to get any sleep at all. We rolled up our gear, some of us grabbed a snack from our C Ration "lights," and then lined up to begin the descent to the road below. There on the road we found a column of three tanks ready to accompany us on the assault. The three platoons of How Company lined up along the road, and after a last brief meeting between Captain Hoey and the platoon leaders the word came back to move out. We moved along on both sides of the road, keeping our intervals, with the tanks clattering along between our two columns.

The road took us east following the base of the hill we had just come down, continued in a slow curve to our right and soon brought us in full view of the mountain standing off to the north. There she was, just as she had appeared the evening before and in our troubled dreams throughout the night, but now larger and even more menacing. And just as on the day before, all the eyes of How Company were drawn to the Crag. Men might force themselves to look elsewhere, at the entrenching tool on the man's pack in front of them perhaps, or back at the hills they had recently come down, but the dark attraction of the mountain exerted too strong a pull and soon heads would turn again, and there she was.

Our artillery, which had been firing sporadically all night, had now opened up in a steady barrage, and the bombardment up on that mountain accompanied us while we continued moving down the road parallel to the base of our objective which lay across the open fields to our left. As we came abreast of the mountain our two columns turned left, leaving the tanks. We waded a small stream that ran parallel to the road and started moving quicktime now toward the mountain as the first incoming mortar and artillery rounds began to explode in the rice paddies to our front and off to our right. We were apparently just beyond the range of their mortars so the fire was off target.

In the meantime the tanks had moved on down the road a way where they did a left flank toward the mountain but just before they turned we heard a tremendous explosion from the area of the first tank. We didn't know it then, but the first tank had hit a land mine that killed the driver and blew a track off the tank. The remaining tanks moved on out into the rice paddies and began to give us covering fire with their 50 caliber machineguns and their 90 mm rifled cannons.

Now the company had to begin a sprint toward the base of the mountain and toward the central spur which was our objective. This was a familiar situation, running exposed across an open field seeking the security of the mountain base where we would be concealed from the defenders high up. I ran huffing with the weight of my pack and rifle, uttering one of my usual self-absorbed prayers, "Oh Lord help me make it to that mountain!" I was one of two hundred and fifty Marines and corpsmen spread out across that field, all in a desperate dash for the safety of the mountain base. We could now hear a splattering of machinegun and rifle fire coming from above, mixed in with the mortar rounds which continued to explode around us. Thanks to our artillery that continued to rain down on that mountaintop and to the tanks that were now firing point blank into the enemy position, the incoming fire was suppressed, sporadic and not very effective.

The roar of battle was deafening. I passed close to one of the tanks clattering through the dry rice paddy like a giant beetle, its turret humming as its 90mm rifled gun swung toward the mountain. When the tank fired its

90 mm cannon the muzzle flash lit up the overcast morning and the shock momentarily blurred my vision and knocked the world out of focus.

How Company took some casualties crossing the rice paddies, but fortunately no one in the 2ⁿᵈ Platoon was hit. We reached the base of the mountain and began moving to the right to reach the central spur of the mountain that was the path to our objective, the one we were going to climb to reach our goal–the summit of the Crag. As we moved along the foot of the mountain we passed some small out buildings and sheds and some dugouts or caves going back into the mountain's base which we took note of as we passed by. I heard rifle shots behind me from someone in our platoon, but I took little notice in the din of battle because we were all intent on getting to the base of the mountain spur.

Once there, Captain Hoey again shouted out the orders for the prearranged assault. There were three objectives up this spur of the mountain, each one about one third of the distance to the top. The 1ˢᵗ Platoon was to go first and secure the first objective while the other platoons provided covering fire. Once that objective was secured, the 2ⁿᵈ Platoon would advance and move through the 1ˢᵗ Platoon toward the second objective while the third platoon provided covering fire. Then the 3ʳᵈ Platoon would move up through the other platoons while they provided covering fire and take the third objective which was in fact the overall objective of How Company–the crest of the Crag. Our hope was that before we reached the top the enemy would see the futility of their situation and withdraw. That was always our hope.

The 1ˢᵗ Platoon started moving up the mountain, not in single file, but along either side of the ridge in a skirmish line. We watched them disappear into the small trees and shrubbery of the mountain and waited. It grew quieter as the fire from our artillery and the tanks in the valley abated a bit. Earlier, when How Company had reached the cover of the mountain, the small arms fire from the mountaintop died down, so the noise level was now considerably reduced. That fact further fueled our hopes that the defenders had fled, though the most likely explanation was that they could no longer see us to shoot at.

After some time Captain Hoey got word on his radio from the 1ˢᵗ Platoon that they had secured their objective, so now it was the 2ⁿᵈ Platoon's turn. Lt. McVeigh led us up the mountain following the backbone of the spur until we came upon the 1ˢᵗ Platoon spread out in defensive positions behind a hump on the ridge. There we formed a skirmish line, passed through them and continued to climb the mountain in ready, crouched positions, staring intently into the trees and undergrowth ahead of us for any sign or movement. We continued to climb for some time until the lieutenant, checking his map, said, "OK, This is it! Take your positions." He then called Captain Hoey on his radio and we all settled in to wait on the 3ʳᵈ Platoon.

After a while Lieutenant Barnes' platoon showed up accompanied by Captain Hoey and Gunny Spell. The Captain and the Gunny remained with us while the 3rd Platoon established a skirmish line and continued the climb to the top of the mountain. We watched them disappear into the trees above us and waited. For some reason it had grown even quieter, perhaps because the artillery and tanks knew we were approaching the summit of the mountain. We lay there and looked at each other and then looked up to the rise in front of us and just waited. The minutes ticked by.

Suddenly the quiet was shattered by the rip of a burp gun followed by three punching reports from a rifle—and then all hell broke loose above us. The roar of small arms fire and mortar fire swept over the mountain and engulfed us. Now Captain Hoey was on the phone with battalion commander, Lt. Colonel Bernard Kelly, calling for artillery fire on the crest of the mountain. We were receiving fire from the ridgeline on our left and Gunny Spell was yelling, "Goddamit, lay down some fire over there!" The Marines in positions to fire obeyed the Gunny.

Shexnayder was behind a tree with his M1 firing at that ridge on our left. He called out to me, "Hey Doc, look there!" When I looked I could see enemy soldiers running down the slope to the southwest. I don't know why they were running in that direction; I guess to get off the mountaintop that was being battered by our artillery. Some were carrying down their wounded on stretchers. Now and then one would be going the other way, back up the mountain, perhaps carrying ammunition to comrades there on the top. While we were taking fire from that direction some of the enemy soldiers seemed oblivious of our presence on that parallel finger of the mountain, and Shexnayder was taking advantage of the opportunity by taking potshots at the scampering NKPA soldiers like they were figures in a carnival shooting gallery.

While we were lying there I overheard Captain Hoey on the phone with the Colonel Kelly. I didn't know the exact topic of conversation, but the colonel was apparently ordering the Skipper to do something that to him, there in the middle of a firefight, seemed not only impractical but stupid. Captain Hoey didn't believe the battalion CO had a full understanding and appreciation of the position we were in on that mountain and he didn't mince words. Whatever the situation, I heard our Skipper let go a furious blast of profanity in his exchange with the colonel, language you don't often hear used by a military man to a superior officer. Captain Hoey was loved by his men, but because his loyalty and concern was more down rather than up, he was not an officer destined to rise high in the ranks.

So far it was the 3rd Platoon primarily engaged in the battle. Most of us were not in positions to provide covering fire because we couldn't see above us; we would be likely to hit our own men if we started firing up the slope. So I was hunkered down studying the weave of my aid kit when Lt. McVeigh gave the word for the 2nd Platoon to move out. We all rose to a crouch and began to move up the slope to join the 3rd Platoon. Now the roar of battle was deafening, machinegun and rifle fire were zipping and buzzing through the trees, and our artillery rounds were fluttering close overhead and exploding on the ridgeline up above us. Just before we moved out the 1st Platoon had joined Captain Hoey and Gunny Spell. Soon they would all be following us to join the 3rd Platoon.

We started out slowly, cautiously, keeping as close to the ground as we could and watching for the guys in the 3rd Platoon. After a while we came up on some Marines in defensive positions behind rocks, mounds of earth and tree trunks. Lt. McVeigh had us stop and take up positions while he questioned some of those guys about what was going on up ahead. While he was trying to get information from them a call came from somewhere up the slope.

"We need a corpsman! Send a corpsman up here!"

Smitty said, "Hey Doc, they need you up there."

"Yeah, I know!"

I rose to a crouch and started moving up the slope.

"Be careful up there, Doc!"

"See you guys after a while," I said.

"Yeah, watch it Doc. We need you. Don't take no chances!"

"Don't worry about me. I'll be all right." I replied, trying to convince myself.

I moved out ahead of my platoon and soon found myself all alone in a saddle of the ridgeline. I could see no one ahead of me and no one behind me, but the sounds of gunfire from above were deafening. I scrambled up to the far rim of the saddle and crouched behind the cover there listening to the bullets flying above my head.

In the explosive din of a firefight it's not possible just by listening to place or locate incoming or outgoing fire, to tell exactly how near or far away the bullets are flying, or to distinguish a bullet hitting near you from a rifle firing near you. But from the sheer racket, the intensity of this battle, I concluded that this rise I was lying behind was being raked by enemy machinegun fire. But I knew I had to go forward. I knew I had to rise up and move over that hump, but I also knew that as soon as I did I would be killed. I had not been so certain I would die since that first Sunflower How patrol back during the Gook Chase.

I took several deep breaths, rose to a low crouch, and then charged over the rise and, much to my amazement, I found myself still alive descending into another saddle of the ridgeline. Now I could see the other members of the 3rd Platoon in defensive positions, behind trees and boulders against the far rise of the saddle engaged with the enemy to their front. Ahead of them was the crest of the mountain and it was there that the enemy was dug in and making their stand. And up on the high ground ahead, riflemen and machine gunners and BAR men were engaged in a pitched battle with the enemy on the ridgeline ahead of them.

And now I saw the reason I had been called forward. Lying there on the reverse slope ahead of me was a long line of wounded Marines that had been dragged down from the firing line to be attended to, and there was the 3rd Platoon corpsman working over them.

I ran up to him and asked, "What can I do?"

"Over there, look at those over there!" and he pointed to some Marines on the far end of the line.

I noticed immediately one who was struggling for breath. He had a sucking bullet wound to the chest and every time he tried to breathe, air would bubble out of the wound and he could get no oxygen, so he was in danger of suffocation. I cut his shirt away to expose the wound, and then I wiped the blood away and sealed up the bullet hole with adhesive tape, turned him over and sealed the other side, then lay him on the wounded side so his good lung would not fill up with blood. He started to breathe easier.

Then I went down the line and found that almost all the injured had suffered bullet wounds. Several of them were machine gunners who had been dragged down from the rise above where the 3rd Platoon was battling it out right now. There were shoulder wounds, arm and leg wounds, one head wound where the bullet had gone through the Marine's helmet, shattered the helmet liner and taken a strip of scalp and hair but hadn't broken the skull. The 3rd Platoon corpsman and I were totally absorbed in administering aid to these wounded Marines, applying battle dressings, staunching bleeding, injecting morphine, and positioning the wounded to minimize the chances of shock.

While we were totally absorbed in our efforts to save these wounded Marines, the battle was raging just a few feet above our heads. The 2nd Platoon had now joined the action up there on the Crag. There were frantic calls coming from above for more ammunition for the machineguns. Our 2nd Platoon machine gunners had already joined those gunners of the 3rd Platoon and contributed their firepower and ammunition, but the intensity of the battle rapidly depleted our supply of ammunition.

One of our BAR men, Joe Sipolski, "Ski," later recalled that he, Swanson, Tate, Smitty and a number of other Marines were put to work loading their rifle ammunition into the empty machinegun belts. Calls went back to the 1st Platoon behind to bring up their cans of ammo for the machine guns and when they arrived they were immediately put to good use. Ski and the other Marines were now free to go forward and add their firepower to the struggle.

One of the members of the 3rd Platoon, Frank "Hoagy" Carmichael, moved forward and when he saw wounded Marines out in the open on the ridgeline ahead, he ran to an exposed position and provided covering fire which suppressed enemy fire until the wounded could be recovered.

By now the battle had taken up the entire morning. Although we had been up since dawn, it took us a while to assemble and move down the road into position for the assault. We certainly did our best to move quickly across the open rice paddies, but the mountain was huge. The climb up took some time, and the caution required in making the ascent slowed our progress even more. Our hopes that the enemy had flown had been dashed; the defenders were there all the while, looking down the slope through the trees, waiting for us. When the 3rd Platoon emerged from the cover of the trees, the North Korean machine gunners opened up and the battle was joined. The intense firefight that started then had been in progress now for two hours and more.

We were now getting re-supplied by trains of *cargadores* who were bringing up ammunition, medical supplies, water and food on their A-frame packs and carrying stretchers to evacuate our wounded back down the mountain. The mountain top was a beehive of activity, with Marines running back and forth carrying weapons and ammunition and shouting messages and orders, trying to be heard over the din of small arms fire and the artillery and mortar barrages that were continuing to erupt on the mountain, while all three of us corpsmen continued to work on the ever growing number of wounded.

By early afternoon the skies had cleared and we were getting some close air support hitting the enemy positions to our front. We had our blaze orange air panels out on the ground out in front to show the Marine pilots our location. How Company had made several attempts to push the enemy off the Crag, but the defenders fought back with counterattacks of their own, so the battle continued to rage back and forth and the wounded continued to be brought back to our makeshift hospital there on the ground.

We had been working there on the wounded for some time when something from the sounds of the battle, perhaps a lessening of fire from the enemy positions, caught my attention. I heard Lt. McVeigh call to the 2nd Platoon and saw Marines rise up from their positions around me and start to move swiftly toward the crest of the mountain. I had just finished binding the wound of a Marine, and when I saw my platoon moving out I grabbed my aid kit and my carbine and jumped in behind a troop of yelling 2nd Platoon Marines and we were headed for the mountaintop.

I leaped across a trench and had not taken ten steps when it hit. There was a sudden black flash above us. My head and chest were crushed with the pressure and in an instant I knew I was dead.

When I came to my senses I was on my hands and knees looking back to the spot where I'd been running. My eyes burned, my head ached and my mouth and nose were filled with the acrid sting of cordite. I examined myself quickly and could find no wounds.

"They have us zeroed in!" flashed through my mind. Gripped with panic, I jumped to my feet and started to run back to the trench. Then I heard them, voices coming from several directions.

"Corpsman! Corpsman!"

"Help me, Doc . . . Oh please God, help me . . . SOMEBODY HELP ME!"

I turned around and moved back to the area where that powerful artillery shell had burst in the air and there I saw something lying on the ground, dark and gray and almost indistinguishable from the earth around it. I moved closer to examine it and discovered it was a human, or what was left of a human. It was a Marine lying on his back. Both legs were gone and there was a foot in a shoe nearby standing upright. His left arm was gone except for a string of skin about two inches wide still connected to a hand lying there on the ground. I couldn't identify this human torso because his face was black from the blast, but I wanted to know who this dead Marine was so I bent over to get a good look, and when I did the name escaped unconsciously from my mouth.

"Putnam!"

When I said his name, two bright blue eyes shot open, the whites of those eyes in stark contrast with his powder-blackened face. I was stunned. How could he possibly be alive?

"Putnam, this is Doc. How you doin'?"

"OK . . . I think I'll be OK." Then he turned his head to the left and reached across with his one remaining limb and picked up his left hand lying there on the ground, and with the strip of skin dangling crazily, he placed the hand gently, palm down on his chest. For the first time since I had been in Korea I felt I was confronted with a situation I could not handle. I kept thinking, "Putnam, you ought to be dead! Why aren't you dead?"

Both legs were gone close to the hips; just covering those wounds with battle dressings would be extremely difficult. And there was the missing arm as well as the possibility that there were other wounds on his body. Strangely there was little blood.

I began scratching through my bag for my largest battle dressings when I saw the 1ˢᵗ Platoon corpsman going by, so I yelled at him and asked for his help. He joined me and before long we managed to get bandages on Sergeant Putnam's stumps and give him a shot of morphine then load him on to a stretcher for the trip down the mountain.

There were still calls for help coming from scattered spots around the area. I heard someone calling from down the eastern slope, and when I went searching for the voice I saw a helmet with the green camouflage cover sticking out of a shallow shell hole. I dropped into the hole and found myself face to face with Smitty. He was sitting up holding his knee and rocking gently back and forth. The kneecap was gone and jagged white bones protruded from the gray flesh.

"Smitty?"

"I'm hurt, Doc!" There was fear in his voice.

"You'll be OK, "I said. I cut his trousers away and soon had his knee securely bound with a battle dressing.

"My back, too. I think I'm hit back there."

"Let's take a look."

I cut his shirt away and found a shallow three-inch wound high up on his back. "You got a flesh wound here but you'll be all right. I bandaged the wound as well as I could, talking all the while.

"I still feel it, on farther down." I could tell from his voice that he was in considerable pain. I tore his shirt on down and exposed a large gaping hole at his waist. Blood and water oozed from the wound, and without realizing it I suddenly stopped talking.

"What is it, Doc? What is it?"

"You got another place down here, but it's not bad. You'll be all right." I lied.

"Am I going to be all right?"

"Sure, sure! You got a good ticket out of here, back to Japan or maybe even the states!"

After I had his wounds bandaged, I removed his helmet and leaned him back against the side of the hole and looked at him. His skin was the color of ashes and his breathing was shallow and dry. He was still in considerable pain so I gave him a shot of morphine.

"Am I going to die, Doc?'

"No! Hell no, Smitty! You got a ticket out of here that's all. Here . . ." I'd fished his New Testament out of his pack and handed it to him. "I'll get some guys here with a stretcher to take you out of here. Just hold on."

When I left Smitty he was leaning back against the beveled wall of the shell hole; the look of worry and pain on his face was beginning to relax some from loss of blood and the morphine. His eyes were half closed and the New Testament had slipped from his hand and was lying on his chest.

One of the other 2nd Platoon Marines who had been calling out for help was PFC Pless. That same artillery shell had taken his arm off halfway between the elbow and the shoulder, and while I was tied up with Putnam and Smitty, the 3rd Platoon corpsman tended to Pless and got him bandaged and moving down the mountain with the rest of the wounded.

By the time we got these latest wounded tended to the 1st Platoon had carried the fight further north on the ridgeline pushing those last stubborn defenders back, and we would discover the following morning when we sent out a patrol that they had abandoned the Crag during the night.

* * *

After the frenzy of the battle had died down on that afternoon of May 31, 1951, we surveyed the scene and saw that the little strip of ground we had fought for was devastated. It looked like the surface of the moon, barren and pock marked, nothing remaining but shattered trees, splintered stone, and brittle dust.

Some of the Marines now moved forward to check out the trenches and bunkers the enemy had used in the defense of this mountain, tallying enemy dead and making sure the Crag had been secured.

A semblance of order was soon restored to the mountain. Platoon leaders called muster and counted heads to determine our losses. *Cargadores* and Marines were getting the last of the wounded down the mountain while we continued to receive ammunition and supplies from the battalion HQ behind us in the valley.

We had eaten nothing since our light snack that morning, so after we had things reasonably squared away some of us built fires and began to heat up C Rations. Men gathered in clusters around the fires and began to recount details of the battle. Conversations were subdued at first but soon grew more animated. As we exchanged our accounts of the battle we found again what we already knew—that each man has his own perspective, his own unique experiences in a firefight. There is no single, unified point of view that can convey the story of a battle because of all the chaos and emotionally charged confusion. If there are two hundred fifty men in the fight there will be two hundred fifty stories, each of which, in spite of seeming conflicts with other accounts, can well be true.

We in the 2nd Platoon were focused on our losses; of particular concern were the conditions of Smitty and Putnam. We later learned that both died on the way to the battalion aid station. Paul Perras and Ed Parungo, Marines who helped carry Sergeant Putnam down the mountain, later recalled that one of the men carrying the stretcher looked at the terribly wounded Marine and asked, "Is he alive?"

Sergeant Putnam replied, "I'm not dead yet."

But he was dead before they reached the bottom of the mountain.

We had not noticed, but while we were battling for the Crag, the clouds had dispersed and the sun had come out, and that May 31st had turned into a beautiful spring day.

After finishing our C Rations, George Brodeur, I and some other Marines descended the reverse slope of the mountain to a point from which we could see some four hundred yards to the east. Marines from the 2nd Battalion who were battling to take the high ground there had called for air support. We watched as a quartet of FU4 Corsairs from the Marine Air Wing approached the mountain from the south. We could see on the ridgeline the Marines' brightly colored air panels laid out on the ground to mark their location.

When the Corsairs reached the mountain they peeled off and one by one swooped down to release their napalm bombs, those wing tanks filled with jellied gasoline. We watched the bombs tumble end over end and smear crimson and orange curling flames along the ridgelines north of the air panels sending up curtains of black smoke. After they had released all their napalm, they began strafing runs. One of the guys sitting there with us suddenly blurted out, "Hey, that plane's strafing the Marines."

We looked, and it sure appeared that one of the planes started strafing on the wrong side of the air panels, which meant he would have been strafing the Marines.

I never did hear if the 2nd Battalion Marines suffered casualties from that strafing run, but I did learn much later that the artillery round that got Smitty and Putnam and Pless and a number of others was a 155 mm "short round" from our own artillery. Those men were all victims of "friendly fire," a tragic but all too common occurrence in warfare.

We also learned later that the gunfire we heard behind us after we had passed the houses and caves at the base of the mountain before we began our ascent came from Shexnayder. He had fired into one of the caves when he saw movement only to discover that what he saw was an old woman trying to hide from the battle. Accidentally killing our own people or innocent civilians was a routine thing. Such incidents in war are not the exception but the rule. We try to make these horrors more palatable by referring to them euphemistically as "collateral damage."

Sitting there on the southern slope of the Crag we could see clearly our battalion command post in the valley below and the battalion aid station, all of which had been set up that day while we were engaged in the battle for the Crag. Their presence there in those tents reflected their confidence that we would be successful in taking our objective. And it was from those positions that they had been able to support us, keep us supplied, and help us evacuate and take care of our wounded. And now from our balcony seats we were watching their activities—trucks moving back and forth over the roads and men moving busily around the tent areas.

While we were thus engaged, we heard the roar of planes close overhead. When we looked up we saw skimming the treetops over the Crag behind us three Corsairs headed south. Smoke was pouring from the cowl of the center plane; the other two on his wingtips were apparently providing their buddy an escort. They had no doubt seen our air panels and knew they had made it back to friendly territory. As they passed over our heads toward the valley, the two wingmen peeled off to left and right and left the burning plane on a trajectory over the battalion CP area. At once that pilot dropped his bombs over an open field, turned his plane upside down with the canopy open and came tumbling out. His parachute quickly opened and he began to float slowly to the ground while his plane continued upside down and crashed at the base of a mountain on the far side of the valley in a big ball of flame.

We had a bird's eye view of the entire drama. As the Marine pilot was floating down to the valley floor, we could see corpsmen running out of the aid station tents and jumping into a cracker box ambulance and a jeep and heading out to meet the pilot as he came down. We saw the dust from the vehicles as they sped to the spot of rescue, and saw that the corpsmen were there to meet him when he hit the ground. The lucky pilot would surely never forget that day. Those pilots looked out for one another.

\* \* \*

Just six months earlier the first African American aviator in the U.S. Navy, Ensign Jesse Brown, was hit by ground fire on a mission near the Chosin Reservoir and was forced to ditch his Corsair in the snow. When his plane hit the ground it struck some hidden obstacle and the engine went flying and the fuselage crumpled from the impact. Two of his wing mates, Lt. William Koenig and Lt. (JG) William Hudner, circled low above him believing Ensign Brown could not have survived the crash, but as they flew over they saw him push his canopy back and release his parachute. At that time Hudner decided he would attempt a wheels up landing beside Brown to render aid.

It was a rough landing jarring and bruising Hudner, but he quickly made it to the other smoking aircraft where he discovered Brown's legs were pinned tight under the instrument panel and that, though conscious and talking, he was probably suffering from internal injuries as well. Hudner had earlier called for a helicopter, and after trying unsuccessfully to free Brown's legs he ran back to his plane and radioed for the chopper to bring an axe and a fire extinguisher. When the chopper arrived the two men now continued to struggle to free Brown, but the axe was useless against the metal that had him trapped. It was bitterly cold, the sun was going down, and the helicopter pilot said he could not fly after dark. So Hudner told Brown they were going back for more help.

Brown had told Hudner earlier that if he didn't make it to tell his wife he loved her. Before the helicopter took off, Hudner had to go back one more time to check on Brown and found him unconscious. Hudner said later, "'I spoke to him anyway, in case he could hear me. I told him we would be back. There was no response. He may have been dead at that time. I like to think he was. If I got any satisfaction out of any of this, it was that we had remained with him until the end'" (Russ, 345).

\* \* \*

Smitty was dead, but I was not with him at the end. For three months we had been tent-mates, had shared the few things we possessed, and had worked together to make it through some hard days. Over that time I had learned to admire his good humor, kindness, and integrity. Even though he had refused to fire his weapon in combat, he never shrank from danger and the whole platoon respected and liked him. As I noted before, he was a natural Christian in the best sense of that word, not dogmatic or self-righteous, but caring and unselfish. He was caught up in a war, but hurting other people was just not in his nature.

For several months How Company had been lucky. Other units had been hit harder, like the Army support force that was decimated in Massacre Valley, and Able and Baker Companies, the ones we relieved that day the Corsair almost got us. On this last day of May we learned once more that it's when your own platoon, your own company, gets hit hard that it hurts the most.

There seems to be some kind of law like Newton's law of gravity that says the power of tragedy to affect us is directly proportional to its magnitude and inversely proportional to its distance from us. When comrades like Smitty and Sergeant Putnam are blown apart we are traumatized and haunted by the experience the rest of our lives. When we learn of KIAs and WIAs in other companies in our battalion it grabs our attention and provokes our compassion and concern but that news has less impact. The farther away the tragedy the less effect it has on us.

A tsunami in the Indian Ocean captured the attention of the world because of its magnitude, 250,000 dead, and because of extensive media coverage. A recent earthquake in Haiti killed 230,000 leaving horrible devastation and disease in its wake. Even though the death toll was much lighter, Hurricane Katrina hit us harder because of its closeness; we were the victims. But as a rule we can read of catastrophes in other countries while having our morning coffee: 30,000 people dead in an earthquake in Iran. We think it unfortunate, though we may not be touched much on an emotional level. One gets used to such stories—wars, pestilence, natural and human disasters. We read about them along with the sports scores. These things seem to happen a long way off–the farther away, the less our concern. What do we care if entire solar systems are sucked into black holes on the far side of the universe?

There is probably a rational explanation for our callousness when it comes to distant calamities. How much tragedy can the human spirit stand? How much empathy can we feel before we ourselves are pulled into the black hole of despair?

Combat is no place for tender hearts. While we cared for our comrades, we didn't dwell long on our losses. We moved on. I never shed a tear for a lost comrade while I was in Korea. I didn't know anyone who did. We cared, but we had the next battle to deal with, the next day to get through. Often it is not until years later with the perspective of time and the advantage of maturity that the realization of the prices paid, the lives cut short, fully sinks in and touches the veteran's heart. That's when the tears come.

How Company's losses for this day were considerable. The Official 3rd Battalion Diary for this day reads:

> 31 May: 3/7 attacked to seize and occupy hill 483 and high ground at TA 1317M with "H" in the assault supported by tanks, artillery, air and mortars. Received intense enemy smallarms, automatic weapons, mortar and artillery fire throughout the attack. After five hours of engagement with an estimated enemy battalion "H" secured hill 483 but was unable to take the high ground at TA1317M. During the consolidation phase of 3/7 on hill 483, "H" received a strong and determined enemy counter attack which was supported by enemy mortar and artillery fire. "H" repelled counter attack and 3/7 continued to consolidate defensive positions vicinity TA1317. Throughout the period 3/7 inflicted an estimated 450 casualties and captured 2 prisoners of war while suffering 2 Marines killed in action and 55 Marines wounded in action.

According to the official roster of How Company for May 31 1951 there were two hundred forty two Marines and three Corpsmen. Those fifty-seven casualties meant that almost one in four in the company suffered wounds that day. The battalion diaries list only two KIAs, Smitty and Putnam, but according to Lt. Barnes PFC Ted Hatfield also died on the Crag. His name was dropped from the June roster so the battalion diaries it seems don't always tell the whole story.

\* \* \*

By taking the Crag How Company had helped open the gateway to Yanggu, and now the war was about to change. My duties in the war were about to change as well.

*George Brodeur*        *Doc Hughes*

*Ralph Tate*

*Third Squad Second Platoon of How Company*

*Sgt Noreiga with Swanson taking aim*

*John Tarver and Bryan Berryman*

*Bookie Turner and Ralph Tate with KMC Friends*

# CHAPTER 14

# Reserve

Two days after the battle for the Crag, the 1st Regiment relieved the 7th Regiment, giving us a chance to replenish our depleted ranks. The town of Yanggu was now ours so the 7th Regiment took respite near there while the other two regiments of the 1st Marine Division took the battle to the enemy north of the town. This break from the action proved to be a time of change for How Company. Not only did we require replacements for the fifty-seven men we had lost on the Crag, but we lost our Skipper as well.

Captain Hoey, because of his angry and profanity-laced dispute with Colonel Kelly over tactics and the artillery coverage up on the Crag, was relieved of his command and replaced by an ex-flyboy, Captain Reed King. The Skipper's firing came as a blow to the whole company. One thing we all knew about Captain Hoey was that above all he cared about his company–he cared about his men. I guess it was a professional weakness on his part that he wasn't concerned enough about his relationships with the brass above him.

I remember once when we stood a regimental inspection by a brigadier general at Hongchon, he told us: "If the general comes before you and asks you a question, by God, stand straight, look him in the eye, and answer him forcefully. After what you guys have been through you don't need to be shy about addressing anyone."

In caring for his men Captain Hoey had something in common with Chesty Puller, the Marine Corps legend whose main concern was also the men who served under him, the man who once said, don't give Marines mom's apple pie and ice cream, give them beer.

If Captain Hoey had had the resources, he would have supplied the entire company with beer and booze and all the ingredients of a grand fare-well party, just as he had done for the platoon leaders and squad leaders back at Pohang-Dong after the Gook Chase when the party was broken up by "Sergeant Ralph," that Luger-toting Chosin Reservoir veteran who tossed the grenade outside the tent and put an end to the revelry and to his own military career.

As it was, the Skipper did come by and say farewell to all of us in the company that he had led so well over the past five months. He warmly thanked us all for our service to the company and to our country during the time we had served under his command. He praised us all highly and showed no bitterness about the circumstances under which he had been relieved of his command. The bond between Captain Hoey and How Company was unusually strong, and the men who served under the Skipper returned his loyalty and affection in equal measure. He was one of those heroes who, rather than go down with medals on his chest, would perhaps go down with a blot on his record. But he was a hero nevertheless.

I don't know why, but I never wrote home and told my folks about Smitty's death. I suppose it was because Mother knew he was my foxhole buddy and that I was afraid it might make her worry more. But as I look back through those letters she carefully preserved I find I rarely mentioned our casualties, I suppose for the same reason.

\* \* \*

Now, finally, after our battle for the Crag and after sixty-one days on the line, we got a break. Along with temporary relief from combat we also got a break in the weather and a chance to look around at the country now decked out in the greenery of late spring.

After climbing those mountains all winter, not to mention getting shot at on a regular basis, most of us had had enough of Korea. But when spring came to the countryside it was impossible not to be captured by the beauty of that land. On one occasion it even jarred me out of my usual prosaic letter writing style when I wrote home on May 13:

> We were coming off the mountain just before we came here and we came through one of the most beautiful places I've ever seen. On both sides of us were rock cliffs all covered with purple, white, pink and all colors of blossoms. The grass and undergrowth were all green and the green trees hung over a clear cold stream that ran through big white rocks, and boy the smell! It was wonderful. The birds were singing & the sun was shining and I didn't have a care in the world. You'd better watch me. I'm liable to settle down over here.

At that time by most standards of measurement Korea was a desperately poor country. In my eight and a half months there I never slept in a building, and the only ones I ever entered were thatch-roofed village houses. I know there were wooden buildings with tile roofs in towns like Hongchon and Chunchon, but mostly we circled those towns staying in the high ground, and I never made it to Seoul. Outside of Pusan I don't remember ever seeing a paved road. But the wealth the country did possess at that time became evident with the coming of spring. It was easy to see why Koreans chose to be buried on hillsides and why they called their country the Land of the Morning Calm.

Poor though they may have been in material wealth, the Korean people were rich in ancient history and culture. The symbol of the country was the tiger; some maps even show the peninsula in the form of a tiger. Like many cultures, the Koreans have their own genesis mythology and the tiger is part of that mythology. The story of how that came to be, in an abbreviated form, is as follows:

Long ago when the earth and the heavens were one and animals could speak like humans, Hwan-in, the god king of the eastern heavens, sent his son, Hwan-ung to earth in the eastern land and told him to build a country there. Hwan-ung brought three spirits with him to earth—the teacher, the general, and the governor. He also brought three thousand souls to establish a new race of people in this new country. He gathered those souls together in the shade of an ancient birch tree on the slope of T'aebaek-san, a rugged 9,100 ft mountain in North Korea, and there began a new nation. The capital of that new country was called Shinshi, the "divine city."

In a cave not far from Shinshi lived a bear and a great Siberian tiger. These animals had been watching this new settlement and saw how happy the humans were, living under the wise rule of Hwan-ung, and one day while they were out lying in the grass the bear said, "wouldn't it be wonderful if we could live like Men!"

The tiger shared the bear's longing to be human, so they both decided to go to Shinshi and express their desire to Hwan-ung. They traveled to the divine city and requested an audience with the wise ruler, and when they were admitted to his presence they asked their question.

"Hwan-ung, we would like to become men. Is there any way you could help us?"

Hwan-ung told them there was a way but warned them it was very difficult. But the desire of the two animals was very strong and they said they would undertake any challenge to become human. So the task they were given was to go to the cave and live in the dark for one hundred days and eat nothing but twenty garlic cloves and a bundle of mugwort.

Because of their strong desire to become human, the tiger and the bear eagerly accepted this challenge and returned to the cave and began their trial. But after twenty days the tiger became hungry and restless and told the bear that if he stayed in the cave he would starve to death and would never become human, so the tiger abandoned his challenge and returned to the mountains to search for food. From that point on he became fierce and was thereafter looked upon as the enemy of man.

But the bear, perhaps because he knew how to hibernate, managed to stay in darkness for the one hundred days. When that time was up the bear moved out into the sunlight, and an amazing transformation had occurred. There was no longer a bear, but in its place was a beautiful young woman standing there in the fresh breeze of the mountains. When she realized that her wish had been fulfilled she headed straight to Shinshi to express her gratitude to Hwan-ung.

The great leader was struck by the beauty of the girl and gave her the name Ung-yo which meant the "girl incarnated from a bear." The beauty of Ung-yo grew with each passing day until at last Hwan-ung asked her to be his wife. Not long after their marriage Ung-yo gave birth to a boy child under a birch tree on the slopes of T'aebaek-san. The boy was named Tan'gun, or lord of the birch trees.

After Hwan-ung went back into heaven, Tan'gun became the father of Korea, or "Choson," which means, "Land of the Morning Calm," or "Land of the Dawn," or "Land of the Morning Freshness."

Tan'gun ruled wisely for ninety-nine years, and then in the last year of his rule an old tiger came to him and lamented the fact that his father had failed his test to become human so many years ago and confided that this failure had caused them both great sorrow. The old tiger asked the great leader, "Must all tigers live always in shame because of my father's impatience?"

Tan'gun replied that the tiger had one last chance to redeem himself and change his fate, but that now the challenge would be even more demanding than that presented to his father. "If you succeed," he said, "you will enjoy all those pleasures of human existence—you will experience the love of family, the pleasures of good food, and all the sights and smells of the beautiful country of Choson, the great feeling of attaining an ambition, realizing a dream."

"But those pleasures," he added, "do not come without a price. You will also know the sorrows of being human. You will suffer the hardships and hunger and cruelty that humans can inflict on one another. You will experience the pain and despair that is the lot of human creatures, and, in short, you will live the long history of my people."

Tan'gun told the tiger that the time was coming when men and animals would no longer be able to talk together. Stroking the tiger's neck he told him that he could give him the power to become human, but only for short periods of time. Then he said to the tiger,

> "You shall not grow older and you will not die. You shall see and experience and remember all that your father will never know. If you accept this task, there will be no turning back... The powers I give you shall be yours until Choson becomes a sovereign kingdom and its people become masters of their own destiny. When they achieve their goal my old friend, you shall

achieve yours...." Spreading his arms outward toward the valleys below, he added, "All they need is here."

Tan'gun gave him his name, the Tiger of Shinshi, and set forth the tasks he has been fulfilling for more than three thousand years....

He is the Tiger of Shinshi, the Warden of Three Thousand Li, Defender of Choson, and Guardian of the Golden Thread. He is the strength and cunning the Korean people have used to defend their homeland. He protects and keeps alive the long and ancient history of Korea and his teachings pass the legacy to each new generation. He is the comforter who brings peace to the spirits of Korea's ancestors and who safeguards and protects the Golden Thread, that which ties and binds the Korean people together throughout time, a thread that must never be broken. (www.koreanhistoryproject.org/Ket/Essays/C01/E0000.html )

So the tiger came to symbolize the Korean people and their country, Choson, the Land of the Morning Calm.

\* \* \*

We Marines in the 2$^{nd}$ Platoon didn't know this story back in the spring of 1951; we just knew the land was beautiful and that we were at last going to get a break. We were going into reserve for two weeks, two whole weeks!

Although at this time I wrote home that How Company had spent sixty-one days on the line, we were rotated off that point duty in the Marine pattern of threes—two companies forward with one in reserve, two battalions forward with one in reserve, and now and then two regiments forward with one in reserve. As noted before there were several reasons for this pattern, most having to do with military readiness, but one of them was humanitarian.

In those days the Marine Corps had no R&R, "rest and recuperation," a program designed to give fighting men an opportunity to return to civilization for a break, perhaps to Japan for a couple of weeks. If there was such a program I never knew of it. We had only heard the term; some guys jokingly referred to it as "I&I" for "intercourse and intoxication." I never personally knew of any Marine receiving such a benefaction. In How Company we had to follow the standard Marine Corps practice and improvise. We had to come up with our own R&R, and the only times we could do that was when we were pulled off the line to go in reserve.

Of course even in reserve we would still have combat training and inspections, but we got to sleep in pyramidal tents and eat hot chow. We would also have some free time to see outdoor movies at night on makeshift screens, to play games and visit friends in other units. And there were a number of talented Marines like Joe Rousseau and others who could sing and play musical instruments and even do stand up comedy. So those few breaks in reserve meant a lot to us. The ones I remember most were the ones after the coming of spring, after the weather warmed up.

On this particular occasion Shexnayder, Hawkshaw, CP and I and about five other Marines settled in to our spacious tent furnished with that great luxury, folding cots. After running ridgelines for a couple of months and sleeping on the ground these accommodations were great luxuries, like the Waldorf Astoria.

Even though we now were served hot meals we still spent time scrounging for food and scuttlebutt. One of the men knew a mess sergeant and was able to come away with some cans of peaches and pears. He was more generous with his buddies than the other Marine had been with the can of peanut butter. Of course that guy had a particular weakness in that case, which he may have cured with his peanut butter orgy.

Most of the food we received, even our hot meals, came out of cans. The camp cooks just had bigger cans with a different selection on the menu, so we welcomed the change. They did get a few foods like potatoes with a fairly long shelf life, but fresh food was a rarity for rifle companies in Korea. That's why we took special notice when CP came in one day eating a handful of fresh berries.

"Hey, What are you eating?" Shexnayder asked him.

"Berries."

"Hell, I can see that! What kind of berries? Where'd you get 'em?"

"Off a tree on that road down by the river."

"Those are mulberries," I said. "Are there many of them down there?"

"A whole tree full."

Shexnayder stood lost in thought for a minute or two and then he said, "Hey, you know what we can do with those berries?" And then he answered his own question. "We can make us some wine."

"How do you make wine?" I asked. "Doesn't it take a long time?"

"We got two weeks," Shexnayder said.

"That's not very long to age wine," someone else threw in.

"Maybe we can do something to hurry it up," Hawkshaw said. "I might be able to get some yeast from my mess sergeant friend and I'll ask him if he knows of any other ingredients we can add."

Shexnayder took charge: "OK, here's what we got to do. CP you go see if you can scrounge up one of those big water cans. Hawkshaw, you go to that mess sergeant and get that yeast and sugar and any other ingredients that might hurry up the process, Doc, you got that new t shirt over there on your bunk, let's use that to gather the berries. Take the covers off your helmets and bring those helmets along. Let's get to work."

We were all ready to follow Shexnayder's directions. Since he was from New Orleans, we figured he was the closest thing we had to an authority in the field of wine making.

This turned out to be one of the most efficient and eager work details I ever served on in my four years in the military. We found that mulberry tree and it really was loaded down with fruit. We used our helmets as buckets and gathered a lot of berries, maybe two or three gallons. Then we took them down to the river and washed them and carried them back to our tent. CP returned with the big water can and after a while Hawkshaw showed up with a bag of sugar, a can of powdered yeast and a brown sack full of potatoes.

"What the hell you going to do with those potatoes?" CP asked.

"Cookie said they might add to the fermentation process," Hawkshaw explained. "What do you think, Shex?"

"Hell, yeah. We'll throw 'em in."

So we set to work. We tied off one end of the tee shirt and poured a helmet full of berries in it, then placed the shirt back in the helmet and began to try to press the juice out of it. It was tough going at first, but then someone came up with a big smooth river rock about the size of a coconut. We began to use that rock and helmet like a mortar and pestle, and before long we were getting a fair amount of juice which we poured into the water can. Hawkshaw in the meantime had taken his bayonet and sliced up the potatoes and had them in a helmet. We repeated the process with the helmet and the rock until we had gone through all the mulberries and were left with a pile of potatoes and a pile of berry mash.

"What do we do with these?" Someone asked Shexnayder.

"Dump 'em in. We're going to have to strain the stuff when it's ready anyway, so just dump it all in. Give me that yeast, Hawkshaw." Shexnayder opened the can with his handy dandy and poured a generous amount into the water can with the other ingredients.

"Now all we need to add is some water," so Shexnayder grabbed the full can of water we kept there in our tent and added probably a couple of gallons of water into the mix, then he swished it around a while and set it down.

"One more thing."

"What's that?"

"We need to dig a hole. Wine has to age underground. Also we don't need for the word to get around about this or somebody's liable to make off with it, so that'll be a way to hide it. We'll need to dig the hole here in the tent."

Digging holes was something we had become very proficient at, so it didn't take us long to have a hole deep enough to set the can in, and then someone came up with a piece of plywood that made an excellent cover for the hole. When we had everything in place Shexnayder set his pack on top of the plywood and our project was safely concealed and the aging process had begun. Now we could turn our attention to other things.

Since we were camped in the valley of the Pukhan-gang River, one of the things we did was take the opportunity to go swimming. The water was shallow in many places, but we followed the river down stream until we came to a fairly deep hole. Several of us stripped down and gingerly stepped out into the cold water, but after a few gasps and a little splashing around we got used to it and proceeded to swim and horse around, trying to duck one another and just having a good time. I had dived down and was swimming under water when I heard a loud, "Crack!"

I immediately surfaced and called out to the other guys, "What was that?"

They said they had heard it too and it sounded like it came from somewhere down stream. Then we heard another loud, "Thwump!" And a few minutes later another, and then another.

"We need to check that out," someone said, so we went to the bank, dried off and dressed and started walking downstream toward the sounds of the explosions. We didn't have our weapons with us since we were in a secure area; we didn't feel threatened, only curious.

When we rounded a bend in the river we saw two ROK soldiers up on a high embankment standing by a wooden box. Down below them was a bare-chested companion in rolled up pants standing knee deep in the river. As we approached we could see they had a wooden box of hand grenades, and what they were doing was pulling the pins and tossing them into the river. They were fishing with the hand grenades. Whenever a fish would float to the surface after an explosion, the guy in the shorts would wade out or swim out to retrieve it. There were only three or four fish lying on the bank, so that was a pretty expensive way to fish. We exchanged bilingual pleasantries with them for a while then returned to our camp.

Korea is rich in history and culture and it is also blessed with a wide variety of wildlife. There really were tigers back in the days of Old Choson and possibly up to the time of the Japanese occupation. There were bear and deer when I was there, although I don't remember ever seeing any, even on the "deer hunt" I took back in Masan when I ended up playing with the kids on the frozen pond.

Some wildlife I do remember, though. Once when a mortar shell landed nearby I saw a fox run out from under a burned-out tank and take off across a field. Another time we were spread out in a skirmish line moving up a slope expecting to encounter enemy resistance when a brace of ring-necked pheasants exploded right in front of me and went flying on up the hill. Needless to say that scared the hell out of me.

One denizen of the Korean mountains that was always near but never visible was the cuckoo. I know they are native to the USA as well, but I don't believe I've ever heard one here.

But over there while sitting around our campfires in the afternoons and evenings the plaintive cries of the cuckoo would often come wafting up to us from the ravines below and keep us company.

I had no trouble identifying the cuckoo because of its distinctive call. But when I wrote home about the beautiful spot I had seen between the two cliffs where the cold stream splashed through big white rocks, I only mentioned the blossoms of all colors and the wonderful smell. I probably could not have identified any of those flowers and few of the trees.

This brings up a thought. When we are young our senses are clear, we see, smell, and hear things vividly and intensely. No need for bifocals or hearing aids (although many of us lost some of our hearing while we were in Korea). Young people see surfaces brightly and older people generally see things in a little more depth. The reasons for this are that our senses become duller as we age while our knowledge grows. If we are paying attention as we go through life we learn the names of things, we learn to discriminate. We may not see as sharply as young people do but we understand more.

My Daddy once said of a man, "he sees the light through a tiny hole." I guess that describes us all, but of course the holes for some are larger than the holes for others. There are different levels of consciousness and awareness among species as there are among individuals in the human race. Is there a pinpoint of light for insects?

Among humans the largest apertures must be for geniuses like Shakespeare and Einstein. I guess the goal for the rest of us should be to try and expand our peepholes. And who knows? Maybe from time to time a beam of light will flash through and enable us to see more deeply into things than we ever thought we could.

Putting names on things is important. Think about the story of Adam and the animals. Before God brought the animals for Adam to name all he could see was "animals." "Hey, Eve, look at all those animals running around out there!" But when God paraded them in front of him and Adam gave each one a name, then he could actually see them, he could discriminate among them. "That's a giraffe! That's a hippopotamus! That's a ringed tail cat!" He named them all from aardvark to zebra. What a wonderful power, the naming of things! I don't suppose it mattered much to the animals what Adam called them, but it made a whole lot of difference for us human beings. God may have created the big world from nothing, but we create our own small worlds with language.

I could enjoy the beauty of the flowers I described to my folks, but I couldn't distinguish among them. Like Adam and the animals, to me they were all just "blossoms." It may seem strange, but we can't really "see" things until we can put names on them. The military understands this principle very well, but the beauties of nature are not the focus of military nomenclature. Henry Reed, a British poet and soldier in World War II, wrote a series of poems called *Lessons of War,* and in the following poem from that series he illustrates the point while he captures the cadences of military instruction:

### Naming of Parts

To-day we have naming of parts. Yesterday
We had daily cleaning. And to-morrow morning,
We shall have what to do after firing. But to-day,
To-day we have naming of parts. Japonica
Glistens like coral in all the neighboring gardens,
    And to-day we have naming of parts.

This is the lower sling swivel. And this
Is the upper sling swivel, whose use you will see,
When you are given your slings. And this is the piling
    swivel,
Which in your case you have not got. The branches
Hold the gardens in their silent, eloquent gestures,
    Which in our case we have not got.

This is the safety-catch, which is always released
With an easy flick of the thumb. And please do not let me
See anyone using his finger. You can do it quite easy
If you have any strength in your thumb. The blossoms
Are fragile and motionless, never letting anyone see
    Any of them using their finger.

And this you can see is the bolt. The purpose of this
Is to open the breech, as you see. We can slide it
Rapidly backwards and forwards
The early bees are assaulting and fumbling the flowers
    They call it easing the spring.

They call it easing the spring: It is perfectly easy
If you have any strength in your thumb: like the bolt,
And the breech, and the cocking-piece, and the point of
    balance,
Which in our case we have not got; and the almond-blossom
Silent in all of the gardens and the bees going backwards
and forwards,
    For to-day we have naming of parts.

I didn't know then that the Korean national flower was the Rose of Sharon. Of course they don't use that Judeo-Christian name; to them it is "*Mugunghwa.*" We also know the flower by the name althea, or hibiscus. There are many varieties growing wild in Korea and it is so important to them that it is mentioned in their national anthem.

\* \* \*

But there in reserve we in the 2nd Platoon had other things on our minds besides nature studies. We came in that evening after the swim and someone asked, "How's that wine doing?"

We went over and moved Shexnayder's pack and bent down and listened.

"Hey, I can hear it. Do you hear it?"

"Yeah, it's working. We're going to have us some fine vintage!"

"Don't think it'll explode, do you?"

"Nah! We'll crack the lid in a day or two and let out the steam."

The next day Hawkshaw and I heard there was an army medical unit down the road a couple of miles that was going to have a good movie that night so we decided to hike down there and take it in. After we had walked a mile or so an army jeep with two guys in it pulled along side us on the road and one of them jumped out with a 45 in his hand.

"Hey, what's up?" we asked.

"Who are you guys?" he wanted to know.

"We're Marines from down the road. Heard there was a movie, thought we would check it out."

"OK, no problem. Jump in we'll give you a ride."

"What's the deal with the 45?" I asked.

"Oh, there's been some Chinks infiltrated into this area. We've got to stay on high alert. Some were spotted a mile or so to the west a couple of nights ago."

The two of them entertained us all the way into the army medical encampment with scary war stories.

After they let us out, Hawkshaw said, "I don't know what they'd do if they met any Chinese with that 45. Throw it at them I guess."

"Yeah," I said. "Here they are ten miles behind the front lines and they have all these dramatic stories. These are the very kind of rear echelon types that will go back home and entertain the ladies with their heroic tales."

The movie was entitled *The Thing!* starring James Arness, later the star of the TV series "Gunsmoke." But here he played an astronaut or pilot who crashed into a bog and mutated into a monster, some kind of vegetative hulk. We didn't get a lot out of it and later returned to our camp up the road lit only by moonlight.

The next day we were going to have a "Smoker," or what some of the guys referred to as "organized grab ass." This was a program where we entertained ourselves with music, recitations, softball and boxing matches. We were the audience and we were the entertainers. I only knew three chords on the guitar, but I had done a little boxing in high school and used to hang out at the YMCA and workout on the speed bags and heavy bags and sometimes spar a few rounds with local guys, so I volunteered to box three rounds.

Gunny Spell was the organizer of the event for How Company. I gave him my name for boxing and he matched me up with a corpsman from another platoon, Bill "Doc" Holliday. Holliday was my size, about 150 pounds, so I felt pretty good about that. I figured I could take him. But there were some big guys in the company with real boxing experience, so we looked forward to some good bouts.

It was about this time we got our first beer ration. I got a can of Carling Black Label and a can of Blatz. I decided I wanted to get away by myself on that beautiful spring day and enjoy my beer. I knew just the place to go. I had seen it about a half-mile from where we were camped when we were on the way to see the movie. We had come upon three houses against the base of a hill with a stream flowing between them. We followed the stream a way and discovered it started as a spring flowing from a long vertical crevice in a stone face of the hill then spilled onto a large fairly flat rock surface where, before making its way on to the river, it filled a basin about the size of a bushel basket which natives in years past had carved into the rock. We had gotten ourselves a drink there so I knew the water was ice cold. I found the spring and dropped my two cans into the cold mossy water then lay back against the slope of the mountain and just kind of melted into the grass. What a day!

While I was lying there soaking in that vibrant Korean spring weather I got to thinking about the first beer I ever had when I was stationed at Mare Island Naval Hospital in Vallejo, California. I could have been still seventeen or maybe just barely eighteen when I walked self-consciously into a bar on the main drag of that sailors' town and took a seat on a barstool. I tried to act self-assured, like this was a routine thing for me. I had seen George Raft and Humphrey Bogart movies and had an idea how this was supposed to be done. But when I looked across the bar into the mirror behind that assorted row of liquor bottles with the little pour caps I could easily see I didn't look like Humphrey Bogart. Even in my Navy uniform with my white hat pushed back on my head I still looked like a kid. But I was determined to see this through.

After attending to a couple of other guys down at the other end of the bar, the bartender came back my way and said, "What'll it be?"

"Schlitz. Give me a Schlitz."

"Tap or bottle?"

"Bottle."

To my relief he said not a word but stepped back to the icebox, retrieved a bottle of Schlitz, popped the cap, picked up a beer glass and came placed them in front of me with a little napkin and told me how much it was. I gave him a bill and he brought me back the change and put it on the bar and I just let it lay there.

Now this was it. I could see myself in the mirror with the bottle of beer in front of me and I knew I was undergoing an important rite of passage. When I left Dallas on the Pullman train with that bunch of new recruits I was a little taken aback when some of them broke out the booze and the cards and the dice. All the way through boot camp and Hospital Corps School I had resisted the evils my parents and my fundamentalist upbringing had warned me about. But now I felt a strong impulse to taste the ways of the world.

But that presented me with a problem here in this bar, and it was the taste. I took a sip of the beer and I didn't like it. How do people drink this stuff? But I couldn't walk out. I had set out to do this thing and I had to see it through. So I sat there looking around with what I thought was an expression that showed that for me drinking beer in a bar was old hat. But in between those confident looks around I had to struggle to choke down that beer. I finally finished all but about a third of the second glass, picked up my change off the bar and made my way out of there.

Beer is an acquired taste, and I later acquired it. Now I was looking forward to the two cans chilling there in the spring. When I took out the first one a kind of frost appeared on the can. Since I didn't have a church key I had to jab a hole in it with my bayonet. These were steel cans with no opening tabs, not the flimsy aluminum ones we have today. In those days it took real strength to crush a beer can with your hands. There was printing on top of the can that gave the name of some fraternal organization that had donated the beer and I hope somehow they learned how much their donation was appreciated. I finished that beer and the second then started following the stream back toward camp.

Other springs fed into the stream and it grew larger as I got closer to our camp. After a while I heard excited voices up ahead of me and as I drew nearer I saw CP and some guys from our platoon and another platoon gathered around a pool in the stream.

"There's one over there. Get him!"

As I drew closer I could see that they were throwing rocks at something in the pool.

"What is it, CP?"

"Frogs, Doc, Frogs. Get you some rocks!"

When I looked I saw little green frogs all around the pool, and I could see from some they'd already smashed that the frogs had bright red bellies. My friends there were caught up in a frenzy of chunking rocks at those frogs.

I didn't join them in this activity, but not because I was above it. I had done my share of blasting away at nature's creatures. Growing up on the outskirts of Dallas near fields and woods, I started out with a single shot bb gun, progressed to a Daisy 500 shot repeater, then to the cowboy hero Red

Ryder bb gun, and finally to the real things, a .22 rifle, and then 410 and 20 gauge shotguns. In those days my friends and I would shoot anything that moved. If nothing moved we'd shoot tin cans, bottles, fence posts.

When I was just starting my hunting career with that single shot bb gun, I was out one day walking through the field when I came up on a cottontail hunkered down in a little grass dome it had made for itself. The rabbit thought it would escape my notice by lying real still. But I saw him. This was meat on the table. I pointed my bb gun down at him, but then the bb rolled out of the barrel on to the ground. I picked it up and dropped it back down the barrel and took aim again. But again the bb rolled out on the ground. On the third try the cottontail lost patience and hopped away into the woods.

But I was not deterred. When I got my 500 shot Daisy bb gun, I and the other boys on the block would go up and down the streets and alleys looking for sparrows we called, "chi chi's," I guess because of the sounds they made. I remember once in my backyard I spotted one on the phone line coming into the house. I took aim and pulled the trigger and I could see the bb make kind of an arc and hit the bird plump in the chest. For a split second it just sat there, and then it swung down in a perfect loop like a gymnast on the high uneven bar; it hung upside down for a second, then dropped to the ground.

I walked over, picked up my quarry and examined it, and then tossed it aside.

We think we're doing things for the first time when we're only repeating actions a million years old. Why were those guys throwing at those frogs? Why do guys like to throw? Why did we like to shoot those chi chi's and anything else that moved in those fields and woods? Why were we climbing these mountains, hiking these ridgelines, sitting around campfires, chasing Chinese? What we were involved in was nothing new.

\* \* \*

That night in the tent we had to check our mulberry wine. When we listened at the plywood cover we could hear this subterranean seething going on; it sounded like the grating movement of tectonic plates.

"What do you think, Shex?"

"That stuff's really working. We got us something going here."

"You think it might explode?"

"I don't think so, but we might ought to relieve the pressure some."

So we removed the plywood cover and lifted the can out of the hole and sat it on the dirt floor of the tent.

"Who wants to loosen up that lid?"

"I'll do it, but you guys better step back some," Shexnayder said. "The secret is to unscrew the lid slowly."

He took both hands and got a good grip on the lid and began to twist. The pressure had tightened the lid to the can, but he struggled and groaned and then we heard this "hissss" and finally a loud "thomp" as he got the lid off.

"God, smell that! That's something. That's potent stuff!"

"We're going to be in business when this stuff is ready," Hawkshaw said.

"We'll have a hell of a party before we leave this camp!" CP was excited.

We got the can back in its hole and covered up, but this time we didn't screw the lid on so tight. We didn't want the whole tent to go up in a mushroom cloud.

The next day we had the Smoker with the boxing matches, music and other entertainment and activities, our "organized grab ass." Bill Holliday and I went at it for three rounds. I wish I could give a blow-by-blow account, but all I remember was that stinging taste I always get in my mouth when I get hit in the nose, and how tired I got. Getting in shape for one activity doesn't prepare you for another and, though I was conditioned to march and climb mountains for hours and days, I was in no shape to go three rounds of boxing. By the time we got to the end of the third round my arms felt like lead. And Holliday was not the pushover I thought he would be. In fact the referee ended up calling it a draw, and that was all right with both of us.

***Doc Hughes and Doc Holliday, Pugilists***

Our fight was just part of the preliminaries. The main bout was between a Chicano Marine and a big machine-gunner, a corporal named Murphy. Now I knew the Chicano fairly well. He and I had talked some about boxing. He was a nice, quiet, unassuming guy, but he was big and strong and looked like a boxer. I think he'd fought Golden Gloves and had some previous boxing experience in the Marines. So my money was on him. Murphy too was big and strong looking, but I didn't think he would be a match for my How Company buddy. But was I wrong! That machine-gunner was aggressive and mean and came at my friend for three rounds, penetrating his defenses with jabs and hooks and just generally working him over. There was no disputing the call when the ref raised Murphy's hand.

The strength and determination of the machine-gunner is one kind of power, but there is another kind of power that is much more useful in life—that is the ability to stand before a crowd and hold their attention, to grab an audience and entertain them. Successful preachers, politicians, and entertainers all understand this power. Some of them develop such ability through hard study and practice while others seem born with a natural gift to entertain. We had a Marine in How Company that fell into that latter category. He was "The Bard."

The Bard was part poet and part court jester. He wasn't in the 2nd Platoon but his reputation had spread throughout How Company and beyond. Those Jarheads in his platoon were fortunate in that they got to enjoy his poems and droll humor around their campfires up on the ridgelines while the rest of us had to wait for these Smokers when the regiment was in reserve.

When the Bard's time came on the program, he began with some topical humor about the recent adventures and misadventures of How Company, with a lot of his barbs aimed at our leadership, Captain Hoey and our platoon leaders. Like the court jesters of old, he could get by with wisecracks that any of the rest of us would have been court-martialed for, and we loved it. The officers seemed to love it too and laughed right along with us. Everyone got an especially big laugh out of the Bard's retelling of Gunny Spell's fall from grace when he attempted to make coffee using Lt. Lowe's whiskey; that is, everyone laughed but Gunny Spell.

While the Bard was going through his monologue, it wasn't long before there were shouts from the crowd, "Brown Side Out! Brown Side Out!"

This phrase requires some explanation. It is the title of a poem the Bard was famous for, a title inspired by the equipment and uniforms Marines wore during World War II and the Korean War. When I look at photos of American fighting men taken during those wars, the first thing I check are the helmets. If the helmets have camouflage covers I know they are Leathernecks. Some of our equipment was reversible, such as our helmet covers and ponchos—brown camouflage on one side and green on the other. Of course the brown side was for fall and winter and the green side was for spring and summer. But during training, orders would come down to roll the packs and gear so one side or the other would be showing—a familiar ritual for these Marines and thus the popularity of the Bard's poem. Here it is:

Brown Side Out

Now I'm not a wheel as you can see
I'm just a shit-bird in the infantry.
I never fought the Jap and I never fought the Kraut,
But I fought the battle of brown-side out.
It happened one morning at reveille,
When the duty came in so merrily,
He was a boot in his teens, a kid still growin'

He took out his whistle and started a blowin'.

"Reveille, reveille. Outa those sacks,
On yer feet and fix those packs."
And as he left with a mighty shout,
"Don't forget, it's brown-side out."

"Brown-side out?" cried a pissed-off Marine,
"You said last night it was gonna be green."

"Quit your bitching and rearrange,
You knew the word was subject to change."

Strainin' and sweatin we changed to brown,
Redone our rolls and settled down,
But about that time the Gunny came in,
"Men, the word's been changed, it's green again."

Switched to green, spirits start to soar,
Then a voice of doom—"It's brown once more."
Can't get it right to save my soul,
My bane in life is that fucking roll (Gogan, quoted on p 115).

There's no way to get the full effect of this poem by reading it on the page. To attain the highest level of appreciation two requirements must be met: the first is having experienced Marine boot camp and combat training, and the second is seeing and hearing the Bard as he made those words come alive with his expressions and antics. He was one entertainer who knew how to work a crowd.

We had some excellent musical entertainment too—singers and musicians. It was amazing how much talent there was in How Company.

Other than knowing a few chords on the guitar and singing a few country songs for friends sitting around in the barracks, I was not a musician. But I loved music, and that was one of the things I missed most while I was in Korea. I had grown up in Dallas listening to the standard music on the radio—country and pop. There were such artists as Eddie Arnold, Ernest Tubbs, Roy Acuff, and Bill Monroe on the country side, and Bing Crosby, Perry Como, Frank Sinatra, Ella Fitzgerald, and Nat King Cole on the pop side. When I was younger, mother took me to several Starlight Operettas at Fair Park where we saw shows like, "The Merry Widow," and "Toy Land." For me that was high culture.

My musical appreciation broadened some after I joined the Navy. I mentioned before my early experience with the Marine corporal in boot camp who caught me sleeping while we were snapping in our rifles and straddled my back and twisted my ears. Well I had a much more positive experience with a couple of Marine PFC's while I was stationed at Mare Island Naval Hospital. One of them had been admitted to the hospital, for a reason I don't recall, and put in a private room off the hall. His friend would come by to see him and bring records to play on a little portable record player. I stopped in from time to time and they would say, "Hey, listen to this! Isn't this great?"

They were listening to some of the early bebop, Charlie Parker and Dizzy Gillespie, and they would scat sing along with the records. That music seemed far out to me but I knew those two guys were cool. If they didn't instill in me an immediate love for bebop, they did encourage me to expand the boundaries of my musical taste. And I did. Two singers I developed a love for while at Mare Island were Billy Eckstine and Sara Vaughn.

Now here in reserve, for the first time in months, I got to hear some stateside music. One of the guys had a Grundig intercontinental radio and we were able to pick up American stations from Japan, and there was Billy Eckstine singing, "If," and "I Apologize," and "I'm Sitting by the Window." I just sat there and soaked it all in.

This was 1951. Some of the recent hits had been "Mona Lisa," by Nat King Cole, "Tennessee Waltz," by Patti Page, "White Christmas," by Bing Crosby, and that enduring classic by the Ames Brothers, "Rag Mop." This was also the year when some disc jockey first used the term "rock and roll." He was trying to introduce black rhythm and blues music into American pop music. His ambition would ultimately be realized, but not for another three years.

A sad note on that year: By the end of 1951 there had been 15,000 Americans killed in Korea and another 75,000 wounded.

\* \* \*

But now in early June things were sailing along smoothly for us there in the valley of the Pukhan-gang River. We should have realized that was cause for concern, for a few days later Gunny Spell came into our tent and told us we were going back to the front the next morning. We were furious.

"But they said we were going to have two weeks, and it's only been nine days!" Someone protested, and then we all pitched in. "Come on, Gunny, say it ain't so. We got five more days!"

"Tough shit, guys. These are orders, so be ready to move out in the morning." Gunny left our tent to spread the good news around the rest of the How Company area.

"What are we going to do now?" Hawkshaw asked, "What are we going to do about our wine?"

CP asked, "Is nine days long enough to make wine?"

Shexnayder said, "Hell no. We needed the full two weeks, but we'll just have to test it out. We can't let all that work go to waste. Here, let's take it out and see how it's doing."

Before we removed the plywood Shexnayder bent down and listened. "It's still working but it's calmed down some, so maybe it will be drinkable."

He removed the plywood cover and lifted the heavy can out of its hiding place and set it down by his cot. He unscrewed the lid and took a sniff, then drew his head back with a wince. "Kind of yeasty and strong, but it might work. Who wants a sample?"

No volunteers. "Look, we've put too much work into this to dump it. Let's let it age for the rest of the day and tonight we'll all have a going away party. I'm game. What d'y'all say?"

"OK, Shex, we'll do it. We'll have ourselves a farewell party tonight."

We spent that day getting our weapons and equipment ready to move out the next day. Some of us bathed in the river and shaved. Those helmets came in handy for gathering mulberries, but they were useful for other things as well. Most of them under their helmet covers were blackened from wood smoke where we had used them to heat water for shaving. Many of us carried tubes of Burma Shave and those high-tech double-edge Gillette blue blade razors, along with a little stainless steel mirror that we would hang on some convenient tree limb to see ourselves while we shaved.

By evening we had completed all our preparations for moving out the next morning, and we found ourselves sitting in our pyramidal tent gathered around that can of mulberry wine. "Well, who wants to start it off?" Shexnayder asked. "Doc, you ready for a cup?"

"Yeah, I guess," and I held out my canteen cup for him to pour.

"Let's see if we have to strain it." He proceeded to carefully pour me about half a cup and we didn't see any big lumps come out so it seemed to be all right.

"I think the potatoes and mulberries have settled to the bottom, so if we are careful pouring I don't think we will have to strain this stuff," Shexnayder said. "OK, the rest of you guys."

And each in turn held out his canteen cup while Shexnayder poured. Then we all sat there on our cots looking at each other, holding our canteen cups and occasionally bringing them to our lips for a tentative sip. But the party was slow getting started. Then a young man poked his head in the flap of the tent and asked, "Hey, is CP in there?"

Indeed he was. This was one of CP's old buddies from George Company who had dropped by to see him before we moved out the next morning.

"Come in, come in," we all warmly invited him in to join our party.

He was a small guy, lively and curious. After some preliminary discussion he finally asked, "What's that y'all are drinking?"

"Wine, wine! We got us some fine mulberry wine here. Would you like a drink?"

216

"Hey, sure. That sounds great!" Then someone came up with a spare canteen cup and Shexnayder poured this kid a generous helping of our mulberry wine.

We all sat around shooting the breeze, asking this young man all about the goings on in George Company while we watched him drink that wine. We would from time to time bring our cups to our lips, but the level in our cups shrank little while we watched CP's friend drink his wine with gusto. After maybe forty-five minutes to an hour of lively conversation the young man began to slow down in his speech. And then a short while later he said he had to go outside to use the bathroom.

There in the tent we continued to discuss the move that was coming up the next day and our anger and disappointment that our reserve time was being cut short by five days. Some of us continued to gingerly sip our mulberry wine, and apparently our experiment had worked to some extent because we began to get a little buzz out of the brew, but none of us had drunk that stuff down the way the young man from George Company had.

When he didn't return to the tent for some time, CP went to the door and called from the open flap for his friend. We heard a groan from outside, so several of us went out and found him lying in the grass and dragged him back into the tent where we laid him on a cot and attended to him until we slowly brought him around.

We were relieved that the George Company Marine gradually regained consciousness and reassured us he was going to be all right. We were also relieved to know that we would not be charged with manslaughter. We also ended up drinking a fair amount of that vintage ourselves with no terrible after-effects, save one. That big rumble that we heard in the can underground was now divided into several smaller rumbles in the bellies of the winemakers.

And so ended the 2nd Platoon's great farewell party in honor of that memorable springtime reserve in the beautiful valley of the Pukhan-gang River. And there were other farewells, for while the 2nd Platoon was saddling up to move back to the high ground, I was preparing to move to a new assignment.

# CHAPTER 15

# The Punchbowl

Captain Hoey and I had joined the company at the same time, December 1950, and now we would be leaving at just about the same time, because not only did How Company require replacements for the company commander and our recent casualties, but also for some of the men who had served their time to be rotated out. At this time, June 10 1951, I was one of those men due for rotation.

One of the things the line corpsman had to look forward to was that after serving a certain term in a rifle company he would be transferred back to the Battalion Aid Station and there serve the remainder of his tour in Korea. It's true the battalion HQ were always set up right behind the front lines, but duty there was a hell of a lot easier and safer than duty in a rifle company. No more long marches and mountain climbing, no more sleeping on the ground, no more C Rations, and best of all no more getting shot at, although there had been occasions when battalion HQs had been overrun, such as happened in Massacre Valley, and times when enemy forces infiltrated into rear areas, and times when they set up mortars and artillery to lob ordinance in on them, but compared to duty in a rifle company, working in the Battalion Aid Station was easy street.

The drawback for me was leaving my platoon. This reservation might strike the outsider as peculiar, to say the least, but the bonds formed in a Marine rifle company are strong and I believe unique. And the corpsman has a special relationship with his platoon, a special responsibility. During my months in Korea I was torn between two desires: Looking for security "in the rear with the gear" and staying with my buddies in How Company. Following are some of the things I wrote home about that relationship:

Feb 20th, after the Gook Chase while I was still on the Hospital Ship, I wrote:

> The day after I left my platoon got in a firefight and one of my boys was killed and one wounded . . . our only casualties so far . . . It is all guerilla warfare. We send out a small party to engage a small party of the enemy. Actually it's a miserable life, but I'm kinda anxious to get back with my platoon. . . .

Then I mention the rotation system set up for line corpsmen:

> . . . they are working on a rotation system so that we are relieved [after] six months, so I only have four more to go and that will be a snap.

Two days later I wrote:

> I'm still on the *Repose*. I'm going back to duty tomorrow. I'm even anxious to get back. I haven't received your packages yet so maybe my platoon is holding them for me.
>
> You know my job is to take care of the guys in my platoon, and I get so used to worrying about them I'm still worrying about them.
>
> It gets kinda hard sometimes because when a guy complains of blisters on his feet, stomachache, sore back, etc. I often have it just as bad, but I do what I can and sympathize with him. They think corpsmen are invulnerable. I try not to let them know any different.

After I had rejoined How Company and replaced Ollie in the 2nd Platoon in early March I wrote:

> Now be good and don't worry about me, don't imagine me suffering and going through hell. Right now I'm where I want to be, (besides being home).

April 19:

> I have got just about four months over here now, and before long I will probably be transferred back to battalion and work in the aid station until I am relieved. Believe me that will be an improvement.

May 7:

> I am no.1 on the list now to go back to battalion, so before long I will be in the rear with the gear. I had the chance once before but I turned it down, so this time I figure I'd better not push my luck any farther. I want you to know that I think your prayers are answered because more than once I thought your little boy wasn't going to make it home, but now it seems pretty certain that I will.

May 13:

> The good word is that I am going back to battalion in a day or
> two. My replacement is already in. I guess he's just going through
> the usual red tape.
>
> I sure hate to leave my platoon. They sure are a swell bunch
> of guys. They all say when I go back they're going to protest
> and tell them to make me stay here. They're just kidding. At
> least I hope they're kidding.

Hope springs eternal, but as was often the case in Korea, those hopes
were dashed. Just two weeks later I wrote:

> May 27: The rotation plan is kinda fouled up now, so I
> may be over here a month or more than I expected, but it won't
> be so bad.
>
> I had a chance to go to Company Mortars day before yester-
> day, but when it comes right down to it, it's kinda hard to leave
> the guys you've been with so long. So I turned it down.
>
> This will have to be a short letter because I think we are
> getting ready to move out. We will cross the 38th again this
> evening. It's been raining quite a bit lately. It rained all last
> night and it's cloudy today.

Four days after that letter How Company fought the battle of the Crag.
Then on the 9th of June I wrote this final letter about my tour of duty with
the 2nd Platoon:

> My relief got here today so I thought I would write and
> give you my new address. We got four [corpsmen] in this Co.
> and boy it sure was good to see them come in . . .
>
> If my writing seems a little jumpy it's because there's a bat-
> tery of 155 howitzers just below us that keep going off.
>
> I hate to leave the platoon, but I feel that I have pushed
> my luck far enough. I hate a bragger and if I sound like I'm
> bragging I'm sorry, but I feel that I have done a pretty good job
> since I have been with "H" Company. In fact I've been told so
> several times, even though it is the first thing in my life I've
> ever done good.

So at last I had made it. I was now "in the rear with the gear." It was to
be a new kind of life, sleeping in pyramidal tents on cots, serving with doctors and other corpsmen rather than Marine riflemen and BAR men. Most

of the corpsmen in the Battalion Aid Station were former line corpsmen, like Charlie Mims, Bill Holliday (the guy I boxed for three rounds at the Smoker), Thompson, Gallagher, Gerald Ford and a few weeks later Ollie Langston who joined us after recuperating from his wounds over in Otsu, Japan. As I recall he got tired of the duty over there and volunteered to return to Korea. I would have thought he would have learned better after that first time he volunteered for duty in Korea.

Now, rather than working alone and being responsible for forty-five men, I would be working with a team which would be responsible for a battalion, about twelve hundred men. We would get the wounded directly off the mountains and provide them with emergency surgery and lifesaving transfusions and treatments before evacuating them on to regimental hospitals where they would get the same kinds of treatment provided in the Army counterpart organizations, the Mobile Army Surgical Hospitals, or MASH units. I was now working with the same people I had watched from the reverse slope of the Crag speed out in ambulances to recover the Marine pilot who had parachuted from his burning Corsair, the same ones who were unable to save Smitty and Putnam, but who did save the other fifty-five wounded from How Company just a few days earlier, a truly remarkable performance.

I had about a week to get adjusted to life in the Battalion Aid Station before the 7th Regiment was put back on the line. After six months in a rifle company, the adjustment came pretty easy. I no longer needed my pack and entrenching tool, or even my Unit One aid kit. I swapped my M2 carbine for a 45-caliber side arm. I had my own cot in a luxurious pyramidal tent and we had such wonderful amenities as radios, hot chow, Cokes and pogey bait snacks. We did have to stand watches throughout the nights, but that was no problem. I could read and listen to music on the radio and I wrote home and told my folks that I was listening to Eddy Arnold sing "Molly Darlin'" and Billy Eckstine singing "If."

One of the doctors working with us at the aid station was Dr. Smith, who I had worked with back at Oak Knoll Naval Hospital. I wrote home and told my folks that he was "a pretty good guy." I also told them they might be hearing from a friend of mine from the 2nd Platoon, Charles Foley, who had been rotated back to the states. I told my folks: "I gave him your address and ph. Number. If he phones why don't you ask him over for dinner. He is really a character. He's always laughing and joking. You'll never find a better guy or a better Marine."

* * *

The objective of the Division now was the Punchbowl, an ancient volcanic crater, a flat basin of earth surrounded by a circle of steep mountains with sharp ridgelines in which the North Koreans and Chinese had built deep and heavy log fortifications, determined to fight there to the death rather than permit UN forces to once again penetrate deep into North Korea. The southern rim of the Punchbowl lay a few miles northeast of Yanggu not far from where How Company had its bitter struggle for the Crag, and about eight miles northeast of the Hwachon Reservoir, that long body of water running east and west, which came into existence when the Pukhan-gang River had been dammed.

Only six weeks earlier we had been on the west side of that same reservoir when the Chinese unleashed their CCF Spring Offensive and we were forced to make that long grueling march south after the battle of Horseshoe Ridge when the ROK division had given way on our left flank. It had been our objective then to disrupt Communist activities in the Iron Triangle which the Chinese had been using for their offensive build up. But our long spring "retrograde" march to close the gap on our flank, followed by the seesaw battles that occurred as we fought our way back north, would be the last of the long thrusts, the deep penetrations by either side. Now, one year after North Korea had invaded South Korea on June 25th 1950, the UN forces, including the ROK divisions, which had had problems in the past, were the strongest they had ever been and it was clear that we had the manpower and the firepower to prevail in any further encounters in this war.

Even now, to our west, UN forces were moving once more to take the southern two towns of the Iron Triangle, Chorwon and Kumhwa, while at the same time the 1st Marine Division was pursuing the enemy in the area of the Punchbowl north of Yanggu, moving back to the positions we had held earlier on the Kansas Line.

It was no coincidence that this was the time the Communist forces began to show some real interest in truce talks. There was much talk now about some kind of peace arrangement, and for our side the time was propitious as well, since there had already been a high level decision by the United States and the UN Command that taking North Korea was not a practical military or political option. So the goal of UN forces now was to secure as advantageous positions as possible along the 38th Parallel in preparation for upcoming peace talks.

Peace talks had always been something that those of us in the 2nd Platoon hoped for. I don't care how gung-ho a man is; I believe any person in combat is ready to welcome a cessation of hostilities. I never knew a man who had experienced a firefight say, "come on, give me some more!" I had volunteered for this war, but six months into it I was ready to see it end. The losses we had suffered on the Crag served to intensify that desire.

So almost exactly one year after the war began, peace talks commenced. Sadly, they would drag on for another two years before the war was finally concluded. Fortunately for us we had no crystal ball, so our spirits were lifted when we learned in early July that peace talks were underway in Kaesong.

The battle for the Crag was in effect one of the final chapters in the accordion phase of the war. There would be no more rapid penetrations north of the 38th Parallel and no more long retreats south to close breaches in the UN line. All the ROK units were fighting better now, and other UN forces had continued to grow in manpower and firepower while the Communist forces had also strengthened their units. Both sides were now fighting to secure positions which would give them some advantage in any kind of final settlement.

Since the war had become positional, new tactics and techniques were required. Digging log-reinforced and sandbagged bunkers and trenches, clearing fields of fire, rolling out great lengths of concertina wire, setting booby traps and antipersonnel mines, these activities would occupy much of the time of the Marines and soldiers in this new phase of the war. Captain Hoey, Charles Foley, I and all the other Marines wounded or rotated out that June never got to experience this new kind of warfare. We had marched, hiked and climbed hundreds of miles in Korea, but we had never built a bunker or rolled out barbed wire to establish a defensive position. We had always been on the move.

Although over half the casualties of the three-year Korean War occurred during that first year of combat, the fighting was by no means over. During the first year our campaigns had covered hundreds of miles horizontally and vertically; from this point on much blood would be shed to gain only a few hundred yards. Both sides were now concentrated and close; the battles from here on out would later be compared to the trench warfare of WWI.

But the 3rd Battalion of the 7th Regiment would have several more battles before they settled into trench warfare. How Company had taken the brunt at the Crag, but now it was George and Item Companies' turn.

\* \* \*

On the 18th of June the 3rd Battalion went back on the line north of Yanggu and was assigned the task of seizing objective 11 on the right flank of the 2nd Battalion on the southern rim of the Punchbowl. On the 19th George Company led off and made the first hundred yards with no opposition, but then they encountered heavy enemy fire from both their front and flanks and were forced to withdraw. Item Company was then ordered to move through a KMC unit on the right flank of George Company and advance on the objective, but they also had trouble because of the unusually rugged terrain and the fact that their radio communications failed, making it impossible to get in position for their assault. In the meantime George

Company had assaulted the objective three more times without success, and after that third attempt had to fight off a counterattack from the enemy.

Finally George Company made its fifth assault on objective 11. This time Item Company was in position to join in the assault, but both met such stiff resistance that they had to withdraw and dig in for the night some 200 yards from their goal, the crest of the hill, objective 11. The next morning the two companies resumed their attacks and found the enemy had abandoned their positions during the night. The two companies took their objective but the battle had exacted a price. The 3rd Battalion had inflicted an estimated 60 KIAs and 110 WIAs on the enemy while suffering 13 Marines KIA and 46 WIA. (3rd Bn Historical Diary)

Those 46 wounded Marines were the first I had to help care for in my new duties as a hospital corpsman in the Battalion Aid Station. It was a relief, however, not to have the sole responsibility. Now I was part of a team. We had doctors who took charge and we corpsmen with our line experience pitched in and gave the wounded Marines the best care possible before sending them back to the Regimental Hospital for emergency surgery and evacuation to hospitals in Japan or the US.

\* \* \*

After this last battle the 3rd Battalion got a break. Rather than jumping off on a new attack, the mission now was to work on defensive positions. Those entrenching tools, the little shovels with the folding blades that we had carried for months and used only sparingly, now became one of the most valuable tools in the Marines' arsenal. And that training in defensive warfare was at last put to full use, even though it went against the history and tradition of the Corps that always preferred to be on the attack. But the world political situation now was dictating the conduct of the war. While the truce talks were beginning in Kaesong, the Marines of the 3rd Battalion were clearing out fields of fire in the rugged mountains of the Punchbowl, digging trenches and log reinforced sandbagged bunkers, setting barbed wire, mines and booby traps, and positioning their machineguns and other weapons to provide the most effective enfilading fire down the north slopes.

The Chinese also saw the truce talks as a chance to build up their forces and construct elaborate defensive positions capable of fending off the greatly superior power of the UN forces, and they set busily to work to do just that. In fact there is no doubt that they used the talks primarily as a delaying tactic to gain an advantage. They realized that the UN forces were now strong enough to push their forces back to the north and perhaps retake the entire peninsula so they took advantage of the delay in the war to build strong defensive positions to ward off any such assault. They dug deep to protect themselves from our superior artillery and from the steady poundings they took from the air, and they constructed redundant positions behind them to some depth so that if they were pushed out of one defensive zone they would have others to fall back on. And of course they brought to the front many more troops and arms and supplies.

While the 3rd Battalion spent the last week of June and the first week of July continuing to strengthen our defensive positions, we were also sending out daily reinforced platoon patrols to feel out the enemy and maintain contact with them; and the artillery of the 11th Marines continued its bombardment of enemy positions, aided by the ever effective Marine Air Wing fighter bombers. So all was not quiet on the central front.

During this period there were two more casualties in the 3rd Battalion, both from How Company—one KIA and one WIA, both victims of booby traps. Lt. Barnes, who was now Executive Officer and at this point in charge of How Company, told me the Marine, Corporal Ralph Richards, was killed when he tripped a booby trap while he and other men from the company were out laying barbed wire. The irony was it was rigged with an American grenade, so the ROK Army unit that had previously occupied the position most likely put the device there. Ralph Richards, as it turned out, was another victim of "friendly fire."

The 1st Marine Division had now been in almost continuous combat for the better part of a year, and the 3rd Battalion had been in the thick of it. Now that UN forces were strong and the front line was approaching a stasis, there was an opportunity to give the division a well-deserved break. Our battalion was pulled off the line on the 7th of July and took up reserve positions near Yanggu and two weeks later the entire division went into reserve well back behind the lines near Hongchon, the city we had liberated in late March.

These weeks were a welcome break for the battalion and all of us there in the Battalion Aid Station. I had not known such ease since I had joined the FMF, either at Camp Pendleton or anywhere in Korea except for that brief stay on the USS *Repose* and in H&S Company at Masan. But that was wintertime; now it was warm, sometimes downright hot.

Around 2 AM on July 2nd I wrote home:

> I'm still living a life of ease, and I guess I will be until I leave this place, which is, who knows when?
>
> There is a creek out in front of the tent here and about 25 yds down the creek there is a spring coming right out of the mountain. The water is ice cold & almost any time of the day you can find me loafing around there chilling off Cokes (when I can get them) or lying out here in front under a shade tree reading a book & trickling my toes in the water. Ah, what a life!

In almost all my letters I brought up the peace talks. Once while we were watching an outdoor movie news came over a jeep radio that China had accepted General Ridgway's proposal for talks, and all the guys in attendance there let out a loud cheer. It's a tough question whether it's better to have false hope or no hope. But our hope for a ceasefire continued to tantalize us like a distant mirage beckons a thirsty man in the desert.

Our weeks in reserve were not all leisure. The Marine Corps doesn't permit troops to sit idle for long, so during our time in reserve all the units participated in a rigorous training program. Even back in Hongchon the drills continued on weapons and tactics. Officer-led squad patrols into the hills were an everyday activity along with inspections and trips to an improvised rifle range. Corpsmen were required to accompany Marines at the rifle range and once while sitting in a "cracker box" ambulance watching the Marines hone their marksmanship I penned a letter home. We also underwent additional training in emergency medical procedures there in the Battalion Aid Station to make sure we were equipped and ready to handle the casualties once we were put back on the line.

Once while the division was in Hongchon, the Commander of the Eighth Army, General Van Fleet, came to see a demonstration of Marine firepower. Machineguns were positioned along a ridgeline targeting an imaginary enemy force in the valley below, and since the attack was to come at night we all waited for darkness. When the Signal was given to open fire the blackness in the valley was illuminated by the most dazzling display of military pyrotechnics I had ever seen. I wrote home that it looked like the 4th of July. Jack Gogan, one of the machine gunners who took part in the demonstration, explained later that some of the guns were firing all tracers and that one of those gunners had described that experience by saying, "there seemed to flow from the gun a stream of liquid fire." General Van Fleet was impressed. James Brady in his book *The Coldest War* says that in the entire history of warfare there had never been a more powerful military force than the 1st Marine Division in Korea in 1951.

We bitched, we complained, we all wanted to go home, we all wanted the war to end. But though we never came right out and said it, we took pride in who we were and what we were doing. I wrote home in June:

> A guy will cuss the infantry and swear that he hates every part of it. But when you're marching back from the front all tired & dirty you see them raise their heads and stiffen their backs. I guess we're all proud of it in a way . . . .One out of seven men are linemen.

That last remark refers to the fact that for each man on the front line there were six backing him up behind the lines. Those were the troops we contemptuously called "rear echelon pogues." That group included not only outfits such as supply and transportation, but also our battalion, regimental, division and higher echelon commanders. All the units we saw filing on to the roads south of Horseshoe Ridge when we began our "spring retrograde" maneuver after the CCF spring offensive broke through the ROK division on our left flank were rear echelon units supporting us. There's no doubt that the infantryman's contempt for the rear echelon types was tinged with envy, but our anger was intensified when we felt that high brass commanders in the rear were playing games by sticking pins in maps with no regard for the price the men on the lines had to pay for their miscalculations.

Of course we knew we were absolutely dependent on those supporting units. But we felt that those guys, like the two army medics we had encountered far back behind the lines, would be the ones to go back home and tell the hairy war stories.

It's been my experience that very few front line combat veterans bring up war stories in their conversations. All those memories are in too private a place to be rolled out for entertainment purposes. But when combat veterans who served together meet, the doors to those past experiences open up, the years melt away, and old men for a time become their younger selves reliving the most intense and dramatic events of their lives.

But now for the rest of my tour in Korea I was going to be one of those rear echelon types. As noted before, my transfer to the Battalion Aid Station coincided with more sweeping changes in the war. Truce talks had begun. Both UN and Communist forces had switched from offense to defense and were now battling for territory to give themselves stronger hands when the final deal would be cut.

At this time when the new emphasis was placed on bunkers, barbed wire and booby traps, the Marines for the first time got body armor. Careful study of wounds suffered in Korea showed that body armor would save a substantial number of lives. Such armor probably would not have saved Sergeant Putnam, but Smitty would very likely have survived had he been so protected.

Late spring and the summer of 1951 provided the longest quiet stretches for the 1st Marine Division and the 3rd Battalion of the 7th Regiment since the war began. There had been that tough battle near the Punchbowl on the 19th of June, then in early July the peace talks began in Kaesong, and both sides in the war for a time concentrated on holding their positions and building defenses, with most of the action coming in the forms of artillery barrages, probing patrols, occasional skirmishes, and heavy US air attacks on enemy supply lines and North Korean cities.

Except for the moves to Hongchon and back to Yanggu, which required us to break down the tents and load all the medical equipment and supplies for the move, I was enjoying my new life of ease in the Battalion Aid Station. Ollie Langston returned that July and he and I and Gallagher, Thompson, Mims, and Holliday spent a good deal of time sitting on a cot and playing poker, using carbine bullets for chips. But those weeks leading up to the first week in September when Ollie and I finally got our orders back to the states were not without incident.

\* \* \*

By the 11<sup>th</sup> of August we were back in Yanggu just south of the Punchbowl where we could hear the tremendous blasts of 155 howitzers reverberating through the mountains and see the MAW planes flying north to unload their ordnance on Communist troops burrowed down in their tunnels and bunkers. The peace talks were not going well and there was that well-grounded suspicion that the enemy was using the talks primarily to stall our forces while they continued their buildup; and when the North Koreans walked out after claiming we had attacked the neutral territory at Kaesong, the site of the talks, General Ridgway lost patience and decided the Communists needed to feel a little more pressure, so he ordered UN forces back in action.

What followed were some of the most celebrated battles of the Korean War. For the Marines it was the battle for the Punchbowl, a circular volcanic valley about three miles wide at the bottom and six miles wide at the top ringed by high, rocky, sharply pointed mountains. For the Army's 2<sup>nd</sup> Division just a few miles away on our left flank, it was the objectives later known as Heartbreak Ridge and Bloody Ridge and an enemy defensive position colorfully dubbed, "Luke the Gook's Castle."

\* \* \*

The last week of August the 7<sup>th</sup> Regiment was ordered back into the fray. I wrote my folks at that time that we had word that a "hurricane" (I suppose typhoon would have been the correct term) was on the way, but I told them I wasn't too concerned about it. As it turned out the winds were no big problem, but the rain it brought was another thing.

On the 27<sup>th</sup> of August we got orders to move out and relieve ROK Army units on the Kansas Line. We folded up our tents and readied our equipment for the move, then sat around in a driving rain from the typhoon, waiting for the trucks to take us on and carry us to and across the shallow Soyang-gang River. But the trucks failed to arrive so we ended up eating our noon meal sitting on the crates and equipment we had readied for the move. We were compensated for our wait by plentiful hot food that the galley crews needed to get rid of before the move. But after that feast we continued to sit in the pouring rain waiting for the trucks until it was time for the evening meal. This time we were back to the old reliable C Rations. Still we waited, and it was not until 9 o'clock that evening that the trucks finally showed up, and it was 10:45 before we got moving. The 3rd Battalion was the last unit to move out, and in the meantime the downpour from the typhoon had grown even more intense.

It took 83 two and a half ton trucks and 27 other vehicles to move the unit, and we didn't reach the regimental assembly area until 4 am. It was another two hours before we reached the battalion assembly area where we were told to stay on the trucks, and it was 7:45 before the convoy moved once again. The trucks were having a difficult time on the muddy rutted road, and finally had to off load us and attempt to back up and turn around and get out of there. Battalion officers were running up and down the long convoy trying to break the log jam and get the trucks moving. At about 2 pm the rest of us began to slog toward the Soyang-gang to prepare for the crossing. The torrential rains by this time had turned this small mountain stream into a rapidly flowing swollen river. Ducks were requested to move troops and equipment across the river, so once more we waited. But we didn't wait long, for soon the word came that the Ducks had been delayed. So the battalion started to ford the river.

By 4 o'clock we in the battalion headquarters units had made it across after much difficulty, but the river continued to rise. How Company followed us, but by this time the river had become a rushing torrent. We watched as they began their crossing and when it seemed clear they would be able to make it we moved out toward our new position. But we didn't appreciate the trouble the company was in.

Two hours later How Company still had not made it across, and their attempt had taken a toll. The swift stream had carried Marines downstream and many of them reached the opposite bank far from the point where they entered the river. When the company started out on the treacherous crossing the water was waist high, but it continued to rise until it was chest level making it impossible for those who came later to keep their footing.

Those who were first to get across saw the difficulties their buddies were in and quickly formed a human chain, reaching out into the swift current to pull the struggling Marines to safety. Still, many lost their footing and their grip on their weapons and equipment and went tumbling into the flood. The battalion diary for that day records, "'H' Company had eighteen casualties in crossing and in addition lost one light machinegun and seven rifles. A minor mountain stream had become a torrent that 'H' Company could not continue to cross in the darkness."

The battalion spent the next three days drying out radios and equipment and recovering from that battle with nature, and after that we were back in the fight. The rifle companies moved up into the high ground to relieve the Korean troops there in the rugged southern peaks of the Punchbowl while we set up our tents in the valley below and got the Battalion Aid Station ready for action. General Ridgway, unhappy with the Communists' recalcitrance and delaying tactics in the truce talks, decided it was time to apply some fire and steel to encourage better cooperation. Also it had been determined that UN positions on the Kansas line could be strengthened and straightened by moving to some higher positions to the north, so the battle now would be to advance to a new objective dubbed the Brown Line where the terrain would be better suited for defense. Now, at the end of August, the war heated up again.

\* \* \*

The battalion CP and the aid station were set up near the base of the southern range of the Punchbowl. The road out of there ran east until it crossed a river where it turned south and ran along a range of lower mountains. A stretch of the road where it turned was exposed to enemy mortar and artillery fire, so vehicles passing through that area often came under fire. It was always a risky business running that gauntlet. When we got wounded off the mountains and sent them south down that road in cracker box ambulances, they almost always came under fire as they sped through the exposed stretch of the road. Fortunately the lag time between the time the enemy could see the vehicles and the time they could get the fire on the road enabled the ambulances to make it through. But it was always a scary run.

Our own heavy artillery, the 11th Marine Regiment, was also moving into position in this valley with their 105 and big 155 howitzers to answer the enemy fire. It was at this time the Battalion Aid Station got an emergency call from the artillery unit reporting someone seriously wounded. Ollie Langston and I took a jeep ambulance and sped out to their location in the field where the artillery was being set up. When we pulled in to the area we were directed to a group of Marines surrounding one of their comrades lying on the ground.

It was an artillery captain, bloodied on the left side of his face and down the left side of his body. We removed a stretcher from the jeep and laid him on it and I leaned down to take a close look at his wounds. There was a bloody socket where his left eye had been. His face, neck, shoulder and arm were peppered with shrapnel lacerations. I took out a battle dressing and began to press it gently to his face to protect the wound and control the bleeding.

"How bad is it, Doc?"

"You'll be all right."

"The eye! How about my eye? Am I going to lose my eye?"

"Nothing that they can't take care of. You're going to be all right. We're going to get you out of here and get you taken care of right now."

And with the help of his Marine comrades Ollie and I quickly got him secured to the jeep and began a more careful journey back to the aid station.

231

This captain, as he searched through the field for a place to set up his artillery, had triggered a bouncing Betty mine, one that when tripped springs up from the ground and explodes at head level. As happens to many people in combat as well as in other varieties of human calamities, the captain came out of the experience alive but with his life forever changed. Tripping that booby trap had taken only a second, but the effects from that second he would carry the rest of his life.

\* \* \*

By this time, around the 1st of September, Ollie and I had received word that we would be relieved soon to return to the states. We were excited about the possibility, but at the same time we were worried because the war had heated up again. We wanted to go home but were afraid conditions there at the Punchbowl would delay our departure. There was even the possibility that if many line corpsmen were lost we might be reassigned to rifle companies up in the mountains.

When Ollie got back to the states he got a letter from Sergeant Naun Juarez about a firefight How Company fought that had taken place at this very time at a spot called Yoke Ridge, just north of the Punchbowl.

> Sept 24 1951
> US Hospital Ship Repose
>
> Hello Doc,
> How are you? Fine I hope. As for me I'm doing great, thanks to God. I just thought of writing and report to you how the Co. is doing. Did we step into shit? I thought I would never get out alive. We jumped off on the attack on the 31st of Aug. Item Co took its objective by 5pm. How Co was to pass by Item Co and take ours, but it was too late to do it so we just tied in with Item Co. All night long we had incoming mail. Mortars and artillery. We had some casualties, not too many. But next day on Sept 1st all Hell tore loose at us. About 2 Bns [battalions] against 2 beat up Cos [companies].
> Item Co had really been clobbered the day before.
> At about 0900 Sept 1st the 2nd Platoon was ordered to send 2 fire teams to the 1st Platoon which was badly shot up after stopping the gooks counterattacks time after time. At about 1000 I was ordered to take my entire squad and reinforce the 1st Platoon again. So we went in and joined the party.
> Things were really popping. A lot of excitement just like the 4th of July. At 1300 I was told to pull 3 men out of anywhere

and plug the gap on the left flank. I took Brodeur, Lawrence, and myself. I couldn't afford to take anyone else and leave a wide gap so I went myself. We were there about five minutes and mortars and artillery came in. Brodeur got hit in the leg and Lawrence got it in the gut. I got pieces on my back and on my left butt. Of the guys that you know that got hit were O'Brien, Noriega, Brodeur, Darchuck, and myself. We had two killed in action. Berryman and Kline.[KIA ten days later on Sanguine.]

The [2nd] Platoon got it around the 9th while H Company was trying to take a hill where the gooks were well entrenched. Nolan had the Platoon. The platoon leader got hit, the platoon Sergeant got it, the right guide was a new Sergeant undependable as far as experience goes in combat. The 3 squad leaders were hit, so Nolan got stuck with the platoon. He was supposed to go home on the 10th of this month. I don't know if he did or not. I got it the 1st of Sept. . . .All this took place up North east Central front, the famous "Punchbowl." The darn mountains get bigger every time. You are lucky you got out of here. The gooks are making use of their mortars and artillery. I've been trying to find out about Demeuse. As far as I can gather he is okay.
[Casualties cited by Juarez here are from both 9/1 and 9/11]

Sergeant Juarez was wounded on the first of September, just as Ollie and I were leaving the Battalion Aid Station. We were worried that we might not get out because the fighting had so intensified, but we had our orders and those orders were honored. Ollie and I and several other rotatees were put aboard a cracker box ambulance for our trip to the rear. We loaded up our gear, got aboard, and the driver took off bouncing down the road to the east until we got to the spot where it turned south through the area exposed to enemy mortar and artillery fire.

Always a fatalist, I thought, "it will be just my luck after eight months of climbing these mountains and surviving all those firefights to be wiped out on my way home, on my way out of here." When we came to that bend in the road, the driver, who had been making this run for a while, slowed down until he reached a certain point, and then he gunned the engine and we went barreling through that exposed stretch of the road. After some minutes at full speed the driver slowed down. We all breathed a sigh of relief. We had made it!

As we bounced on down the road, Ollie took out a can of C Rations and opened it with his handy dandy and began to eat. When I saw him do that I grabbed the can and threw it out the window. "We're not eating anymore of that crap," I told him. "From now on we're going to eat real food, hot chow!" (I know I did that because Ollie told me—many years later.)

We didn't go far to the rear that first night and found ourselves rolling out our sleeping bags and bedding down near a battery of 155 howitzers. We didn't get a lot of sleep because the tremendous blasts from those cannon lifted us off the ground each time they fired and the salvos continued all through the night. Also we didn't really feel like sleeping because we were so excited about going home.

One of our group managed to come up with a bottle of grain alcohol. Since we were having trouble sleeping we thought we might as well have a little celebration. But we couldn't drink that stuff straight. We had to find something to mix it with. One enterprising member of the group went scrounging around and returned with a large can of grapefruit sections. We decided that would do, so we opened the can and poured some of the sections along with the juice into our canteen cups then laced it with the grain alcohol and enjoyed a nutritious libation.

\* \* \*

The next day we were on our way to Wonju where we were put aboard a C 47 and flown to Pusan. Once there we were housed in long tents and given some of our back pay in that GI money called scrip. We spent a few days there in a fenced-in compound playing poker on the bunks in the tents. A lot of money changed hands. We all started out with a fairly equal amount, but by the time we left some of the guys had big wads of money and some had empty pockets. I managed to win some and bought some money orders and sent my winnings home so I wouldn't be able to lose it later.

Korean peddlers gathered around the fence of the compound selling their wares, the most popular of which was booze. They had not only the Japanese Suntory, but also American brands like Seagram's 7.

We had time now to write home and on Friday, September 7[th] I wrote the following:

> Dearest Folks,
>
> Well here I am in beautiful Pusan. I never thought I would be so glad to see all the grass roofed houses & slums, but to me it's just like New York. Ah! That fragrant aroma of honey buckets!
>
> The reason I haven't written before is because just after the last letter I wrote the Third Battalion was put back on the lines and the going was pretty rough. Two corpsmen were killed and two more were evacuated so I wasn't sure whether I was coming home or going back to "H" Company, but I made it.

We leave Korea Mon. the 10[th] for Japan. We will be there about three days and then we leave for the states. Oh, Happy Day!

I don't know whether we will land in San Diego or San Francisco, but it doesn't really matter.

Ollie Langston is going home also . . .

Well be good and stand by for a shock.

Love, Charles

I had not been home since I got out of boot camp in late November of 1948 when I was seventeen. I had turned twenty in July while working in the Aid Station, so it had been just about three years since I had been home.

In that letter I told my folks that I was bringing a friend home with me and not to write anymore because I would probably be home before I got the letters. But mother had written me a couple before she got the one above and they are the only two I have from her, since they were returned and she saved them along with the letters I had written from Korea.

She wrote on Aug 28:

. . . We heard on the radio this morning where there was quite a bit of fighting around Yanggu so I am beginning to be afraid they may call in the Marines if they haven't already. So do be careful and don't volunteer for any front line duties . . .

Do let us hear from you every chance you get. We will be looking every day for that letter telling us you will be coming home.

Be careful and send us some more pictures if you get any. We really are thrilled to get them.

Love from all of us to you,
Mother, Daddy & Mary Alice

Two days later she wrote after receiving the letter I wrote on Aug 23rd telling her I was coming home.

Dallas, Texas
Aug 30, 1951
Thursday

Just got the letter with the good news and I am so happy I don't know what to do. Sure hope and pray nothing happens to keep everything from working out as planned and that you really will be starting home soon....

I am afraid the Marines have been called back to the front by now, but that won't keep you from coming home....So do be careful and take care of yourself and try hard to get home safe and sound...

I am so happy thinking about you coming home that I can hardly write. I want to hurry and get this mailed so you can get it and get started home...

Do let us hear from you and be as careful as you can. We will be lying awake too thinking about your coming home.

Love to you from all of us,

Mother, Daddy, & Mary Alice

These excerpts from a mother's letters many years ago, expressions of love and concern from a family– mother, dad, and baby sister (today all gone)–show clearly that it's not just young men who bear the burdens of warfare. Families, and mothers in particular, often endure more real agonies than the men doing the fighting. The intensity of my mother's feelings, normally the strongest and most rational member of the family, can be seen in her belief that getting that letter in the mail would somehow expedite my journey home.

Every fighting man in Korea must have been getting similar expressions of love and concern from his family, and so it surely has been from the beginning of warfare, and warfare is older than history. Sadly, every mother did not get the good news my mother did.

\* \* \*

We left Korea Monday, the 10th of September, 1951. Finally, after being in the Navy for over three years, I would be assigned aboard a ship, but it would be a troop ship and I would not be part of the crew, I would be a troop. The ship was the *General William Mitchell*, a troop transport, and before letting us board they sprayed us down for lice. I had seen some problems with parasites in Korea such as round worms, intestinal parasites GIs got from digging up onions from village gardens to flavor their cans of C Rations, but I had never seen lice. Still, that was the required procedure so we had to submit to them spraying white powder down our collars and into our pants. But we were going home. What did we care?

# CHAPTER 16

# <u>Sanguine</u>

On the 11th of September 1951, (a date, 9/11, that would, fifty years later, be seared into the consciousness of every American and people around the world), Ollie and I and all the Marines and Corpsmen being rotated home weren't aware, as we toured the city of Yokosuka buying cheap souvenirs and touring bars looking for women, that our comrades back in How Company were facing one of their fiercest battles of the war, that they would have a half century head start on the rest of us in remembering 9/11. These were men we had served many months with, hiked hundreds of miles and climbed countless mountains and faced many battles with, men such as Marcel Shexnayder, Ralph Tate, "Hoagy" Carmichael, George Brodeur, "Hawkshaw" Hannah, Dean Nighswonger, George Nightwine. And there were a number of others who had joined the company after the battle of the Crag, men such as Wadie Moore, Roy Westerman, Bob Nichols, Tom Martin, and many others who deserve remembering. They were men with whom we had formed bonds stronger than any we were ever likely to have again with anyone outside our immediate families. But now our thoughts were on home, and our buddies in How Company back at the Punchbowl were on their own. Our links to them had been severed, at least for now.

The war had indeed entered a new phase. Both sides now accepted the reality that neither was going to succeed in driving the other from the peninsula. The Communists understood that the UN had the superior fire-power. The UN under the leadership of the United States and President Truman realized the horrendous costs in lives and money an all-out war with China, and perhaps the Soviet Union, would exact on the world. So each side struggled to gain the most advantageous positions for the final truce, which seemed likely would come from the peace talks now underway. It was in part the realization that, at some point, both sides would be frozen in place that contributed to the intensity of the battles in the fall of 1951.

UN forces were still situated pretty much along the Kansas Line, about forty miles north of Hongchon, but General Van Fleet wanted to keep his troops active. In the area of the Punchbowl and the mountain ridges to the west there was a sag in the UN lines that put our forces in vulnerable positions since the enemy held the high ground to the north. So the decision was made to move north of the Punchbowl to what was designated as the Hays Line and capture those strong defensive positions, straighten the UN lines, and thereby give UN forces the defensive advantage.

But during the relative lull of battle in July and part of August, the Chinese and North Korean Peoples Army had worked steadily to construct deep and elaborate defensive positions in the mountains north of the Punchbowl and in the ridgelines to the west. So when the UN assault began, the North Koreans and Chinese were ready. The battle had just gotten underway when Ollie and I made that mad dash in the cracker box ambulance on our way to the rear. The timing for us was most fortunate.

On that same day, as Sergeant Naun Juarez later wrote Ollie, the 2nd Platoon of How Company was hard hit in a battle at Yoke Ridge on the northern rim of the Punchbowl. But there would be worse to come ten days later at the battle for Sanguine Hill on September 11.

The push to straighten the UN lines produced some of the most violent clashes of the war. During the opening days of the month just four or five miles west of the Punchbowl the Army's 2nd Division, spearheaded by two ROK regiments, assaulted a steep, north-south running mountain which later earned the name "Bloody Ridge." The struggle for that mountain and the one just north of it, "Heartbreak Ridge," lasted for over a month and produced some of the highest casualty counts, on both sides, of the entire war. The Chinese and North Koreans had used the time of the lull to construct networked trenches and dig deep log-reinforced bunkers that could withstand just about anything except a direct hit from 155mm Long Tom artillery.

The mountains of the Punchbowl and Bloody Ridge and Heartbreak Hill had been denuded of trees by our blistering artillery and air assaults, but still the enemy was secure in their deep bunkers and determined to hold their positions at all costs. Because of the scarred surfaces of the mountains it was difficult if not impossible to locate the enemy bunkers and defensive positions for the artillery, so ultimately the only weapon that could dislodge them was the one that is always called on to get the job done in warfare—the infantry.

After the battle for Yoke Ridge on the northern rim of the Punchbowl on the 1st of September, How Company along with the other units of the 3rd Battalion continued building up defensive positions along the ridge, laying barbed wire, digging emplacements and clearing fields of fire. At the same time all three companies were sending out daily patrols and directing mortar, artillery and air strikes on known enemy positions. During this time some strange and unsettling things had been happening. On the 4th and 5th of September the 5th Marine Regiment which was on the Kansas Line five miles behind the 7th Marines, was attacked, while there on the Hays

Line patrols sometimes penetrated 2,000 yards to the north without meeting resistance.

Although there may have been problems determining exactly where enemy forces were located, there was no question that How Company would meet resistance in its next assignment because more enemy troops had been spotted moving south into the zone of the 1st Marine Division. It was discovered that the 1st NKPA III Corps had relieved the 2nd NKPA Division II Corps, and it wasn't long before they began to hit the Marines with heavy 76mm artillery and mortar fire. These fresh enemy troops had moved in to the deep fortifications their comrades had been digging and preparing for the past several weeks, and they were ready for battle.

\* \* \*

By the 10th of September UN forces were ready to take on these fresh troops and assault the heavily defended mountains northeast of the Punchbowl and begin the push north. The 1st Division ordered the 7th Regiment to jump off at 0300 hours on September 11 and take objectives Able and Baker, which were the well-defended hills 673 and 749. The areas they were assaulting were midpoints on the way to the final objective, Kanmubong Ridge some 5000 yards north of their position on Yoke Ridge. It fell to How Company on hill 602 on the eastern most part of Yoke Ridge to spearhead the attack by moving down into the valley, crossing a small creek which fed the Soyang-gang River, and taking an intermediate objective, hill 680. When the orders came no one understood what a toll this "intermediate" objective would take on the men of How Company or how this nondescript hill would earn the name "Sanguine."

"Sanguine," a word meaning rosy or cheerful, has another meaning more appropriate for the Marines of How Company who fought for hill 680 on the 11th and 12th of September—that meaning is "bloody." The battle that took place there turned out to be How Company's "Bloody Ridge."

The two hundred plus men of How Company were a small but important and effective element in the September assault, which involved thousands of UN forces across a broad front stretching from northeast of the Punchbowl all the way west to the corner of the Iron Triangle. General Van Fleet had wanted his troops to remain active, so he should have been pleased with what followed, because his forces were about to see some of the most intense action of the war, and How Company was right in the middle of it.

Lt. Dwight Young, now the CO of How Company, gave the order to roust the men out of their sleeping bags some time after midnight. The company was assembled, issued extra ammo and hand grenades, and given their final instructions. At 0230 they moved out in the dark on this rainy, foggy night and made their way single file down the rocky trail leading to the creek below. Visibility was so bad each man had to hold his hand to the back of the man in front in order to keep the company together, and the steep and rocky trail caused many men to stumble and fall in the difficult descent to the valley below. By the time How Company reached the creek and was ready to begin the assault on hill 680, daylight had come.

The 3$^{rd}$ Platoon was to lead the attack and the other platoons would leapfrog them on the way to the objective, the crest of hill 680. Early morning fog had provided some cover for the Marines as they began their ascent, but by 0730 the fog had lifted and exposed them to the waiting and well-entrenched enemy above. These North Korean troops, like the Marines, had been preparing fortifications and clearing fields of fire for weeks and they were ready.

At the Crag the 1st Platoon had reached that first objective without opposition, but on this day the 3$^{rd}$ Platoon was not so lucky. When the curtain of fog lifted they were fully exposed to the enemy above who had them in the sights of their heavy maxim machine guns, burp guns and rifles, and they cut loose at the Marines of How Company with blistering effectiveness. To add to the hail of small arms fire, the North Koreans began to drop 82mm mortars on the exposed Marines adding to their difficulties. The 1$^{st}$ and 2$^{nd}$ Platoons quickly joined the battle and within less than an hour there were many How Company casualties, including two platoon leaders.

One of those two was the leader of the 3$^{rd}$ Platoon, Lt. Tom Carline, who lay exposed to enemy fire with an almost certain likelihood of being killed. When Hoagy Carmichael spotted him he dashed through the mortar rounds and gunfire, picked up the lieutenant and carried him to safety. He had demonstrated similar courage in the battle for the Crag, and for each of these spontaneous acts of bravery he later received the bronze star.

*Frank "Hoagy" Carmichael*

Roy Westerman, a young Marine from Arkansas following Lt. Carline up Sanguine was hit in the waist and stumbled to the ground. When he checked to see where he was hit he found the bullet had struck an ammo clip on his belt and in his hurried search he could find no wound; so he picked up his M1 and continued to move up the hill. Almost immediately he was hit in the head and everything went black. The battle stopped for him that instant. The Marines who saw him on the ground lying still with such a terrible head wound believed him to be dead. A corpsman did get to him and put a battle dressing over the wound and pulled his cap down over his head to staunch the flow of blood, but even he could not have given Roy much hope for survival. Yet many days later Roy woke up in the hospital. He had suffered a grievous head wound and there was considerable brain damage, but he had enough of a very good brain left and lot of spirit and courage as well to see it through—and he did. One surprise he got when he woke up came when he looked down at a sore spot on his waist and saw the stitches that had been required to close up that first wound. He had been hit twice after all.

George Brodeur was also a casualty on this day. He was wounded in several places but still able to walk, so he was given orders to escort two prisoners to the rear on his way to get medical assistance. As he passed the 81mm mortars, someone yelled out, "Hey Brodeur!" He turned to see Lt. McVeigh waving at him. When he arrived at the forward aid station a corpsman said, "Hey, man. You're bleeding." But the corpsmen seemed more interested in the two prisoners than the wounded Marine.

As the enfilading machine gun fire from the enemy emplacements continued to sweep the slope of hill 680, the Marines of How Company scrambled to find cover and positions from which to return fire, and they were having some success. But by 9 o'clock that morning they were pinned down some fifty yards from the top. At this point Item Company was ordered to move forward to help How Company push to the top of the hill. But Item Company, some distance to the rear, was unable to get in position to join the fray until after noon, and in the confusion of battle they somehow lost their way and rather than advancing up the western spur of the hill and coming at the enemy from the flank they ended up on the eastern spur with How Company. From that point on both companies continued to fight together in an effort to dislodge the North Koreans from the deep bunkers above.

Because they were in those strongly fortified bunkers, in effect looking down the throats of the assaulting Marines, the North Koreans with their small arms and machine gun fire were able to take a terrible toll on the attackers. During the desperate struggle that morning the Marines' 81mm mortars were dueling it out with the North Korean's 82mm mortars, and in one of the terrible ironies of the battle Second Lieutenant Thomas McVeigh, the spirited leader of the 2nd Platoon at the Crag, the man who had just a short time ago called out to Brodeur, was killed by an enemy mortar round. A further irony was that he had just recently been transferred to that mortar platoon, a relatively safer assignment. But on this day that mortar platoon was anything but safe. Their command post suffered a direct hit killing Lt. McVeigh and causing a number of other casualties. The death of "Lefty" McVeigh, Colombia University graduate and a young leader of men, cut short a most promising life. The following passage from a recent issue of

his hometown newspaper shows that, even after more than a half century his
sacrifice had not been forgotten:

> Appropriately held on Sept. 11, the Village of Stewart
> Manor [NY] rededicated a memorial to two local heroes who
> died exactly 50 years apart to the day: Marine Lieutenant
> Thomas McVeigh, killed in action in Korea at "Bloody Ridge"
> Sept. 11, 1951, and David Leistman, killed in the North Tower
> of the World Trade Center Sept. 11, 2001.
>
> A football star and honor student during his days at
> Sewanhaka High School, McVeigh graduated from Columbia
> University and was called into active service four days after he
> entered St. John's University to study law. Leistman, a bond
> trader at Cantor Fitzgerald, grew up in Stewart Manor, also
> attended Sewanhaka High School and became an All-American
> lacrosse player while attending school at nearby Adelphi
> University.
>
> For many years, a plaque honoring Lt. McVeigh stood adja-
> cent to Stewart Manor Village Hall, at the corner of Chester and
> Covert Avenues. In 2001, when the Village of Stewart Manor
> chose to erect a September 11, 2001 memorial on Stewart Manor
> Country Club grounds for Leistman and all others who perished
> during the terrorist attacks, McVeigh's plaque was moved as
> well (The *Floral Park Dispatch*, Jan 07, 2005).

* * *

Because of the great advantages the enemy had of terrain and position, there was a desperate need for the Marines to bring artillery and air
power against hill 680. The men responsible for getting the fire to the
right spots were the forward observers. One of the artillery FO's, Sergeant
Jim Dettman, wrote about this day many years later to Wadie (long "a"
as in "wade") Moore, the then eighteen-year-old Marine who had been his
radioman. Every man in any battle has his own story to tell. This is Jim
Dettman's, or part of it anyway:

> I was with Lt. Young [H Company CO] at the Bn CP when
> he received the attack orders for the 11th of September. We
> were to jump off in the attack at about 3a.m. on the 11th. Our
> objective was hill 680. On the 10th of September, I with Lt.
> Young marked concentrations on the objective, possible mortar
> positions and possible troop concentrations. When we jumped
> off, to call in artillery all I had to do was shoot a new azimuth.

If you can remember, it was raining at approximately 2 or 3 in the morning and fog had set in. We moved out at that time on 11 Sept. We had to hold each other's hand as not to get lost. When we got to the line of departure we fanned out. I am not sure which platoon was leading the attack. If you can remember we were about half way up the ridge when we saw 4 or 5 gooks sitting around a fire. One of them got up and started to urinate when he saw us. He yelled and all hell broke loose.

Your squad covered me while I adjusted artillery and after about 30 minutes we moved to a better position of observation. Just as we got to a bunker, I yelled to you, "I will get in the bunker you cover me." You said, "No...I will get in the bunker and you cover me." That is what we did. We fired VT [variable time], PD [point detonating] and time delay fuses on the forward slopes, reverse slopes as close as 50 yards to ourselves. This went on for about 30 minutes.

It seemed only seconds after you got into the bunker when a heavy maxim machine gun, small arms and mortars opened up on us. I heard you on my left crawling out of the bunker. When I saw you I thought your complete face was shot off. I asked, "Can you make it?" You gurgled back, "I will make it." I told you to crawl straight ahead until you felt like you were going to fall forward, then turn right and go down the slope to the Company CP and the Corpsman. When I turned to see you leave, I swore I could see right through your head. A short time later I was hit.

When I got to the wounded collection point you were lying on a stretcher with your head bandaged. You were a death like grey in color and I asked the Corpsman if you were dead. You rose up on both elbows and gurgled, "I will make it, Sergeant." You were then evacuated before me and I lost all records of what happened to you.

This letter from Sergeant Jim Dettman FO to his radioman, written forty-six years after the battle for Sanguine Hill was fought, reflects clearly the intensity and violence and confusion of that struggle.

Another remembrance of Wadie Moore and that fateful day came from my comrade and fellow veteran of the Crag and many other battles of How Company in 1951, BAR man Joe Sipolski. The following is part of a letter he wrote to Moore in October 1999:

I often think of that day 11ᵗʰ [of] September. I remember that night march to Sanguine. That empty, tight knot in my stomach was a little tighter that morning. It didn't take long to get in the fight. It looked like half the 1ˢᵗ Platoon was wiped out in minutes, as the wounded were working their way through our position. It was not a morale builder. I was working my way to the right of the main finger and was surprised to see how close we were to the bunkers above. I tried to get a few shots off but my BAR was jammed. As we worked our way to the right and up the hill, all hell was breaking loose. I hit the ground, but obviously not in a good spot. Shrapnel hit me in the shoulder and a bullet hit my left forearm and traveled nine inches up through my arm. I worked my way back to the wounded area, was shot up with morphine, and later started the trip back down the hill with another Marine who had a bullet wound through his thigh. He had just been with How Co. for 5 days. By late afternoon we were back near the first medical area. This is where I learned of the death of my [former] platoon leader Lt. McVeigh. His bunker took a direct hit that same [day]. He had recently been transferred back to heavy mortars.

It was just starting to get dark when I reached the first hospital tent. I was told to go into a little room on the left and have a doctor check my arm. I walked into this tiny room in the tent, just enough room for three operating tables. On the first table was a Marine who appeared to have a bullet hole clean through his chest. He was sitting up. On the table to the right was a Marine with his foot hanging only by the skin. On the center table was a Marine lying half propped up with 2 doctors working on him. His face had been blown open and I could see inside his head. The docs were talking to him as they worked, and he was trying to answer back with gurgling sounds. I could hardly believe the Marine was alive. I stayed for a short period of time watching them work when a feeling of guilt overcame me.

I walked out of the room and told a corpsman, "I don't belong in there with those Marines; they're fighting for their lives." By this time it was dark outside. I was loaded on a truck and sent back to the larger hospital in the rear where I was operated on at 11 o'clock that night. Don't remember a thing till next morning when I was flown out to Japan.

*Wadie Moore*

Joe Sipolski never identifies the Marine on the center table. He didn't have to.

*Joe Sipolski*

\* \* \*

The battle for Sanguine continued throughout the morning. How company was unable to get closer than fifty yards to the crest of the hill and they continued to receive heavy small arms and mortar fire. The direct hit on their mortar platoon and the death of Lt. McVeigh was a real blow to the company. The many casualties the company suffered, including two platoon leaders, made the attainment of their objective even more difficult.

When Item Company arrived after noon it seemed there might now be a strong enough force to push to the top of the hill. Even though Sergeant Dettman had been wounded, the 11th Regiment artillery had the range of the enemy and there was a forward observer with Item Company, so hill 680 continued to be pounded by our artillery. Also since the weather had cleared the air panels were laid out and an air strike was called. When the air strike was completed at 2pm How and Item Companies moved out together in an assault, but they were met by fierce resistance from North Koreans popping out of their bunkers to unleash withering fire on the attackers, and within fifteen minutes the Marines were driven back to their starting point.

For the next hour 4.2 mortars and artillery rained upon the enemy there on the top of Sanguine, and another air strike was called, pounding the hill with napalm, rockets, and 50-caliber machine gun fire. Shortly after 3pm the two companies again assaulted the hill and a few of the men made it to the top, but their casualties were so heavy they could not hold the position. When the enemy counterattacked the Marines returned the way they had come dragging their wounded and dead with them. This time they fell back a hundred yards from the crest of hill 680 where they regrouped and reorganized before moving back to set up defensive positions that evening near the hilltop.

All night long the Marines in How and Item Companies received incoming mail from the North Koreans' 82mm mortars and 76mm cannons. The Marines gave as good as they got in this exchange of volleys throughout the night, and with the coming of daylight George Company joined the other two embattled companies of the 3rd Battalion and all three companies were ready to make the final push for the summit.

By 10:28 the prize was won. The punishment the enemy had suffered the day before and through the night, coupled with the increased strength of the Marine assault force, turned the tide. But even though the enemy had abandoned the hill, they had not abandoned the fight. All through the day they continued to lob mortar rounds on the hill and hit the Marines with their 76mm artillery, causing the casualty rate to continue to rise. And the enemy had not completely given up on Sanguine. That night, shortly before 11 o'clock, they launched one more counterattack, but the 3rd Battalion Marines were not about to give back this battered hill they had fought so hard for. They drove back the attackers in a fifteen-minute firefight, and now there was no question of who was the victor in the battle for Sanguine.

On the following day the 3rd Battalion of the 1st Regiment relieved the 3rd Battalion of the 7th Regiment. The casualty figures for 3/7 for the month of September 1951 were 36 KIA, 2 DOW and 323 WIA. How Company suffered a major share of those casualties in the battle for Sanguine Hill, paying possibly the highest price in the shortest period for any battle by any company during the Korean War. Bob Nichols reported that in the 24-hour period, September 11-12, How company had 15 KIA, 2 DOW, 141 WIA evacuated, and of the 41 members who walked off the hill 30 of them were walking wounded, for a total of 187 casualties out of the under-strength company of approximately 198. Joe Sipolski learned later that he had lost two more of his buddies in the battle. His fire team leader, Bryan Berryman, and Palmer Kline were among the KIA.

\* \* \*

There in Japan Ollie and I and all the rotatees were unaware of the struggle our comrades in How Company were going through. As noted earlier, tragedies affect us directly proportional to their magnitude and inversely proportional to their distance from us. If we don't know about a tragedy, however, it doesn't affect us at all. Mayhem can occur right next door, but if we don't know about it we're not bothered. So even though our friends were only a few hundred miles from us we didn't know about Yoke Ridge and Sanguine Hill and therefore were unaffected by their latest hardships and losses.

We spent about three days in Japan; it was there I bought the flashy dragon jackets and wooden thong shoes, and the "Ronson" cigarette lighter made out of an American beer can. I also bought the 78rpm records, "China Night," and the Korean folk song, "Arirang," and other Japanese and Korean songs.

Back aboard the *William Mitchell*, preparing to sail, I remember looking up on a high cliff there in Yokosuka harbor to the silhouettes of trees against the evening sky, large trees but with shapes like the miniature Bonsai. I promised myself that someday in more peaceful times I would come back to Japan, the Land of the Rising Sun, and to Korea, the Land of the Morning Calm, but my life took me in other directions and I was never able to keep that promise to myself.

It was warm when we started our voyage across the Pacific. I remember sitting out on the fantail of the *William Mitchell* at night and looking back at the blue-green phosphorescent wake stretching back as far as we could see and feeling the thrumming of the engines vibrating all the way up through to the deck we were sitting on.

But the ship took a northern route, somewhere toward the coast of Alaska, so within a few days the weather turned cold and we ended up staying below deck crammed into the multi-tiered bunk areas of the troop ship. Then the weather got rough. The ship reared and pitched in the heavy seas, and at times the screws would come out of the water and we could feel the ship vibrate as the propellers spun in the air. Many of the troops got sick and spent a great deal of time in the head. I was feeling none too good myself, but I managed to keep my chow down. I had Korean mountain legs; I didn't have sea legs.

We found out that our port of return would be San Francisco, not San Diego. When we arrived we sailed in under the Golden Gate Bridge where we were met by several fireboats that pulled alongside and greeted us with a tremendous display of waterpower, their nozzles firing great arcs of water into the air as they escorted us in to our berth. I don't know how strong the public support for the war was at this time, but at least officially we were given a grand welcome home.

# CHAPTER 17

# Return

Returning from the war in Korea to the United States was like taking a journey back through the looking glass. All the rules changed again. When we went on liberty in San Francisco we were in high spirits, happy to be back in the good old USA, and with money in our pockets we were ready to do the town. The city may have welcomed us with fireboats as we entered the harbor, but now on the streets of San Francisco we were just young Jarheads looking for a good time, and indeed we were. But we carried inside recent memories that others could not discern or care about. It's not possible by looking at people to know what they've been through, and it's a sad comment on life that most people don't care anyway. Some veterans became touchy and hostile and could explode over some real or imagined slight or insult. I understood their feelings but I never had that problem. I did have one problem with a civilian that day, though.

Three of us were walking down the sidewalk in our Marine green uniforms, I with my Navy 3rd Class Petty Officer's stripe on my shoulder, when a sporty looking man in a sharp suit called us to the side of a building, looking furtively around like he was in some kind of trouble.

"Hey, men! Look here! I'm in a scrape," he said with desperation in his voice. "I got a woman waiting for me up here in this hotel, and I lost all my cash out at the track this afternoon. Look, I got this watch, brand new—two hundred-fifty bucks." He shot the cuff of his white shirt under his suit coat and revealed a beautiful gold watch with a gold band. The numerals were encrusted with diamonds and there was the name, "Elgin." I certainly was no connoisseur of watches, but Elgin was a known and respected brand at that time and the watch was beautiful.

"How much do you want for it?" I asked.

"Forty bucks! Only forty bucks! My woman's gonna leave if I don't get up there!"

I looked at my companions and looked at the watch, then succumbed to the temptation to get such a beautiful and valuable watch for only forty dollars. I reached in my pocket and pulled out a roll of bills and peeled off two twenties and handed them to the man. He slipped the watch off his wrist and handed it to me.

My companions and I continued our stroll down the sidewalk and I found myself frequently checking the time on my beautiful new watch. But for some reason as we walked I began to feel uneasy, some kind of delayed reaction was setting in. I tried to convince myself that I had made a steal with that purchase, but still a nagging doubt was there. As we continued our progress down the street I saw a jewelry store ahead. Just for the heck of it, I thought, I'll stop in there and have the jeweler take a look at my fine watch.

The jeweler took the watch over the counter and popped the back off, replaced it and handed it back to me.

"Well, how much is it worth?" I asked anxiously.

"About seven bucks."

"Seven bucks?"

"Yeah, seven bucks."

"The guy I bought it from said it was worth two hundred fifty!"

"Those guys buy these watches by the boxful and sell them on the street to unsuspecting guys like you. Too bad."

When we were back on the sidewalk I said, "Let's go get that son of a bitch!" My companions were with me and we double-timed it back the several blocks to where I had made the purchase, but of course the man was nowhere in sight. And I knew there would be no point in going in the hotel to try to find the guy and his "woman," since that was only part of the line he used to gull easy marks like me. By now he was far away on some other corner waiting for the next dupe to come by.

Welcome home, Korean veteran.

We did take a trip to Oak Knoll Naval Hospital across the Oakland Bay Bridge to see our friend James Pless who had lost an arm at the Crag. We had a good visit with Pless and I got to tour the wards I had worked on hardly a year before. The wards were white World War II barracks-type buildings built on rolling hills. Oak was part of its name, but it was the eucalyptus trees that gave the hospital its distinctive appearance and aroma. This was the place where I had had the honor of assisting in a colonoscopy examination of an admiral, and where I had gotten to know some of the first casualties of the Korean War. I had been fascinated by their stories then about that conflict, and their stories had whetted my desire to go and see for myself what the war was like. And now I had seen for myself.

The Marine with the gunstock splinters in his side and the one with the gangrenous arm were no longer there, of course, and were hopefully recovered from their wounds and well on their way to rehabilitation, but the wards were still full of men with wounds of every kind, many with a long difficult road to recovery ahead. That artillery captain who lost an eye and part of his face could have been there, I don't know. And very likely some of the H-3-7 Marines wounded at Yoke Ridge and Sanguine would show up in these wards before long. Oak Knoll Naval Hospital, like others around the country and in Japan, had received a steady flow of wounded GI's ever since the war had begun fifteen months earlier.

\* \* \*

I guess that letter mother hurried to get in the mail did the trick, because I did at long last have that reunion with my family—my mother, dad, and my twelve-year-old sister, Mary Alice, and my two married sisters, and grandmothers and aunts and uncles and cousins. I had not been home since my leave after boot camp almost three years earlier, so I was a little uncomfortable seeing all those people again. Many of them asked what it had been like over there, but what do you say?

My dear old uncle Howard from Ft. Worth, with his wavy hair and urbane manner, pulled his cigar from his mouth, his Mason ring shining on his finger, squinted at me through his rimless glasses, winked, and said, "You really saw it over there, Boy! Didn't you?"

Somewhere I had picked me up a sharp looking khaki Marine uniform and I wore that with my two rows of ribbons to a church party there in Dallas and met a number of pretty girls, one of whom I would know much better in a few years.

\* \* \*

When I was rotated out of Korea I was given my choice of duty. I could stay with the Marines in the FMF or go back to the Navy. And I could choose the area stateside where I would like to serve. I chose to go back to the Navy, and since I had served over two years in the sunny state of California, I thought it would be good to finish out my enlistment in that vacation state on the other side of the country, Florida.

There is no question that of the four years I spent in the service, my year with the Marines made the most indelible impression on me, and it is what I most identify with when I think of my military service. But the thing that drew me to the FMF was my desire to see combat, and since that desire had been more than satisfied, I was ready to complete my enlistment on a quiet Navy base. So I ended up in the Infirmary at Whiting Field, an auxiliary air base at Milton, Florida, not far from the main base at Pensacola where most of the Corsair pilots in Korea started their training. But my experiences there, while sometimes exciting, were considerably different from those I had in a Marine rifle company.

The Naval Cadets at Pensacola, many of whom no doubt would end up in Korea, went through one phase of flight training at our base and we in the dispensary took care of their medical needs. Occasionally we would take cadets to the main base at Pensacola to undergo the centrifuge test. The student pilot would be placed in a cockpit-like pod suspended from a long arm. As the pod began to spin around and pick up speed the cadet's position went from perpendicular to horizontal. After a while a light flashed and a horn sounded, and as the centrifuge slowed down the cadet returned from horizontal to perpendicular. He had been instructed to hold down two buttons with his thumbs as long as he could. When he lost consciousness his thumbs relaxed, the horn sounded, and the light flashed telling the testers how many G's the young man could take before losing consciousness.

In my final eleven months in the service there at Whiting Field, our main excitement came in making ambulance runs to pick up drunken sailors who had wrecked their cars on the way back from the clubs and bars of Pensacola. One wreck was particularly gruesome–three people with compound, complex fractures and severe internal injuries. We spent several hours working on them in the emergency room before we had them transported back to the hospital at Pensacola. After we got them on their way, the doctor singled me out to compliment the way I had helped handle the emergency. If I had performed well in the emergency there was a reason. I had had some recent experience dealing with trauma.

The most bizarre case I remember from that time was a sailor who was brought in with the skin torn off the bottoms of both his feet and gravel rocks imbedded into the raw flesh. In the emergency room, as we worked on the man who was in considerable pain, we tried to get from his drunken companion their story.

As we understood the man's account, the two had had a great time that night in the bars of Pensacola, and since his friend was in no condition to drive he, who was hardly in better condition, agreed to do the service. It was a warm night and, since this was before auto air conditioning, they headed back to Milton with their windows down. The passenger, in order to rest comfortably, took off his shoes and socks. The driver all the while tried his best to keep the road in focus while his shipmate, after a bit of jumbled conversation, fell asleep with his head on his arm resting on the car window. Somewhere, somehow along the way, the sleeping man's hand fell on the door handle and the door came open. They were going at a pretty good clip when this happened and when the driver saw the door start to open he put his foot on the brake. The sudden slowing of the car caused the door to swing forward sending the barefooted man out over the pavement which was racing below his feet while he hung desperately to the car door. His feet for a time skied across the asphalt and then as the driver pulled to the shoulder his feet scooted across the gravel and produced the wounds we were now treating at the Infirmary.

\* \* \*

As I finished out my enlistment in Florida, I corresponded from time to time with some of the Marines I had served with in How Company, but the contacts became fewer and fewer. Once while hitchhiking from Dallas back to Milton I stopped in New Orleans and gave Marcel Shexnayder a call. I told him I was just passing through and wanted to say hi, but he insisted on coming to pick me up and have me meet his family. It happened that he was just about to get married and he wanted me to meet his fiancée. I remember Marcel, being of French derivation, told me he was marrying an Italian girl— no, he said, "Hightalian" girl. He and all their families were in party mode and we had a great time as he took me around and introduced me, "Doc," to everyone. We wined and dined and had a great time, and Marcel wanted me to stay over for the wedding, but I had to report back to duty so I couldn't.

When Marcel dropped me back on the highway at about 2 am my head was reeling a bit from all the partying. There was a soldier also trying to catch a ride so we joined forces on the theory that two thumbs are better than one. After a while two men in a big Mercury stopped for us and we climbed into the back seat and roared off. I was pretty well bushed from the long journey and the celebrations, so after some perfunctory conversation between the driver and us, I promptly dozed off. Some time later I was awakened by the soldier poking me in the side. When I looked he was pointing between the two men at the speedometer there on the dashboard. I rose and looked over the shoulders of the men in the front seat and saw the needle bouncing between 95 and 100. It was a sobering experience.

What was the etiquette there? If someone does you a big favor and gives you a ride then puts your life at risk, is it OK to say something? We couldn't decide so we said nothing and yet somehow managed to survive.

While the war continued in Korea for almost another two years after I returned, I spent that time finishing up my enlistment in Florida and my first year of college. The war was behind me now, and though I kept up with the news, anxious for the war to end, I went on with my life. Soon all the guys I knew would have been rotated out and another crew would be there in the bunkers toughing it out.

\* \* \*

In the spring of 1952 the 1st Marine Division was moved to the west coast of Korea near Panmunjom and continued to fight in that region until the war ended over a year later. How Company was in the middle of much of the conflict, and it was there in the battle for Bunker Hill that Hospital Corpsman John E. Kilmer became the second member of How Company to win the Congressional Medal of Honor, joining 2nd Lt. Robert Reem who had also received his award posthumously during the Chosin Operation. Kilmer's citation reads in part, that he

> ...repeatedly braved intense enemy mortar, artillery, and
> sniper fire to move from one position to another, administering
> aid to the wounded and expediting their evacuation. Painfully
> wounded himself when struck by mortar fragments while mov-
> ing to the aid of a casualty, he persisted in his efforts and inched
> his way to the side of the stricken marine through a hail of enemy
> shells falling all around him. Undaunted by the devastating hos-
> tile fire, he skillfully administered first aid to his comrade and,
> as another mounting barrage of enemy fire shattered the immedi-
> ate area, unhesitatingly shielded the wounded man with his body.
> ( www.medalofhonor.com/JohnKilmer )

That final year of positional trench warfare saw many battles like the
one for Bunker Hill where Kilmer died carrying out his duties. An interesting footnote says of Kilmer and his fellow corpsmen during this phase of the
war: "Hospitalman Kilmer, a distant cousin of poet Joyce Kilmer, became
the first of four corpsmen serving with the 1[st] Marine Division to be awarded
the Medal of Honor during the trench warfare in western Korea" (Meid &
Yingling, 127).

One other member of How Company was awarded the Congressional
Medal of Honor, the only one to live to accept the award, and that was
Second Lieutenant George H. O'Brien, Jr. at the battle for the Hook, which
followed the struggle for Bunker Hill. His courageous leadership in that
battle and his character is revealed clearly online at the following website,
http://www.medalofhonor.com/GeorgeHOBrien.htm. In part the descriptions of O'Brien's leadership reads as follows:

> ...as a rifle platoon commander of Company H, in action
> against enemy aggressor forces. With his platoon subjected to
> an intense mortar and artillery bombardment while prepar-
> ing to assault a vitally important hill position on the main line
> of resistance which had been overrun by a numerically superior
> enemy force on the preceding night, 2d Lt. O'Brien leaped from
> his trench when the attack signal was given and, shouting for his
> men to follow, raced across an exposed saddle and up the enemy-
> held hill through a virtual hail of deadly small-arms, artillery, and
> mortar fire. Although shot through the arm and thrown to the
> ground by hostile automatic-weapons fire as he neared the well-
> entrenched enemy position, he bravely regained his feet, waved his
> men onward, and continued to spearhead the assault, pausing only
> long enough to go to the aid of a wounded marine. Encountering
> the enemy at close range, he proceeded to hurl hand grenades into
> the bunkers and, utilizing his carbine to best advantage in savage

hand-to-hand combat, succeeded in killing at least 3 of the enemy. Struck down by the concussion of grenades on 3 occasions during the subsequent action, he steadfastly refused to be evacuated for medical treatment and continued to lead his platoon in the assault for a period of nearly 4 hours...

Hospital Corpsman Kilmer was killed a week before I was discharged from the Navy; the following month I enrolled at Abilene Christian College in west Texas.

Going back and forth between Dallas and Abilene I drove through Ft Worth where a Chicano veteran of How Company lived, and once I stopped and visited with him. I regret that I can't remember his name, but I do remember he had been shot in the arm and that we talked about his treatment and rehabilitation and his plans for the future. I did communicate with Charles Foley and a few of my other buddies from Korea back then, but as the years passed the strong ties that had bound me to the men of H-3-7 were loosened, and over time I lost contact with them.

* * *

On July 27 1953 the Korean War finally came to an end. By then our dead had been buried, our wounded hospitalized and rehabilitated to the extent possible, and those of us who survived had gone on with our lives. One author says of the ending of the war,

> In essence, everything that occurred in Korea after the summer of 1951 was a waste of time and lives. The issue had been decided: the North Korean military adventure had failed, the UN attempt to impose a military solution had failed, and the Chinese attempt to force the UN out of Korea had failed. (Hoyt, 230)

We left the mountains of Korea, we left the war, we left history behind, and the powerful bond that had held us together during those months of combat, of winter cold, summer heat, travails, triumphs and tragedies, were memories now. Military units live on with new personnel and new conflicts, but the group of men, How Company, 3rd Battalion, 7th Regiment, 1st Marine Division, that rifle company of the Korean War, was no more. Just as we had come together from different backgrounds and different places to make up How Company, after the war we all went our separate ways. Like standing on the rear platform of a train and watching a town fall away in the distance, growing ever smaller and less distinct, the names and faces and memories of those comrades dimmed with time, but for me they could never be lost. Some of those names and faces and memories I knew I would take to my grave.

Like all of us who made it back alive from Korea I went on with my life, but through the years from time to time I would puzzle over the question: what was that thing I had been so intensely a part of? Why do young men generation after generation find themselves brothers in arms like those of us in How Company climbing the mountains of Korea listening to the thunder of cannons reverberating across the valleys? And when we found ourselves caught up in the most horrible human enterprise imaginable, the slaughter of other human beings, why did it seem so ordinary?

Sprawled around in the smoke of campfires heating our C Rations, smoking cigarettes, drinking coffee, talking and laughing, knowing we were going to move out in the morning and likely be in another firefight before the next nightfall, seemed to us a natural thing to be doing, like we were following some familiar pattern much older than our own experience. There is no question that strong bonds were forged among those of us in How Company in the crucible of combat there in Korea, and it's clear that such bonds are the universal experience of men whose survival depends on the courage and loyalty of their comrades. But those strong bonds are purchased at a dear price.

That price is war.

# CHAPTER 18

# War

In an early scene of Stanley Kubrick's movie, "2001 A Space Odyssey," a clan of hirsute primates is scavenging the carcass of some giant prehistoric creature when another clan appears over a rise and looks down on their kindred gorging themselves below. Being of the same or closely similar species, one might reasonably expect the first group to invite the late arrivals down to the feast, or at least move over and make room for them at the table, but these were proto humans and reason played no part in such interactions. When they become aware of the intruders the primal emotions of greed, fear and anger take over and, not yet having developed language, those in possession of the carcass attempt to drive off the marauders with loud grunts, snorts, and violent gestures; but hunger draws the newcomers ever closer to the food and the defending clan. The "warriors" of each group move to the fore, confronting one another with even louder displays of threatening behavior, but it appears the defenders will not be able to hold off their hungry cousins. Then at the height of these raucous displays, a defender picks up what looks to be a long leg bone and lays one of the opposing warriors upside the head. All the loud displays cease as both sides stare in shock and surprise at the fallen warrior lying there on the ground. They had all witnessed something new, something prodigious—the use of a weapon.

The latecomers confronted with this new and awful circumstance begin to back off and withdraw from the field, leaving the first clan to continue their feast. The weapon-wielding warrior, elated by his innovation and discovery, hurls the bone into the air, the camera following it as it whirls upward into the blue sky where, after a dramatic interlude, it morphs into a spinning space station, a giant wheel turning in orbit above the earth. At this point the strains of the Blue Danube Waltz fill the theater and contribute an emotional dimension to that brief trip the audience has just taken through a few million years of human history.

The movie is fantasy, science fiction, but the idea that the development of weapons and the development of human technology and civilization are inextricably connected is real. And humans didn't need the movie's mysterious monolith from outer space to spark their creativity. They did it on their own thanks to the development of upright posture, bipedal gait, amazing prehensile hands with opposing thumbs, growing brains, and the emergence of language, each of which synergistically stoked the others. Weapons, tools, technology all grew together in an autocatalytic process which has in recent decades accelerated to warp speed. Would our space satellites be circling the earth today if there had been no Cold War, if nations on both sides had not felt threatened, felt fear and anger toward one another? Are orbiting satellites not just the latest manifestations of the technology begun when that bone was hurled in the air?

\* \* \*

We all came out of Africa a million or so years ago, and we were all hunters following the game. Stone was the material of our first weapons and remained the raw material for our technology for untold millennia. I marvel when I find an arrowhead like the one I recently found in my back yard while I was transplanting that burning bush, (which interestingly enough is not native to this country, but to Korea). God didn't speak to me out of the bush like he did to Moses, but the arrowhead I dug up from the ground was a kind of silent messenger, nevertheless. I examined it closely, studied the carefully chipped edges, the point and the fluted neck intelligently crafted to fit an arrow shaft. A purposeful human hand chipped every flake from this artifact and valued it before losing it in a hunt or a battle, and holding it somehow connected me to the person who had shaped it. It occurs to me as I examine the collection of arrowheads, stone axes and scrapers my son and I have retrieved from Caddo Indian campsites along the Ouachita River nearby, that nothing we make in our high-tech society will endure like the tools and weapons of our earliest ancestors.

Like the imaginary primates in "2001 a Space Odyssey," our earliest forebears spent the great part of their lives searching for food. They were hunters and gatherers and competitors for game and hunting territory, so those tools developed for the hunt served equally well as weapons in combat. But our forebears were also social creatures so they had, as we continue to have, a great capacity for friendly interaction and social cooperation. They must have developed early on, when confronted with perceived strangers and potential competitors, the ability to quickly categorize other human beings, as we still do today, as "them," the aliens, the enemies, and "us," members of our own group. So the tools developed to bring down game in a cooperative hunt became weapons to bring down enemies in a tribal conflict. No doubt many hunting parties quickly converted to war parties when they encountered rival bands of hunters.

Our most distant ancestors may not have been "killer apes" as one anthropologist, Robert Ardrey, has suggested, but they were, under the right circumstances, certainly able to kill their fellow humans with little or no compunction just as we are still able to do in the twenty first century. How we are able to kill one another so readily and on such large scales has long puzzled scholars and students of history. John Keegan, the distinguished historian of war has a good deal to say concerning the academic inquiry into the question of why men fight in *A History of Warfare* in a section headed, "War and the Anthropologists."

I believe most scientists today would agree that these cultural and psychosocial combative traits have a genetic basis, and if that is the case we should recognize that we humans are genetically predisposed to hunting and war just as we are predisposed to many other behaviors, many of them benevolent and altruistic and admirable. Why do young boys and men love to compete, to run races, to wrestle and box, to see who can throw things the farthest, footballs, baseballs, javelins, rocks–all the skills required for ancient hunting and warfare? Why do they enjoy organized sports, many of them little more than mock warfare? (I don't want to violate the principles of political correctness here. I do know girls and young women also enjoy these activities, but I believe it's clear that, at least up until the last decade, war has been the province and profession of men.) Even in the midst of the war there in Korea we in How Company entertained ourselves by wrestling with the *cargadores*, and holding boxing matches during our "Smokers," and throwing rocks at little red-bellied frogs.

Having taught college for thirty years I remember being involved in numerous encounters between us academic professors on one side and administrators on the other over what we believed were the excessive expenditures for varsity sports, particularly football. In large schools athletic programs are often self-supporting, but in small regional universities such as the one where I taught those programs are a drain on the general budget, and we resented it. In addition to support from the university's general funds, profits from the bookstore were also used to subsidize our less than spectacular football program. Many of us in the academic faculty dreamed of having a small liberal arts university where students participated in intramural athletics and academics. But ours was a losing cause. The desire from our students and alumni to get out there and root for their football team, their "warriors," was too powerful for a gaggle of namby-pamby professors to overcome. A defender of athletic programs at some university once taunted the academics: "Let's see you fill up a stadium with a reading of Shakespeare's sonnets!"

Well, maybe not the sonnets. But Shakespeare understood very well the drama and appeal of warfare, and used that understanding better than any other writer to fill theaters and entertain audiences. That is another problem with war—it is so damned entertaining, at least for the reader, the spectator, and the historian. Drama is a Greek word meaning "thing done," or "action," and certainly war is the ultimate human action or drama. We even speak of "theaters of war" using another Greek word, "theater."

The Romans understood well the human fascination with combat and made gladiatorial and other martial contests the main attractions in their spectacle entertainments; the Caesars found that for the most part they could keep citizens pacified with bread and circuses. And of course the Romans lined up by the thousands to witness the triumphal parades of the victorious Caesars returning from far-flung battles, displaying with great pomp their tributes of war.

The millions of soldiers who have suffered and died, and the multitudinous innocent victims of war, however, have never appreciated war's entertainment value. While football and other sports have the same compelling ingredients of conflict, strategy, spirit and struggle, and clear and decisive outcomes, they are played only for the glory of the day, or for the season, and then the outcomes are quickly forgotten. Wars, which have been with us since our beginnings, are fought for keeps, for ultimate stakes, and their outcomes can change history forever.

We don't have to go back far in our history to find our hunter-gatherer ancestors; take away our technological trappings, and we are still those same people. Stone Age tribes still exist and it was just a twinkling of time ago that we all followed that same pattern of existence. Under our thin veneer of civilization the impulses for that ancient way of life are still strong. Visit a few deer camps in Arkansas during hunting season and you will see that those old traditions are very much alive. And the hunting instinct cuts across cultural and class lines. Prince Charles is outspoken in defense of the royal foxhunt while wealthy Americans have access to more than 3000 "canned hunting" operations in this country where they can shoot pen-raised birds and mammals for a fee. Former Vice President Cheney, who famously made news as a result of a mishap on a quail hunt when he shot a fellow hunter in the face with his Perazzi Brescia 28 gauge shotgun (price $10, 000 to $500,000), was reported to have killed more than 70 pheasants on a single "canned hunt" in 2003.

Our impulse for war also lies just beneath the thin veneer of civilization. There is little difference, physical or mental, between people today driving around in SUVs and talking on cell phones and our hunter-gatherer ancestors twenty thousand years ago. Why else did boys have so much fun playing cowboys and Indians in my day, a pastime which I suppose today has been replaced by video combat games, and why do grown men enjoy taking to the woods to engage in mock "paint ball" warfare? Hunting and warfare are inextricably connected and are still very much a part of our human nature.

\* \* \*

Our most destructive activity, war, has given us our greatest heroes. The most admired men throughout history have been warriors. And there are good reasons for our adulation. Just as the hunters had to be successful in bringing home game, the warriors had to be successful in fending off attacks and in bringing home booty and spoils and claiming new territory from rival clans if the tribe was to survive. In primitive societies the same skills and weapons were required for success in both activities, and tribal champions no doubt excelled in both hunting and warfare. The Darwinian dynamic applies to human societies as it does to all life on earth. What would the Cheetah look like if it had never had to run down its prey? What would the gazelle look like if it had never had to flee its predators? Human societies faced the same kinds of challenges for their survival and were shaped by the struggle. Robinson Jeffers recognized this and wrote the following poem celebrating war:

### The Bloody Sire

It is not bad. Let them play.
Let the guns bark and the bombing-plane
Speak his prodigious blasphemies.
It is not bad, it is high time,
Stark violence is still the sire of all the world's values.

What but the wolf's tooth chiseled so fine
The fleet limbs of the antelope?
What but fear winged the birds and hunger
Gemmed with such eyes the great goshawks head?
Violence has been the sire of all the world's values.

Who would remember Helen's face
Lacking the terrible halo of spears?
Who formed Christ but Herod and Caesar,
The cruel and bloody victories of Caesar?
Violence has been the sire of all the world's values.

Never weep, let them play,
Old violence is not too old to beget new values.

We don't have to go so far as the poet and celebrate war and violence, and we can hope there's a touch of irony in his poem. The challenge we face today is to try to find a way out of our bloody heritage.

While our ancient race may have been strengthened when only the strongest were left standing on the battlefield, it's difficult to imagine any advantages of biological selection for humans that might come from modern warfare, just as it's difficult to imagine what improvements can come to wild game, such as deer, when the natural predators that culled the weakest are replaced with hunters in deer stands with high powered rifles and scopes looking for big bucks with huge racks.

While today technology has changed the dynamic, we can still recognize that all life, including human life, has reached its present state through violent struggle and competition, and it doesn't take a great leap of imagination to see that those human groups in the past with the strongest and bravest and most physically skillful young men had the greatest chance for survival. It's no wonder then that successful tribes selected from among those young men their champions, their heroes to celebrate. Often they made those heroes their "chiefs" and "kings."

\* \* \*

The characteristics which will most likely shape the future evolution of man if we are to continue to progress will not be physical strength and prowess, however, but intelligence and wisdom. Of course there have been those in recent times who have not understood this, including the leaders of the Axis powers in World War II. Benito Mussolini, called by some the "sawdust Caesar," believed in the invigorating power of modern war. He said "The Italian proletariat needs a blood bath for its force to be renewed." He later said, "War alone brings up to its highest tension all human energy and puts the stamp of nobility upon the peoples who have the courage to face it."

By 1945 I had graduated from selling magazines from door to door to throwing a *Dallas Morning News* paper route. I and a number of other borderline juvenile delinquents would gather at Wylie's Corner, an all-night service station and convenience store at the corner of Beckley and Saner Avenue, around 4:30 each morning to retrieve our bundle of papers and sit together while we folded them and stored them snugly in our canvas bags in preparation for setting out on our bicycles to fling them onto the porches of subscribers along our routes. Today we're lucky if our paper makes it over the curb, but in those days if the paper didn't land on the porch we got a complaint, or as we called them, "kicks."

Daily the news was about the war, but in late April of that year I got a call from my manager one morning—it must have been a weekend because I wasn't in school—and he told me he would be dropping off a bundle of extras for me at Wylie's Corner to peddle up and down the streets.

Selling extras was a new experience for me, but I rode my bike down to Wylie's Corner, picked up the extras and then set out on foot down my route calling out, "Extra! Extra! Read all about it! Mussolini is dead!" I took my cue from newsboys I had seen cry out like that in movies.

At first I was a little embarrassed and didn't call out very loud, but after a while, as people started coming out of their houses to buy a paper, I became bolder and raised my voice and raised my profits. When they placed that nickel in my hand I would give them a copy of the paper with the picture of Mussolini and his mistress Claretta Petacci hanging upside down between the pumps of a gas station in Milan along with other members of their ill-fated gang. They had been caught by their own countrymen while trying to flee dressed as German soldiers. So much for that stamp of nobility.

\* \* \*

While the characteristics of intelligence and wisdom may determine man's evolutionary future, physical prowess and conflict are what have made us who we are today. No wonder then that the history of war plays such a dominant role in the history of man. Library shelves are weighted down with innumerable volumes recounting stories of war and deeds of heroes. And many conflicts and heroes in the long millennia of prehistory never got into books because there was no written language. But we can be sure those heroes and battles were celebrated and passed down in song and story by early people gathered around fires at night in places like Lascaux, France, where talented artists seventeen thousand years ago created in caves there beautiful wall paintings of extinct bison, ibexes, wooly rhinoceros, and other migrating game on which our nomadic ancestors depended for life.

Our forebears following the game herds across Europe and other Stone Age hunter-gatherers around the world were no doubt entertained and edified by their preliterate tribal historians and troubadours with tales of heroes, legendary hunters and warriors, while sitting around campfires at night. The stories were surely memorized, embellished, and passed down from generation to generation by poets following ancient oral tradition. With the rise of civilization, however, the nature of war changed, and with the development of writing man found a way to pass down stories and history even when the story tellers and historians who generated the accounts were no more.

In the four and a half billion-year history of the earth and the million or so year history of man it is astounding how recent a phenomenon civilization is. The last ice age, the Pleistocene period, ended just over ten thousand years ago, and it was only after that that man developed agriculture, domesticated animals, learned to plow and plant, and was able to abandon his nomadic ways. We know that the first cities developed in Mesopotamia between the Tigris and Euphrates Rivers and along the fertile Nile River in Egypt. These things we all learned in elementary school. The significance of these developments in the history of war is that this new way of producing food meant that warriors were no longer required to double as hunters. And since agriculture provided surpluses that rarely existed among hunter-gatherers, war became a specialization and warriors now had a profession.

The fact that civilization had arrived did not mean that man was civilized. The old competitive, marauding ways did not cease with the rise of cities. If the ruler of a city or the king of a land wanted to preserve his domain he had to have means of defending it, so he built up an army to provide that protection. Under this new arrangement the loose band of warriors of old now became an organized military. And if a ruler built up a strong army to defend his realm and saw a weaker neighbor close by just sitting there for the taking, why not lead his army over to appropriate that land and wealth and increase his own domain? So the struggle that had gone on from time immemorial continued: offense and defense–attack and defend. And in all these societies the men most respected and admired were the warriors, the men who won victories, who brought new territory and wealth to the country, the men who repelled the heathen at the walls of the city. They were the heroes that enabled those societies to exist, so we should not be surprised at their exalted status.

With the rise of civilizations and the armies which defended them and enabled them to expand their power, there arose theoreticians of war, men who understood that war was an adjunct of statecraft and set about to spell out the principles and strategies that were essential for successful warfare. One of the earliest surviving works on the subject is from 4[th] century China, Sun Tzu's *Art of War,* a work which presents many principles of warfare that are eternally valid. Classical writers such as Herodotus, Thucydides, and Xenophon expounded on the subject in detail and in the middle ages Machiavelli, author of the classic work, *The Prince,* wrote his own treatise also entitled *The Art of War* which went through twenty-one editions in the sixteenth century alone. Carl von Clausewitz, a veteran of the Prussian Wars of the 19[th] century, added to the genre with his often quoted study entitled *On War.* And today libraries, particularly at military academies, have shelves lined with books on warriors and on the art and science of warfare.

The first such warrior king we know of came from Mesopotamia. He was Gilgamesh, king of Uruk around 2700 BCE (Keegan, 133). We know about him because, after being transmitted orally for generations, his story was at last written down and thus became the earliest recorded heroic tale—*The Epic of Gilgamesh.* He and his half-animal sidekick, Enkidu, battle Humbaba, monster of the cedar forests of Lebanon and bring new trade and wealth to their country. Gilgamesh faces many challenges and overcomes them all except one, his long journey to the land of Dilmun in search of Upnatishtim who had survived the Great Flood and become one of the immortals. He wanted to find for himself from Upnatishtim the secret of immortality. But he failed in his quest and the great hero of our earliest epic, as is the common lot, had to accept his own mortality. It is in this work that we find the earliest version of the story of the flood told in Genesis.

Western literature began with a story of war. The Homeric epics, the *Iliad* and the *Odyssey,* have preserved in our collective memories tales of a war that occurred over three millennia ago. We all know the story of how the Trojan, Paris, stole from the Greek Meneleus, his wife, Helen, the most beautiful woman in the world, "the face that launched a thousand ships," and fled with her to Troy. And we know that Meneleus then went to his brother, Agamemnon, first among kings, to seek help in avenging this Trojan outrage, and in so doing set in motion a war that would last ten years. The conflict began with the first marine operation we know of, the amphibious assault by the Greeks on the city of Troy.

In addition to entertaining people through all these years, Homer's epics provide us with the two major archetypes of military leaders in Achilles and Odysseus. Achilles is the professional warrior, the straight-ahead fighter who relies on his strength and courage and his confidence that no man is his equal in combat. When given the choice between a long uneventful life and a short glorious life, he chose the latter. He exults in his profession and relishes the contest, and the Trojans soon learn to fear his battle cry.

Odysseus, on the other hand, while also a courageous warrior, is more of a strategist and diplomat. He can be deadly in a fight, as the suitors of his wife, Penelope, find out when he returns to his home in Ithaca, but he seems happiest when he can best his opponents by using his wits. And on his long journey home we see a man with great curiosity, open to whatever experiences life brings him, fascinated by other cultures and ways of life. Nations today still need both types of leaders, the Achilles and the Odysseus, the straight-ahead fighters and the intellectually gifted strategists.

While war is the subject of our earliest literature, it is also the subject of our earliest historians. Herodotus, the father of history, tells us of the Persian Wars that threatened the very existence of Athens, Sparta and other Greek city-states. We learn from him that great story of the Spartan king, Leonidas, who with a small band of Spartans, Thespians, and other Greek soldiers held off Xerxes and his million-man Persian army in the narrow mountain pass of Thermopylae. Their courageous fight to the death gave the Greeks time to prepare their defenses against the invading army and gave Western Civilization a hero to admire for the ages. The Greek victory in that war in 480 BCE set the stage for the greatest flowering of culture in human history. We owe a lot to our warriors, our military heroes.

Victor Hanson in his study of war, *Carnage and Culture,* presents the thesis that Western Civilization–beginning with the Greeks who gave the world, among other things, the ideas of democracy, the celebration of the individual, and respect for reason and science–has produced the deadliest and most efficient fighting forces in the world. According to him we in the United States are inheritors of a culture of warfare that began with the Greeks who, he says,

> fought much differently than their adversaries and . . . [the] unique
> Hellenic characteristics of battle—a sense of personal freedom,

superior discipline, matchless weapons, egalitarian camaraderie, individual initiative, constant tactical adaptation and flexibility, preference for shock battle of heavy infantry—were themselves the murderous dividends of Hellenic culture at large. The peculiar way Greeks killed grew out of consensual government, equality among the middling classes, civilian audit of military affairs, and politics apart from religion, freedom and individualism, and rationalism (Hanson, 4).

The author goes on to give many examples of conflicts between Western armies and those from other cultures to make his point that Western armies that permitted some degree of latitude and autonomy to their troops always had the upper hand in battle, and that those Eastern powers from Persia on down who impressed and coerced their hapless subjects into the ranks with no voice in the conduct of a war could never match the ferocity of those fighters who had some stake and some say in the conflict.

The most destructive wars, he points out, have been those where two Western powers fought one another, as happened in the Peloponnesian War between Sparta and Athens. Thucydides, considered by some to be the greatest historian of all times, wrote the history of that war, which followed by only five decades the Greek victory over Persia. In his study of the war that brought an end to the Golden Age of Greece that had blossomed during that scant five decades, Thucydides carefully analyzes and dissects the causes of that civil war between Sparta and Athens in an attempt to understand how wars, which can protect and defend nations, can also be the means of their destruction and downfall.

In history as in literature the warrior hero has continued to be celebrated down through the ages: Aeneas, the legendary Roman hero who escaped from burning Troy and eventually established the ruling lineage of Rome according to the poet, Virgil; Alexander the Great, the factual historical warrior from Macedonia who spread Greek culture in all his military campaigns following the Peloponnesian War, and who had conquered the known world before his death at the age of thirty two; the Biblical warriors, such as David, Joshua, and the desperado, Samson, who, among his other exploits, reportedly slew one thousand Philistines with the jawbone of an ass; the Caesars and military leaders documented in Gibbon's classic work, *The Decline and Fall of the Roman Empire*; the knights and Crusaders of the Middle Ages, and the list goes on to include the many warriors and heroes from cultures throughout the world. These warrior heroes have furnished material for our myths and legends, poetry and drama, and continue to serve as examples of leadership, courage, ingenuity and daring, and their stories continue to entertain and inspire us to this day.

There are too many English heroes to enumerate—the many kings and lords in the many battles, heroes like Sir Walter Raleigh, Admiral Nelson, Lord Wellington, all the way up to those RAF pilots in the Battle of Britain, about whom Churchill said, "Never have so many owed so much to so few." And we have not even mentioned Napoleon and the many other military heroes of Europe and the other countries of the world. But I believe the point is made. Although many important and significant events have taken place since the beginning of human history, the majority of those making it into books are stories of wars, battles, and warriors.

We in the United States don't lag behind the rest of the world when it comes to warrior heroes. Every war we have fought has provided us with exemplars of those qualities we admire, from The Revolutionary War to Vietnam, heroes from George Washington to Sergeant York, Audie Murphy, and Chesty Puller. We have heroes from the Indian Wars, from the battle of the Alamo, and many heroes from both sides in that greatest crisis of our nation, the Civil War. And a fair number of those heroes have gone on to fill high leadership positions in government at state and national levels, including the office of President. After Washington there were other warrior presidents, such as Andrew Jackson, Ulysses S. Grant, Theodore Roosevelt, Dwight D. Eisenhower, John F. Kennedy and George H.W. Bush. We owe our very existence to all the warriors, known and forgotten, who have preserved this country and the principles on which it was founded—freedom, democracy, equality, human rights. These ideals should always be propagated with moral suasion but defended with military force when necessary. While wars are often senseless and always destructive, we know they are sometimes necessary.

But there are terrible downsides to any war. In the entire history of man we have killed enough of one another to populate another planet. On the other side of the glory, excitement, and drama of war is the terrible toll war takes in human suffering. Even when war is waged for the noblest purposes, the suffering of innocents is always beyond imagining.

\* \* \*

I know of no other conflict where the line between the forces of good and evil was more clearly drawn than when the Allies and the Axis powers faced off in World War II. And certainly the Nazi blitzkrieg that swept across Europe and the Holocaust that followed, and the murderous Japanese attack on the Philippines and China that resulted in such atrocities as the "Rape of Nanking" and the Bataan Death March, and the surprise attack on Pearl Harbor, were evils that had to be met with force. But countering those evils resulted in additional tragedies too numerous to mention. Just a few examples are the firebombing of Dresden, the firebombing of Japan and the A-bombing of Hiroshima and Nagasaki, and the examples go on and on.

In each of these cases and in every war fought for whatever reason, the most pitiful tragedy is the toll taken on innocent civilians, on women, children, the elderly. And along with that terrible toll is the great price we pay in the loss of the best and bravest of the young men we send off to fight.

In spite of such terrible costs, man has never for long been able to resist the call to war. Throughout history and prehistory, the reasons for which men fought wars, except in cases of self-defense, were seldom noble. The first leaders were often Alpha males, big strong warriors who attained their office by courageous deeds and force of arms, though no doubt intelligence was a useful adjunct. But many times these warriors would contrive to pass their power to their offspring who might not be so powerful and noble and might even be depraved, and those heritors of power often emulated their sires and sought to bring glory to themselves and their domains by attacking their neighbors.

The successful leaders assumed the title of "Chief" or "King" or some other lordly title, and eventually succeeded in getting the populace to accept the proposition that they ruled by "Divine Right." One way to serve God was to be obedient to the king. There developed over the years the idea that king and country were one, and the people's loyalty to their country was expressed through their loyalty to the king. That, in those days, was patriotism. Illiterate peasants, farmers, craftsmen, and poor young men from around the country would be rounded up, impressed into military service, and sent off to die for the glory of the king in a war that was often nothing more than a royal family feud. King and country could be a great rallying cry, as we see in the closing lines of that great speech provided to *Henry V* by Shakespeare before the battle of Agincourt on Saint Crispin's day:

> And Crispin Crispian shall ne'er go by,
> From this day to the ending of the world,
> But we in it shall be remembered;
> We few, we happy few, we band of brothers;
> For he to-day that sheds his blood with me
> Shall be my brother; be he ne'er so vile,
> This day shall gentle his condition:
> And gentlemen in England now a-bed
> Shall think themselves accursed they were not here,
> And hold their manhoods cheap whiles any speaks
> That fought with us upon Saint Crispin's day.

We see here that the way to rouse troops for battle is not by an appeal to their reason, for the French greatly outnumbered the English in this battle, but rather, as King Henry does so brilliantly, by stirring their emotions.

We would not be human without emotions. Emotions are what give value to everything we love and cherish—our families, our country, art and music, and the beautiful planet we live on, our sense of wonder at all the marvels of the universe. Without emotions we would be robots. But human emotions also have the potential to wreak havoc and are in fact one of the most powerful weapons in any war. The most effective military leaders throughout history have been those who knew how to arouse and channel that power. Morally that power is neutral; it can be used for good, as it was by Winston Churchill and Franklin Roosevelt during World War II, or for evil, as practiced by the propaganda machine of Adolph Hitler. When the flags are waving and the martial music is playing few can resist. The masses have always been vulnerable to charismatic madmen. The classic Nazi film, *Triumph of the Will*, demonstrates powerfully the way skillful propagandists can manipulate the emotions of the masses. First stir the blood then spill the blood.

Patriotism is not the only way to reach the emotions. Another reliable trigger for our emotion is religion. The old nationalistic wars were often fought under the cry "For God and Country!" or "For God and King!" There have been many rationales for war, such as Alexander's campaign to bring the excellence of Hellenic civilization to the benighted regions of the world, or the many campaigns of the Caesars and Emperors to bring the rights of Roman citizenship to the barbaric hinterlands of the Empire, but in all these cases the major purpose for the wars was simply to expand the hegemony of a particular power and promote the glory of the leader. Often, however, alongside state powers there have existed influential ecclesiastic powers that helped create a special category of war, the "Holy War"—as fine an example of an oxymoron as can be found.

Prophets who claimed the power to speak for God have instigated some of those wars in the past, and the "religious wars" which followed were often the bloodiest of them all. The Old Testament records more than a few such battles. Just one of them from 1st Samuel 15 will illustrate:

The prophet Samuel commands Saul to "Go smite Amalek, and utterly destroy all that they have, and spare them not, but slay both man and woman, infant and suckling, ox, sheep, camel and ass." Later when Samuel learns that Saul has destroyed Amalek and killed all the men, women, children and babies but has kept some of the prize livestock and spared the life of King A-gag, he is furious. The prophet tells Saul that the Lord is grieved that Saul has spared A-gag and then demands that the unfortunate king be brought before him. When he is brought in, A-gag, realizing the danger he is in, talks fast in pleading tones trying to save his life, but to no avail. The scripture says Samuel drew his sword and "hewed A-gag to pieces before the Lord in Gil-gal."

There are certain prophecies that are safe: "There will be wars and rumors of wars." "It will be hot in Arkansas next summer." These kinds of "prophecies" we can all make. But when men from any age presume to speak for God and offer to reveal the future to us and tell us what God wants us to do, when they claim to have some special understanding of any scripture from any religion and presume to tell us what God's will is, we should take care. We are warned to "beware of false prophets." From my own observations and experience I would shorten that warning by one word. "Beware of prophets!"

Throughout history political leaders have used war as a method for gaining and expanding power while religious leaders and religions have provided divine justification for the slaughter. There have been many so-called "holy wars," or "jihads," in which one group of believers set out to put the "infidels" to the sword. Even followers of Jesus, the Prince of Peace, ironically have resorted to war on numerous occasions to gain power and impose their will on non-believers. There were not only the Crusades of the Middle Ages whose purpose was to take the Holy Land from the Muslims who had been on a military expansion of their own, but also the power struggles in Europe between feudal lords and popes throughout the Middle Ages and continuing into the Age of Discovery and the Renaissance and Reformation.

The Conquistadores combined their search for gold with the mission to spread their religion to the benighted inhabitants of the New World, and men such as Cortez, shocked to see the Aztecs cut the beating hearts of their sacrificial victims from their bodies in practicing their religion, were not reluctant to hack to death any of those recalcitrant natives who refused to accept Spanish dominance and the Lord Jesus Christ.

In our own national history some justified the taking of the land from Native Americans as "Manifest Destiny," which is very close if not identical to claiming that North America was the European settlers' "Promised Land."

The planet we inhabit could very well be dubbed "Battlefield Earth." The soil everywhere is drenched in blood and tears. Just about everyone in the world lives on land that was taken from someone else by force. I heard a story once about a scholar who went to study the natives of a particular country and began by asking one the question, "Where did you get this land?"

"I got it from my father," the native answered.

"Where did he get it?"

"He got it from his father."

"And where did he get it?"

"He got it from his father."

"And where did he get it?"

"He took it from those people who were here before."

How can we ever go back and right all the injustices of the past? At some point we are going to have to accept the boundaries as we find them, the status quo, and resolve to stop the aggressive wars and learn to live under law and in peace.

* * *

It occurs to me that one of the greatest curses that can befall a child is to be born into a people with a blood grievance, to be taught from the cradle that it is his duty to exact vengeance on some other hated group which has inflicted hurt and injustice on the child's people in the past. We can look around the world today and see many examples of peoples nursing their injuries and looking for revenge. Children born into those societies have their lives stolen from them. There can never be an end to such cycles of violence. The Greeks came to understand this, though they were unable to escape that destructive cycle themselves.

Aeschylus in his *Oresteia* trilogy follows his protagonist, Orestes, one of those individuals doomed to be an avenger. It is his solemn, divine duty to avenge the death of his father, Agamemnon. The problem was that Agamemnon was brutally slain by Orestes' mother, Clytemnestra, and since there was also a divine injunction against matricide, Orestes was caught in a double bind. He was duty bound to kill his mother, but in doing so he would be condemned as a parricide.

It's true the murder of Agamemnon was only the latest in a complex history of blood and vengeance in that family, the House of Atreus, going back generations. Agamemnon had sacrificed his daughter, Iphigenia, to placate the gods before setting off for the Trojan War, and Clytemnestra avenged her daughter's death by killing Agamemnon. Orestes now was obligated to kill his mother, and so he does, but afterwards he is pursued around the world and tormented by the vengeful spirits, the Furies.

By the end of the third play of the trilogy the gods and the audience, with Aeschylus' help, come to understand that the old idea of vengeance as justice, the idea that the next of kin should serve as the avenger, can never lead to true justice, can never lead to any kind of stasis or resolution. At some point there must be atonement, there must be some way out of the endless cycle of retribution. Orestes at last finds that atonement when the gods acknowledge their own culpability in these human tragedies; then, finally, after Orestes' long travail, the Furies are replaced by friendly spirits, the Eumenides, and Orestes can find peace at last.

Jesus in his Sermon on the Mount showed us a way out of the cycle of retribution, that fearful symmetry of vengeance—an eye for an eye. But we have already discussed the impracticality of his recommendations. There are many Christians, but how many practice the principles he taught in that sermon? Maybe when the lion lies down with the lamb we will be able to turn the other cheek, but I don't see that happening anytime soon.

Yet Jesus' message has a deep and powerful appeal to all of us. He offers us a way out, but before we can follow that way we have to overcome our own nature that has been shaped by a million years of struggle and conflict. He is in effect telling us that we must do away with our deepest and most primal instincts, our natural tendency to categorize people as "them" and "us," telling us that we must eliminate the label of "them" and recognize everyone as "us." Love is his answer, but time after time throughout history love has been overpowered by human rage and aggression.

Much of the tragedy of the human condition comes from the fact that we are able to love one another and kill one another. It is likely that Cain loved his brother Abel, but that didn't stop him from murdering him. We would all like to see an end to the eternal strife, to the suffering we inflict on one another, an end to our lamentations, an end to war. And perhaps we could find peace in the valley if war weren't so deeply embedded in our hearts.

* * *

Beating our swords into plowshares is going to be devilishly hard because swords (weapons) have been integral to our nature and cultures much longer than plowshares (agriculture, civilization), so it is clear that putting an end to war will not be easy. If insanity is, as they say, repeating an action over and over expecting to get a different result, then the human race is clearly insane. We fight war after war and the outcome is always the same: bloodshed, destruction, suffering and grief.

# CHAPTER 19

# After Korea–Wars Cold and Hot

While humans are not given the powers of prophecy we are permitted to make predictions based on inductive reasoning, on our experience. We can be very precise with some of our forecasts, such as the times of the rising and setting of the sun and the changes of tides and seasons. Other phenomena, such as the weather, earthquakes and tsunamis, are more difficult. The former we can predict with mathematical precision; they follow purely rational patterns. The latter involve chaotic elements beyond our capacity to compute; the seething molten core of the earth is always taking us by surprise with earthquakes and erupting volcanoes. Above ground the earth's atmosphere and the weather it produces, such as hurricanes and tornadoes, often catch us unprepared. But while we cannot predict the timing of natural disasters as we can with sunrise and seasons, we can with certainty predict they will come.

These two natural forces have counterparts in man's psyche—his capacity for reason and his emotions. War is irrational. It draws its devastating power from our emotions. It has more similarities with tsunamis and hurricanes than with the regular fluctuations of the tides. We don't know exactly when wars will erupt, but because of the volatility of human emotions we know they will come, thus the prophet was on safe ground when he said there will be wars and rumors of wars. Like other members of my generation, I can attest to the truth of that prophecy. I have been witness to wars for a major portion of my life and was intimately involved in one of them.

That war, the Korean War, can be understood only in the broader context of World War II and Vietnam. All three wars are linked, first by one life span, three score years and ten. Second, they are linked by participants in those wars. Just as Chesty Puller and Gunny Spell and all the senior officers and NCOs in the Korean War were veterans of World War II, so were many of the senior military leaders in Vietnam veterans of the Korean War. Korean veterans were the kid brothers of the Greatest Generation, while Vietnam veterans were their sons. The families of Chesty Puller and his son,

Lewis Jr., are representative of many American families that saw their men go off to fight in all three wars.

A third way the three wars are linked is geopolitically. The defeat of Nazi Germany and imperial Japan did not bring an end to division in the world but led instead to a new one. The victors, the former Allied forces, now divided amoeba-like into two new opposing camps–China under Mao Tse Tung who had vanquished the Nationalist leader Chaing Kai Shek to Formosa and The Soviet Bloc under the iron-fisted rule of Joseph Stalin on one side, and the United States and Western Europe on the other. This new division between Communism and the Free World shaped international relations for the next forty years and ushered into history the conflict that came to be known as the Cold War.

I spent four years of my childhood and early teens, along with my family and everyone else in the world, following the greatest drama in the history of mankind–the struggle between the Allied and Axis powers in World War II. Not since Satan and his angels rebelled against God in Milton's *Paradise Lost* had the forces of good and evil been arrayed so powerfully against each other in such absolute warfare. Everyone understood that the outcome of the struggle in that great conflict would determine the future of the planet. Because of my experiences with the Marine Corps in Korea, the Pacific War is of particular interest to me, but in Dallas from December 1941 until the summer of 1945 my family followed greedily every bit of news from every theater of the war. We had that map of Europe on the wall in our living room where we followed Patton's progress across France and Germany marking the spots with colored pins where we believed my sister's husband, Sergeant Johnnie George, and his tank destroyer outfit were. We didn't have television, cable news or the Internet, but we combed the daily papers and listened to radio bulletins from reporters like Edward R. Murrow and Eric Severeid and eagerly exchanged news items with our neighbors. There were many houses up and down Alabama Street with stars for their service men proudly displayed in their windows.

I missed that war because I was too young, but three years after the war ended, during peace time, I joined the navy to escape high school and see the world and, through a series of personal decisions and happenstance, found myself a little over two years later climbing the mountains of Korea in a Marine rifle company. My experience in the Fleet Marine Force, however, would not be my last assignment as a Cold War warrior.

* * *

I graduated from the University of Texas in 1957 with a degree in political science. I settled on that major after I could see my grades in pre-med weren't going to get me in med school. To make that supremely important decision about the future course of my life, I simply looked through my transcript and plotted the shortest route to a degree. And I made it. But what do you do with a bachelor's degree in liberal arts that is not worth much in the marketplace? I puzzled over that question my last semester in school, then one day as I was walking down a hallway a shiny silver notice on a bulletin board caught my eye. It asked the questions, "Do you have an analytical mind?" and "Would you like to work for your nation's intelligence service?" I read the rest of the notice, about how representatives would be on campus to conduct interviews and decided to give it a try. After going through the interview and a battery of tests, I had a job. I would be working for the National Security Agency and was to report for duty that June at Arlington, Virginia.

For the next nine years I worked at NSA and later at the Air Force Security Service as a cryptanalyst, an instructor of cryptanalysis, a writer of instructional manuals for cryptanalysis, an editor of textbooks in communications intelligence, and finally as Chief of the Editing and Publications Branch of the USAFSS School at Goodfellow AFB, Texas. When I first started out with NSA, after undergoing the lengthy process of a security clearance investigation and a program of courses in the Russian language, cryptology, linguistics, probability theory, and related subjects, I began working on Russian military codes and ciphers at the new NSA main facility at Fort Meade, Maryland, unofficially dubbed the "Puzzle Palace." Our work was top secret and at that time everything was hush-hush. We were told that if anyone asked where we worked we should say only that we worked for the Defense Department. In those days NSA stood for "no such agency."

Things have changed since then. The work there is still highly classified, but today NSA has a web page with a great deal of information on its operations and history. Over the years the agency has gained an unprecedented ability to eavesdrop on every kind of electronic signal and communication from any place on the globe. While this technology enables the United States to keep track of our enemies, there were charges early in 2006 that the agency's snooping powers have been used illegally against our own citizens. If those charges prove true they represent a real threat to democracy. Some political leaders have claimed we must sacrifice some of our privacy in order to protect ourselves from terrorists. We should, however, remember the warning, that people who are willing to surrender a little freedom for a little more security will ultimately lose both.

The jobs I held for nine years I mention here because they were part of the continuation of the Cold War during the interlude between Korea and Vietnam. What both sides did during that period was to work assiduously to assess the military capabilities of each other. We routinely sent our military planes on missions along the borders of the Soviet Union in order to provoke them into scrambling their aircraft so we could monitor their communications and identify their military units, aircraft, personnel and operational procedures. The Soviets, at the same time, would cruise along our coasts with their "fishing trawlers" laden with sophisticated electronic equipment to accumulate the same kind of information about our defenses. Each side wanted to know as much about the other as possible in case the unthinkable happened.

That year, 1957, NSA hired a large number of college graduates from around the country in what was called the Promotion and Training Agreement program, or PATA. We entered the program in classes where we were eventually sorted out for different specializations, such as linguists, traffic analysts, and cryptanalysts in Communications Intelligence, or COMINT, or in one of the several specializations in Communications Security, or COMSEC, the organization responsible for maintaining the security of our own communications. In COMINT we received intercepts from all around the world, copied them on large sheets of lined paper, and worked in pencil trying to decipher and decode the messages and reconstruct the encrypting systems. The traffic analysts worked on the message externals in order to identify aircraft and chains of command and diagram the organizational structures of military facilities. The methods and techniques of encryption and cryptanalysis used in those days were primitive compared to what must be used today, and while NSA has always had the most powerful computers in the world, I suspect that all the rooms full of consoles with their whirling tapes in 1957 didn't have the computing power of the laptop I'm typing on now.

When we weren't working at the Puzzle Palace we PATA people socialized with one another, since we knew no one else in D.C. in those days; we had parties at one another's apartments, cooked spaghetti and drank Chianti and saw the sights together. One night that first October several of us were driving around the city with the car radio on when we heard the news that the Soviets had put the first ever satellite into orbit, a little sphere they called "Sputnik." The radio station after breaking the news broadcast the "beep beep beep" that thing was sending down from space, and as we listened we looked at one another in wonderment. What did this mean for us, for the United States? This achievement clearly showed that the Soviet Union was ahead of us in the space race and it gave us an even greater sense of urgency about the work we were doing at NSA. It also led to an intense reappraisal of our education system throughout the country, particularly in the sciences.

Two years later a number of us were walking down a sidewalk at the NSA compound when we looked up and saw a huge jet liner with a big red star on the tail gliding in toward the Washington D.C. airport. The plane was carrying Nikita Khruschev, who had come to the U.S. to visit President Eisenhower at Camp David and at his home at Gettysburg to talk over relations between the two superpowers. We joked with one another about hearing the clicks of the cameras as the plane passed over the compound.

Any good will engendered by that meeting was soured only eight months later when Gary Powers was shot down over the Soviet Union in his high-altitude U2 spy plane. President Eisenhower was embarrassed when, after he had claimed it was a weather plane that had strayed off course, the Soviets produced not only the cameras that were on the plane but the pilot himself who admitted the nature of his mission. A couple of months later one of our reconnaissance planes, an RB 47, was shot down in the area of the Bering Sea while on an intelligence mission, and while we claimed the plane was over international waters, it was later discovered that it too had violated the airspace of the USSR. Later Eisenhower acknowledged that had the Soviets sent a spy plane intruding into our air space as the U2 had done in theirs he would have considered that an act of war.

In between those two events a story broke that was of particular interest to us PATA recruits. Two of the people hired in our program, William Martin and Bernon Mitchell, had defected to the Soviet Union. It was hard to believe that anyone who had gone through the rigorous screening and security procedures we had endured could do such a thing, but there they were, their pictures in *Time* magazine. They had not been in my class but I recognized their faces, having seen them in the halls around the Coke machines during our breaks while we were in school. Later these two defectors came out with a lame rationale for their perfidy that was published in TASS. They said they had been disillusioned to learn that the U.S. lied about its spying on the Soviet Union and the fact that we even spied on our own allies.

How could two people who chose intelligence as their profession be so naïve about the nature of the business? They were like Captain Renault in *Casablanca* who was "shocked! shocked!" to learn there was gambling in Rick's nightclub. I have speculated on the motives of Martin and Mitchell over the years, but whatever their motives might have been for betraying their country, I always believed the two men got their just punishment— sentenced to live much of the rest of their lives in that drab, unhappy totalitarian system.

But at least the four decades of the Cold war never saw a direct clash between the two superpowers, and the period between Korea and Vietnam provided a ten-year respite from any hot wars. The principle of mutually assured destruction, or MAD, seemed to work in restraining the two sides. Therein is some hope for mankind, the hope that we can use reason when we face imminent annihilation. For threats that are not so immediate but just as real—conventional warfare, hunger, disease, global warming and other threats to our environment, to those things that have given us and our fellow creatures on this small blue planet life and that sustain us—it may take

longer. If we made it through those four dark decades of the Cold War, however, we know there is hope. Reason saved us then, and that is what we must
look to for deliverance in the future. We might also pray for a little luck.

Though we came close to open conflict in that forty-year era of brink-
manship, sanity prevailed. The Cuban Missile Crisis was as close as we got
to the Dr. Strangelove scenario, but we had many other tense moments
throughout the Cold War. Fortunately, for the most part, the two superpowers were content to aid and abet their surrogates in the struggle, as the
Chinese and Soviets did in the Korean War and Vietnam, and as we later did
in Afghanistan, and as both sides did throughout those decades in far-flung
places around the globe.

\* \* \*

In 1966, after four years in the military and nine years working for
the Defense Department, I decided to make a career change. Up until that
time the direction of my life had been set willy-nilly, as much by chance as
by choice. I had never planned to be a hospital corpsman and I had never
planned to be a cryptanalyst. Now I was thirty-five years old with a wife
and two young children and I knew the longer I waited to change careers
the harder the move would be. It was like standing on the rear platform of
an accelerating train preparing to jump. The longer you wait the more it's
going to hurt when you hit the ground.

We all made the jump together and discovered the pain came in the form
of living for five years on frugal rations while I attended graduate school at
Texas Tech University in Lubbock. This time in making my career choice I
drew upon the advice of Robert Frost in his poem "Two Tramps in Mudtime:"
I joined my vocation and my avocation. I had always loved to read, even when
flunking out of high school. In Korea I always carried a book or two in my
pack to read while camped in the mountains. Now at last I would follow my
own path. My major would be literature and linguistics. What could be better than getting paid to read good books and talk about them?

If only that had been all there was to it.

The truth was I had to teach half time, for the first two years only
freshman composition, and there were all the graduate classes to attend and
papers to write, and the pay as a teaching assistant would have been insult-
ing to Bob Cratchit. Anyone who has ever taught freshman English will
tell you that the bane of that job is all the themes that have to be read and
graded. But the good thing about teaching that course is the interaction you
get with young people, and the fact that in that one course there is no limit
to the wide range of topics you can discuss.

Since writing and thinking are of a piece and since eighteen and nineteen year-olds are interested in what's happening now, that period of the late

nineteen-sixties and early nineteen-seventies provided no end of lively topics for classroom discussions and essays. Of course personal topics are always the most popular—first dates, pledging a sorority, the death of a grandparent. (One student described in sad detail how her gravely ill grandfather "lapsed into a comma.") But the broader subjects received much attention. Martin Luther King Jr.'s "I Have a Dream" speech of 1963 and the social revolution it was part of still provided good topics, but the topic that continued to draw most interest from my students during this time was the war in Vietnam, because that was a subject that affected them directly. When confronted with the draft many young men who had been uninterested in higher learning before suddenly became desirous of expanding their minds and getting a college education—along with the military deferment that came with it.

I discovered then that even though I had changed careers I had not been able to escape the Cold War. In those days nobody could. The whole nation was now focused on Vietnam, although just as it is in all wars, those with family and friends in the conflict and those fearing they might have to go were more attuned to the details than the rest of us.

\* \* \*

No family better dramatizes the glory and tragedy of war than that of Chesty Puller, the Marine Corps legend, winner of five Navy Crosses, the hero of battles ranging from the Banana Wars to Korea.

Chesty was in the prime of his career as a warrior when World War II broke out and as fate would have it, he wound up in exactly the right place at the right time to stop the Japanese advance in the Pacific when he and his greatly outnumbered battalion heroically beat back the furious assault on his sector of the perimeter at Henderson Field on Guadalcanal. That battle turned out to be the high water mark for Japan. From that point on, though there were many bloody struggles ahead, the outcome of the Pacific war seemed assured. Chesty Puller and millions of other young American men had the opportunity at that time to fight many battles against evil powers in an unambiguously good war and they had the entire nation and free world behind them. And for all those who didn't survive the conflict, such as my boyhood neighbor and friend, Felix Ezell, there was no doubt in the hearts and minds of their families and countrymen that they had died for a worthy cause.

Twenty-five years later Lewis Puller Jr., the son that Chesty adored, found himself wading chest deep through leech infested rice paddies of the Riviera district of Vietnam. He and his generation had not been so fortunate in the hand they were dealt. This time our country had gone to war on its own without the support of the rest of the Free World, and not against an enemy that had attacked us or was trying to conquer the world, but against people fighting to expel foreign forces from their land. It's true that many of us, out of fear, were deluded into believing that Communism was a powerful, alien force on the move to rule the world and that the only thing that could stop it was military force. And many of us bought in to the Domino Theory, believing that if one country in Southeast Asia fell, its neighbors would soon follow. So we were primed to accept President Johnson's claim, later proven false, that our ships had been attacked in the Gulf of Tonkin and follow him off to war, into what was to become the quagmire of Vietnam.

Unlike his father who led a charmed life while surviving many battles throughout a long career, who was given the opportunity to defend his country against a real threat from an evil power, who came home to a hero's welcome, Lewis Puller Jr. after only two months in Vietnam found his body and life shattered by an improvised booby trap made from an American 155 mm howitzer shell. He lost both legs while following in his father's footsteps and suffered multiple other wounds and severe complications. During his long and painful recovery his weight once dropped below 70 pounds.

As did many who fought in that war, Lewis came home to a long and painful convalescence while being greeted with indifference from the public and neglect from the very government that sent him into that tragic conflict. The best he could do to come to terms with his experience was to recognize, as he said in his Pulitzer Prize winning autobiography, *Fortunate Son*, "that while the Vietnam War was a tragic mistake and never should have been fought, my role in it had been as honorable as circumstances would permit" (428).

While teaching at Texas Tech I didn't learn that Chesty Puller's son had been grievously wounded, but we did get daily reports about the progress being made in Vietnam, progress measured by the grim and sad statistic, "body count." The idea was that if we just kept raising the pressure, kept the "rolling thunder" air attacks going against the North and kept killing more Communists, the Viet Cong and the North Vietnamese would sooner or later have to buckle under. That never happened.

The families and loved ones of the 58,000 who died in Vietnam would never be able to feel the consolation that comforted their counterparts in World War II, to feel secure in the knowledge that their young men had died for a worthy cause. We lost that war because we were never able to win the support of the Vietnamese people, and as the war dragged on year after year without any progress and as the casualties mounted, the discontent at home grew until finally our own country was torn apart.

\* \* \*

The My Lai Massacre occurred in March of 1968 when Lieutenant William Calley and his platoon shot and killed more than three hundred unarmed old men, women, and children and left them in a ditch. We didn't learn about it in this country for over a year because the military and the U.S. government sat on the shameful story, hoping it would never get out; but when the news finally broke in the fall of 1969 it added new fuel to the antiwar movement that was spreading across the country. It also created even more turmoil in the hearts of Lewis Puller Jr. and other Vietnam veterans who were struggling with rehabilitation, readjustment, and their mixed feelings about the war, trying to understand why they had not been warmly welcomed home like veterans of past wars and what it was they had paid such a high price for.

There were many stories in the news about the war and the protests against the war that provided topics for class discussions and essays. As Bob Dylan said in his song, the times they were a changin'. The focus of the protests had expanded from civil rights to the war to finally the entire American power structure, both corporate and governmental. The youth of America began to manifest their rebellion in their music, in their dress, and in their hairstyles.

The Beatles had something to do with boys first growing their hair long, and later other rock groups and young icons continued to set the fashion trends with bell-bottom pants, tie-dyed shirts, beads, and other stylistic innovations designed to drive their parents nuts. Experimentation with drugs became a big thing, and soon the hippie movement was in full stride with gurus such as Timothy Leary advising young people to turn on, tune in, and drop out.

In August of 1969 a milestone was reached at a hog farm in upper New York state when a half million young people assembled for the greatest rock concert in history, a landmark event that would become the cynosure of the counterculture movement—Woodstock. According to the testimonials, no one who attended that event would ever be able to forget it including more than a few Vietnam vets. One of the groups performing there was Creedence Clearwater Revival led by John Fogerty who wrote the protest song from which Lewis Puller Jr. took the title for his autobiography. The song, which came out that year, summed up a widely prevalent attitude about the war and is worth taking a look at for that reason:

Fortunate Son

Some folks are born made to wave the flag,
Oh they're red, white, and blue,
And when the band plays "Hail to the Chief,"
Oh, they point a cannon at you, Lord.

>It ain't me, it ain't me
>I ain't no senator's son,
>It ain't me, it ain't me,
>I ain't no fortunate one, no.

Some folks are born silver spoon in hand,
Lord, don't they help themselves, oh.
But when the taxman come to the door,
The house look like a rummage sale, yes.

>It ain't me, it ain't me,
>I ain't no millionaire's son
>It ain't me, it ain't me,
>I ain't no fortunate one, no.

Yeah, some folks inherit star spangled eyes,
Oh, they send you down to war, Lord,
And when you ask them how much should we give,
Oh, they only answer, more, more, more, yo,

>It ain't me, it ain't me,
>I ain't no military son,
>It ain't me, it ain't me,
>I ain't no fortunate one,

>It ain't me, it ain't me,
>I ain't no fortunate one, no no no,
>It ain't me, it ain't me,
>I ain't no fortunate son, no no no.

Song lyrics don't often make great poetry written out on the page, but they can be very powerful in performance, and here this song reveals what the Army platoon leader James McDonough and Lewis Jr. both recognized in Vietnam: sons of the wealthy and powerful, the ones who start wars and profit from them, mostly got a pass.

These young protesters of the 60's and 70's were the sons and daughters of the Greatest Generation; their fathers had fought in the Good War against an enemy that attacked us with the intent to conquer and enslave us. In that war everyone contributed, all shared the sacrifices. That was not the case in Vietnam, where the blood and sacrifice came largely from the working class, from minorities and the less-educated.

\* \* \*

I remember when the first male students started coming to class with long hair. One of them, who said he let his hair grow long because he played in a rock band, wrote an essay about the hostility he faced because of his provocative hairstyle, how he was the recipient of gratuitous insults from people in checkout lines and from passers by on the street. As his teacher I assumed a professional air of sympathy and understanding, but I must confess I too was a little put off by those early pioneers in tonsorial iconoclasm. When I asked myself why such things bothered me, my answer was that men just didn't wear long hair. I had been around for better than three and a half decades and I knew for a fact that men didn't wear long hair—unless they were classical musicians or scientific geniuses like Albert Einstein. I had grown up getting a haircut every week—for a number of years nothing but flattops with whitewalls. But in spite of the resistance of people like me to the youthful styles of the 60's and 70's, they caught on and spread and soon we were all infected.

I remember once while driving my family on vacation to Colorado I propped my elbow on the window of our Volkswagen Beetle and reached up behind my neck and found I could pull the hair there between my finger and thumb. I thought, "This is the first time in my life I have ever been able to do this." It wasn't long before beards and long hair were common and we all were wearing bellbottom pants and wide ties. Alexander Pope had it right about style when he said, "Be not the first by whom the new is tried/ Nor yet the last to lay the old aside."

But there were a lot more serious things going on during this period than fashion. When I was an undergraduate in the 1950's after the Korean War had ended, life on campus was pretty dull. The only controversial topic that came up at the University of Texas while I was there in Austin was the question of whether a black woman graduate student should be given a role in a university-produced opera (the undergraduate school was still segregated). For the most part students were content to focus on material goals, on getting their degrees and securing a sound financial future. Things were different a decade later on campuses around the country and at Texas Tech in Lubbock, because in the intervening years two major upheavals had taken place—the Civil Rights movement and the protests against the war in Vietnam.

\* \* \*

Shortly after the concert at Woodstock the news broke about the My Lai Massacre. Since current events were grist for the discussion and essay mill in my freshman English classes, I tossed this one out for my students to consider. What do you think, I asked, about this incident where U.S. soldiers entered the town of My Lai and massacred over three hundred unarmed civilians including women, children, babies and the elderly?

Most were shocked that our American boys could commit such an atrocity, but there were a couple of young men sprawled on the back row who took issue with their classmates. Willie Morris, the editor of the campus newspaper, the *Daily Texan,* while I was at Austin, wrote in the autobiographical account of his early career, *North Toward Home,* that the smartest students often sat at the back of class and made D's. I understand what he meant, but these weren't two of them, at least as far as the smartest is concerned. One of them spoke up:

"I don't blame those guys. I would have done the same thing. Those people were trying to do the same thing to them. This is war."

When other students protested that those killed weren't soldiers but unarmed civilians, these two guys weren't impressed.

"Yeah," the other one spoke up, "but those civilians planted booby traps and helped those Vietcong who were killing our guys."

"But children and babies?" A girl protested, "How can you kill children and babies? If we do things like that how can we claim to be the good guys? How are we different from the Nazis?"

"Lots 'a bad things happen in war, and this is war."

The thing that tipped these two guys off was the swagger in their voices, their grins at each other as they looked around the room to check out the effect their macho words were having on their classmates. We went on with the discussion and I did as I usually did, called on those students I thought would lead the dialog in the right direction. We generally concluded that this atrocity was a terrible stain on our fighting men inflicted by only a small minority of our troops. We came to a kind of consensus: American soldiers must be held to higher standards because they are Americans—while killing is part of their job, they must be highly trained, they must be disciplined, they must always use discretion, and, though it may appear paradoxical, they must be humanitarian killers.

Tragedies such as the one at My Lai occurred, not just because it was a dirty war with its free fire zones, carpet bombing, forced relocations and agent orange, but because of the lowering of standards that put a man like William Calley in a position of leadership, and because too many of our troops suffered from a lack of adequate training and discipline. I told those callow young men in my class that I gave them more credit than they gave themselves, that I didn't believe they would murder unarmed old men, women and children. I certainly hoped they wouldn't.

Chances were they would never be faced with that opportunity anyway unless they flunked out of college and lost their deferments.

\* \* \*

On the last day of April 1970 President Nixon announced on national television that we had launched a massive invasion into Cambodia with combined U.S and South Vietnamese forces. The reason, he said, was "not for the purpose of expanding the war into Cambodia, but for the purpose of ending the war in Vietnam, and winning the just peace we all desire." He had defeated Hubert Humphrey in 1968 in part on the promise that he would get us out of Vietnam, but like Lyndon Johnson before him he suffered from the illusion that just one more turn of the screw might bring capitulation from the enemy. That invasion did nothing to bring about a "just peace," but it did throw gasoline on the smoldering protests around the country, and one of the places where flames erupted was the campus of Kent State University in Ohio.

The day after Nixon announced the invasion of Cambodia students on that campus angry about the war clashed with their administration and with local law enforcement, breaking windows and threatening to burn the ROTC building. ROTC programs were targets for protesters on campuses across the country at that time. When the protests swelled the National Guard was called in, and for four days the demonstrations continued to rock the campus. The students finally did succeed in burning down the ROTC building, an old World War II barracks type building scheduled for demolition, while the National Guard, armed with M1s loaded with live ammunition, attempted to disperse the students by firing tear gas into the crowds.

The trouble on campus that began on Friday, the 1ˢᵗ of May, culminated the following Monday, May 4ᵗʰ, when the following tragedy unfolded:

> Members of Troop G, while advancing up the hill, continued to glance back at the parking lot, where the most militant and vocal students were located. The students assumed the confrontation was over. Many students began to walk to their next classes. As the guard reached the crest of Blanket Hill, near the Pagoda of Taylor Hall, about a dozen members of Troop G simultaneously turned around 180 degrees, aimed and fired their weapons into the crowd in the Prentice Hall parking lot. The 1975 civil trials proved there was a verbal command to fire.
>
> A total of 67 shots were fired in 13 seconds. Four students, Allison Krause, Jeffery Miller, Sandra Scheuer and William Schroeder were killed. Nine students were wounded: Joseph Lewis, John Cleary, Thomas Grace, Robbie Stamps, Donald Scott MacKenzie, Alan Canfora, Douglas Wrentmore, James Russell and Dean Kahler. Of the wounded, 1 was permanently paralyzed, and several were seriously maimed. All were full

time students (May 4[th] Taskforce, http://dept.kent.edu/may4/chrono.htm, 6).

To the blood of our fighting men in Vietnam, to the victims of the My Lai massacre and the countless other Vietnamese victims of the war, now was added the blood of more of our own children, and in this case both the killers and the killed were our own. World War II had united us, throughout the Korean War we had held together as a nation, but the War in Vietnam tore us apart. Not since the Civil War over a hundred years before had an issue so bitterly divided our country.

The invasion of Cambodia did not end the war, and the killings at Kent State only further inflamed the anti-war movement, leading to more violent demonstrations and to more protest songs such as "Ohio" by Crosby, Stills, Nash, and Young, a song which proved to be another rallying anthem for the anti-war movement.

\* \* \*

Because of that war, Lyndon Johnson, one of the most powerful and gifted political leaders of the twentieth century, left the stage in part a tragic figure. Having grown up in Texas and gone to college there I was familiar with Johnson's political career from the time he was called "Landslide Lyndon" because of his narrow margin of victory in his first campaign for the U.S. Senate, a victory which his opponents attributed to some questionable votes he got down in Duvall County. In record time, however, he became master of the Senate as Majority Leader; the most rapid rise to power in the history of that body.

I attended Abilene Christian my first two years of college, and there in 1953 Johnson came and spoke to our assembly. I recall that he spoke about the legislative process and the bills Congress was working on, but what I remember most clearly was that as he spoke a quiet buzz sounded. He took that occasion to pull back his cuff and show us his wristwatch, the source of the buzz. I'm sure he had set the alarm to go off during his talk just so he could proudly share that amazing technological novelty with us. We were impressed.

Four years later, after I had started to work for the National Security Agency, while I was waiting for the investigation for my security clearance to be completed, I was sent to the Library of Congress to do research on the cryptography of the Civil War. I knew that assignment was just busy work to keep me out of the way until my clearance came in, but I found the study fascinating—about Lincoln and the telegraph office and the telegraph operators who were the NSA of that time. One of the interesting facts I learned was that the North deciphered every secret telegraph message they intercepted, while the South never deciphered one from the North. Those Yankee telegraph operators began the tradition of American code breakers that has been carried on to this day.

When I needed a break from this research I would sometimes walk out the front of the Thomas Jefferson building of the Library, past the fountain of Neptune and his court, and across the long Capital lawn and into the great domed building. There were no barriers then and no guards stopped me, so I found it easy to go up into the balcony and look down on the lawmakers below carrying out the nation's business. More than once I saw Lyndon Johnson moving about on the floor of the Senate, pressing the flesh with other senators and conferring with his Republican counterpart, the Minority Leader William Knowland of California.

Shortly after I returned to Texas in1960 to set up a course in cryptanalysis for the Air Force Security Service at Goodfellow AFB, Johnson became Vice President, then after the tragic assassination of John F. Kennedy in Dallas in November 1963 he became President. He and Lady Bird made frequent visits to their ranch on the Pedernales River near Austin and would sometimes be pictured with his two beagles, Him and Her. Because of his love for the breed we bought a beagle and named him Lyndon. We were proud Texas Democrats and were proud of our President, who, for all his long and successful legislative career, would be remembered primarily for two major actions—The Civil Rights Act of July 1964 and the Gulf of Tonkin Resolution which came only a month later.

He surprised many people by strongly supporting the Civil Rights Act, bringing to bear his enormous persuasive and legislative skills to overcome strong Southern Democratic opposition and lukewarm support from many Republicans. He finally broke the logjam when he persuaded the Republican leader, Senator Everett Dirksen, to come over to his side. No other politician of that day could have succeeded in steering that law through congress, a law which for the first time protected minority voting rights and provided equal access to housing for all regardless of race.

Being a Southerner helped him in the fight, and he was aided as well by the strong sentiment throughout the country for the recently assassinated young president who had sought this legislation. There is no question however that, even though coming from the racist South and having gained office by soliciting the support of racist individuals and organizations, Johnson pushed the Civil Rights Act through Congress because he believed in it, because he knew it was the right thing to do. As do all leaders who possess an element of greatness, he knew to look to the future and not get stuck in the past. It has been reported that after he had signed the bill he said to his Vice President, Hubert Humphrey, "I've just signed the South over to the Republican Party."

That party and Richard Nixon saw the opportunities now available, and with their "Southern Strategy" of "positive polarization" succeeded over the next few years by using carefully selected code words such as "law and order," and "state's rights" to exploit wide-spread racial attitudes and change the solid blue South to the solid red South. Most of my family and most of the Democratic folks I grew up with in Texas are today Republicans, and few of them could tell you clearly how that change came about.

But it was Vietnam that brought an end to Johnson's distinguished political career, the war that he came to call his "bitch mistress." He had paid little attention to the problems in that country while he was busy with his campaign against Barry Goldwater and later while he was working to get the Civil Rights Act through Congress. During that time he left the conduct of the struggle largely in the hands of Secretary of Defense Robert MacNamara and the commander on the ground, General William Westmoreland. During the campaign he had spoken out against sending more American troops to the conflict and against conducting air strikes north of the 17th parallel. He said with his characteristic Texas intonation, "We don't want our American boys to do the fighting for Asian boys," and repeated that sentiment on several occasions (Evans and Novak, 532). But when he got the word about the alleged attacks on the destroyers *Maddox* and *Turner Joy* in August 1964, even though our ships were assisting South Vietnamese forces in raids on North Vietnamese coastal facilities, he saw that as a provocation he could not ignore.

Being a strong leader accustomed to overcoming opposition, and being sensitive to the criticisms coming from conservatives of both parties who claimed he had not been firm enough in standing up to the Communists, Lyndon Johnson determined he would strike back. In an interview with the newsman David Brinkley he stated flatly that he was not going to be the first American president to lose a war. When he announced the attack on our ships the nation rallied to the support of the President as it always does in a perceived crisis, and he was able quickly to get the Gulf of Tonkin Resolution passed through Congress. With that approval in hand, without going to the United Nations, as Truman had, and without seeking any kind of international coalition, he gave the order to retaliate, and with that order he took the fateful step that set in motion the ten-year tragedy that was the Vietnam War.

Four years later, after raising the ante again and again in a fruitless effort to bring the enemy to heel, a tired and discouraged Lyndon Johnson surprised the country and the world when he announced that he would not seek nor would he accept the nomination for a second term.

\* \* \*

Nixon won a narrow victory over Hubert Humphrey in 1968, in part with the slogan, "Peace with Honor," but over the next four years we had neither while the violence continued to escalate both in Vietnam and at home. By 1975, with Nixon out of office in disgrace, with our South Vietnamese allies totally routed and defeated, our country found that the only thing it could salvage from that tragic and costly war were lessons for the future. But we have unfortunately too often had short memories. The philosopher George Santayana's well-known comment that "those who cannot remember the past are condemned to repeat it," should be a caution to all of us. What, then, are the lessons we should have learned from the war in Vietnam? One obvious place to look for answers is to one of the architects of that war, Robert MacNamara.

Robert MacNamara was the only major insider who ever came forward to present a detailed account of the fateful step-by-step process that led our country into the tragedy of Vietnam. The octogenarian, still sharp of mind three decades later, went about the country and the world like the Ancient Mariner, seemingly compelled to share his cautionary tale with those who would listen, and he did so courageously in the face of a good deal of residual hostility directed against him because of his part in that war. He authored several books on the subject and appeared in the Academy Award winning documentary, *The Fog of War,* directed by Errol Morris, a film which grabs the viewer's attention and holds it to the end while at the same time impart-ing a great deal of information about this sad chapter in American history.

In his book *In Retrospect*, MacNamara presents a detailed account of our descent into the quagmire of Vietnam. He starts out with the following statement of purpose and an admission:

> I want to put Vietnam in context.
> We in the Kennedy and Johnson administrations who partici-pated in the decisions on Vietnam acted according to what we thought were the principles and traditions of this nation. We made our decisions in light of those values.
> Yet we were wrong, terribly wrong. We owe it to future genera-tions to explain why (MacNamara, xx).

The man who was Secretary of Defense for seven years under two presi-dents does an admirable job recounting the fateful steps that led us deeper and deeper into the morass of that conflict. (See Appendix) The reader of his book begins to understand how the best and the brightest advisors, how strong and capable leaders with the best of intentions, once started down that slippery slope, could not extricate themselves and the nation from a war whose tragic dimensions would challenge the dramatic skills of Sophocles.

To Robert MacNamara's authoritative analysis I would simply add from my observations that we should never get involved in any military campaign where we have to fight from circles—an idea that could be called the Custer

Principle. If a front line can't be established and maintained with some confidence that the people behind you won't shoot you in the back or blow you up, then the clear message is you're not wanted in that country. When the natives don't view you as deliverers but rather as aliens and occupiers, then your campaign is going to fail, no matter how unselfish and noble your motives or how high-tech and powerful your military forces. That was one big difference between Korea and Vietnam. We were drawn into both wars because of our mistaken belief in the Domino Theory, but in Korea we had the support of the people we were defending and, with the exception of that early struggle when North Korea invaded and caught the U.S and South Korea off guard and pushed us back into a circle around Pusan and again when the Chinese poured across the border setting the stage for the dramatic breakout from the Chosin Reservoir, we never had to fight from within perimeters.

A war that has to be fought from circles is the kind of war most likely to lead to low morale, the kind that pressures troops into becoming insensitive, callous and hostile to the citizens of that country. Such conditions of daily stress and uncertainty, where any civilian can prove to be a hostile, invite dishonorable conduct from our own forces. When we put our young people into conflicts like that and bad things happen, the responsibility for the tragedy cannot be placed only on the soldiers involved, but should be shared all the way to the top, by those who should have provided better training, and especially by those who sent them into a war that had to be fought from circles in the first place.

Another lesson it would be helpful to learn from the Vietnam War is that we should not get involved in conflicts that are, in Lewis Puller Jr.'s words, "fought apart from the mainstream of America." If a struggle requires the blood of our young people then we should see that those troops are drawn from all classes of our society, that all Americans are called upon to contribute, either through service or financial sacrifice. We should not have wars where segments of our society bear a disproportional burden while others bear none, where some prosper from the war while others pay in blood. The military-industrial complex that President Eisenhower warned us about has never been healthier than it is today, but our fighting men and women are not the ones reaping the profits.

Only if we all feel some pain can we begin to understand the cost of war. I realize that what I am recommending here is a draft system that is fair, with no exemptions—and raising taxes on everyone to pay for the war. I also realize the chances of such a proposal ever making it through Congress or getting the signature of a President are nil. And since I am making unrealizable recommendations, I will make one more. I believe the windfall profits defense industries make in wartime should be distributed among the service men and women who fight the war and their families. Wouldn't that be something?

\* \* \*

In order for democracies to function properly each person must act as an independent, informed, free thinking, rational citizen prepared to question authority, to question political leaders and their decisions. But we don't behave like that. In times of crisis we tend to move instantaneously together like a school of fish. When our leaders appear before the nation and tell us we have been attacked, or that we are in jeopardy, we seldom call on them to lay out their evidence in detail so we may all subject it to rational analysis and then make a collective decision about what action would be in the best interest of our country. We are more likely to accept whatever our leaders tell us, and if they say war is the required response, we are inclined to jump on the bandwagon and set off down the road to war. The reason we behave like that, I think, comes from deep in our natures and has very ancient origins.

We all need to recognize, however, that in order for democracy to work, there must be dissent, and the voices of dissent must be heard. Many times opposition comes from misguided people and cranks, but sometimes those protesting actions of our government are people who have clearer vision than the rest of us, people who march to different drummers, men like Henry David Thoreau and Martin Luther King Jr., people whose greatness is often only understood by later generations. All dissenters, however, must be prepared for the opprobrium they will receive from their fellow citizens. Emily Dickinson wrote a little poem about such dissenters:

> Much Madness is divinest Sense—
> To a discerning eye—
> Much Sense—the starkest Madness—
> 'Tis the Majority
> In this, as All, prevail—
> Assent—and you are sane—
> Demur—you're straightway dangerous—
> And handled with a Chain—

Only two members from both houses of Congress voted against the Gulf of Tonkin Resolution, and one of them, Senator Wayne Morse from Oregon, was in fact accused of being mentally unbalanced, of being mad. He and Ernest Gruening, Senator from Alaska, the only two voices speaking out against taking our country to war, were both vilified, and it took a decade and more for the country to recognize that they had been right and the rest of us had been wrong.

Leaders of armies and nations, such as Henry V at Agincourt and all those before and since, have known where our buttons are located and they know how to push them. And we always respond. And when we all assemble and start off down the road to war those rare individuals such as Wayne Morse who question the direction we are heading are going to get swept aside. When someone falsely yells "fire" in a crowded theater, the unfortunate person who stands in the lobby attempting to reason with the stampeding crowd, attempting to explain to them that there really is no fire, is going to get crushed. We humans are not purely rational animals; we are emotional creatures with an intermittent and often fragile capacity for reason. Unfortunately when martial music is playing and flags are waving emotion trumps reason every time.

There is one rational justification for war, however, that fires the emotions of all citizens and produces no dissenters—that is the right to respond when attacked. The right of self-defense is universally recognized.

\* \* \*

On September 11, 2001 our country suffered a vicious and unprovoked attack which killed thousands of innocent people when four passenger planes were hijacked and flown into the Pentagon, the Twin Towers of the World Trade Center in New York City, and into a field in Pennsylvania. Across the country Americans watched their TV screens in horror as one of the planes crashed into the second Tower with its full load of passengers and fuel penetrating and bursting through to the other side in a great ball of flame. Later we saw pictures of desperate humans leaning out of windows gasping for breath and others leaping to their deaths to escape the inferno at their backs. We watched as each tower in turn collapsed, sending up suffocating clouds of poisonous dust and debris. The horror of that day shocked the world and unified the nation in a way we had not seen since the bombing of Pearl Harbor. In fact, this attack was more mindless and vicious since more people were killed, all innocent victims. Those haunting, indelible images of that day will forever remain in the consciousnesses of those of us who witnessed the atrocity.

While we were still reeling from the attack President Bush spoke through a bullhorn from the ruins of the World Trade Center where he consoled the grieved and rallied the country and assured the world that those who were behind that monstrous act would be pursued and punished. And the hunt quickly got underway. From the moment of the attack we as a nation were committed to pursuing the monsters who perpetrated this heinous act and killing them or bringing them to justice. We understood that we were at war.

We knew who was behind the attack and as soon as our forces could be deployed to Afghanistan we were in pursuit of Osama Bin Laden and Al Qaeda as well as the radical Islamic Taliban who had brutalized the Afghan people and provided a haven and training base for the terrorists. Our military performed admirably in that inaccessible, rugged, and forbidding land and killed and captured many of the terrorists and their Taliban supporters and drove the rest of them into the mountains bordering Pakistan. We arranged elections in that country and Hamid Karzai became the first democratically elected president in that country's history, though that government remains widely corrupt and ineffectual.

But Afghanistan, historically known as "the graveyard of empires," remains a dangerous place, desperately poor with a predominantly illiterate population, an economy largely dependent on opium poppy crops, and still ruled throughout the countryside primarily by warlords. But at least some schools have reopened and girls have access to education while many terrorists have been killed, captured, or chased to the hills. The Taliban remain a force to be reckoned with, however, and now, over ten years later, new terrorists are being recruited while Osama and his Ayman al-Zawahri have not been captured or killed. So the hunt goes on. In 2009 President Obama inherited the war in Afghanistan from his predecessor, and unfortunately no prophet anywhere can tell us when we will be out of that country.

\* \* \*

A year and a half after 9/11 our attention was directed away from Afghanistan and Osama and toward Iraq and Sadaam Hussein. Our national leaders convinced many Americans that there was a connection between Sadaam and Al Qaeda, and that Iraq had something to do with the attacks on the World Trade Center and the Pentagon. We were further warned that Sadaam was working diligently to build up an arsenal of weapons of mass destruction and that the first evidence of his efforts could come in the form of a mushroom cloud. So now, added to our outrage over the horror of 9/11, was added the fear that we could become victims of a nuclear attack from Iraq.

Our blood had been both spilled and stirred by the 9/11 attack and there was a widespread need in the country to strike back at someone. Our cars and SUVs were emblazoned with American flags and patriotic slogans and we were primed to respond to a call to war. While Osama had eluded us, by God we knew where Saddam was, and we could get him!

Those who questioned the wisdom of invading Iraq, even military leaders and heroes of earlier wars, were likely to be accused of not recognizing what a monster Saddam was, of not recognizing that the world would be better off without him and his two depraved sons, or, worst of all, of being "unpatriotic," of not supporting our troops.

Most notable among those voices of dissent was that of General Brent Scowcroft, National Security Advisor under President Ford and the first President Bush. A close friend of the first President Bush, he had been a key player in the first Gulf War and is well versed in the history and politics of the Middle East. Finding himself unable to get the ear of the decision makers in the administration of George W. Bush, he resorted to writing an op-ed in the *Wall Street Journal* entitled, "Don't Invade Iraq." He pointed out that such an action would inflame the region and make the war on terror much more difficult. Richard Clarke, the counterterrorism czar for both Bill Clinton and George W. Bush, was incredulous when he learned we were about to invade Iraq. He tried to explain to the president that Iraq had not attacked us.

It takes one kind of courage to fight a war and another kind to stand up to national leaders and tell them they are headed in the wrong direction. The Marine Corps has always had leaders with both the courage to fight battles and the courage to speak truth to power, from General Smedley Butler with his often repeated remark that "war is a racket," to Generals Shoup and Greene who were outspoken during the Vietnam War. In the lead-up to the Iraq war, top Marine leaders such as retired four-star Marine Generals Joseph Hoar and Anthony Zinni joined Brent Scowcroft in speaking out against the invasion. Both Hoar and Zinni had been CENTCOM Commanders responsible for keeping Sadaam contained, and neither saw the dictator as an imminent threat to this country. Zinni resigned his position as President Bush's special envoy to the Middle East because of his opposition to the war.

In April of 2003 Zinni had spoken to the midshipmen at the U.S. Naval Academy in a program hosted by their Center for the Study of Military Ethics, and there he chose for his topic, "The Obligation to Speak the Truth." Years before in Vietnam when a soldier had asked him why they were there, he said he gave the young man the party line rather than telling him what he really thought. Afterwards he was troubled by his dissembling answer and decided from then on to speak the truth. He told the midshipmen assembled there at Annapolis that "speaking the truth could be painful and costly, but it was a duty. Often those who need to hear it won't like it and may even punish you for it; but you owe the truth to your country, your leaders, and your troops." General Zinni went on to say:

> I have been amazed that men who bravely faced death on the battlefield are later, as senior officers, cowed and unwilling to stand up for what is right or to point out what is wrong. There are many reasons for this, from careerism and the hope of personal gain, to political expediency, to a false sense of obedience, to a kind of "Charge of the Light Brigade" mentality: As long as guys are dying out there, it is morally reprehensible to criticize the flawed policies

and tactics that put them in that predicament. Bullshit (Clancy with Zinni, 425).

He makes the point that while we speak up when our troops are sent into battle with faulty equipment, we are reluctant to speak out when the policies that commit our young people to war are flawed. But that is the time we are morally obligated to speak out, he says. "If you make a political mistake, the troops have to pay for it with their blood. Our political and military leaders must be held accountable for their mistakes."

Before we invaded Iraq Army Chief of Staff General Eric Shinseki testified that twice the number of troops would be needed to control the countryside after the first phase of the operation was completed, but his advice along with that from and other top military leaders was ignored. Once our forces were lined up along the Iraqi border it was clear nothing Sadaam could have said or done would have stopped us. It was a slam-dunk. Our buttons had been pushed and we were going to have ourselves a war.

* * *

In this war there was no question that our military would prevail since it was a battle between the world's only superpower and a small country whose technology and military was, according to Thomas Friedman of *The New York Times*, on the level of the Flintstones. So the military campaign went as expected. And after our armed forces had swept through Iraq dispensing "shock and awe," our nation felt proud when the President's fighter plane (piloted by a naval aviator) landed on the deck of the carrier USS *Abraham Lincoln*, and he strode across the deck in his flight suit and addressed the crew under the big banner, "MISSION ACCOMPLISHED."

But those original feelings of euphoria proved to be premature because looting, chaos and growing hostility toward the American occupation quickly followed our military success. The President's "Bring 'em on!" proved to be very imprudent. We soon learned that rather than being welcomed with flowers, many of the Iraqi people were greeting us with hostility, with gunfire, car bombs and improvised explosive devices. The majority of Iraqis saw us as occupiers rather than liberators. After the first successful military phase of the operation was completed, looting, violence and chaos followed. Our soldiers found themselves once more fighting from circles, from "Green Zones," never sure whether an Iraqi would offer a friendly greeting or detonate a suicide bomb. And just as in Vietnam, fighting from circles and the inadequate training of our troops led to accusations of abuse against our service men. The scandal of the abuse of prisoners by American soldiers at Abu Ghraib Prison reverberated through the Islamic world and tarnished the cause of the United States in the Middle East. So many things went wrong.

Now Iraq became a magnet for jihadists from all over the world. President Mubarak of Egypt had warned Bush that if he invaded Iraq he would create a hundred Osamas. But his advice, along with the other voices questioning the wisdom of attacking Iraq, had been drowned out in the general clamor for war.

After the terrorist attacks of 9/11 the United States had the support of every nation in the world including Islamic nations and their peoples, except for the relatively few fanatical Jihadists. People around the world were saying, "We are all Americans." But our support in the world took a nosedive after we invaded Iraq. We went to war without the support of most of the world and most of our major NATO allies, including France and Germany, and without the approval of a single Islamic nation.

The truth is that the United States with the most powerful military the world has ever seen can easily defeat a country like Iraq and depose a ruthless despot like Sadaam, but it is equally true that we cannot win the war on terror with military power alone. As Brent Scowcroft has emphatically pointed out, the most important tool for countering terrorism is diplomacy. The tentacles of the Jihadists have found their way into just about every country on the globe, and it is only by systematically and thoroughly sharing intelligence with those countries that we can hope to wage an effective war on terrorism, and to do that we must show respect for other countries and not come across to the world as arrogant. For a politician to be a leader in a democratic nation he or she must win the support of the people; for a nation to be a leader among the countries of the world it must win the support of those countries. If we are going to be successful in the war against terror we need to do a better job of working with other nations.

Sadaam Hussein was indeed a very bad guy who needed to be deposed, a swaggering tyrant who had brutalized and murdered his own people and made war on his neighbors; but Iraq was clearly not an imminent threat to our country as we were being told, and Sadaam was not the only tyrant in the world brutalizing his people. Even if he had had WMD, which he did not, he would not have been a threat since we had him in a box. And as the official 9/11 Report brought out there was no Iraqi connection with the terrorist attack on our country. The nation's top anti-terrorist expert, Richard Clarke, told the president that Iraq had nothing to do with the attack, that it was Al Qaeda. The President and his administration as well as the Congress had heard testimony from top military and civilian leaders that Sadaam was contained and offered no military threat to our country.

\* \* \*

After our two stated reasons for invading Iraq, weapons of mass destruction and links to Al Qaeda, proved groundless, the administration fell back on a third justification for the war, one that could never have inspired our nation to go to war in the first place, and that was to bring democracy to the Middle East. Using our military power to impose democracy in that part of the world had actually been the driving idea of the neo-conservatives, or "neocons," a group of civilians in the Defense Department and the White House. The pro-war faction included Paul Wolfowitz, Richard Perle, Douglas Feith, and Secretary Rumsfeld, as well as Vice President Cheney and other members of the Executive Branch, a group labeled "chicken hawks" by opponents of the war because these neocons had all diligently avoided serving in Vietnam. Many high-ranking military were leery of this group believing, along with General Zinni, that decisions to go to war are best made by men who had "smelled a little powder." Our current Secretary of Defense, the man who has supervised our two recent wars while serving in two administrations, Robert Gates, in his speech of February 25, 2011 to the cadets at West Point said, "Any future defense secretary who advises the president to again send a big American land army into Asia or into the Middle East or Africa should 'have his head examined.'"

President Bush was right in his belief that democracies are much less likely to harbor terrorists or attack one another. It is reasonable to believe that as democracy spreads the world will become a safer place. But invading other countries is not a good way to bring freedom to the world. Democracy imposed by force, as former Secretary of State Madeline Albright has said, is an oxymoron. Revolutions must come from within, from the citizens of the country.

As I write this the world is witnessing popular revolts in Tunisia, Egypt, Libya, and other areas of the Middle East. No one knows how these uprisings will turn out or how far this hunger for freedom will spread, but because of the pervasive nature of modern communications and the availability of news and information on the Internet, through Face Book, Twitter, You Tube, we do know despotic leaders can no longer keep their people in the dark. If citizens are prohibited from assembling in public places they can contact one another and organize online. Thanks to the digital revolution the world has become a global community and monarchies, theocracies and other autocratic governments around the world have good cause to be uneasy.

The road to democracy for these aspiring people will not be smooth or easy, but as one protester said, "I have tasted freedom today, and the taste of freedom is sweet." Once people experience liberty they are not likely to passively submit to the yoke again, and President Obama and Secretary of State Hillary Clinton have pledged to support people who want a voice in their governments. The United States will have an important role to play in coming democratic revolutions around the world, but it will not be with our military might. Rather we must do what we do best—lead by example, by offering encouragement and support and by standing with all people around the world who hunger for freedom.

There have been arguments lately over "American Exceptionalism," with some putting forward the idea that we are some kind of "chosen people." But we owe our exceptionalism, not to divine providence, but to the genius and wisdom of our founding fathers who wrote the Declaration of Independence, the Federalist Papers, and our Constitution, and to those wise citizens and legislators who subsequently amended the Constitution to help us form a more perfect union. (And America is still a work in progress.) So it is not the land we live on or the kind of people we are, as great as these may be, that makes the United States exceptional; it is the ideals on which our country was founded, ideals which are universally valid and can be aspired to by all people.

\* \* \*

In launching his "preemptive" war President Bush broke with a long-standing tradition in American foreign affairs of fighting only defensive wars. In the past the pattern was for someone else to start the war and for us to finish it, or at least for our country to offer some plausible claim of an attack against us or our allies to serve as a rationale for going to war, as we did when we entered the Korean conflict after North Korea invaded South Korea, and in Vietnam with the Gulf of Tonkin Resolution.

The war against terror was thrust on us, it is a war of necessity, but the invasion of Iraq was a war of choice, a war which diverted us from our pursuit of Osama and Al Qaeda. No one knowledgeable about the events of this period thought Iraq had attacked us on 9/11. The commission appointed by President Bush to study the intelligence failures leading up to the war, headed by Republican Laurence Silberman and Democrat Charles Robb, reported on March 31, 2005, that the assumptions that led to the invasion of Iraq had been "dead wrong." Our invasion of Iraq, based on such shaky and poorly interpreted intelligence, will doubtless make it much more difficult for the United States to get other nations to follow us on similar operations in the future. Today the belligerent leaders Kim Jong Il and Mahmoud Ahmadinejad either have or soon will have nuclear weapons and the ability to deliver them. And now with Iraq removed as a bulwark against Iran the Middle East has become a much more dangerous place. Retired Army general William Odom, who headed the National Security Agency under President Reagan, called the invasion of Iraq "the greatest strategic disaster in United States history."

We must all hope that history will salvage something from our sacrifices. We all share President Bush's hope that the future will see a democratic Middle East and a safer world, that something of lasting value will be purchased with the blood of our soldiers and the innocent victims of that war. The greatest hope for the Middle East, however, appears to be the swelling demands for liberty from the citizens in that part of the world. What force could be more threatening to the terrorists, to death-loving Al Qaeda and the Jihadists, than a tsunami of hope and freedom sweeping across their land?

# CHAPTER 20
# The Brotherhood

I was uneasy as my wife and I walked across the motel parking lot in Branson, Missouri, to my first H-3-7 reunion in May of 2001. As we approached the room reserved for the Korean War veterans of How Company we could see other "mature" couples like ourselves filing into the room, many of the men wearing their red "H-3-7 1st Marine Division Korea" caps. We exchanged greetings with them as we entered the building. I recognized no one, but everyone was friendly and when we entered the room we signed in and were given nametags. The man sitting behind the sign-in table greeted us warmly and said they were really glad to have a corpsman at the meeting. I learned a bit later I was the only corpsman there, though Ollie Langston had attended an earlier reunion. Men were standing around visiting with one another and couples were seated chatting at tables where there were a few picture albums on display. I scanned the faces of the men standing around, trying to connect any one of them with my memories, but I was having no luck. Then a stocky man with a white mustache wearing his red Korea cap who had been standing behind the check-in table approached me and stuck out his hand.

"Doc! You're Doc? I've been thinking about you for fifty years. Jack Thein, I'm Jack Thein." As I studied the nametag on his shirt he added, "The name rhymes with 'wine.'"

We shook hands and I realized he had seen the "Doc" on my nametag, but I could see he had no doubt he had the right man.

"You took care of me May thirty-first. Remember that day?"

None of us who had been there would ever forget the Crag. Jack went on to tell me that he had been a machine gunner that day when they had positioned their guns on that knob and fought back furious counterattacks by the Chinese defenders. Those gunners drew heavy defilading fire from the enemy that took a heavy toll. Jack said he was an assistant gunner and when the gunner was hit, he crawled forward and took his position and was immediately hit himself. He was the one who had been hit in the head. The bullet went through his helmet and splintered the helmet liner and embedded fragments all through his scalp, taking some scalp and hair with it, but didn't fracture his skull. He pulled off his cap and ran his hand across his head showing me that time as well as the bullet had taken a toll on his hair.

He said, "Doc, you know you put a battle dressing on my head and tied it so tight under my chin that I couldn't open my mouth. I kept that wound tag for years and somehow misplaced it a few years ago."

"Boy, that's too bad, Jack. I would love to have seen it."

Jack had stayed in the Marines and retired as a Master Sergeant and was now living in Florida.

As we moved around the room shaking hands and introducing ourselves, the questions we always asked were, what platoon were you in and when were you in Korea? How company had usually somewhere in the neighborhood of two hundred fifty men. But the war lasted three years, and with replacements for casualties and regular rotation, the number of How Company Korean veterans would have been over a thousand. At a gathering of about seventy veterans, the odds of meeting men who served in your forty-man platoon during the time you were there were not great; still there were contacts.

One of the men I met was Ralph Tate. I didn't recognize him when I first saw him, but when I looked at his album of Korean War pictures there on the table I remembered the young man in the photographs. He had joined How Company in March with the 6[th] Replacement draft and had made that cold train ride with John Tarver, Lawrence Hansen, Hal Tardio and me and many others from Pusan to Wonju in March of 51, right after the battle for Cloverleaf where Ollie had been wounded. So Ralph had been through a lot. He was there at Izabitch, and Morae Kogae Pass, the Crag, Yoke Ridge, Sanguine, and all the battles in between. He and his pretty wife, Betty, now live in Tennessee.

It takes time to explore the connections, the experiences shared so many years ago. But one connection was established quickly at that meeting. I met Hardie Richards and his wife Betty (there were a number of wives at that meeting named Betty, and that helped me with my faulty memory). He, like Jack Thein, had been a machine gunner at the Crag, and he was the one who had been shot through the chest and was struggling for breath when I found him lined up with the other wounded there on the Crag. He certainly had done his job and I was only doing mine when I taped that chest wound so he could breathe, but both he and his wife Betty insisted on thanking me, as they said, for saving his life.

When I attended my first meeting there in Branson I had only recently been working to reestablish contact with these men I had served with a half-century earlier and there was a lot I as yet didn't know. For example, John Tarver was at the meeting, the man who had written Hal Tardio's mother the letter from the hospital in Japan where he was recovering from his wounds about the death of her son at Izabitch. Later, when I got a copy of his letter and found out about him, I called him at his home in Oklahoma and talked to him, but on this day at Branson he was right there in the room and I didn't understand our connection so we didn't visit.

I later discovered after going over the attendance list and the How Company roster for May 1951 that there were at least twelve other men there besides myself who had been at the battle for the Crag. One of them was the man who greeted us at the sign-in table, Ed Parungo. He was the Marine who had helped carry Sergeant Putnam down the hill, the one who heard Putnam, after someone asked if he were still alive, answer, "I'm not dead yet."

This was an amazing thing for me, seeing these men who had been part of How Company all those years ago. I had accepted the fact that I would carry the memories of that war privately with me to my grave, but here I was walking among men who shared many of those experiences with me and had many other memories of their own.

Even now I have trouble explaining to myself how this discovery from the past came about. Certainly for me it could never have happened without the Internet. I believe I started out a few years ago when I found the Korean War Page and looked up my pup tent buddy, Smitty, Alfred Smith from Pennsylvania, and found him listed among the KIA's. Then I looked up Hal Tardio, James Putnam and others. As my interest was whetted by these explorations, I got the idea to try to call Ollie Langston, but he had been such a heavy smoker I wasn't sure he would still be around. I remembered he was from Banning, California, so I began searching the white pages on the Internet until I somehow found his number and gave him a call. I was delighted when he answered the phone and we immediately resumed a lapsed friendship and began to share memories, not only from Korea, but from Mare Island Naval Hospital and Oak Knoll Naval Hospital as well. Fortunately we had both kicked the smoking habit some time before, so we were able to share again those memories from long ago as we continue to do by email. After making those first contacts, piece-by-piece I found I was able to begin reconstructing friendships and memories from that time long past.

\* \* \*

Because they have been forged in the crucible of battle, the bonds among combat veterans are strong, and when a group like the H-3-7 Brotherhood have the opportunity to reunite many years after the conflict that first brought them together it's as if they share a secret language, a language they have kept inside, knowing that if they spoke it no one would understand. For that reason there is a tendency at reunions for the wives to move to separate tables and socialize while the men gather in groups and share war stories. Who can blame these tolerant women for that? Who would want to be immersed in a conversation, no matter how animated and entertaining, if it were carried on in a foreign tongue?

Brotherhoods are as old as war. In ancient times tribes and clans went to war together and returned together, so when the fighting was over the brotherhood was made up of the survivors and the association didn't end with the fighting. It doesn't always work that way in modern nation states where brotherhoods are often created when men are called from all points of the country and fused into a single fighting unit; they are close for the duration of the conflict, and when it is over they go their separate ways. Many veterans never get the chance to reunite with their comrades. Sergeant Johnnie George, my brother-in-law in the Tank Destroyers who fought under Patton in World War II, never did. Perhaps if he had had access to the Internet he could have reunited with men from his old unit and shared stories and validated his memories with them.

Of course there are a number of veterans' organizations such as the American Legion and Veterans of Foreign wars that offer fellowship to veterans, but in these large general organizations the chances of meeting up with men who served with you are not great, so I never had the desire to join. Smedley Butler, one of Chesty Puller's heroes and one of only two Marines to be awarded Congressional Medals of Honor for two different actions, vociferously attacked the American Legion believing its leadership represented the corporate interests of the country rather than veterans, probably because they appeared to him to support wars too readily and to support wars that were good for the financiers rather than the young men sent out to fight them. I'm sure members of that organization don't see it that way and that they and other veterans' organizations provide many useful services to their memberships.

I can personally attest to the value of communing with old comrades, but to gauge the genuinely profound effects such reunions can have on a veteran we need only to remember the case of Lewis Puller Jr.—the gathering of veterans' families for the dedication of the Vietnam Memorial, the parting of the crowd to admit Lewis' wheelchair amid calls of "welcome home, brother," the reaching out of hands to touch his back and arms, hands of veterans who didn't know his name, who needed no explanation regarding his severe physical limitations. He shared with them on that occasion what he called their "exquisite anguish," and in their company he felt the healing power of that polished black granite wall that had finally brought for those gathered there some sense of closure, the wall that he and others had worked so hard to bring into existence, the memorial that would now preserve the names of all those American men who had lost their lives in that tragic war. He said of that reunion, "I was at last back among the men who had fought with me in the now-distant rice paddies and jungles of Vietnam, and I felt safe and at ease in their company" (Puller Jr., 436).

As powerful and moving as such sessions of healing can be we all know that they would not be necessary if we could put an end to wars. But wars seem to keep coming at a fairly steady pace—for the United States alone five significant ones along with several lesser ones during the lifetimes of the generation of H-3-7 veterans. These wars have been varied in their justifications and outcomes, but each has left in its wake a band of brothers, veterans of the conflict whose lives have been changed by their experiences. The same has been true in all countries for all wars. Lewis Puller Jr. tells about a group of Russian veterans of the Afghanistan campaign who attended the dedication of the Vietnam Memorial. He was struck by how readily they identified with the Vietnam veterans, how both groups in exchanging experiences discovered they had much in common from those two wars that concluded with similar results. And Lewis's visit with Vietcong vets after the war proved to be a communion of brothers as well. He found himself among comrades when he hopped up on a bed with his former enemies and fellow amputees, and swapped stories warmly and in friendship.

While the situations and conditions that lead to war are many and various, the experiences of warriors throughout the ages have been remarkably consistent. Historically there is a large brotherhood of warriors that stretches back over the millennia, back to our prehistoric ancestors in Africa, Asia, Europe and the New World, all the way back to that fictional scene from *2001 A Space Odyssey* that depicts a true event in the evolution of man—the discovery or invention of weapons.

General George Patton believed he was the reincarnation of Hannibal. I don't buy that, but he was a representative of an ancient archetype. He, like Achilles and Chesty Puller, was a straight-ahead fighter. Patterns of human behavior are repeated and pass through generations like waves, and one of those recurring patterns is war. It is an ancient script recast each generation with new actors—armed young men traveling in bands over great distances, working as teams, on guard against the enemy, sharing food and stories around campfires, and ready when necessary to go into battle for the clan, the tribe, the nation, but always primarily for the brotherhood. These things are part of our heritage and I believe part of our human nature, though we can certainly hope they don't constitute our destiny.

\* \* \*

As I continued around the room I ran into a silver haired man whose face looked somehow familiar. I glanced down at his nametag and saw "George Barnes." Could this be Lt. Barnes, our 2nd Platoon leader at the Long Valley, the long retrograde maneuver after the CCF Spring Offensive near Horseshoe Ridge, and Izabitch? It was indeed, and after I introduced myself and he recognized me as "Doc," we spent some time sharing memories and comparing notes. We had both been in that platoon together for only about a month, but we had been close then as he, the platoon leader, the platoon sergeant, and I the corpsman, and Smitty the runner made up the platoon CP. We four were always in close proximity. We were as close as a four-man fire team.

How many people can remember details of events that occurred over such a short period a half-century ago? Well, it depends on the intensity of the experience, of course. There are many experiences that produce lasting memories and no doubt such experiences are common to everyone. But sad to say war is perhaps the one human enterprise that leaves the most indelible imprint in the minds and spirits and long-term memories of those who have gone through it. So Lt. Barnes (Lt. Col. Ret) and I had no trouble remembering events and names from the time we both served in the 2$^{nd}$ Platoon. Being the platoon leader gave him a unique perspective of our shared history in Korea, and he was able to clarify and shed light on many of my memories.

As I continued around the room meeting members of the H-3-7 Brotherhood, I was curious to find out what lay behind the success of this remarkable organization. To an outsider I suppose we would have appeared to be just a group of old veterans shooting the bull about the old days, and maybe that's what we were, old men sitting around wearing our trifocal glasses, hearing aids, and some of us leaning on walking canes, a number of us having gone through bypass surgery, cancer surgery and various other insults that come with years, not to mention the many scars we carried, both physical and otherwise, ever since Korea. But to borrow another book's title, "We Were Marines Once, and Young," and no one outside this group could understand what it meant to us seeing our comrades from so many years ago. The memories we called up as we talked to each other were not of old men, but of young men with strong legs and backs, sharp vision and hearing, young men who could climb those Korean mountains day after day and stand together in the fiercest firefight. With our perspective of age we could see across the years to the young men we had been.

When I was a child I thought there were just three groups of people: kids, adults, and old people. It seemed to me that those categories were pretty well immutable. Time moved so slowly then it almost seemed to stand still. But the older I got the more quickly time flew by. At some point I realized, as Bill Cosby has expressed it, that we are all on the same conveyer belt, and people shouldn't be pigeonholed in any age group. Our life is a continuum and each of us will occupy every stage of the continuum. We old folks who are gliding along toward the end of that belt understand this.

What I learned as I moved around the room and talked to people was that there were a number of veterans who deserved credit for the birth of the H-3-7 Brotherhood. I don't know firsthand how the organization came about, but I do know one of my first contacts on the Internet was with Bob

Nichols who joined How Company about the time I was leaving Korea. Bob, who was a fire team leader in the 3<sup>rd</sup> platoon, seems to me to be more than a sparkplug, something more like the engine of the Brotherhood. He is the one who takes care of business, who arranges our meetings and keeps us all posted by email about our brothers and upcoming activities. He also looks out after the needs of individuals in the organization and keeps us informed on veterans' rights.

Ed Parungo, the man who was sitting at the sign-in table, is Bob's dedicated factotum who handles the money and many of the chores and details of the organization. I understand that Bob Cameron and Willie Williams provided some of the early impetus in establishing the Brotherhood, and that Jack Gogan and Bill Burnett served as early historians. Tom Martin and Ralph Tate, along with "Ace" Martucci and Joe Sipolski all played a part in getting things going, but as Jean Moore told me, Bob "Nic" Nichols is truly the "Daddy" of the Brotherhood as it is today, and Nic tells me authoritatively the following:

> The founders of H-3-7 Brotherhood and Survivors are: John "Jack" Gogan, Tom Martin, Wadie "Cyclops" Moore, Bob "Nic" Nichols and Ralph Tate. The first Brotherhood Reunion was held October 17-19 1996 in Mobile, Alabama.

There was one man who stood out in the room there, not because of his size, because he was small in stature. He stood out because of his sharp khaki Marine uniform, neatly creased, with his buck sergeant stripes and ribbons proudly displayed, and his good humored and dignified manner. He wore a large white patch or bandage over his right eye with a red USMC affixed, and moved about the room accompanied by his attentive wife greeting and joking with the people in the room.

I soon learned that this was Wadie Moore accompanied by his wife Jean; Wadie the Marine who had accompanied the FO Jim Dettman up on Sanguine that bloody day 9/11/51 and was so badly wounded when an incoming round hit the hole he was in that no one thought he could live. Dettman, who verbally guided the blinded man out of that hole and down the hill, said he thought Wadie's whole face had been shot off. Joe Sipolski, badly wounded in the arm himself that day, when he later saw the medics working over Wadie, left the tent out of deference to the more severely wounded man. He said he could see inside Wadie's head.

The trip down the mountain was rough on Wadie. To get to the helicopters they had to drag him across a river with other wounded and he got soaking wet, and it was cold. He remembered hearing a sergeant who was in charge of the evacuation yell matter-of-factly, "Get that man floating down river. Get him!" But he was told later that getting chilled like that in the

cold water no doubt slowed his circulation and bleeding and very likely
helped him survive his grievous wound.

He shared his memories of what happened to him at the hospital after
that helicopter ride with Mackey Murdock:

> "There were lights shining on my face. I looked up at those
> people over me and asked, 'Am I going to make it?'
> "'We can't tell you,' was all they would say. There was a
> Catholic priest and a Jewish rabbi leaning over me with the
> doctors.
> "I guess it was sometime after that I woke with the worst
> pain I ever experienced. It was my combat boots. They were still
> on and shrunk from all that river water. You talk about hurting."

In that last statement we see another quality that endeared Wadie to his
friends and family—his wry sense of humor.

After receiving preliminary treatment in Japan and Honolulu Wadie
wound up at my former duty post, Oak Knoll Naval Hospital. He must
have gotten there not too long after I had stopped by to visit Jim Pless who
lost an arm on the Crag.

Wadie goes on to tell Murdock what happened at Oak Knoll.

> There I met a young Navy surgeon, Commander Joseph R.
> Connelly...I was seriously wounded, emotionally traumatized,
> and my life was going to hell if he didn't turn it around.
> The first thing he did was remove my bandages and poke a
> mirror in front of me. "Look at what you're going to live with
> the rest of your life."
> My eye was gone. There was a hole in my head, and there
> was little left of my nose.
> "'Yes you are deformed, but you must remember there are
> others worse. I want you to promise me you'll never let another
> doctor work on you. I'm the best in the world, believe it. I'm
> gonna fix you up, but you'll never be pretty, and we're gonna be
> together a long, long time" (Murdock, 118-119).

It was a long hard struggle for Wadie, but to borrow some words from
William Faulkner, he not only endured, he prevailed. He married his hometown sweetheart who was there at the meeting with him. Murdock con-
cludes his account of Sergeant Moore like this:

> The only thing stronger than the bond that grew between
> Moore and Commander Connelly was the love that developed for a

hometown girl named Norma Jean Henderson. They were married October 23, 1952. Wadie stayed under the doctor's care for three years (Murdock, 224).

After being medically discharged from the Marines, Wadie took up a love of his that would be his life-long vocation—education. He returned to school on the GI Bill, as did many of us who were World War II and Korean veterans, and capped off his education with a Doctor of Education degree. He taught at several different colleges and universities, concluding his teaching career at Cumberland College in Williamsburg, Kentucky, where he attained the rank of full professor.

While Wadie was being evacuated, not knowing if he was going to make it, he uttered a prayer: "God, if you see fit, put me in a peaceful place with my buddies."

The prayers I uttered in Korea, I must confess, never rose to that level of courage and selflessness.

Most of us there at that meeting had fought other battles after Korea—battles with illness, depression, PTSD, (post traumatic stress disorder, a condition we had never heard of then), the bottle, family difficulties, and the many other slings and arrows that life throws at folks. Not that we were a particularly afflicted group of people, however, because we weren't. But who can make it into his seventies without taking some rough knocks? The fact that we were all gathered together there in good spirits was evidence that we were survivors. Many, however, were not there. At each meeting Bob Nichols distributes two lists of H-3-7 personnel, one a list of live, active veterans who have been located, and the other a list of KIA's, DOW's and those who have died since the war. But one of our brothers was not there, not because he was dead, but because he was in prison. That was "Hoagy" Carmichael, a special case.

Hoagy had won a Bronze Star at the battle of the Crag. That commendation reads in part:

> For heroic achievement in connection with operations against the enemy while serving as a member of H Company, 3rd Battalion, 7th Marines, 1st Marine Division in Korea on 31 May 1951. Corporal Carmichael while serving as a rifleman in a rifle company defending a strategic ridge against enemy forces employing intense automatic weapons and hand grenade fire, causing many casualties. In order to provide covering fire for the evacuation of the wounded, he courageously advanced to a forward position swept by concentrated enemy fire, completely disregarding his own personal safety. His covering fire temporarily halted the advance of the enemy, thus permitting the wounded to be carried to safety. His heroic actions undoubtedly saved the lives of his wounded comrades and was an inspiration to those who served with him...

On 9/11/51 he won another Bronze Star in the battle for Sanguine where he again demonstrated his courage. That citation reads in part: "Corporal Carmichael's Platoon Leader was lying exposed to continuing heavy enemy fire. Corporal Carmichael completely disregarding his own safety went forward and carried his Platoon Leader to safety. His heroic actions saved the life of his Platoon Leader..."

Hoagy was the kind of man you would want with you in a fight. But there are other situations in life where his company might not have been all that helpful. I don't remember him from Korea although the man in the photograph I have since seen looks familiar. I believe he was in another platoon, but we both were there at the battle for the Crag. Wadie Moore knew him better and here's what his wife Jean emailed me about Hoagy.

> Wadie played poker one time with Hoagy and lost about three hundred dollars in a short period of time. Wadie did not like Hoagy in Korea. He said Hoagy was street smart and a smart mouth. He did see Hoagy risk his life to save Lt. Tom Carline. Hoagy received two Bronze Stars. Carline was Wadie's Lt.
>
> Bob Nichols located Hoagy in prison. [They had both been fireteam leaders in the same squad.] He asked us to visit him before the Branson reunion. We were impressed with how articulate he [Hoagy] was. Hoagy had spent the better part of his life after Korea in the prison system. He was very bright. Such a shame he wasted his life. Gail and Bob Nichols started to work on trying to get Hoagy paroled. We visited with him several times. Bill and Betty Burnett, Ike Stanley, Bob and Gail also visited. Hoagy was so glad to see us and receive mail. He could not believe anyone cared enough to donate to a fund to get him out. The sad part is, we did not succeed.
>
> He did not want to be buried on prison grounds. Some of the money that How Company donated to his fund was used to claim his body.

When I asked the obvious question, what had Hoagy done that caused him to end up spending most of his life in prison, I was told that he had beaten his step-dad for spending over ten thousand dollars he had sent home while he was in the Marines and that he had also killed a man who was trying to introduce his wife to drugs and prostitution.

After he was convicted he escaped from prison, stole a police car and went to Chicago or some distant place, but he was captured and ended up back in the Texas State Prison System. He was now a three-time loser and Texas law is inflexible when a man has used up his three strikes.

At our meeting there in Branson Wadie spoke to our group and told us about Hoagy and explained about the fund that had been set up to help him. He also spoke to us about other business and while doing so set on the table in front of him a steel machinegun ammunition box. I'm sure most of the men there knew the purpose of that box, but I didn't. I learned from Wadie that day that the box contained the names of all our How Company comrades who had died in Korea or in the years since the war, and that at each meeting we would add the names of those who had died that year and we would continue this process until the end. The box would go to the last surviving member of the company and be buried with him.

There were scheduled activities typical for such reunions—dinner and a show on the paddleboat, *Branson Belle,* and free time to tour the museums and shops. Back in our meeting room we bought tickets to support the Brotherhood and drew for prizes which had been donated by members, and enjoyed a lot more visiting. And as at all such meetings we posed for a group picture. I was especially honored at that picture session when the two machine gunners, Hardie Richards and Jack Thein, wanted to sit on either side of me.

I missed the 2002 meeting in Nevada but returned to the 2003 meeting held once more in Branson. I saw many of the men I had seen two years before and some new ones as well, though not all those I met two years earlier had returned. Jack Thein was not there.

Bob Nichols, who keeps us informed by email about our members, had told us that Hoagy Carmichael was terminally ill with cancer and that the attempts to get him paroled from prison had been unsuccessful. He had also told us that Wadie Moore had recently undergone heart bypass surgery so we were not sure if he would be able to attend. We were all happily surprised when Wadie showed up in his sharp uniform with the sergeant stripes and ribbons. This time, though, he was clutching a large red heart-shaped pillow to his chest over the painful scars of his recent operation, and, as usual, he was escorted and protected by his wife, Jean.

Bob Nichols and his How Company helpers were the brains and brawn of the outfit, but Wadie, with his dignity, good humor and quick wit, seemed to me to be the spirit of the Brotherhood. We always looked forward to him presiding over the drawings and entertaining us in the process, but this time, because of his recent surgery, we weren't sure he would be able to do it. But he did. After some music from a beautiful blond at a grand piano, Wadie walked out in the darkened amphitheater-like clubroom, took the microphone, and entertained us once more with his good natured and sardonic wit and wisdom.

\* \* \*

Hoagy died Nov. 10, 2002. He was seventy years old. Wadie Moore delivered the eulogy with a delegation of the H-3-7 Brotherhood in attendance. Hoagy's obituary read in part,

> Serving twelve and one half months in Korea, he was promoted to sergeant. Wounded twice in action, he spent two months in the hospital and was medically discharged Aug. 5, 1952. Frank received two bronze stars with V's for valor for heroic action under fire and one for saving the life of Lt. Tom Carline, his platoon leader.
>
> Survivors are special friends, only next of kin and legally appointed guardians, Bob and Gail Nichols and the Brotherhood of Survivors of How Company, Third Battalion, Seventh Regiment, First Marine Division.

After fifty years of conflict, travail, imprisonment and loneliness, and fifty years after he had left Korea, Frank "Hoagy" Carmichael received a funeral service with full military honors. The only family in attendance were members of the H-3-7 Brotherhood. Hoagy's body was cremated and Wadie brought his ashes with him to the 2003 meeting of the Brotherhood.

Wadie Moore died fourteen months after delivering Hoagy's eulogy. He too was buried with full military honors in his dress blue Marine uniform at Shiloh Cemetery just outside Commerce, Texas. But while members of the Brotherhood were the only family present for the funeral of Hoagy, family and friends along with a delegation from the H-3-7 Brotherhood filled the church for Wadie's funeral.

It would be hard to find a starker contrast than that between the paths these two Marines of How Company took after Korea. There are no simple answers to the complexities of human character, but whatever the reason, Hoagy went down the path of conflict and violence. One wrong step often leads to another until a person is no longer able go back to the point where he began and take a different road. There is a natural desire to blame the war for Hoagy's troubles, blame the battles and violence that he faced so courageously. But many others faced the same kinds of challenges and managed to come home and live constructive lives.

Hoagy's life was tragic, but Wadie's was a triumph over adversity. His son Kevin in his eulogy said of his father:

> Wadie Moore was many things, a warrior, a teacher, a mentor, a life guide, a friend, a husband, a father, a gentleman, a wise man and a generous man. He fought his entire life, either to have life, or to improve the lives of those around him. He did so with grace,

dignity, humor and love. I will miss him...we all will miss him...I think that were he here to speak to us, he would tell us that the greatest way to eulogize him, to pay him tribute and honor, would be to live life to the fullest, and to fight to improve ourselves and the lives of others.

At the ceremony there were nine of us present from the H-3-7 Brotherhood, but there was one other Marine veteran present and that was the tall BAR man from George Company who had made the cold train ride from Pusan to Wonju back in early March of 1951with the 6<sup>th</sup> Replacement Draft and those of us returning to duty from Casual Company. He was one of the Marines who retrieved the bodies of Tardio and Hansen from that rocky mountain fortress, Izabitch. Today he is Jim Nicholson, MD, still practicing medicine in the city of Greenville, Texas, and a long time friend of Wadie and Jean Moore. While he had not been Wadie's primary care physician, he had followed his case closely and continuously offered his counsel and support.

As we gathered around the grave there at Shiloh Cemetery and listened to the rifle team fire its final salute and watched the Marine Honor Guard carefully remove and fold the United States flag from the coffin, those of us who looked to the foot of Wadie's grave saw a new dark bronze grave marker with shiny letters. There we read:

> ### *Frank J Carmichael*
> ### *Sergeant US Marine Corps*
> ### *Korea*
> ### *Mar 25 1932 ✝ Nov 10 2002*
> ### *Purple Heart*
> ### *Bronze Star Medal*

At a meeting in May 2004 in Washington DC Wadie's name, along with the names of twelve other members of the Brotherhood, was placed in the steel ammo box. The prayer he had uttered fifty-two years earlier when, grievously wounded, he had been dragged down off Sanguine mountain and through the cold water of the Soyang-gang River, had now been answered. Wadie Moore was at last in a peaceful place with his buddies.

*Wadie Moore 70<sup>th</sup> Birthday*

*H-3-7 Brotherhood 2003*
*Ed Parungo, Wadie Moore, Bob Nichols front and center*

*Memorial to How Company, 3rd Battalion, 7th
Regiment Korea 1950-1953
The USMC University Quantico, Virginia*

*H-3-7 Memorial Dedication Ceremony October 2007*

# H-3-7 Casualties and Awards Korea 1950-1953

| | |
|---|---|
| Killed in Action | 181 |
| Missing in Action | 21 |
| Wounded in Action | 603 |
| Medal of Honor | 3 |
| Navy Cross | 7 |
| Silver Star | 34 |
| Bronze Star with V | 71 |
| Purple Heart | 784 |
| Other Medals / Commendations | 27 |

# EPILOGUE

# The Land of the
# Morning Calm

In December of 1950, as Ollie and I and our class of hospital corpsmen of the 4th Replacement Draft were island hopping across the Pacific on our way to Korea all decked out in our new Marine combat gear, we were in a sense taking a journey back through recent history. Our first stop at Hawaii found us near Pearl Harbor, the target of the surprise attack by Japan nine years earlier when the U.S. Pacific fleet was caught that quiet Sunday morning moored at harbor on the date that would live in infamy. Next, after refueling stops on Johnston Island and Kwajalein, we landed on Guam in the Marianas, the place that had been the launching platform for the B 29 missions that had devastated Japan with incendiary attacks less than six years earlier, even before the A bombs were dropped on Hiroshima and Nagasaki; our next stop was Tokyo where according to Robert MacNamara one hundred thousand people were killed in a single night of incendiary bombing in the summer of 1945. From there we went to the ancient and storied city of Otsu and a week later we traveled by train to Sasebo not far from Nagasaki, the second and hopefully the last city ever to suffer the hell of an atomic explosion. At Sasebo we boarded the *Takuja Maru* for the short cruise to Korea. At every point on our journey we had passed through recent history and met people who could tell vivid stories about the late war.

Now we were headed for a new war in an old land. When we disembarked at Pusan we found ourselves entering not the recent past but the distant past; Korea was an unlikely arena for a war that turned out to be indirectly a struggle between the world's two superpowers. This country, sometimes called the "Hermit Kingdom," had for centuries taken great pains to remain outside the contests for power that swirled about its periphery, to avoid getting caught up in the rivalries of its more powerful neighbors, China and Japan. Rather than seek out technological innovations and trade from the West as Japan had done, Korea for centuries had discouraged visitors, preferring its isolation and solitude to the tumultuous and unpredictable conflicts that were part of the wider world. By escaping those conflicts, however, it had to a great extent escaped history.

317

But early in the twentieth century history intruded on The Land of the Morning Calm in the form of Japanese imperial expansion. Throughout her history China had been the major cultural and economic influence on Korea, sometimes exerting that influence through military dominance, but more often by diplomacy and example. The Koreans, although proud of their own language and heritage, truly admired China's ancient history and remarkable civilization and freely adopted elements from the culture of that giant neighbor to their north. Buddhism from India and Confucianism from China helped shape the religious, educational, cultural and governmental institutions of Korea. The nobility and ruling *yangban* class of Korea followed the teachings of Confucius and required members to take exams based on Confucian principles before they were accepted for civil service jobs. Korea was in effect a "tributary" state of China, but after a brief war between her two powerful neighbors at the end of the nineteenth century, Japan, which easily won that war, became the dominant foreign influence. By 1910 Korea had been reduced to nothing more than a colony of that nascent imperial power.

The Hermit Kingdom, which had always been an agrarian society, was now forcibly introduced to western technology by way of Japan. The Japanese brought manufacturing to the larger cities of the country and introduced governmental reforms replacing the hereditary *yangban* civil service class with one based on open competitive exams that measured practical managerial skills rather than a knowledge of Confucian philosophy. But along with these western-influenced reforms came increasingly oppressive measures designed to impose the Japanese culture on the Korean people, even to the point of requiring the Japanese language to be taught in schools and requiring children to be given Japanese rather than Korean names. The history of the Japanese colonial period in Korea is a sad and troubled one that culminated in World War II when Japan forced two hundred thousand young Korean women to serve as "comfort women" for Japanese troops and forced many other citizens to serve virtually as slave labor to stoke the imperial war machine.

The iron grip of that colonial rule did not end until the defeat of the Axis powers in 1945, and when relief finally came the Korean people learned to their heartbreak that the price of their deliverance was the news that their nation had been arbitrarily divided into two hostile camps with the line of demarcation being the 38th parallel. Now, rather than being caught between the neighboring powers of China and Japan, the Land of the Morning Calm had become a pawn in the struggle between the world's two superpowers. The division of the country after World War II set the stage for the Korean War, the saddest kind of war—one that pits brother against brother.

Relativity doesn't apply only to physics. If there are still stone-age cultures on earth, it's clear that historical time is also relative. History does not progress with technological and social advances coming in lock step around the globe. World societies measured by Western standards, (and there are many who might legitimately question whether those are the proper criteria), are clearly at different stages of development. The Korea we entered in December 1950 was, to a great extent, because of its own wishes, a land that time had forgotten. As a nineteen year old high school dropout I was in no position to evaluate that country's history or culture, but after our convoy pulled out of Pusan and left behind the paved roads and tiled-roof buildings of that city, I began an eight-month journey through that country, covering hundreds of miles almost entirely on foot, a journey that provided me with a more intimate experience of Korea's landscape and geography than I'll ever have of any area of my native land. And I did learn something about the people too, and I came to admire what I saw.

What I didn't see after we left Pusan, however, were paved roads, automobiles or factory-manufactured products. The technology in the countryside through which we moved was comparable to that of medieval Europe. The villages we saw were, when not disrupted by war, self-sufficient, and the people we met could provide for their own needs. They grew their own food in the summer and preserved and stored it for winter using various age-old techniques, including that Korean specialty of pickled and fermented spicy cabbages and other vegetables, *kimchi*. They cared for their oxen and other farm animals and kept them in sheds near their houses when they were not grazing or working.

The tools and farm equipment I remember seeing were hand-made, and, like the A-frames of the *cargadores*, were most often hewn from wood with the flat facets made by the shaping blades clearly visible. The Koreans who lived in the countryside had a lot in common with folks here in the Ozarks a hundred and fifty years ago and our frontier ancestors before that. Aside from bartering at local markets for special items and selling and buying with small amounts of money, the food they produced and the implements they made supplied all their needs.

Before the war intruded into their lives the people in these villages followed the eternal rhythms of the seasons and marked the passage of time with the lunar calendar. Each September they celebrate the harvest with one of their happiest holidays, *Chusok*, the Korean Thanksgiving. At this time rural people, as well as those from villages, small towns and cities, prepare special foods and give thanks for the harvest, visit family tombs—those grave mounds we frequently passed on the hillsides—and pay respects to their ancestors. The other big holiday is the Korean New Year, or *Sol*, which is set, as are all Korean holidays, according to the lunar calendar.

We saw some civilians as we moved through villages and towns and we relied on our interpreters and *cargadores*, but during most of my tour we saw the Korean people primarily on the periphery of our vision. They were not the main focus of our attention. Our lives in How Company were determined by the ebb and flow of the war, by the circadian passage of time, and by the orders that came down to us on a daily basis. But eight months of hiking through a land can't help but leave impressions. Often from our positions in the high ground we would look down on clusters of thatched-roofed traditional houses and see smoke rising from *ondol* kitchen fires. Beyond the houses and the surrounding family gardens terraced rice paddies extended out in all directions until, like the waters of an alpine lake, they touched the bases of the T'aebaek and Sobaek Mountains that bounded the valleys they lived in.

One comfort I discovered in that land halfway around the world was that everyone in the northern hemisphere shares the same sky, the same sun, moon and starry constellations. So the night skies followed us to Korea and provided us with a touch of home. Sitting around our fires on clear nights we could view the Big Dipper, Little Dipper, the Milky Way and the whole familiar celestial panoply, and know that our families and friends back home could be watching the same show when it was nighttime there. But of course most of those folks were snug in their houses. We in the 2$^{nd}$ Platoon did not have that option so we consequently became intimate with the night sky, with the turning constellations and the phases of the moon, from full when rising at dusk in the east to crescent when setting at dusk in the west, its darker portion lit with earthshine and sometimes attended by a brilliant white Venus. But for us the night sky was just a show. For the people in the villages below the heavens regulated their lives. It was their yearly guide and calendar, so they were much more familiar with and knowledgeable about the stars than we could ever be. The night skies were part of the beauty of Korea, but no country can lay claim to the stars.

As I noted in my letters home we didn't often stop to take in the beauty of the country. It's hard to appreciate the landscape when you're struggling to make it up a mountain weighted down with a heavy pack and a rifle and preoccupied with who might be waiting for you on top. But there were times when the beauty would not be ignored as that letter I wrote home in May illustrated, the letter describing the lush green canyon we had recently passed through where clear ice-cold water tumbled over white rocks, where we were surrounded by a profusion of red, purple and yellow flowers and intoxicated by their perfume while being serenaded by a choir of birds.

There likely was among them the Korean national flower, *Mugunghwa*, that we call rose of Sharon, and the native shrub, burning bush. They would have been hard to recognize at any rate, because the rose of Sharon wouldn't bloom for another couple of months and the burning bush wouldn't reach its glory until late autumn. Though I would be able to recognize either now in any season (because I have them in my back yard), I couldn't have then. I regret I didn't have a couple of nature guidebooks in my pack so I could have identified some of those plants and birds and taken some notes. But I probably wouldn't have been willing to tote the extra weight anyway, and what do most nineteen year-olds care about such things? So, sadly, my descriptions were limited to general categories, to colors, sounds and smells. As noted before, we can't truly see things until we can discriminate among them, until we put names on them. And they can't be private names; we must learn the *commun*al names so we can *commun*icate our observations and discoveries to others.

Did God command Adam to name the flowers too? I think He probably gave that job to Eve. She would have been the one to name the flowers and the birds as well. God must have noticed as Adam was naming the animals, being the instinctive hunter his race would become, that he was paying too much attention to the beasts that would provide succulent meat for his table. God surely recognized in Adam man's predatory and warlike potential and attempted to soften that tendency by providing him with "a help meet for him." Robert Frost describes in the following sonnet the changes wrought upon Adam when he received this gift from God:

### Never Again Would Birds' Song Be the Same

He would declare and could himself believe
That birds there in all the garden round
From having heard the daylong voice of Eve
Had added to their own an oversound,
Her tone of meaning but without the words.
Admittedly an eloquence so soft
Could only have had an influence on birds
When call or laughter carried it aloft.
Be that as may be, she was in their song.
Moreover her voice upon their voices crossed
Had now persisted in the woods so long
That probably it never would be lost.
Never again would birds' song be the same.
And to do that to birds was why she came.

More often the vistas of the country provided only backgrounds for the things we were focused on, but they slipped into our consciousnesses nevertheless. I was in Korea long enough to witness the succession of seasons from early winter to the threshold of fall, beginning with the frozen bean fields at Masan where I had a pleasant interlude playing with the children on the frozen pond. Next came the bleak, bitterly cold mountains we climbed searching for guerillas in the area around Andong west of Pohang in January. It was there my epiphany of war came while standing on the mountaintop and watching the tracers fly through the darkness below, there where I thought my tour in Korea and my life would end on that first night patrol, and there where we killed the guerilla on the frozen river and destroyed the little village of Kitty Dong.

I have remembered that scene many times over the years and wondered about the old man and young girl who came out and stood by the door looking up at us. Could they or any of the inhabitants of that village have escaped? And how was it we were able to go off and leave that village in flames with so little thought about what we had done? Such is the calculus of combat: men who wipe away tears in a sentimental movie about some appealing little anthropomorphic cartoon creature can step through the looking glass into that other world of war and kill other human beings without compunction.

We are all crazy bastards.

We saw few civilians during that operation west of Pohang. There was a typhus outbreak in the area that took a toll that winter and, for those who escaped the disease, the weather was so bitter cold most of them must have been staying in their houses taking what comfort they could from *ondol*, their ingenious floor heating system. Trudging down the curving mountain roads in our heavy parkas and mittens we could see wide expanses of snow-spotted mountain ranges surrounding us, often with black clouds of napalm smoke hanging in the air while gull-winged Corsairs circled above. My memories of that experience are like images from a black and white movie. There was a kind of grandeur to the panorama, no doubt, but we were not the ones to appreciate it.

We really began to explore the geography of Korea from late February when we set out on Operation Killer, moving north from Wonju. For the next three months we moved in that accordion war, sometimes north and sometimes south, along the line from Wonju to Hongchon to Chunchon and on to the Iron Triangle near the Hwachon Reservoir, almost always following the high ground. Operation Ripper beginning in early March took us to the southern side of the Iron Triangle where we were dug in until the Chinese spring offensive of April 22$^{nd}$. It was there the ROK units on our left flank gave way and forced us to abandon our positions east of Horseshoe Ridge and begin that long retrograde march south.

From time to time while we were advancing north we would meet lines of refugees fleeing south, carrying what possessions they could in ox-drawn carts and on their heads and backs. Most of them wore unbleached white, loose-fitting cotton clothes, *hanbok*, the traditional dress of Korea that provided the model for the uniforms of *Tai Kwan Do*. Many wore black boat-shaped shoes with heavy cotton socks. All of these practical fashions were developed long ago for comfortable living in *hanok*, the traditional Korean house.

***Refugees West of Pohang***

We would also meet Korean civilians when we entered settlements looking for water or information on the whereabouts of the enemy, village elders in their *yangban* attire with their little black horsehair top hats and wispy white chin whiskers, Papa-sans and Mama-sans and children, but never young women. And there were the many sick calls I conducted for villagers, treating wounds and injuries and illness, dispensing my paltry nostrums while practicing the laying on of hands and listening to symptoms in a language I couldn't understand. I don't believe in my entire life I have ever been so appreciated. And for doing so little.

We lived in the mountains of Korea for months; we experienced them up close and viewed them in the distance. We said many harsh words about those mountains, stumbling up steep trails, struggling to reach the top, then cursing when we got there only to find another higher peak ahead of us. But often from our positions in the high ground, sitting around campfires on quiet evenings with the pleasant smell of wood smoke in the air, we were able to forget our resentments and take in the landscape, and at those times there was no ignoring the beauty of the mountains. We saw them in snow and in rain, shrouded in fog, and spread out in bright sunlight. We passed by grave mounds in peaceful spots where the spirit of the mountains, *San-Shin*, was believed to dwell.

We never saw a tiger or a bear, but we saw fox and pheasants and other birds and though we never actually spotted one, the cries of cuckoos coming up from the canyons below often kept us company. The most persistent sounds accompanying us there in the mountains, however, continued to be the thunder of our own artillery, sometimes in concert with thunder from the skies, rolling together through the canyons.

The bitter cold weather eased up in March when we had a few sunny days interspersed with snow, rain, sleet and slush. And then in April we had all that on a single day. On April 11, the day MacArthur got relieved, I wrote home that it rained, snowed, sleeted, and the sun came out within the space of an hour. But it was not until our next advance north in early May after we had stopped the Chinese April offensive that springtime truly came to the Land of the Morning Calm.

Once spring really set in we were able to discard our heavy winter gear, lighten our load, and watch the green return to the mountains. And spring in Korea is something to behold. Five thousand miles away and half that many years earlier, in a land at the same latitude, that annual rebirth of life inspired the following song:

> For, lo, the winter is past, the rain is over and gone. The flowers appear on the earth; the time of the singing of birds is come, and the voice of the turtle [dove] is heard in our land; the fig tree putteth forth her green figs, and the vines with the tender grapes give a good smell. Arise, my love, my fair one, and come away.

The poet who wrote these verses in "The Song of Solomon" was, like the Japanese master of Haiku, Basho, a poet of love and sensuality, but he didn't do a whole lot better at naming flowers and birds than I did, although he did get the figs and grapes. But I could have done that. What he does though in this beautiful celebration of love and life is begin his song by naming *Mugunghwa*, the Korean national flower,

> I am the rose of Sharon, and the lily of the valleys.

In that spring of 1951 we in the 2nd Platoon along with the rest of How Company were positioned on a ridgeline south of Chunchon looking down on the forlorn and largely abandoned city stretched out on the plain before us. There were no lights, no high-rise buildings, no cars, no public transportation; the mostly empty buildings were dark box-like structures with pitched tile or tin roofs, and though we could not determine from our position, it is likely the only traffic on the dirt roads were a few wary pedestrians and the occasional oxcart. Most of the residents had fled south toward Hongchon to escape the fighting. We were preparing to move the next morning in a circle to the east, taking the high country as we went in order to avoid the necessity of house-to-house combat. The Chinese held to the high ground for the same reasons we did. Neither side wanted to be caught in the open flat valley with the enemy looking down on them from above—so we would fight them in the mountains.

Sitting around our small campfires that evening after our accustomed C Ration meal we would have been drinking coffee from our blackened canteen cups, cleaning our rifles, and checking our gear, while shooting the breeze and waiting for Lt. McVeigh and the platoon sergeant to come back with the word from Captain Hoey about our plans for the following day. Smitty and I would have our sleeping bags rolled out on our ponchos in the area of the platoon CP while guys like Sheksnayder, Sipolski, Tate, Putnam, Tarver, Brodeur and all the rest of the platoon would be strung out along the ridge-line on the alert, taking advantage of the trenches and foxholes which had been dug when the ground had been fought over previously, deepening and modifying them where needed, ready to take up their defensive positions in an instant.

After Lt. McVeigh and the Sarge came back and gave us our orders for the next day and set the watch for the night, we would have sat around our dwindling campfires (built carefully just down the reverse slope) and watched the day dying behind the mountains west of Chunchon. Gunny Spell might have come around growling out some last minute cautions and concerns. And if the sky had been mostly clear we would have seen a beautiful sunset as we often did in the mountains of Korea, but if it had been overcast the sun would have set out of our view. Whatever the case, the sun did set and the fires went out leaving How Company on the mountain and Chunchon in the valley below in darkness.

\* \* \*

When the sun came up—more than fifty years later—all the foreign armies were long gone from the mountains. The capital of Kangwon Province, Chunchon City, is now a bustling metropolis with a population of a quarter of a million people. The two rivers, the Soyang-gang and the Pukhan-gang, have been dammed and great shimmering lakes with sandy resort beaches now beckon not only residents from the nearby city, but also vacationers from around the country. Where before only pedestrians and oxcarts plied the dirt roads of the town passing between the low, dark buildings, now thousands of automobiles mostly Korean made—Hyundai, Daewoo, and Kia—fill the hundreds of miles of paved streets lined with high-rise buildings punctuated with shops and restaurants advertised with colorful signs and billboards along the way. Maple trees and flower gardens make their contributions to the scene, especially the yellow *forsythia,* the city flower of Chunchon. The people also add to the color of the city because now, rather than wearing the traditional white *hanbok,* they wear western style clothes—jeans, T-shirts with logos, athletic shoes—attire that might be found in any American,

European, or Japanese city. And in this place where once I held sick call for long lines of local citizens with my bag of battle dressings, gauze, tape, antiseptics, morphine, and APCs, there are now more than a hundred and sixty medical facilities. There are also over a hundred public schools, two junior colleges and a university with graduate schools.

Time has long since healed the bomb-shattered trees along the ridgelines surrounding the city, and the trails formerly followed by fighting men groaning under their heavy loads and cursing the climb are now followed by holiday hikers, no doubt some with nature guidebooks to enable them to put names on things, to help them identify plants, flowers, and birds—maybe hoping to spot the official city bird, the mountain magpie.

I wonder what a young couple on such an outing might think as they pass by those old scars in the earth, the overgrown foxholes and trenches and occasional bunker collapsed back into the ground. If they are like many young people I know, with their minds absorbed by things of the present, they would likely give them little thought; such artifacts would be of concern primarily to historians, or maybe archaeologists. But if they happened to be among the few wise young people who listen to their grandparents, they would understand the connection between those scars in the earth and the thriving city below.

A new day has truly dawned over all South Korea. In slightly over fifty years the population of South Korea has doubled, from somewhere around twenty million to forty million. In 1950 more than three-fourths of the people lived in the country, while today more than-four fifths live in cities. The population of Seoul grew from one million in 1950 to eleven million in 2005, placing it in the category with other great cities such as New York and Los Angeles. Where I had never seen a privately owned motor vehicle or a paved road after leaving Pusan in December of 1950, now there are thousands of miles of paved highways and millions of cars, many of them traveling up and down superhighways such as the expressways between Seoul and Pusan. Where we traveled many miles up and down and along side the dirt road going from Wonju to Hoengsong, to Hongchon and to Chunchon, now that road is the Jungang expressway that goes all the way south to Taegu where it connects with other highways and expressways that lead to every point on the southern peninsula. And in place of the cold, drafty train cars the 6th Replacement Draft and I rode from Masan to Wonju, today South Korea is one of only five countries in the world with bullet trains that speed passengers and commuters between major metropolitan centers. Four Korean cities, including Pusan and Seoul, have extensive and modern subway systems to serve their citizens and visitors from around the world.

In the five decades since the end of the war in 1953 South Korea has advanced, both technologically and materially, five centuries. No country in the history of the planet has ever come so far so fast. On practically every front, starting from virtually zero, the nation has made incredible progress in industries ranging from automobile manufacturing to shipbuilding; but perhaps its most spectacular achievements have been in the area of technology—semiconductors, television, multimedia, and all kinds of electronic devices and equipment. These dramatic successes have been the products of huge state-supported conglomerates or *chaebols* with familiar names such as Samsung, Daewoo, and Hyundai. And the successes of the *chaebols* were made possible by aggressive governmental policies and by the hard work and determination of the Korean people dedicated to education and self-improvement. Who could have recognized all those years ago the potential, the latent talent of the refugees fleeing south on the road from Chunchon to Hongchon and all their fellow citizens?

The miraculous transformation did not come, however, without struggle and pain, nor did it come without loss. Improvements came slowly that first decade in the aftermath of the three-year conflict, as the country worked to recover from the devastation of the war. And the path to democracy was neither easy nor quick. Park Chung-Hee, who came to power in 1963, did introduce important economic reforms that set the country on the path to better times, but he was impatient of democratic processes and insensitive to human rights. His strongman leadership continued until he was assassinated in 1979. Following that disturbing event, another military strong man, Chun Doo-Hwan, assumed leadership of the country in what amounted to a coup. After Chun took over pro-democracy riots broke out around the country, the most violent in Kwangju where hundreds of people, many of them students, were killed by the military in a ruthless suppression of the uprising. There were unfounded accusations that somehow the United States had been involved in the coup, sparking protests against our government. The three years from 1979 through 1981 greatly strained the diplomatic relations between our two countries. And the "Kwangju Massacre," as it was called, with ethnic and provincial overtones, left resentments that still rankle today.

The 1980s, a period of rapid economic growth in South Korea, saw a great improvement in personal incomes as more and more rural residents moved to the cities to pursue education and take well-paying jobs offered by the *chaebols* and all the service industries that grew up around them. There were some economic rough spots and setbacks in the 1990's but the migration of rural populations to the cities continued, the aspiration for learning and the growth of educational institutions accelerated, and the miraculous transformation of South Korea would not be denied. Millions of people who a generation or two earlier would have been living in traditional rural thatched-roofed *hanok* were now living in cities, many in high-rise apartments, riding on subways or buses or driving their own automobiles to their high-tech jobs.

Such rapid growth inevitably brought with it social and environmental problems. In the rush to accommodate the influx of businesses and people into the cities, the aesthetics of planning and architecture did not always receive the highest priority, and there were many people who for various reasons were unable to share in the new prosperity. And just as in every country that has undergone rapid industrialization there have been problems with environmental pollution, though these problems are now being addressed. Modern South Korea is, like the rest of us, a work in progress. One thing is certain, however—it can never again be accurately referred to as "The Hermit Kingdom."

Progress never comes without a price. Ralph Waldo Emerson points out in his essay "Compensation" that for every gain there is something lost and for every loss something is gained. I don't believe that's always the case, but the tremendous economic gains South Koreans have made over the last few decades have clearly diminished one thing they hold dear, and that is their strong connections to and identification with their home villages and towns. While many of them have left their ancestral homes to work in cities, their hearts are elsewhere. Koreans, one of the most ethnically homogenous people on earth, have always derived a strong sense of identity from place, from the town or village where they, their parents and ancestors were born. That is the reason their highways are jammed with travelers on holidays such as *Chusok*, with people headed "home" to reestablish those familial connections, to celebrate traditional ceremonies and rites, to share special meals, and to visit the graves of their ancestors. At these times the celebrants abandon their jeans, T-shirts, Nike's and Reebok's and dress themselves in traditional *hanbok*; but now rather than the plain white cotton of former times, the traditional Korean dress is often brightly colored and made from the finest silks and fabrics. On these happy occasions workers are able to leave the noise and congestion of the city and flee back to those places where they have their historical roots, to the rural villages and towns where they can feel, at least for a little while, that they are back home in "The Land of the Morning Calm."

The Korean people lost much more than contact with their home towns in that three-year conflict often called The Forgotten War. We may know the statistics from the combat—that 34,000 Americans lost their lives while many more were wounded and crippled, that 16,000 UN troops were killed, that 415,000 South Korean soldiers died, and that on the other side 520,000 North Korean and 900,000 Chinese troops were killed—a terrible toll by any account. What is too often forgotten even when we remember The Forgotten War is that a there were a million civilian casualties in South Korea—dead, wounded and missing—and probably twice that many in North Korea, which suffered from heavy U.S. bombing. Nearly seventy percent of the total casualties in the war were civilians (Cummings, http://csf.colorado.edu/bcas/sample/doc1-bc-htm). And millions of other civilians were driven from their homes, and untold numbers of widows and orphans were left in the aftermath of battle. Added to all this suffering were the many families who were permanently separated when they fled as refugees from the fighting, never able to return to their homes that now lay on the other side of the demarcation line.

We are unable to appreciate the real cost of war because of a failure of imagination and because of that formula by which we seem to measure tragedy—directly according to its magnitude and inversely according to its distance from us. Of course no mathematical equation can capture anything as complex and subjective as human loss. And there are too many variables in measuring the magnitude of a tragedy—did it happen to "them" or "us"? Did it happen to my family members, my countrymen, or me, or did it happen to someone else, someone different from us? The pain we feel when we learn a brother or sister is injured in Timbuktu is immediate and intense and undiminished by the miles between us. So clearly distance, as we have seen, can be measured in kinship, years, or miles. While the grievous hurt of the Korean War has been receding into the past as the new South Korea has been advancing into a brighter future, the wounds inflicted in those dark days can never fully heal until that country is reunited and reconciled and all its people are free.

* * *

In the game of war, Korea was the hand my generation, the younger brothers of the "Greatest Generation," was dealt. And historians as well as those of us who were destined to play out that hand are left to confront a couple of questions: First, where does that war fit into the historical range from disastrous and tragic to necessary and justified? And second, was it worth it? I will heed the advice of my old professor and not presume to answer either, but I have, as I know he intended us to do, pondered those questions.

As to the justification for the war, it seems to me that Korea falls somewhere between World War II and Vietnam. With the long perspective of years it appears the early reactions from such American leaders as Secretary of State Dean Acheson and Senator Tom Connally, that South Korea was not a vital interest of ours, were probably right, that the forceful unification of Korea by Kim Il-sung would not have endangered the security of the United States. We know that for certain today because we now know that the Communist system was destined to rot from within, that it carried within itself its own death gene. (China, rather than collapsing, has for some time been undergoing a metamorphosis to capitalism, which hopefully will some day conclude in democracy.) But we knew none of this then; we know it today only in hindsight.

On the other hand, in 1950 the Soviet Union seemed powerful and was still several decades away from its own implosion, so if we had failed to act Red China and Russia might have been emboldened to undertake other adventures. When North Korean forces swept across the 38th Parallel in June we were not directly attacked as we had been at Pearl Harbor, but we did have our military advisors there working with the South Korean troops, and the invasion was clearly a violation of the agreement that partitioned that land after World War II. So we had clear justification for interceding to stop the North Korean invasion. Also President Truman got the support of the United Nations (thanks to the fact that the Soviets were boycotting that body at the time) so we went in with broad international support. That was not the case in Vietnam where we went in alone. But we got into both Asian land wars in part because of the same unwarranted concern, our fear of the body snatchers—the Domino Theory.

As to the second question, whether the war was worth it: We have seen the casualty counts, the terrible devastation and disruption of lives the war inflicted on the people of Korea in the three years of conflict that swept up and down that peninsula. Had we not intervened the war would have been over in a few months and a million and more lives would have been saved. And the post World War II dream of the Korean people would have been realized: Their country would have been once more unified. But at what cost?

The Defense Department released a satellite photograph of the Korean peninsula taken one night in 2001 that illustrates dramatically the old adage that a picture is worth a thousand words (www.globalsecurity.org/military/world/dprk/dprk-dark.htm). In this photograph, from the 38th Parallel south, the country looks like an enlarged swath of the brightest part of the Milky Way—lights from coast to coast shining like diamonds. North of that line of demarcation is blackness. Where could be found a more convincing contrast between totalitarianism and freedom, more striking evidence of what each side in the conflict had to offer the people of Korea?

On the other hand, how do we measure the human cost exacted by the Korean War, the toll in human suffering that was the price for turning on those lights? I think of Tardio, Hansen, Gross, Smitty, Putnam, Hatfield, Lt. McVeigh, and the more than a hundred and thirty other members of How Company who died in that war and never had the chance to have a family or to see their children grow up. How are such losses to be measured? I am also mindful of the countless others unknown to me, civilian and military, on both sides of the conflict, who suffered and died, people who also had comrades, family and friends who cared about them. Where is the instrument to gauge such losses?

So this is where I wind up: Since I am unable to put a price on human suffering, I am unable to answer the question of whether the war was worth it. The people of South Korea who suffered the most and gained the most are in a better position to consider that question. But the economic miracle that has transformed South Korea from an agrarian, basically pre-industrial economy to a prosperous, high-tech modern society has provided some assurance to people around the globe that something of great value did result from the war.

It took some time to arrive at anything like a balanced assessment of the Korean War, but as Edwin Hoyt sees it,

> In the 1980's...it was becoming clear that the Korean War was not a failure, but a success, in the end. It started as a brave action. One man, general MacArthur changed the nature of the war, when he insisted on driving to the Yalu River. Had he stopped at the 38th parallel and been content to repel aggression, the war would have been "won" in the fall of 1950. Instead it took the UN nearly three more years to attain the same end.
>
> Yet, for the first and only time in history, men of many nations banded together in the common cause of preventing an aggressive force from having its way in world politics (294).

In 1988 over 13,000 athletes accompanied by 30,000 family members from 160 countries converged on Seoul, Korea, from all over the world for the 24th Olympiad. Over 300,000 tourists came to that city for the occasion, and over the sixteen days of the celebration more than 3,000,000 spectators filed into the new 100,000-seat stadium to watch the ceremonies and enjoy the competitions. South Korea in honor of their ancient heritage chose, as symbol and logo for the Olympic games of 1988, Hodori, the Korean tiger cub.

Who could have imagined thirty-five years earlier that the war-devastated capital city would so soon play host to such a world-class spectacle and celebration? In South Korea the competition had moved from the battlefield to the playing field. Wouldn't it be wonderful if humanity could someday totally sublimate its impulses for war and channel them into athletics and other kinds of peaceful competitions? Perhaps we humanities professors should have looked a little more deeply into the value of varsity athletics before we attempted to have them abolished from our campus.

Since I have not had the chance to return to Korea I get my impressions of the conditions there indirectly, through reading and the media, and of course we all see their automobiles on our streets and highways and their electronic products in our stores. But it's clear that the Korean people have progressed on all fronts, not just in economics and technology.

Once while listening to a radio station from New York City I heard a beautiful piece of music that caught my attention. I wanted to find out what the music was and who was playing it, so I listened closely as it concluded. I learned the work was Tchaikovsky's "Variations on a Rococo Theme for Cello and Orchestra" conducted by Mstislav Rostropovitch. The featured cellist was Han-na Chang of South Korea who had recorded the piece in 1983 when she was thirteen. Since she made that recording she has gone on to win many awards, including the 1994 International Rostropovitch Cello Competition, and has performed with major orchestras all over the world. She is representative of many artists from her country who have appeared on the national and world scene since the end of the Korean War. Could such gifts have flourished, I wonder, if the United States had not come to the defense of South Korea, if a satellite photograph today revealed a peninsula totally shrouded in darkness?

After our H-3-7 Brotherhood reunion in Washington D.C. in 2004, my wife and I drove on up to New York City for a holiday and while there took advantage of the subways to get around town. As we boarded one of them we found ourselves standing up as "straphangers," as we sometimes used to do on those old Dallas streetcars, but here we were actually holding on to a perpendicular bar. There was one empty spot facing the aisle beside a pretty Asian girl, so I guided my wife to the seat. The young lady immediately rose and insisted I take her place and I insisted that no, I couldn't do that, but she would not sit back down. After some time I finally relented and took the seat and the girl stood holding the bar.

We struck up a conversation and I asked her name and where she was from. She said her name was Pora, that she was from Seoul, Korea, and that she was in New York to visit her sister who lived there. I told her we had just come from a reunion of a Marine rifle company that had fought in the Korean War. She looked to be about twenty-three years old, so it's difficult to imagine how she might feel about a war that concluded twenty-seven years before she was born. Since the demilitarized zone, the DMZ, is only a few miles north of Seoul, however, with a million-man North Korean army on the other, side she was probably much more familiar with her nation's recent history than I was of my own at her age. World War I ended only thirteen years before I was born and I never gave that war much thought.

I did take this opportunity to test her tolerance by springing a little of my rusty Korean vocabulary on her. We learned that she was a graduate student in Seoul studying to be an English teacher. I told her that had been my profession, but while my area had been literature, hers was to be teaching English to speakers of other languages, Korean being the main one I suppose. Our pleasant visit with this beautiful young woman proved to be a bright conclusion to the 2004 meeting of the H-3-7 Brotherhood, and I got from our brief conversation reassurance that good things have indeed followed from all the sacrifices made by so many people so long ago.

When I reflected later on her kindness in insisting I take her seat, however, it occurred to me: "Now I'm a papa-san." She was acting out of native courtesy, for from ancient times Korean young people have been taught to be kind and respectful to their elders.

\* \* \*

Today, if a resident of Chunchon were to start out on a journey northwest, just thirty miles as the crow flies, he would find himself at the southwest corner of the Iron Triangle, that old battleground we had contested years before, at the town of Chorwon on the DMZ, the line of demarcation established when the truce between North Korea and the UN forces was finally signed in 1953. Today that two and a half-mile wide strip, stretching a hundred and fifty miles across the peninsula from coast to , is the most heavily mined and militarized area on earth. Guards on both sides continually patrol the barbed-wire fences while from strategically located watchtowers they observe each other warily through binoculars. Over the past half-century there have been a number of violations of the line, stealthy intrusions and violent incidents both on land and in costal waters in which Americans and Koreans have died.

In spite of this continuing hostility there have been in recent years efforts from both sides, but more particularly from South Korea, to ease tensions and strengthen ties between the two halves of the divided country. One hopeful sign is that North Korea has opened up an economic zone at Kaesong where they allow South Korean companies to establish plants and hire local citizens. And more companies are working to extend and expand these cooperative efforts. While the North restricts travel to the South, many South Koreans travel to vacation spots along the eastern coast of North Korea, and more importantly a number of families that were divided by the war have been able to visit their ancestral homes and reunite with some of their long lost relatives. It is clear that there is a deep yearning for healing, for reunification on both sides of that divided country.

As it turned out, by clearing out all human habitation from the three hundred and seventy-five square miles of the DMZ, the warring sides have created what has become perhaps East Asia's most remarkable wildlife refuge. There near Chorwon, in that zone now restored to the condition all Korea must have been like in the days of Old Choson, a man, Lim Sun Nam, is searching for that ancient symbol of Korean national unity—the tiger. Norimitsu Onishi, who tells the story of Mr. Lim, elaborates:

> This natural barrier traverses wetlands, rice paddies, prairies, hills, forests and mountains for more that 150 miles. Enclosed by barbed wire and left virtually untouched since it was created in

1953, the zone has become a haven for birds and plants that are seldom seen elsewhere on the peninsula. Migratory birds, including the endangered black-faced spoonbill and white-naped and red-crowned cranes, fly in and out, oblivious to land barriers. Rare animals like the Asiatic black bear, the Eurasian lynx, goral antelopes—and maybe even a tiger—make this area their year-round home (Onisi, *New York Times*, Sept 5 2004).

A number of individuals and organizations in South Korea and in other parts of the world are working to preserve the DMZ as a wildlife refuge when the country is finally reunified, but there will be a struggle because the North is not that interested in environmental issues and the South is strongly focused on economic development.

In the meantime Mr. Lim, who has been searching for a tiger for seven years without seeing one, has not given up hope. He believes he has found paw prints, but skeptics claim that those are the prints of large dogs, that the last tigers were killed by Japanese colonial forces many years before. But the search continues. The tiger that all Koreans want to find is the one that could heal their nation, the one who was there with Tan'gun at the birth of Old Choson:

> He is the Tiger of Shinshi, the Warden of Three Thousand Li, Defender of Choson, and Guardian of the Golden Thread. He is the strength and cunning the Korean people have used to defend their homeland. He protects and keeps alive the long and ancient history of Korea and his teachings pass the legacy to each new generation. He is the comforter who brings peace to the spirits of Korea's ancestors and who safeguards and protects the Golden Thread, that which ties and binds the Korean people together throughout time, a thread that must never be broken.

# Korean War Chronology 1950-1951

| | |
|---|---|
| August 1945 | Korea divided at 38[th] Parallel |
| June 25 1950 | North Korea invades South Korea. The war begins. |
| June 28 1950 | Seoul falls to the North Korea People's Army (NKPA). |
| July 1 1950 | First American ground troops in Korea, Task Force Smith, followed by General William Dean and Army 24[th] Division. |
| July 20 1950 | General Dean is taken prisoner. |
| August 1 1950 | UN Forces pushed back to the Pusan Perimeter. |
| August 17 1950 | First UN victory when US Marines assault No Name Ridge. |
| September 15 1950 | US Marines land at Inchon |
| September 28 1950 | UN forces retake Seoul. |
| October 7 1950 | US forces cross the 38[th] Parallel. |
| October 16 1950 | First Chinese troops enter the war. |
| November 1 1950 | Chinese begin major offensive. |
| November 21 1950 | First Marine Division reaches the Yalu River. |
| November 27 1950 | First Marine Division encircled by Chinese Communist Forces (CCF) near the Chosin Reservoir. |

| | |
|---|---|
| December 10 1950 | Marines break out of the encirclement at Chosin Reservoir. |
| December 25 1950 | CCF cross the 38$^{th}$ Parallel pushing south. |
| December 27 1950 | General Walton Walker killed in jeep accident. General Matthew Ridgway takes command of the U.S 8$^{th}$ Army. |
| | The 4$^{th}$ Replacement Draft lands at Pusan. |
| January 1 1951 | CCF and NKPA begin massive offensive. |
| January 4 1951 | CCF and NKPA recapture Seoul. |
| January 7 1951 | CCF and NKPA recapture Wonju. |
| January 14 1951 | UN forces halt Communist offensive at the 37$^{th}$ parallel. |
| January 15 1951 | First Marine Division Guerilla operation west of Pohang. |
| January 25 1951 | UN forces begin counter offensive. |
| February 10 1951 | UN forces recapture Inchon. |
| February 11 1951 | CCF and NKPA begin counter offensive. Battle at Hoengsong results in Massacre Valley. |
| February 15 1951 | Communist offensive stopped at Chipyong-ni and Wonju. |
| February 18 1951 | UN forces launch Killer Offensive. |
| March 1 1951 | H-3-7 battle for Cloverleaf Hill |
| March 7 1951 | UN forces launch Ripper Offensive. |
| March 8 1951 | H-3-7 relieves Able and Baker Companies after battle for Chinese stronghold. |
| March 15 1951 | UN forces recapture Seoul. |

March 17 1951   MacArthur visits Marines Seventh Regiment.

March 21 1951   Marines recapture Chunchon.

April 2 1951    H-3-7 among the first to re-cross the 38th Parallel

April 6 1951    Ridgway gives orders to move against the Iron Triangle.

April 11 1951    MacArthur is relieved as Supreme Commander of UN forces and replaced by Ridgway. Van Fleet takes command of 8th Army.

April 21 1951    First Marine Division moves to Line Quantico through heavy wood smoke.

April 22 1951    CCF unleashes its Spring Offensive. Marines battle for Horseshoe Ridge and then begin the long retrograde march south.

April 24 1951    General O.P. Smith relieved as Commander of the First Marine Division and replaced by General Gerald Thomas.

May 1 1951     Chinese Spring Offensive stopped north of Seoul.

         H-3-7's 2nd Platoon's struggle at Izabitch.

May 10 1951    CCF begins second phase of Spring Offensive.

May 16 1951    Marines of the Third Battalion, Seventh Regiment repulse CCF at Morae Kogae Pass.

May 20 1951    UN forces halt the second phase of the CCF Spring Offensive.

May 28 1951    UN forces recapture Hwachon and Inge.

May 31 1951    H-3-7 takes the Crag opening the way to Yanggu.

June 10-16 1951   Marines battle for the Punchbowl.

June 13 1951    UN forces recapture Chorwon and Kumhwa.

July 10 1951          Truce Talks begin at Kaesong.

August 18-Sept 5 1951 Battle of Bloody Ridge

August 27 1951        Soyang flood

September 1 1951      H-3-7 Assault on Yoke Ridge

September 11 1951     H-3-7 The Battle for Sanguine

October 25 1951       Truce talks resumed at Panmunjom

# Abbreviations

| | |
|---|---|
| BAR | Browning Automatic Rifle |
| C119 | Flying Boxcar transport plane |
| CCF | Chinese Communist Forces |
| CO | Commanding Officer |
| CP | Command Post |
| DOW | Died of wounds |
| F4U | Corsair fighter bomber |
| FAC | Forward Air Controller |
| FMF | Fleet Marine Force |
| FO | Forward Observer |
| HE | High Explosive |
| KIA | Killed in action |
| KMC | Korean Marine Corps |
| M1 | Model of Garand rifle, the primary weapon of Marine infantrymen in the Korean War |
| MAW | Marine Air Wing |
| MIA | Missing in action |
| MLR | Main line of resistance (the front line) |

**Continued...**

| MSR | Main supply route |
| NCO | Non-commissioned officer |
| NKPA | North Korea People's Army |
| OY | Light observation plane |
| PD | Point detonating artillery fuse |
| POW | Prisoner of War |
| R&R | Rest and Relaxation (recuperation) from combat |
| RCT | Regimental Combat Team |
| ROK | Republic of Korea Army |
| T34 | Soviet tank |
| UN | United Nations |
| VT | Variable time artillery fuse |
| WP | White phosphorus artillery or mortar shell |

# Appendix

Appendix

From Robert S. MacNamara, *In Retrospect*, pp. 321-324

It is sometimes said that the post-Cold War world will be so different from the world of the past that the lessons of Vietnam will be inapplicable or of no relevance to the twenty-first century. I disagree. That said, if we are to learn from our experience in Vietnam, we must first pinpoint our failures. There were eleven major causes for our disaster in Vietnam:

1. We misjudged then—as we have since—the geopolitical intentions of our adversaries (in this case, North Vietnam and the Vietcong, supported by China and the Soviet Union), and we exaggerated the dangers to the United States of their actions.
2. We viewed the people and leaders of South Vietnam in terms of our own experience. We saw in them a thirst for—and a determination to fight for—freedom and democracy. We totally misjudged the political forces within the country.
3. We underestimated the power of nationalism to motivate a people (in this case the North Vietnamese and Vietcong) to fight and die for their beliefs and values—and we continue to do so today in many parts of the world.
4. Our misjudgments of friend and foe alike reflected our profound ignorance of the history, culture, and politics of the people in the area, and the personalities and habits of their leaders....
5. We failed then—as we have since—to recognize the limitations of modern, high-technology military equipment, forces, and doctrine in confronting unconventional, highly motivated people's movements. We failed as well to adapt our military tactics to the task of winning the hearts and minds of people from a totally different culture.
6. We failed to draw Congress and the American people into a full and frank discussion and debate of the pros and cons of a large-scale military involvement in Southeast Asia before we initiated the action.
7. After the action got under way and unanticipated events forced us off our planned course, we failed to retain popular support in part because we did not explain fully what was happening and why we were doing what we did. We had not prepared the public to under-

stand the complex events we faced and how to react constructively to the need for changes in course as the nation confronted uncharted seas in an alien environment. A nation's deepest strength lies not in its military prowess but, rather, in the unity of its people. We failed to maintain it.

8. We did not recognize that neither our people nor our leaders are omniscient. Where our own security is not directly at stake, our judgment of what is in another people's or country's best interest should be put to the test of open discussion in international forums. We do not have the God-given right to shape every nation in our own image or as we choose.

9. We did not hold to the principle the U.S. military action—other than in response to direct threats to our own security—should be carried out only in conjunction with multinational forces supported fully (and not merely cosmetically) by the international community.

10. We failed to recognize that in international affairs, as in other aspects of life, there may be problems for which there are no immediate solutions. For one whose life has been dedicated to the belief and practice of problem solving, this is particularly hard to admit. But at times we may have to live with an imperfect, untidy world.

11. Underlying many of these errors lay our failure to organize the top echelons of the executive branch to deal effectively with the extraordinarily complex range of political and military issues, involving great risks and costs—including, above all else, loss of life—associated with the application of military force under substantial constraints over a long period of time.... We thus failed to analyze and debate our actions in Southeast Asia—our objectives, the risks and costs of alternative ways of dealing with them, and the necessity of changing course when failure was clear—with the intensity and thoroughness that characterized the debates of the Executive Committee during the Cuban Missile Crisis.

These were our major failures, in their essence. Though set forth separately, they are all in some way linked: failure in one area contributed to our confounded failure in another. Each became a turn in a terrible knot.

# Works Cited and References

Blair, Clay. *The Forgotten War*. New York: Time Books, 1987

Brown, Ronald J. Lt. Col. (Ret.) "Counteroffensive: U.S. Marines from Pohang to No Name Line." Korean War Commemorative Series, U.S. Marine Corps Historical Center, Washington Navy Yard, DC, 2001

Clancy, Tom, with Anthony Zinni and Tony Koltz. *Battle Ready*. New York: G.P. Putnam's Sons, 2004

Coleman, J.D. *Wonju:The Gettysburg of the Korean War*. Washington D.C. Brassey's Inc. 2000.

Evans & Novak.*Lyndon B. Johnson: The Exercise of Power*. New American Library, Inc., 1966

Forty, George. *At War in Korea*. New York: Bonanza Books, 1985

Giangreco, D.M. *War in Korea*. Novato, CA: Presidio, 2001

Gogan, John Patrick. *The Hard Way: The Story of H-3-7, A Marine Rifle Company, Korea*—1951. Chattanooga, TN: Published by John Patrick Gogan, Target Graphics

Gordon M. and Trainor B.*Cobra II: The Inside Story of the Invasion and Occupation of Iraq.*New York: Pantheon Books, 2006

Hanson, Victor Davis. *Carnage and Culture*. New York: Anchor Books, 2002

Hickey, Michael. *The Korean War: The West Confronts Communism*. Woodstock & New York: The Overlook Press, 2000

Hoyt, Edwin P. *The Bloody Road to Panmunjom*. New York: Stein and Day, 1985

Keegan, John. *The Book of War.*New York: Penguin Books, 1999

Keegan, John. *A History of Warfare.* New York: Alfred A. Knopf, 1994

McDonough, James R. *Platoon Leader.* New York: Bantam Books, 1986

MacNamara, Robert S. *In Retrospect.* New York: Vintage Books, 1996

Meid and Yingling.*US Marine Operations in Korea Vol V. –Operations in West Korea.* Washington D.C.: United States Marine Corps—Historical Division, 1972

Montross, Kuokka, Hicks. *US Marine Operations in Korea Vol IV—The East-Central Front.* Washington D.C.: United States Marine Corps—Historical Division, 1962

Murdock, Mackey. *Texas Veterans Remember Korea.* Plano, Texas: Republic of Texas Press, 2002

Nicholson, Jim. *George-3-7th Marines: A Brief Glimpse Through Time of a Group of YoungMarines.* Unpublished Manuscript

Puller, Lewis B. Jr.*Fortunate Son.* New York: Bantam Books, 1993

Ridgway, Matthew B. *The Korean War.* Garden City, NY: Da Capo Press, 1967

Russ, Martin. *Breakout: the Chosin Reservoir Campaign, Korea 1950.* New York: Fromm International, 1999

Tucker, Spencer C. Ed. *Encyclopedia of the Korean War.* Santa Barbara, CA: Checkmark Books, 2002

Whelan, Richard. *Drawing the Line: The Korean War, 1950-1953.* Boston: Little Brown & Company, 1990

Wilson, Jim. *Retreat, Hell!* New York:Pocket Books, 1989

Zinni, Anthony. *The Battle for Peace.* New York: Palgrave, 2006

## On-line Sources

http://www.koreanwar.org/html/korean_war_databases.html Korean War Project

http://korea50.army.mil/index.html Korean War 50th Anniversary Commemoration

http://www.koreaaward.com/korea.htm About Korea

http://www.paperlessarchives.com/korean_war_history.html 12 vol. "paperless" history of the Korean War

http://hqinet001.hqmc.usmc.mil/HD/Home_Page.htm USMC History and Museums Division

http://www.kmike.com/MarineCorpsKorea/Marines.htm Brief History of the Marine Corps During the Korean War

http://www.usmc.mil/marinelink/mcn2000.nsf/frontpagenews Official USMC webpage

# Index

11281721R00215

Made in the USA
Charleston, SC
12 February 2012